GENOCIDE AND POLITICAL GROUPS

Genocide and Political Groups

DR. DAVID L. NERSESSIAN

Visiting Assistant Professor of Law
Boston University School of Law

OXFORD
UNIVERSITY PRESS

OXFORD
UNIVERSITY PRESS

Great Clarendon Street, Oxford, OX2 6DP,
United Kingdom

Oxford University Press is a department of the University of Oxford. It furthers the University's objective of excellence in research, scholarship, and education by publishing worldwide. Oxford is a registered trade mark of Oxford University Press in the UK and in certain other countries

First Edition published in 2010

Published in the United States of America by Oxford University Press
198 Madison Avenue, New York, NY 10016, United States of America

British Library Cataloguing in Publication Data
Data available

Library of Congress Cataloging in Publication Data
Data available

ISBN 978–0–19–958890–9

For Suzanne
Always the brightest star in my universe.
DLN

Foreword

The gravest crimes do not always elicit the deepest or clearest thinking. The enormity of the crime of genocide, magnified immeasurably by the fact that it is not an abstract conception but a bloody reality of contemporary life, has been met by an unusually robust response from the international community. More than 140 States have ratified the 1948 Convention on the Prevention and Punishment of the Crime of Genocide, including some States that are generally averse to the kind of compulsory dispute settlement procedures for which that Convention provides. Yet, despite this rare demonstration of support for the aims of the Convention, the content and implications of its provisions are not often analysed in depth.

The Genocide Convention proceeds from the premise that the killing of individuals, motivated not by who they are or what they have done but rather by the accident of their membership of a group is a particularly gross violation of civilized standards, standing out even against the background of the brutality and crudeness of a body of law that is content to regard the killing of non-combatants as being (within limits) collateral damage. For the aim of killing a group is, by definition, an aim which not only fails to respect the objective of distinguishing between combatants and non-combatants but repudiates that distinction entirely. So it is that the Convention declares it a crime under international law to do certain acts, such as killing, or inflicting harsh conditions on a group, with the intention of bringing about the physical destruction of the group in whole or in part. And genocide is committed with the first bullet: the shooting of the first person in pursuit of a policy of genocide is enough to constitute the offence. The curiosity of the Convention is that it only protects certain groups, however. National, ethnical, racial and religious groups alone are singled out for protection, according to the definition of genocide in the Convention.

This produces paradoxical results. Stalin's use of the state apparatus to eliminate 20 million people in the great purges of Kulaks, intellectuals and others deemed unfit for the Soviet paradise; Mao's killings during the Great Leap Forward and the Cultural Revolution; and the killing fields of the Khmer Rouge in Cambodia: none of these counted as genocide, because the victims were defined not by nationality, ethnicity, race or religion, but by other elements of their background or allegiance. They were the victims of what might be called political genocide.

Dr Nersessian pursues two main themes in this study. The first is to ask why political genocide should be excluded from genocide, given that it is an outrage to moral decency which actually occurs—and on a massive scale—and is not obviously morally distinct from other forms of genocide that are forbidden under the 1948 Convention. The second is to analyse precisely what constitutes the crime of genocide, in terms of the necessary acts and intentions which make up the crime, in order to pin down precisely what the law against genocide is seeking to prevent. From these two threads he weaves a thoughtful and valuable critique of the current law on genocide, arguing that it is no longer adequate to address the forms of mass killing from which the world now suffers.

The book grew out of an Oxford doctoral thesis which we supervised jointly, from our respective viewpoints as a criminal lawyer and an international lawyer. It is a great pleasure to see the text escape the confines of the university library, and be brought before a wider audience.

Andrew Ashworth
Vaughan Lowe
Oxford
January 2010

Acknowledgements

I feel privileged to have had the opportunity to write this book. Over ten years in the making, the journey that led to this publication began when I stumbled across a copy of the Genocide Convention early in my time at Oxford and became fascinated with the short international treaty whose content has so much to say about humanity itself. That chance occurrence—if there is such a thing—marked the beginning of a journey for me not only into a new and exciting area of law, but also into a broad range of interpersonal connections with a great many people on both sides of the Atlantic. In a book that seeks to contribute to our understanding of the fundamental value of human existence in concert with others, I would be remiss not to publicly thank the many individuals who influenced, taught, supported, challenged, and brought out the best in me—both personally and professionally—and thereby enabled this writing to come into existence.

I owe a large debt to my doctoral supervisors, Professors Vaughan Lowe (Chichele Professor of International Law) and Andrew Ashworth (Vinerian Professor of English Law), both fellows of All Souls College at Oxford University. I was fortunate indeed to have had the opportunity to work with two scholars at the top of their fields whose tremendous intellectual capabilities were matched evenly by their genuine commitment to teaching and personal warm-heartedness. I feel truly privileged—twice over—to have worked with them, and their example inspires me even today.

I am grateful to St Catherine's College for providing me with a 'home away from home' for several years and for being everything one could hope for from an Oxford college (and more). The College's Master, Roger Ainsworth, and Emeritus Fellow Wilfrid Knapp in particular have become great friends over the years. I also was the recipient of much sage counsel from my former College advisor, Michael Spence (now Vice-Chancellor and Principal of the University of Sydney). Many thanks as well to Craig Klafter, a fellow Catz alumnus who believed in me from the start and first encouraged me to apply to Oxford while he was Assistant to the President at Boston University. Craig (who now is Pro Vice-Chancellor—External at Oxford Brookes University) has been a great friend and supporter over the years.

I have been fortunate to work with great people in the United States as well. I spent time at Harvard Law School as a Visiting Researcher in the International Legal Studies program, which provided not only the opportunity to work in one of the finest law libraries in the world, but also to become part of a whole new community of students, researchers, and academics. Detlev Vagts (Bemis Professor of International Law, Emeritus) was particularly generous, not only in sponsoring my time at Harvard, but also in sharing his encyclopaedic knowledge of international law and fifty-plus years of experience in the HLS faculty. More recently, my colleagues at Boston University School of Law provided many helpful refinements as this writing progressed through its final stages.

Last, but hardly least, I want to thank my family for their support, sacrifices, and love. My children, Zach and Nikki, have never known a time where their father was not working, in one form or another, on the research and writing that became this book. My kids are remarkable, delightful, and full of all that is best in life, and I cherish their many teachings about enjoyment, wonder, enthusiasm, and the other important qualities of a life lived well.

There is one person, however, to whom I am grateful above all others: my wife, Suzanne. For many years now, she has been my travelling companion on the road that led to this publication. She has put up with innumerable long days and nights, lost weekends and vacation time, the existential angst that can only strike a doctoral candidate in his early 30s, relocating five times in nearly as many years, solo parenting for weeks on end while I was out of the country researching and teaching, a grumpy husband's 'occasional' bouts of ill temper, and a plethora of other spousal indignities. And yet there she remains, at my side, leaving me at a loss for words to convey how much she enriches my life, how truly inspiring I find her to be, and how grateful I am for her companionship on our journeys together, both past and future.

It is to Suzanne that this book is dedicated.

David Nersessian
Boston
January 2010

Table of Contents

Notes on Citations and Related References

With minor exceptions, all authorities herein are cited in accordance with the Oxford Standard for Citation of Legal Authorities (OSCOLA).

The initial references to scholarly articles and periodical literature within each chapter are accompanied by a full OSCOLA citation. Subsequent references to the same work within that chapter are cross-referenced by author to the footnote containing the initial appearance. Each chapter is self-contained. There are no cross-references to footnotes in preceding or later chapters.

To provide less cumbersome internal citations, books are referenced by author, page and year—eg, Drost 100 (1959). For authors of multiple works, the italicized abbreviation preceding the bibliography description further identifies the volume—eg, *Ashworth, Principles* 100 (1999).

United Nations documents and other international materials are referenced by the underlined abbreviation accompanying the full document citation in the bibliography, together with the document's date and UN document number. Subsequent references to the same document within that chapter are cross-referenced to the footnote containing the initial appearance. Each chapter is self-contained. There are no cross-references to footnotes in preceding or later chapters.

Some parts of this work—later modified and substantially revised—appeared previously in the following journal publications by the author:

'The Contours of Genocidal Intent: Troubling Jurisprudence from the International Criminal Tribunals' (2002) 37 Texas ILJ 231

'The Razor's Edge: Defining and Protecting Human Groups Under the Genocide Convention' (2004) 36 Cornell ILJ 101

'Whoops—I Committed Genocide! The Anomaly of Constructive Liability for Serious International Crimes' (2006) 30 Fletcher Forum 81

'Comparative Approaches to Punishing Hate—The Intersection of Genocide and Crimes Against Humanity' (2007) 43 Stanford JIL 221

The masculine pronoun is used herein for the sole reason that it corresponds to the gender of the author.

Table of Cases

Table of Legislation

Table of Selected International Materials

Table of Common Abbreviations

D	Defendant / Accused / Alleged Perpetrator or Offender (in relation to a criminal offence)
EC/SOC	United Nations Economic & Social Council
UNHRC	United Nations Human Rights Committee
ICC	International Criminal Court
ICJ	International Court of Justice
ICTR	International Criminal Tribunal for Rwanda
ICTY	International Criminal Tribunal for the Former Yugoslavia
ILC	International Law Commission
ILM	International Legal Materials
IMT	International Military Tribunal at Nuremberg
IMTFE	International Military Tribunal for the Far East
JCE	Joint Criminal Enterprise
PCIJ	Permanent Court of International Justice
SC-SL	Special Court for Sierra Leone
UN	United Nations
UNGA	United Nations General Assembly
UNSC	United Nations Security Council
V	Victim (in relation to a criminal offence)

Introduction

The Yugoslav diplomat and author Ivo Andrić captured a regrettable phenomenon of human nature in his compelling description of atrocities against Serbs at the start of World War I: 'That wild beast, which lives in man and does not dare to show itself until the barriers of law and custom have been removed, was now set free.'[1] Narratives of the wild beast abound: Turkish massacres of Armenians during World War I, the Holocaust during World War II, and more recent tragedies in Andrić's homeland, where more than 7,500 men and boys were massacred at Srebrenica.[2] Ten times that number died scarcely two years earlier in Rwanda.[3] A decade into the new millennium, massacres and other violence against tribal peoples in Darfur continue to draw worldwide attention and condemnation.[4]

A common term ascribed to such atrocities is 'genocide.' Beginning with the Holocaust, the international community[5] started treating genocide as fundamentally criminal under international law, rather than an unfortunate by-product of the shadow side of state sovereignty. The crime is defined through the 1948 Convention on the Prevention and Punishment of the Crime of Genocide, which specifies that certain enumerated acts against national, ethnic, racial or religious groups are criminal under international law. Participation is extensive: some 141 states have ratified the Genocide Convention and domesticated the offence.[6] An additional 36 states are either signatories or parties to the ICC Statute, which mirrors the prohibition on genocide in the Genocide Convention.[7]

But a critical (and controversial) decision was made sixty years ago during the drafting process. The Genocide Convention excludes political groups, which limits its protections solely to national, ethnic, racial, and religious collectives. Acts intended to physically or biologically destroy the four enumerated collectives are condemned as 'genocide,' whereas identical criminal conduct—directed

[1] Andrić 282 (1945).

[2] *Krstic (AC)* [2004] ICTY ¶¶19–21; SR Ratner, 'The Genocide Convention After Fifty Years: Contemporary Strategies for Combating a Crime Against Humanity' (1998) 92 ASILPROC 1, 1 (nearly 100,000 killed throughout the conflict—mostly Bosnian Muslims).

[3] C Cisse, 'The End of a Culture of Impunity in Rwanda?' (1998) 1 YB-IHL 161, 162 (estimated killings of some 800,000 men, women, and children).

[4] 'Documenting Atrocities in Darfur, Bureau of Democracy, Human Rights, and Labour and the Bureau of Intelligence and Research' (9 Sep 2004) US State Dept Pub No 11182; UNSC Res 1593 (31 Mar 2005) UN Doc S/Res/1593 (referring the Darfur crisis to the ICC).

[5] Professor Reisman's definition of 'international community' is useful: 'the broadest range of official and unofficial international and national decision makers…'. WM Reisman, 'Why Regime Change is (Almost Always) a Bad Idea' (2004) 98 AJIL 516, 520.

[6] Appendix A, Table IV.

[7] Appendix A, Table III.

instead at political groups—is not. This leads to anomalous results in international criminal law.

Consider a narrative. Two men lay dead on the floor of Mubuga Church in Rwanda in 1994. One is a 'politically-moderate' Hutu, the other an 'ethnic' Tutsi. They were massacred at the same time, in the same way, by the same villains and for the same underlying reason (to create a Tutsi-free Rwanda). But international law segregates the irrefutable commonalities of their deaths with legal terminology. One is a victim of genocide; the other is a victim of some other (lesser) crime. The factual reality of their destruction is divided in the courtroom through legal texts of inclusion and exclusion.

This book provides a comprehensive analysis of whether this state of affairs continues to make sense today, if indeed it ever did. It aims to ascertain whether, notwithstanding the decision in 1948, a stand-alone crime of political genocide should be recognized under international law. It critically assesses the legitimacy and wisdom of moving beyond the Genocide Convention's present text and extending its protections to political groups under the same basic structure.[8] It does so with a primary focus on individual criminal responsibility, although the related question of state responsibility[9] also is addressed where appropriate.

The focus on political groups and individual criminal responsibility by no means suggests that the law on genocide is settled in other respects. Far from it. There is much controversy, for example, over the peculiar definition of genocide,[10] other shortcomings of the Convention,[11] and the historic absence of international prosecution for the crime.[12] Issues such as the proper forum in which to prosecute

[8] To provide less cumbersome terminology, conduct against political groups that would constitute genocide against racial, national, religious or ethnic groups is referenced herein as 'political genocide.'

[9] The Convention provides for the 'responsibility' of states under international law but does not specify whether this liability is civil or criminal in nature. Genocide Convention art IX. The ILC has studied state responsibility—including deeply complex issues of whether states themselves even can commit crimes—for over 50 years: Report of the International Law Commission on the Work of its 51st Session (3 May–23 Jul 1999) UN Doc A/54/10 ¶¶49–53. Ultimately, the ILC dropped the proposed criminal framework in favour of one more closely tied to jus cogens norms under the VCLT. Report of the International Law Commission on the Work of its Fifty-Third Session (23 Apr–1 Jun and 2 Jul–10 Aug 2001) UN Doc A/56/10 ¶¶45–49.

[10] Bassiouni, CAH 204 (1999) (querying whether 'it is logical to have a legal scheme whereby the intentional killing of a single person can be genocide and the killing of millions of persons without intent to destroy the protected group in whole or in part is not covered by the same convention, or at least by another one.'); D Luban, 'Calling Genocide by its Rightful Name: Lemkin's Word, Darfur, and the UN Report' (2006) 7 Chicago JIL 303, 319–20 (advocating modification to include an express alternate reference to the crime against humanity of extermination, ostensibly 'to bring [genocide] into line with its moral reality.').

[11] *Cf* A Schlogel, 'Genocide' in 2 Bernhardt 541 (1993) (criticizing jurisdictional provisions). For an article by article critique, see Robinson 53–118 (1960).

[12] Only at the end of the 20th century did the UN seek direct enforcement of the Convention by including genocide in the mandates of the ICTY and ICTR. Both tribunals were created by the UN Security Council under its Chapter VII powers to address threats to international peace and security. For details on the legal basis for establishing the tribunals, see I Morris and Scharf, The ICTY 37–48 (1995) and I Morris and Scharf, The ICTR 75–109 (1998). The first criminal

offenders, the basis of asserting jurisdiction over both offender and offence, the role of human rights norms and fair trial procedures, and other similar questions certainly impact the way in which genocide is investigated and prosecuted on the world stage. Significant grey area also remains in matters such as the use of amnesties to end conflicts threatening international peace and security, international cooperation in investigations and evidence-gathering, extradition and rendition, and the enforcement of penalties issued by international tribunals.

All of these issues—and many others—play an important role in the implementation of the prohibition on genocide under international law. But they are well covered elsewhere[13] and will be put aside here to facilitate a deeper study of human groups, genocide, and political genocide. Background material is limited to what is necessary to underscore the nature of genocide as *sui generis* and to facilitate the application of this unique crime to political collectives.

Given the focus on individual criminal responsibility, the analysis also centres principally on only one of the Genocide Convention's twin aims: punishment. This is not to suggest that preventing genocide is not equally (if not more) important.[14] Indeed, a robust critique has been the international community's historic lack of political will to prevent genocides from occurring in the first place.[15] (The UN clearly held itself directly responsible for its failures to prevent the genocide in Rwanda, for example.[16]) But the question of prevention necessarily intertwines with broader questions of *jus ad bellum*, humanitarian intervention,[17] and the

judgment on genocide in an international forum was not rendered until late 1998. *Akayesu (TC)* [1998] ICTR ¶1. Ongoing international enforcement is contemplated through the ICC. ICC Statute arts 5–6.

[13] *Cf* Cassese, ICL (2003) and Mettraux (2005).

[14] State responsibility for failing to prevent genocide was discussed extensively by the ICJ in its judgment in the 13-year legal dispute between Bosnia and Serbia. *Application of Genocide Convention—Merits* [2007] ICJ 1.

[15] On the failure to intervene, see Fein (1993) (advocating humanitarian intervention as response to genocide) and IPEP Report (7 Jul 2000) 40 ILM 141, 157–61 (chastising non-intervention), 230–31 (calling for reform). Reform may soon become reality. The Secretary-General has unveiled an action plan to prevent future genocides, which includes the appointment of a Special Advisor for Genocide Prevention. The Special Advisor's tripartite responsibilities include: (i) working with the UN High Commissioner on Human Rights to collect information on existing or threatened genocides; (ii) acting as an early-warning mechanism for the Security Council and other parts of the UN system; and (iii) making recommendations to the UN Security Council on actions to prevent and halt genocide. '"Risk of Genocide Remains Frighteningly Real," Secretary-General Tells Human Rights Commission as He Launches New Plan to Prevent Genocide' UN Press Release (7 Apr 2004) UN Doc SG/SM/9197.

[16] Report of the Independent Inquiry into the Actions of the United Nations During the 1994 Genocide in Rwanda (16 Dec 1999) UN Doc S/1999/1257.

[17] There has been some movement toward more precisely defining the grounds justifying the use of force on humanitarian grounds. '2005 World Summit Outcome' UNGA Res 60/1 (15 Sep 2005) UN Doc A/Res/60/1 ¶139 ('The international community, through the United Nations, also has the responsibility . . . to help to protect populations from genocide, war crimes, ethnic cleansing and crimes against humanity. In this context, we are prepared to take collective action, in a timely and decisive manner, through the Security Council, in accordance with the Charter . . . should peaceful

authorization of force by the UN Security Council,[18] all of which are beyond the scope of the present work.

The need to consider fully—and more importantly to act upon—these issues is great. World events continue to demonstrate that the capacity of human beings to draw upon the most base and violent aspects of their natures is equally potent today as it was when the Genocide Convention was first drafted in 1948. Genocide regrettably remains one of the most vexing social problems of our time. More regrettable still, its spectre looms to threaten our collective tomorrow as well. It is unlikely any time soon that genocide will be referenced as an historic problem for a world that has evolved beyond such violence.

My hope for this book is to make some meaningful contribution to the debate insofar as it relates to the application of the concept of genocide to one important collective—political groups. Whatever the justifications back in 1948, there is little reason to continue to deny the Convention's protections to political groups today. Continuing to do so denies the fundamental reality of the ongoing use of genocide as a barbaric tool to achieve political supremacy.[19] Even as this book goes to press, the death toll of tribal peoples in Darfur continues to mount, even as questions loom about the prosecution of senior government officials for genocide in the International Criminal Court.[20]

The analysis of genocide and political groups is set forth principally in eight parts. Chapter 1 details the rapid development of genocide from an academic concept to a substantive international crime. Chapter 2 focuses upon the *actus reus* of genocide, outlining both the conduct elements of the offence and the complexities of identifying the contours of protected groups. Chapter 3 addresses the *mens rea* of genocide. It discusses the crime's unique specific intent requirements and analyses the discriminatory targeting of protected groups for destruction.

Chapter 4 analyses whether political groups merit equal treatment to the four groups enumerated in the Genocide Convention. It discusses first what human 'groups' really are and the inherent difficulties of defining them for legal and social purposes. It then proposes a new understanding of groups for purposes of the crime of genocide. This theory links the legal protection of groups to certain

means be inadequate and national authorities are manifestly failing to protect their populations from genocide, war crimes, ethnic cleansing and crimes against humanity.').

18 G Verdirame, 'The Genocide Definition in the Jurisprudence of the Ad Hoc Tribunals' (2000) 49 ICLQ 578, 583 ('Ultimately, the question of an effective prevention of genocide cannot be separated from that of the legality of humanitarian intervention.... [T]he use of force—either by an individual state or a group of states, or by the Security Council using its Chapter VII powers—is often the only method that can effectively stop or limit the commission of genocidal acts.').

19 *Al Bashir—Request for Arrest Warrant* [2008] ICC 1, 3 (alleging that 'Al Bashir decided and set out to destroy in part the Fur, Masalit and Zaghawa groups, on account of their ethnicity. *His motives were largely political.* His pretext was a "counterinsurgency". His intent was genocide.') (Emphasis added).

20 *Al Bashir (Arrest Warrant—TC)* [2009] ICC 1 ¶¶147–223 (declining to issue arrest warrant on genocide charge); *Al Bashir (Leave to Appeal—TC)* [2009] ICC 1, 5–6 (prosecutor's appeal on genocide issue).

individual rights of a *collective nature* that give rise to the group's existence in this context. This sets the stage for a subsequent analysis that demonstrates that political collectives have many similar characteristics to the existing four groups, such that they likewise should be specifically protected from physical and biological destruction 'as such.'

Chapter 5 addresses the question of whether, as some suggest, political genocide is prohibited *already* by virtue of post-Convention developments in customary international law. It provides the most comprehensive empirical study of state practice and *opinio juris* on genocide and political genocide undertaken to date. This analysis demonstrates conclusively that, although some states criminalize political genocide as a matter of domestic province, there is no basis to conclude that the crime otherwise exists as a free-standing offence under customary international law.

Chapter 6 explores the relationship between genocide and other offences under international law, focusing on crimes against humanity (eg, extermination, torture, and other forms of group violence, as well as unlawful persecution on discriminatory grounds). In some circumstances, crimes against humanity cover similar ground because they outlaw large-scale violence and prohibit serious discrimination based upon membership in certain human groups. The availability of such offences is offered frequently as a sufficient justification not to include political groups within the concept of genocide. Chapter 6 demonstrates that, for a number of reasons, these other crimes are neither a workable nor a sufficient proxy for a separate international prohibition on political genocide.

Chapter 7 discusses why political genocide *should* be proscribed as a separate international crime. It evaluates political genocide in light of the underlying theoretical justifications for international criminal regulation as well as the overall goals of the international criminal justice system. Ultimately, it concludes that the international community should create a separate offence of political genocide to squarely address this conduct.

Chapter 8 explores the manner in which a crime of political genocide might be recognized. It suggests that the optimal way to proceed is through an optional protocol to the 1948 Genocide Convention paired with an amendment to the Statute of the International Criminal Court. It proposes draft treaty language to achieve this end and also explores the political realities and potential objections that must be addressed in order to make the proposed offence a reality.

International criminal law is a rapidly-evolving field, and any publication dealing with it in that sense is aiming at a moving target. My hope is that the state of international and domestic law reflected in this work is current as of early 2010.

1

Defining a Crime Without a Name

'Genocide' is an extraordinarily powerful term. The Genocide Convention labels it an 'odious scourge' on the face of humanity.[1] Others nominate genocide as 'the ultimate crime, the pinnacle of evil.'[2] The word itself conveys the most reprehensible form of criminal conduct, all too often committed on a massive scale that devastates regions and even nations for generations to come.[3] But apart from the shared horror that the word conveys, what exactly is 'genocide,' and how do this crime and the legal mechanisms proscribing it fit within the overall scheme of international law?

The term 'genocide' was coined by law professor Raphael Lemkin, who combined the Greek *genos* (race or tribe) with the Latin *cide* (killing).[4] Although the term is modern, it denotes conduct that has transpired for millennia. Historical examples include the Roman sacking of Carthage in 146 BCE[5] and '[s]pecial wholesale massacres . . . by Genghis Khan and by Tamerlane'.[6] Early 20th century examples include Germany's massacre of tribal Hereros in South-West Africa in 1904 and the mass slaughter of Armenians in the crumbling Ottoman Empire during World War I.[7]

The most well-known modern genocide is the Nazi Holocaust during World War II. While the wholesale extermination of Jews was still underway in 1944, Lemkin, a Polish Jew who barely escaped the Nazi invasion of Poland, published a comprehensive study of atrocities by the Axis Powers. Lemkin conceived the neologism 'genocide' as applied in the context of German occupation practice throughout Europe:

> [G]enocide does not necessarily mean the immediate destruction of a nation, except when accomplished by mass killings of all members of a nation. It is intended rather to signify

[1] Genocide Convention pmbl.

[2] SR Ratner, 'The Genocide Convention After Fifty Years: Contemporary Strategies for Combating a Crime Against Humanity' (1998) 92 ASILPROC 1, 7.

[3] Before the word itself even existed, Winston Churchill recognized the true depths of Nazi atrocities and chillingly referenced 'the presence of a crime without a name'. R Lemkin, 'Genocide' (1946) 15 Am Scholar 227, 227.

[4] Lemkin 79 (1944). Lemkin also called it 'ethnocide,' using the Greek *ethnos* (nation). ibid 79 n 1. 'Ethnocide' in modern discourse generally means the destruction of culture without physical extermination of group members. Fein 10 (1993).

[5] F Chalk and K Jonassohn, 'The History and Sociology of Genocidal Killings' in Charny 39, 42 (1988).

[6] Lemkin 80 n 4.

[7] Harff 3 (1984).

a coordinated plan of different actions aiming at the destruction of essential foundations of the life of national groups, *with the aim of annihilating the groups themselves.* The objectives of such a plan would be disintegration of the political and social institutions, of culture, language, national feelings, religion, and the economic existence of national groups, and the destruction of the personal security, liberty, health, dignity, and even the lives of the individuals belonging to such groups. *Genocide is directed against the national group as an entity, and the actions involved are directed against individuals, not in their individual capacity, but as members of the national group* (emphasis added).[8]

Lemkin saw genocide as a multi-faceted attack on all aspects of a group's existence. He identified eight techniques—political, social, cultural, economic, biological, physical, religious and moral genocide—each aimed at destroying a different dimension of group life.[9] Lemkin agreed, however, that the most widely accepted varieties were physical, biological, and cultural genocide.[10] Physical genocide is the tangible annihilation of the group through the direct or indirect killing of its members.[11] Biological genocide covers measures imposed to decrease the reproductive capacity or fertility of the group.[12] Cultural genocide is the destruction of the group's unique cultural, linguistic, and religious characteristics.[13]

A. Genocide as a legal concept

Lemkin's descriptive concept of genocide merged quickly into legal terminology and criminal proceedings soon after World War II ended. The victorious Allies determined that Nazi offences could not go unpunished[14] and convened an international military tribunal for this purpose.[15] The IMT's mandate covered Germany's aggressive military activities abroad as crimes against peace and war

[8] Lemkin 79 (1944). [9] ibid 79–90.

[10] R Lemkin, 'Genocide as a Crime Under International Law' (15 Jan 1948) UN Bull 70–1.

[11] Lemkin 87–9 (1944). [12] ibid 86–7.

[13] Cultural genocide includes the abolition of a group's language and the restriction of education in the ways of the targeted group. It also entails the destruction of religious institutions, theft or destruction of religious objects, and persecution or killing of clergy. Artistic, literary, and cultural activities are restricted or outlawed and national treasures, libraries, archives, museums, artefacts, and art galleries are destroyed or confiscated. ibid 84–5, 89. For a paradigm of cultural genocide, see Greiser [1946] 13 LRTWC 70 (Pol Sup Nat'l Trib) (educational, linguistic, religious, cultural, and scientific destruction in Poland).

[14] London Agreement 280. Nineteen other states subsequently acceded to the Agreement. ibid n 1 (Australia, Belgium, Czechoslovakia, Denmark, Ethiopia, Greece, Haiti, Honduras, India, Luxembourg, the Netherlands, New Zealand, Norway, Panama, Paraguay, Poland, Uruguay, Venezuela, and Yugoslavia). Parallel prosecutions were undertaken against Japanese war criminals. IMTFE Charter; *Araki* [IMTFE 1946] 101–3 IMTFE Proceedings 48413–858.

[15] The IMT was limited to high-level offenders. IMT Charter art 1. Lower-level criminals were returned to the states where they committed their crimes for trial before national or military courts. ibid arts 4, 6.

crimes.[16] Nazi abuses against other civilian populations (including Germany's own) were addressed through the separate concept of crimes against humanity.[17]

Genocide was not included in the IMT Charter but appeared in the indictment describing Nazi offences:

deliberate and systematic genocide; viz, the extermination of racial and national groups, against the civilian populations of certain occupied territories in order to destroy particular races and classes of people, and national, racial, or religious groups, particularly Jews, Poles, and Gypsies.[18]

Similar descriptions appeared in the prosecutors' closing arguments:

Genocide was not restricted to extermination of the Jewish people or of the Gypsies. It was applied in different forms to Yugoslavia, to the non-German inhabitants of Alsace-Lorraine, to the people of the Low Countries and of Norway. The technique varied from nation to nation, from people to people. The long-term aim was the same in all cases.[19]

[The defendants engaged in] the scientific and systematic extermination of millions of human beings and more especially of certain national or religious groups whose existence hampered the hegemony of the German race. This is a crime so monstrous, so undreamt of in history... that the term 'genocide' has had to be coined to define it and an accumulation of documents and testimonies has been needed to make it credible.[20]

A number of Nazi party principals, policymakers and collaborators were convicted of crimes against humanity, war crimes and crimes against peace.[21] Although none were convicted directly of 'genocide', these early efforts to grapple with massive criminality through new terminology set the stage for the evolution of genocide into a separate criminal offence.

The substantive legal content of genocide began to emerge soon after Nuremberg in several trials of high-level Nazi offenders under Allied Control Council Law No 10 (CC10).[22] CC10 expanded the concept of crimes against humanity but, like the IMT Charter, contained no specific reference to genocide.[23] Nevertheless, two American courts applying CC10 convicted defendants of crimes against humanity based on their commission of acts of genocide.[24]

[16] ibid art 6(a)–(b). War crimes delineate permissible methods of warfare and are distinguished from ordinary murder, destruction of property, etc through mandatory contextual elements that limit their application to armed conflict. International humanitarian law is reflected principally in the Geneva Conventions, which were adopted shortly after World War II. Geneva Conventions I–IV; ICC Statute art 8(2)(a) (prohibiting acts against 'persons or property protected under the provisions of the relevant Geneva Conventions'), 8(2)(b) (detailing '[o]ther serious violations of the laws and customs applicable in international armed conflict'), and 8(2)(c),(d) (acts prohibited in 'armed conflicts not of an international character.').

[17] IMT Charter art 6(c).

[18] *IMT Indictment* [1946] 2 IMT Proceedings 45.

[19] *Göring* [IMT 1946] 19 IMT Proceedings 1, 497 (British prosecutor).

[20] ibid 531 (French prosecutor).

[21] ibid 366–7.

[22] CC10 established a uniform basis for prosecutions in the four Allied occupation zones, whether those trials took place before French, British, Russian, or American tribunals. Taylor 277–335 (1949). The trials under CC10 are further detailed in Chapter 6.

[23] CC10 art II(1)(c).

[24] *Justice* [USMT 1947] 3 TWC 1; *RuSHA* [USMT 1948] 4 TWC 599.

The *Justice*[25] case involved abuses of the German legal system by Nazi lawyers, prosecutors and judges. Proceedings focused upon Germany's *Nacht und Nebel* (Night and Fog) Decree, which required the death penalty even for trivial offences by foreign nationals.[26] Trials were allowed in occupied territories only if the death penalty would be imposed and carried out immediately; otherwise, defendants were returned to Germany for trial.[27] Defendants were denied even the most basic due process, including the right to present evidence, to confront charges and to prepare a defence.[28] Thousands of prisoners—some acquitted locally—were tried in Germany and subsequently executed or sentenced to concentration camps.[29]

The *Justice* tribunal labelled genocide 'the prime illustration of a crime against humanity under [CC10]' and held that '[w]hether the crime against humanity [genocide] is the product of statute or of common international law, or, as we believe, of both, we find no injustice to persons tried for such crimes.'[30] The former chief prosecutor and a former judge in Berlin were convicted of genocide for furthering Nazi race policy by perverting German laws on high treason.[31] The court found that each defendant 'was an accessory to and took a consenting part in the crime of genocide',[32] which itself was 'the prime illustration of a crime against humanity under [CC10]'.[33]

RuSHA[34] dealt with genocide arising out of Nazi race policy in occupied territories. The defendants were government officials that implemented Reich decrees against Jews and other racial and ethnic groups in order to 'safeguard the supposed superiority of "Nordic" blood, and to exterminate and suppress all sources which might "dilute" or "taint" it.'[35] They kidnapped children of 'racial value' for 'Germanization', forced abortions, prevented marriage and reproduction, criminalized racial 'inferiors' from having sexual intercourse with Germans, and systematically exterminated 'undesirable' racial elements.[36] Thirteen defendants were convicted of crimes against humanity based upon this 'systematic programme of genocide' aimed at the 'destruction of foreign nations and ethnic groups'.[37]

The genocide convictions under CC10 represented an evolution of the concept from a descriptive term at Nuremberg to a substantive offence (albeit a sub-set of the wider concept of crimes against humanity). Even before the American trials under CC10, however, genocide had been prosecuted as a criminal offence in Poland. The Polish Supreme National Tribunal embraced and applied Raphael Lemkin's descriptive framework as falling within a special domestic law aimed at

[25] *Justice* [USMT 1947] 3 TWC 1. [26] ibid 1035–7. [27] ibid.
[28] ibid 1046–7. [29] ibid 1046–52. [30] ibid 983. [31] ibid 1120–56.
[32] ibid 1128. [33] ibid 1156. [34] *RuSHA* [USMT 1948] 4 TWC 599.
[35] ibid 626. [36] ibid 609–17.
[37] ibid 609. The court drew explicitly upon Lemkin's academic writings in its legal findings: ibid 626.

Poland's former Nazi occupiers[38] and convicted three high-ranking Nazi officials of the offence.

Artur Greiser was the Nazi party chief governing occupied territory in Western Poland.[39] His orders and policies led directly to the deaths of thousands of Jews and Poles, the destruction of schools and religious institutions, and the starvation of sick children and pregnant women (which significantly impacted Polish fertility).[40] The court recognized this conduct as physical, biological, and cultural genocide, characterizing Greiser's actions as a 'totalitarian genocidal attack on the rights of small and medium nations to exist, and to have an identity and culture of their own.'[41] He was convicted and hanged.[42]

The second case involved Amon Goeth, former commandant of the forced labour camp at Plaszów (Kraków), Poland.[43] Goeth caused thousands of deaths by liquidating the Kraków and Tarnów ghettos and transporting the inhabitants to concentration camps.[44] The Tribunal found Goeth guilty of physical genocide ('the policy of extermination . . . against the Jewish and Polish nations') as well as biological and cultural genocide ('[t]he wholesale extermination of Jews and also of Poles had all the characteristics of genocide in the biological meaning of this term, and embraced in addition the destruction of the cultural life of these nations').[45] Goeth too was hanged.[46]

The third case involved Rudolf Hoess, deposed commandant of the Auschwitz concentration camp.[47] Hoess was held personally responsible for the deaths of 2.5 million people.[48] Trial proceedings detailed extensive medical experiments on Jewish victims involving sterilization, castration, and abortion.[49] The court labelled Nazi plans to biologically and culturally exterminate conquered nations 'an attempt on the most organic bases of the human relationship such as the right to live and the right to existence.'[50] The medical experiments, in particular, were held preparatory to genocide as scientific explorations of methods to destroy the reproductive power of conquered nations.[51] Hoess too was convicted and hanged.[52]

[38] Polish Decree on Punishment (31 Aug 1944) reproduced in (1948) 7 LRTWC 82, 84:
'*Article* 1. []Any person who, assisting the authorities of the German State . . .
(1) took part in committing acts of murder against the civilian population, members of the armed forces or prisoners of war; or
(2) by giving information or detaining, acted to the detriment of persons wanted or persecuted by the said authorities on political, national, religious or racial grounds—
is liable to the death penalty.'

[39] *Greiser* [1946] 13 LRTWC 70 (Pol Sup Nat'l Trib) 70–1.

[40] ibid 105.

[41] ibid 114.

[42] ibid 104.

[43] *Goeth* [1947] 7 LRTWC 1 (Pol Sup Nat'l Trib). Stephen Spielberg later dramatized Goeth's crimes. *Schindler's List* (Universal Pictures 1993).

[44] ibid 2–4.

[45] ibid 9.

[46] ibid 4.

[47] *Hoess* [1947] 7 LRTWC 11 (Pol Sup Nat'l Trib).

[48] ibid 17.

[49] ibid 14–16.

[50] ibid 24.

[51] ibid 25. Under the Convention, such acts are genocide in and of themselves. Genocide Convention art II(d).

[52] *Hoess* [1947] 7 LRTWC 11 (Pol Sup Nat'l Trib) 17. After trial in Warsaw, Hoess was returned to Auschwitz and hanged in front of its crematorium. Smoleń 21 (1999).

B. The Genocide Convention

In a few short years, genocide evolved from an academic concept, to a descriptive reference at Nuremberg, to a type of crime against humanity, and finally to a substantive offence under domestic law. This momentum culminated in a multilateral treaty addressing genocide as a separate international offence—distinct from crimes against humanity and domestic law.

As discussed in much greater detail in Chapter 5, the Genocide Convention that exists today was the product of three UN General Assembly resolutions, three multinational drafting committees, three working drafts, and the participation of numerous states, voting blocs and ideological constituencies. The final draft of the treaty was approved unanimously by the General Assembly in December 1948[53] and achieved sufficient ratification two years later, entering into force in January 1951.[54]

The Genocide Convention provides that genocide unquestionably is an international crime: '[t]he Contracting Parties confirm that Genocide, whether committed in time of peace or in time of war, is a crime under international law which they undertake to prevent and to punish.'[55] It confirms the worldwide application of the international prohibition on genocide in all possible circumstances. Acts of genocide create criminal responsibility for individuals[56] and legal responsibility for states.[57]

The Convention defines the crime as:

> [A]ny of the following acts committed with intent to destroy, in whole or in part, a national, ethnical,[58] racial or religious group, as such:
> (a) Killing members of the group;
> (b) Causing serious bodily or mental harm to members of the group;
> (c) Deliberately inflicting on the group conditions of life calculated to bring about its physical destruction in whole or in part;
> (d) Imposing measures intended to prevent births within the group;
> (e) Forcibly transferring children of the group to another group.[59]

The Convention protects *people* and criminalizes physical and biological genocide only.[60] The object of protection is the group itself. Although '[g]roups consist of individuals, and therefore destructive action must, in the last analysis, be

[53] UNGA Res 260-A (III) (9 Dec 1948) UN Doc A/810.

[54] Bassiouni, Conventions 1224 (1997).

[55] Genocide Convention art I.

[56] ibid art IV.

[57] ibid art IX; *Application of Genocide Convention—Merits* [2007] ICJ 1 ¶¶159–69, 428–50.

[58] Several texts replicating the Convention replace 'ethnical' with 'ethnic.' *Cf* [1996] Draft Code art 17. Others do not. *Cf* ICC Statute art 6. This writing uses 'ethnic,' crediting the Draft Code's effort 'to reflect modern English usage without in any way affecting the substance of the provision'. [1996] Draft Code art 17 cmt 9.

[59] Genocide Convention art II.

[60] Article II(a), (b), and (c) cover physical genocide. Article II(d) and (e) cover biological genocide: [1996] Draft Code art 17 cmt 12.

taken against individuals [,] ... these *individuals are important not per se but only as members of the group to which they belong.*' (Emphasis added).[61] Cultural genocide was deleted from the final text because a majority of the drafters saw it as analytically distinct,[62] although there was much disagreement on the point.[63]

There is no requirement under the Convention that a genocidaire[64] achieve his aims or that the group actually suffer total or partial destruction. The crime is complete when certain enumerated acts are committed against group members with the requisite intent.[65] Genocide thus is defined as an inchoate offence *vis à vis* the protected groups. Inchoate offences criminalize certain acts committed with a particular mental state, whether or not those acts actually lead to the injury contemplated (eg, attempts).[66] This is in contrast to result-oriented offences, which require the act in question actually to achieve a specified result (eg, murder).[67] The actual destruction of all or part of the group simply is not required.

Genocide under the Convention thus is far more restrictive than Lemkin's original conception. Offences against a group's property,[68] cultural heritage,[69] or social fabric (including expulsion from traditional homeland or locale)[70] are not covered. It is physical and biological violence perpetrated against group members, rather than a broad attack on the group's holistic existence, that is punishable as genocide under international law.

The definition of genocide—clearly the product of compromise—is hardly perfect. Its technical oddities prompted Professor Bassiouni to query whether 'it

[61] Robinson 58 (1960).

[62] Official Records (6th Comm 1948) (SR83) 206 (approved 25–16, 4 abstentions, 13 absences); ibid (SR63) 8 (Fr) (nature of cultural genocide).

[63] Compare ibid (SR83) 198–9 (Den) (arguing that logic and proportion mitigated against including 'in the same convention both mass murders in gas chambers and the closing of libraries.') with ibid 196 (Venez) (arguing that groups could be destroyed by attacks on culture even absent the physical destruction of their members). The drafters took no position on the viability of the concept itself, leaving it to be addressed through another international instrument. Genocide: Draft Convention and Report of the Economic and Social Council, Report of the Sixth Committee (3 Dec 1948) UN Doc A/760 ¶11.

[64] As used here, this term denotes individuals that in fact have engaged in all constituent elements of the crime of genocide—in contrast to the practice of international tribunals to refer to individuals *charged* with such offences as an 'accused.' *Cf* ICTY Statute art 21 ('Rights of the accused'). The alternate term 'genocidist' is little used today. *Cf* Robinson 77 (1960).

[65] Drost 82 (1959).

[66] AJ Ashworth, 'Defining Criminal Offences Without Harm' in Smith 8 (1987).

[67] ibid.

[68] Property crimes can constitute physical genocide under some circumstances. For example, intentionally destroying or removing food, water, clothing, shelter, or medicine, the absence of which causes death or serious injury, probably violates arts II(a), II(b), and/or II(c). Robinson 63–4 (1960).

[69] The prohibition on the removal of children in art II(e) provides limited cultural protection in addition to ensuring the biological survival of the group through its later generations. This is discussed in Chapter 2.

[70] Ratner (n 2) 2; *Eichmann (TC)* [1961] 36 ILR 5 (Isr Dist Ct) 230 (dismissing genocide charges for deporting Jews before mid-1941, which were not proven to have been accomplished with the specific intent to destroy the group).

is logical to have a legal scheme whereby the intentional killing of a single person can be genocide and the killing of millions of persons without intent to destroy the protected group in whole or in part is not covered by the same convention, or at least by another one.'[71]

Bassiouni's point is a good one. Whether a 'better' definition of the offence could have been achieved when the Convention was drafted, and what this superior conception would look like, are important questions. They are, however, separate matters that cannot be addressed here. For present purposes, the definition of the crime of genocide as it appears in the Convention is simply accepted at face value.[72]

Under the Convention, genocide requires proof of three specific elements:

1. One or more prohibited acts;
2. Against members of a national, racial, ethnical or religious group;
3. Committed with intent to destroy, in whole or in part, the protected group 'as such.'[73]

The first two comprise the *actus reus* or conduct elements of the crime.[74] The third is genocide's *mens rea*, or personal fault element.[75] *Actus reus* is analysed in Chapter 2 and *mens rea* in Chapter 3.[76]

[71] Bassiouni, CAH 204 (1999).

[72] There clearly is logic behind the definition. In theory, it empowers the international community to stop genocides in their early stages before significant destruction actually occurs. *Application of Genocide Convention—Merits* [2007] ICJ 1 ¶438 ('for a State to be held responsible for breaching its obligation of prevention, it does not need to be proven that the State concerned definitely had the power to prevent the genocide; it is sufficient that it had the means to do so and that it manifestly refrained from using them.'). It also identifies 'the singular evil of genocide' and places the 'focus on the communal rather than the individual aspect of the crime.': D Luban, 'A Theory of Crimes Against Humanity' 29 Yale JIL 85, 97 n 44.

[73] Genocide Convention art II.

[74] *Jelisic (TC)* [1999] ICTY ¶62.

[75] ibid.

[76] As detailed in Chapter 6, the ICC specifies a fourth (jurisdictional) element: that '[t]he conduct took place in the context of a manifest [objective] pattern of similar conduct directed against [the target group] or was conduct that itself could effect such destruction.' Elements of Crimes art 6(a)–(e). This restriction, which sensibly delineates matters of international concern *a priori*, applies only in the ICC.

2

Conduct Elements

In any system of criminal justice, individual responsibility is grounded in personal autonomy. It requires that offenders voluntarily engage in certain prohibited acts (the *actus reus* of the offence).[1] This is no less true for international crimes, which have their conduct elements specified either by treaty (eg, the ICC Statute) or through customary international law (eg, the customary principles codified in the ICTY and ICTR Statutes). That said, international crimes typically manifest on a far greater scale than domestic offences. It therefore is worthwhile to briefly discuss some of the unique provisions of international criminal justice before turning to the conduct elements of the specific crime of genocide.

Although massive scale is not a technical requirement of all international crimes, the reality is that culpability for the criminal activity at issue often extends across thousands (or even tens or hundreds of thousands) of individuals, ranging from the highest-level actors planning and ordering crimes to individual perpetrators carrying them out on the ground. International criminal law responds to this lengthy chain of criminal responsibility in three principal ways.

First, it takes a broad view on how individual actors can perpetrate an international offence, either individually[2] or in concert with others through a 'joint criminal enterprise' (JCE). JCE covers situations where the conduct elements of a crime are diffused through multiple actors but the fault of each individual is not reduced. Each participant is liable as a co-perpetrator, provided that he actually participates and intends 'to engage in the common criminal action.'[3]

[1] The broad conditions of criminal liability include: (i) voluntary act requirements; (ii) absence of justification; (iii) positive fault requirements; and (iv) negative fault requirements. Ashworth, Principles 96–7 (2003).

[2] Personal commission is the broadest form of perpetration and includes both the actual execution of a crime and culpable omissions leading to it. *Kajelijeli (TC)* [2003] ICTR ¶764; [1996] Draft Code art 2(3)(b) cmt ¶7.

[3] Cassese, ICL 181–2 (2003). There are two primary methods of commission via JCE. Type-1 covers groups like the Einsatzgruppen–Nazi killing squads that massacred Jews and other 'undesirables' in occupied territories during World War II. *Einsatzgruppen* [USMT 1948] 4 TWC 1. Type-2 is a variant of the first, where offenders actively participate in a general *system* of ill treatment (eg, a concentration camp, a slave labour factory, etc) with personal knowledge and the intent to further the system's ends. *Vasiljevic (AC)* [2004] ICTY ¶¶100–1; *Hadamar* [USMT 1945] 1 LRTWC 46 (medical personnel who poisoned over 400 allied prisoners in a sanatorium, where the 'production line of death' included an administrator, a doctor, three nurses, clerical employees

Second, international criminal law casts a wide net of secondary liability[4] for planning,[5] instigating,[6] ordering,[7] or aiding and abetting[8] international crimes. It also recognizes limited forms of the three main types of inchoate offences—attempts,[9] incitement,[10] and conspiracy.[11]

Finally, international criminal law recognizes two forms of constructive liability to hold individuals directly liable for offences committed by others: (i) 'extended' joint criminal enterprise (where a willing participant in a JCE can be held liable for collateral offences committed by other members);[12] and

who falsified death records, and a caretaker who disposed of bodies); Cassese, ICL 182–5 (2003) (additional discussion).

[4] ICTY Statute art 7(1); ICTR Statute art 6(1); ICC Statute art 25(3)(a)–(c).

[5] Planning covers the design of a course of criminal conduct by one or more persons, provided that the accused is substantially involved in formulating or endorsing the plan. *Kajelijeli (TC)* [2003] ICTR ¶761. Unlike conspiracy, planning can be accomplished by one person.

[6] Instigating is prompting another to commit a crime where the prompting substantially contributes to the actual commission of the offence. *Kordic & Cerkez (AC)* [2004] ICTY ¶27. Unlike incitement, instigation need be neither direct nor public.

[7] Ordering is using a formal or informal position of authority to instruct another to commit a crime. ibid ¶28. Ordering is an abuse of authority involving twin wrongs: failing to ensure the lawful conduct of subordinates and the separate breach of an obligation to exercise authority lawfully. [1996] Draft Code art 2(3)(b) cmt ¶8.

[8] Aiding and abetting includes encouraging, supporting or assisting in the commission of a specific offence: (i) with knowledge that the conduct will help the principal to commit it; and (ii) where the assistance has a substantial effect on the actual commission of the offence. *Tadic (Merits—AC)* [1999] ICTY ¶229. There are theoretical distinctions between aiding and abetting and the crime of complicity, premised largely upon the unique nature of genocide, but in application they are treated as largely co-extensive. G Dawson and R Boynton, 'Reconciling Complicity in Genocide and Aiding and Abetting Genocide in the Jurisprudence of the United Nations Ad Hoc Tribunals' (2008) 21 Harv HRJ 241, 277–9.

[9] The ICTY and ICTR Statutes recognize attempts only for genocide. ICTR Statute art 2(3)(d); ICTY Statute art 4(3)(d). The ICC Statute is more progressive and includes attempts to commit any crime in the ICC's jurisdiction that is prevented by reasons independent of an accused's wishes. ICC Statute art 25(3)(f). This includes both complete attempts, where he completes all acts intended without the desired consequence (eg, where D shoots at V intending to murder him but misses), and incomplete attempts, where D is deprived of the chance to commit certain acts (eg, where D intends to murder V but is apprehended en route).

[10] Incitement includes all forms of pressure, threat or persuasion. *Kajelijeli (TC)* [2003] ICTR ¶850; Cassese, ICL 189 (2003) ('psychological or physical measures designed to prompt somebody else to commit a crime').

[11] Conspiracy is recognized in the ICTY and ICTR only for genocide and is not covered at all in the ICC. ICTR Statute art 2(3)(b); ICTY Statute art 4(3)(b), ICC Statute art 25(3). Unlike planning, which requires that the crime in question actually transpire, a conspiracy exists the instant a criminal agreement is reached. *Musema (TC)* [2000] ICTR ¶194.

[12] Extended JCE is recognized in domestic law as well. Simester and Sullivan 219–26 (2003) (theoretical bases for JCE); *Powell and Daniels* [1998] 1 Cr App R 261 (UK HL) (upholding murder conviction where it was foreseeable that co-venturer might kill during a drug deal). Liability can be so-constructed for any crime, even serious offences like genocide. *Milosevic (Motion to Acquit—TC)* [2004] ICTY ¶¶246, 248. A similar analysis applies to foreseeable offences outside a 'system' of ill treatment in a type-2 JCE. S Powles, 'Joint Criminal Enterprise—Criminal Liability by Prosecutorial Ingenuity and Judicial Creativity?' (2004) 2 Oxford JICJ 606, 609–10.

(ii) command or superior responsibility (where commanders are held liable for offences committed by subordinates that they failed to prevent or punish).[13]

The broad range of tools in the prosecutorial arsenal thus allows individuals to be held responsible for international crimes in many ways. In cases involving genocide, for example, depending on the perpetrator's conduct and mental state, he is potentially liable for:

1. The crime of genocide itself, as defined in Article II of the Genocide Convention (committed either individually or through a JCE);
2. Secondary liability for genocide (aiding and abetting, ordering, instigating or planning acts of genocide committed by others);
3. Inchoate liability either for attempted genocide (when he has the *mens rea* for genocide but fails to actually commit the offence himself) or for incitement or conspiracy to commit genocide; and
4. Constructive liability for acts of genocide committed by others, either as a collateral crime committed by co-participants in a JCE or by his civilian or military subordinates via the command responsibility doctrine.[14]

These interlocking modes of criminal liability present complex analytical questions in and of themselves. In particular, deep theoretical conflicts arise when the doctrines of 'extended' JCE and 'command responsibility' are applied to specific intent offences such as genocide, which normally are restricted to a narrow range of conduct undertaken with a highly-specific mental state. As noted above, extended JCE and command responsibility hold individuals liable for the offences committed by others, even when they did not personally engage in the prohibited conduct and when they acted with far less blameworthy *mens rea*.

As important as these issues are, they fall outside the scope of the present work. There is extensive discourse[15] (including other writing by the author)[16] analysing how the deeper theoretical questions play out in the prosecution of international

[13] *Blagojevic (TC)* [2005] ICTY ¶790. Note that command responsibility is a distinct form of liability from the direct criminal responsibility of commanders who actually order subordinates to commit criminal acts.

[14] The categories are not entirely insular. As noted previously, an offender may be liable both for committing an offence and for conspiring with others or instigating it. He may also be secondarily liable for offences committed by others and directly liable for the identical offence committed himself, though not for the same course of conduct. *Ntakirutimana (AC)* [2004] ICTR ¶508 (determination that accused committed genocide does not preclude convicting him of aiding and abetting genocide by others).

[15] *Cf* Schabas 361–2 (2009); MJ Osiel, 'Obeying Orders: Atrocity, Military Discipline and the Law of War' (1998) 86 Cal LR 944, 1040 (breadth of liability for 'atrocity by connivance,' while problematic, 'is necessary to prevent superiors from slipping between the cracks of criminal liability by insulating themselves from detailed knowledge of their subordinates criminal activities.').

[16] D Nersessian, 'Whoops—I Committed Genocide! The Anomaly of Constructive Liability for Serious International Crimes' (2006) 30 Fletcher F World Aff 81.

crimes. For present purposes, it suffices simply to remain mindful of the many avenues through which individual criminal responsibility for genocide may be pursued.

A. The prohibited acts

Article II is restrictive. Only the five listed acts are covered. Despite the general sense that genocide applies to cases of mass slaughter, a protected group need not actually be destroyed. Genocide is completed when a prohibited act is committed against a group member with intent to destroy the group.[17] There is no numeric threshold of victims.[18]

Genocide thus is an inchoate offence *vis à vis* the protected group. Inchoate offences criminalize the doing of certain acts with a particular mental state, whether or not the intended harm occurs (eg, attempts).[19] This contrasts with results-oriented offences, where the act actually must achieve a prohibited result to complete the offence (eg, murder).[20]

Killing members of the group

Article II(a) covers the direct killing[21] of members of the group. It deals with situations such as the Holocaust, where millions of Jews were murdered in an effort to destroy the Jewish race in Europe. The material aspects are satisfied if the victim dies and if that death results from an unlawful act or omission.[22]

Causing serious bodily or mental harm

Article II(b) prohibits '[c]ausing serious bodily or mental harm to members of the group.'[23] It includes:

> enslavement, starvation, deportation, and persecution of the [members of the protected group]... [and] their detention in ghettos, transit camps and concentration camps in conditions which were designed to cause their degradation, deprivation of their rights as human beings, and to suppress them and cause them inhumane suffering and torture.[24]

17 Drost 82 (1959). 18 *Kajelijeli (TC)* [2003] ICTR ¶809.
19 AJ Ashworth, 'Defining Criminal Offences Without Harm' in Smith 8 (1987).
20 ibid. 21 This is interchangeable with 'caused death.' Elements of Crimes art 6(a) n 2.
22 *Akayesu (TC)* [1998] ICTR ¶588. 23 Genocide Convention art II(b).
24 *Eichmann (TC)* [1961] 36 ILR 5 (Isr Dist Ct) 238. Although *Eichmann* was a domestic case, its international character is evident. The court justified applying Israeli law to Eichmann's crimes in occupied Europe in part based on universal jurisdiction over the crime of genocide. ibid 26.

The provision covers 'bodily or mental torture, inhumane or degrading treatment, rape, sexual violence and persecution,'[25] as well as forced impregnation,[26] death threats during interrogation[27] and the imposition of mind-altering drugs.[28] Article II(b) also covers broader conduct such as forced displacement and terrorizing the local populace.[29]

Seriousness is assessed on a case-by-case basis,[30] and there is some debate over what constitutes 'serious mental injury.' American legislation, for example, requires '*permanent* impairment of the mental facilities' (emphasis added)[31] arising out of 'physical intrusion of the body (such as the injection of drugs, acts of torture, electric shock, etc).'[32] This position, meant to discourage specious allegations,[33] has some historical support. The *travaux* reflect the view of some states that mental injury alone could not destroy a group.[34]

The permanency qualification applies only in US domestic law, however. Nothing in the Convention limits mental harm by duration or source. It requires only serious injury 'that results in a grave and long-term disadvantage to a person's ability to lead a normal and constructive life'.[35] Both international criminal tribunals have held that that mental injury need not be permanent or irremediable under customary international law,[36] and no such restriction applies in the ICC.[37]

Imposing destructive conditions of life

Article II(c) prohibits '[d]eliberately inflicting on the group conditions of life calculated to bring about its physical destruction in whole or in part'.[38] It covers acts without the temporal immediacy of 'killing' under Article II(a) and contemplates the extermination of a group over time.[39]

Article II(c) does not specifically delineate the proscribed conduct. This was intentional and stems from the practical impossibility of specifying in advance all acts that qualify.[40] The determination is made case-by-case under the totality of the circumstances.[41] It clearly includes 'placing a group on a subsistence [starvation] diet, reducing required medical services below a minimum, [and]

[25] *Musema (TC)* [2000] ICTR ¶156.

[26] Forced impregnation can be accomplished by artificial means but also may constitute rape as 'a physical invasion of a sexual nature'. *Akayesu (TC)* [1998] ICTR ¶598. *Cf* SK Fisher, 'Occupation of the Womb: Forced Impregnation as Genocide' (1996) 46 Duke LJ 91.

[27] *Akayesu (TC)* [1998] ICTR ¶¶711–12.

[28] Proxmire Act (1988) 18 USC s 1091(a)(3).

[29] *Jokic (TC)* [2005] ICTY ¶¶644–54.

[30] *Kajelijeli (TC)* [2003] ICTR ¶815.

[31] Proxmire Act (1988) 18 USC s 1091(a)(3).

[32] MN Leich, 'Contemporary Practice of the United States Relating to International Law' (1986) 80 AJIL 612, 619.

[33] LeBlanc 107 (1991).

[34] Official Records (6th Comm 1948) (SR81) (UK).

[35] *Krstic (TC)* [2001] ICTY ¶513.

[36] *Stakic (TC)* [2003] ICTY ¶516; *Musema (TC)* [2000] ICTR ¶157.

[37] Elements of Crimes art 6(b).

[38] Genocide Convention art II(c).

[39] *Akayesu (TC)* [1998] ICTR ¶505.

[40] Robinson 63 (1960).

[41] ibid.

withholding sufficient living accommodations'.[42] It also covers deportations and expulsions committed with the requisite intent[43] and other acts of 'slow death' such as eliminating the necessities of life or imposing excessive work or physical exertion upon the group.[44]

Preventing births within the group

Article II(d), which prohibits '[i]mposing measures to prevent births within the group',[45] had its genesis in the Nazis'

> gigantic plan to change permanently the population balance in occupied Europe in their favour.... [and] to wipe out entirely the national-biological power of the neighbours of Germany so that Germany might win a permanent victory,... [where] even in the case of Germany's defeat the neighbours would be so weakened that Germany would be able to recover her strength in later years.[46]

The coercive element is critical. Voluntary birth control programmes, even if state-sponsored, are not genocide.[47] Article II(d) covers all measures imposed to prevent reproduction and 'was broadly conceived as encompassing castration, compulsory abortion, sterilization and the segregation of the sexes'.[48] Less directly, it includes forced birth control and prohibitions on marriage,[49] as well as rape perpetrated in societal contexts that stigmatize the victim and render them socially unfit for subsequent marriage or procreation.[50] The same holds true with forced impregnation, where the victim is forced to carry an unwanted foetus and often suffers stigmatization that disrupts her primary family and social relationships even after the child is born.[51]

The measures can be mental or physical and include threats and trauma impeding procreation.[52] Selective deportation (eg, all males, all females of child-bearing years, etc) qualifies,[53] as do killings focused on one gender.[54] It also can

[42] ibid 63–4.

[43] Daes 72 (1973). Forced relocation without the intent to destroy the group is not genocide. *Krstic (AC)* [2004] ICTY ¶33.

[44] *Kayishema (TC)* [1999] ICTR ¶¶115–16; Lemkin 87–9 (1944).

[45] Genocide Convention art II(d).

[46] R Lemkin, 'Genocide as a Crime under International Law' (1947) 41 AJIL 145, 147.

[47] [1996] Draft Code art 17 cmt 16.

[48] M Lippman, 'The Convention on the Prevention and Punishment of the Crime of Genocide: Fifty Years Later' (1998) 15 Arizona JICL 414, 457.

[49] *Musema (TC)* [2000] ICTR ¶158.

[50] 'Women and peace and security' UNSC Res 1888 (30 Sept 2009) UN Doc S/RES/1888 ¶15 (encouraging 'leaders at the national and local level, including traditional leaders where they exist and religious leaders, to play a more active role in sensitizing communities on sexual violence to avoid marginalization and stigmatization of victims, to assist with their social reintegration, and to combat a culture of impunity for these crimes').

[51] *Akayesu (TC)* [1998] ICTR ¶¶508, 598; Fisher (n 102).

[52] *Akayesu (TC)* [1998] ICTR ¶508.

[53] [1996] Draft Code art 17 cmt 15; Daes 72 (1973).

[54] *Krstic (AC)* [2004] ICTY ¶28 (targeting of young Muslim males in Srebrenica had 'severe procreative implications for the Srebrenica Muslim community, potentially consigning [it] to extinction.').

be accomplished by imposing a starvation diet that reduces the overall birth rate or lowers the survival capacity of children born to undernourished parents.[55]

Transferring the children of the group

Article II(e) prohibits '[f]orcibly transferring children of the group to another group'[56] but does not define 'children'. The US legislation defines a child as a person under the age of eighteen,[57] which appears consonant with other international law.[58] The violations contemplated by this provision were analysed at length in *RuSHA*, where 'racially valuable' children of foreign nationals were removed for 'Germanization'.[59]

The prohibition includes not only direct removal, but also threats, coercion or intimidation leading to it.[60] Removal alone is insufficient—children must be transferred to another *group*, ostensibly to another protected group (racial, ethnic, national or religious).[61] Article II(e) prevents group characteristics (religion, etc) from being replaced by alien characteristics from a different group. Removing children for political 're-education' thus is not genocide because the characteristic of 'political identity' is not covered by the Convention.[62]

The removal of children clearly is physically and biologically destructive. The removal violates Articles II(a) (if the children are killed), II(b) (serious mental injury to parents and children from breaking up the family), and II(d) (group members are less likely to reproduce if they know their children will be taken). But despite the overlap, the Convention provides special protection with the proviso of transfer to another *group*. In this sense, Article II(e) is 'strangely out of place in the [C]onvention'.[63]

The reason for this is that Article II(e) returns weak notions of cultural genocide to the treaty. The drafters agreed that removing children had physically and biologically destructive effects.[64] But the *travaux* reflect the further view that transferring children into foreign environments where they would be indoctrinated into the customs, language, religion and values of another group was 'tantamount to the destruction of the group, whose future depended on that next generation'.[65] This damage to the *group* occurs even if the children were

[55] Lemkin 86 (1944).
[56] Genocide Convention art II(e).
[57] Proxmire Act (1988) 18 USC s 1093(1).
[58] CRC (20 Nov 1989) 1577 UNTS 3 art 1. The role of domestic law is unclear. If a state treats persons under 18 as adults or those over 18 as children, it is unclear whether such provisions override age specifications drawn from international law. They might well do so. The Convention protects the group 'as such'—which means that offenders may be required to take the victim group as they find it.
[59] *RuSHA* [USMT 1948] 4 TWC 599.
[60] *Rutaganda (TC)* [1999] ICTR ¶53.
[61] ibid ¶55.
[62] It would constitute political genocide as defined herein, however.
[63] LeBlanc 115 (1991).
[64] Official Records (6th Comm 1948) (SR82) 186.
[65] ibid (SR83) 195 (1948) (Venez).

not harmed physically or emotionally and even if they were provided a higher standard of material life.[66]

This was precisely the issue in *Kruger*, which involved 'Stolen Generations' of Australian Aborigines removed from their tribes between 1925 and 1949.[67] The civil claimants in *Kruger* were removed as children pursuant to legislation allowing the Australian government 'to undertake the care, custody and control of any Aborigine'.[68] They alleged that the Ordinance violated both the Genocide Convention and 'a pre-existing rule of international law involving a prohibition upon genocide'.[69]

The *Kruger* Court denied the Aborigines' claim on two grounds. First, the Ordinance pre-dated the Convention by thirty years and thus did not violate the treaty.[70] Second, even if a pre-existing prohibition on genocide existed under customary international law, the Ordinance was not genocide because it was enacted in the best interests of the Aboriginal population, without the intent to destroy the Aboriginal group.[71]

B. The protected groups

The Genocide Convention covers four restrictive categories of protected groups. By definition, the offence can be perpetrated only against members of national, ethnic, racial or religious groups.[72] Individuals here are a means to an end. If an individual lacks membership in a protected group, genocide cannot occur with respect to that victim, even if the offender ultimately intends to destroy a protected group. Thus, attacks on politically moderate Hutu in 1994 Rwanda were not genocide,[73] even though they were perpetrated as an integral part of the overall scheme to destroy ethnic Tutsis.[74] So, too, for atrocities by the Khmer Rouge, where attacks on economic and political groups proceeded in tandem with genocide against ethnic, national and religious groups.[75]

The Convention does not define the groups it protects, and the question often is not easy to answer:

> [T]he concepts of national, ethnical, racial and religious groups have been researched extensively and... at present, there are no generally and internationally accepted precise

[66] ibid.

[67] *Kruger* (1997) 126 ALR 126 (Austr High Ct).

[68] ibid 126–7.

[69] ibid 160–1.

[70] ibid 161, 174 , 232.

[71] ibid 161, 175, 190, 232. As discussed in Chapter 3, the *mens rea* of genocide is exacting and often the outcome-determining factor.

[72] Genocide Convention art II.

[73] *Akayesu (TC)* [1998] ICTR ¶¶710, 720–1.

[74] Attacks on Hutu were crimes against humanity, which are detailed in Chapter 6.

[75] J Abrams, 'Universal Jurisdiction: Myths, Realities and Prospects: The Atrocities in Cambodia and Kosovo: Observations on the Codification of Genocide' (2001) 35 New England LR 303, 304–6.

definitions thereof. Each of these concepts must be assessed in the light of a particular political, social and cultural context.[76]

The determination of whether a group is 'protected' under the Convention begs the predicate queries of what 'groups' are in the first place and why they deserve legal protection 'as such.' The groups reflected in the final draft of the Convention were much debated in all three versions of the treaty. The theoretical grounds for including some groups and excluding others are especially important when considering whether parallel coverage for other types of human groups is justified.

The conception of groups—what they are, how the law defines them, their importance in society—is a critical part of the analysis herein. At the risk of putting the cart before the horse, those deeper issues are put aside for now. The next section provides a *general* overview of the baseline characteristics of racial, ethnic, religious and national groups. These matters distinguish the groups from each other and help to define the *actus reus* of the offence. The brief explication on group characteristics is followed by an analysis of the methodologies used to ascertain the contours of protected groups under the Convention. The harder questions are left for Chapter 4, which delves more deeply into the theoretical and philosophical issues of group identity and protecting groups 'as such'.

Racial groups

Racial groups are defined principally through external physical appearance.[77] They include 'individuals whose identity as such is distinctive in terms of physical characteristics or biological descent'.[78] The group is based upon 'hereditary physical traits often identified with a geographical region, irrespective of linguistic, cultural, national, or religious factors.'[79]

The references to biology and heredity confirm that physical appearance must be examined for the *collective* in light of the overall features of the group. The fact that individual group members possess racial characteristics to greater or lesser degrees does not remove them from the group. Lighter skinned Blacks, for example, do not lose membership in the group because their skin pigmentation is different. It is the general composition of the racial group, rather than characteristics specific to any individual, that forms the salient inquiry.

[76] *Rutaganda (TC)* [1999] ICTR ¶56; see also *Krstic (TC)* [2001] ICTY ¶557 (group's 'religious, ethnical, or national characteristics must be identified within the socio-historic context which it inhabits.').

[77] Drost 62 (1959).

[78] Proxmire Act (1988) 18 USC s 1093(6).

[79] *Akayesu (TC)* [1998] ICTR ¶514.

Ethnic groups

An 'ethnic group is generally defined as a group whose members share a common language or culture'[80] or other social characteristics.[81] The ILC distinguished them from racial groups as follows:

> [T]he ethnic bond is more cultural. It is based on cultural values and is characterized by a way of life, a way of thinking and the same way of looking at life and things. On a deeper level, the ethnic group is based on a cosmogony.[82]

The distinction between race and ethnicity is hardly clear in application. Some suggest that the concepts are nearly identical. The UNHCR[83] suggests that race includes 'all kinds of ethnic groups that are referred to as 'races' in common usage. Frequently it also will entail membership of a specific social group of common descent forming a minority within a larger population'.[84] A small minority of seven states, mostly in South America, also equate the concepts in their domestic legislation.[85]

The concept proved particularly vexing for the ICTR, where it proved nearly impossible to separate ethnic Hutu and Tutsi based upon physical appearance.[86] As detailed in Chapter 4, the Trial Chamber in *Akayesu* resorted to dramatic interpretive lengths in recognizing Rwandan Tutsi as an ethnic group.[87] In the process, it deviated from its own stated criteria defining ethnicity as a social characteristic, relying instead on questionable inferences drawn from the *travaux préparatoires* of the Genocide Convention.

Religious groups

International instruments make little attempt to define religion, instead aiming at a broader 'catalogue of rights in the sphere of religion, under the heading of

[80] ibid ¶513.

[81] Official Records (6th Comm 1948) (SR73) 97–8 (Swed); ibid (SR75) 115–16 (Swed).

[82] 'Fourth Report on the Draft Code of Offences Against the Peace and Security of Mankind' (1986) UN Doc A/CN4/398 ¶58.

[83] Concepts borrowed from refugee law do not apply directly to criminal offences. *Kupreskic (TC)* [2000] ICTY ¶589 ('It would be contrary to the principle of legality to convict someone of persecution based on a definition found in international refugee law or human rights law.... [because] the net of 'persecution' is cast much wider than is legally justified for the purposes of imposing individual criminal responsibility.'). They are useful by analogy for understanding the distinctions between groups, however.

[84] UNHCR Refugee Handbook ¶68. Similar issues arise with nationality. ibid ¶74 (nationality 'is not to be understood only as "citizenship." It refers also to membership of an ethnic or linguistic group and may occasionally overlap with the term "race."').

[85] Appendix A, Table I (Brazil, Costa Rica, Guatemala, Bolivia, Nicaragua, Paraguay and Lithuania). This is discussed in greater detail in Chapter 5.

[86] Sunga 112 (1997) ('Given the high rate of intermarriage in Rwanda and a common language, religion and geographic area of habitation over several centuries, it is unlikely that the Hutus and Tutsis can be distinguished from each other on an exclusively anthropological basis, despite distinct origins and histories.').

[87] *Akayesu (TC)* [1998] ICTR ¶516.

thought, conscience and religion'.[88] The ICTR opined that a 'religious group is one whose members share the same religion, denomination or mode of worship'.[89] This functional definition grounded in the objective *practices* of group members seems narrow in light of the broader view in human rights law. Other applications account for subjective *belief systems* and define religious groups as having a 'common religious *creed*, *beliefs*, doctrines, practices or rituals'. (Emphasis added.)[90]

There is room for controversy over whether non-religious or atheistic groups qualify. Such groups presumably could be comprised of individuals from a variety of faiths who rejected their religious heritage. In this light, they hardly are a homogeneous 'group'. Nevertheless, they appear to share common practices and a similar belief system. The concept of religious groups should be sufficiently flexible to include atheists and other non-theists targeted for genocide, based either on their internal 'beliefs' or their functional 'mode of worship' (not worshiping at all).[91] This accords with the trend of international thought on the issue.[92]

National groups

'National' groups include those 'whose identity as such is distinctive in terms of nationality or national origins'.[93] This formulation allows simultaneous membership in multiple national groups—that of birth origin and that of current citizenship. The ICJ dealt with nationality in *Nottebohm*, which arose out of Frederic Nottebohm's arrest and permanent expulsion from Guatemala.[94] The concept of nationality was the central issue because Liechtenstein had standing to press diplomatic claims only if Nottebohm genuinely was its citizen.[95]

The ICJ held that Liechtenstein's domestic assessment was not dispositive and that nationality was a separate question under international law.[96] The ICJ described nationality as:

> a legal bond having its basis [in] a *social fact* of attachment, a genuine connection of existence, interests, and sentiments, together with the existence of reciprocal rights and duties. It may be said to constitute the juridical expression of the fact that the individual

[88] Lerner (2003) 77. [89] *Akayesu (TC)* [1998] ICTR ¶515.

[90] Proxmire Act (1988) 18 USC s 1093(7).

[91] *Akayesu (TC)* [1998] ICTR ¶515. See also M Lippman, 'Genocide: The Crime of the Century—The Jurisprudence of Death at the Dawn of the new Millennium' (2001) 23 Houston JIL 467, 475 ('The term 'religious' encompasses theistic, non-theistic, and atheistic groups that are united by a single spiritual ideal.').

[92] Declaration on Religious Belief UNGA Res 36/55 (25 Nov 1981) UN Doc A/36/684 art 1(1) ('Everyone shall have the right to freedom of thought, conscience, and religion. This right shall include freedom to have a religion or whatever belief of his choice. . . .').

[93] Proxmire Act (1988) 18 USC s 1093(6). [94] *Nottebohm* [1955] ICJ 4, 6–7.

[95] ibid 17. [96] ibid 21.

upon whom it is conferred... is in fact more closely connected to the population of the State conferring nationality than with that of any other State.' (Emphasis added.)[97]

Nottebohm is best understood in the unique context of ICJ jurisdiction.[98] The ILC opined that *Nottebohm* dealt solely 'with the admissibility of a claim for diplomatic protection and did not imply that a person could be generally treated as stateless'.[99] Nevertheless, its dictum on 'dominant and effective nationality' has been adopted and applied in contexts beyond the ICJ for other purposes.[100] The ICTR cited *Nottebohm* and defined a national group as 'a collection of people who are perceived to share a common legal bond based on common citizenship, coupled with reciprocity of rights and duties'.[101] Group members' personal conceptions of their own nationality thus are not dispositive.[102] The emphasis on the *legal* aspects of nationality ('rights and duties' and 'a common legal bond') ensures that political groups are not treated as 'national groups'.[103]

Overlapping groups

The groups enumerated in the Convention are not inherently distinct, which enables some to be protected on multiple grounds. Persons of Jewish descent, for example, are covered as ethnic and religious groups and perhaps as national groups as well.[104] Tribal groups fall under the Convention[105] and may satisfy the criteria for all four categories.[106] The groups are not necessarily insular:

[97] ibid 23.

[98] *Flegenheimer Claim (Italy v US)* (1958) 25 ILR 91 (Italy/US Conciliation Comm) 153 (whether or not it was 'effective', the international claims tribunal was not generally empowered to deny a state's decision to confer nationality).

[99] 'Draft Articles on Nationality of Stateless Persons in Relation to the Succession of States' in Report of the International Law Commission on the work of its 51st Session (3 May–23 Jul 1999) UN Doc A/54/10 art 19 cmt 3.

[100] *Cf Iran v United States Case No A/18* (6 Apr 1984) Decision No DEC 32-A18-FT (Iran/US Claims Trib) ('In determining the dominant and effective nationality, the Tribunal will consider all relevant factors, including habitual residence, centre of interests, family ties, participation in public life and other evidence of attachment.').

[101] *Akayesu (TC)* [1998] ICTR ¶512.

[102] Self-identification can be dispositive in other contexts. *Cf* CERD General Recommendation No 8 (22 Aug 1990) UN Doc A/45/18 (group 'identification shall, if no justification exists to the contrary, be based upon self-identification by the individual concerned.').

[103] Official Records (6th Comm 1948) (SR75) 113, 115 (Pol and Swed).

[104] *Eichmann (TC)* [1961] 36 ILR 5 (Isr Dist Ct) 53 (referencing 'the Jewish State, which would open the gates of the homeland wide to every Jew, and confer upon the Jewish People the status of a fully privileged member of the comity of nations.').

[105] For example, the Australian Federal Court dismissed claims of genocide by Aboriginal groups on substantive and procedural grounds but never suggested that the plaintiffs were not protected under the Convention. *Nulyarimma v Thompson* (1999) 165 ALR 621 (Fed Ct Austr).

[106] [1996] Draft Code art 17 cmt 9. There must be some correspondence to the existing categories of protected groups, however. SC Darfur Report (25 Jan 2005) ¶497 ('tribes may fall under the notion of genocide set out in international law only if... they also exhibit the characteristics of one of the four categories of group protected by international law.').

National, ethnical, racial or religious groups are not clearly defined in the Convention or elsewhere.... The preparatory work of the Convention shows that setting out such a list was designed more to describe a single phenomenon, roughly corresponding to what was recognized, before the second world war, as 'national minorities,' rather than to refer to several distinct prototypes of human groups.[107]

There also is potential overlap between protected and unprotected groups. Political groups, for example, were deliberately excluded from the final text of the Convention.[108] Nevertheless, some have claimed that 'political groups which are at the same time national groups are protected under the Convention'.[109]

The point is technically accurate but hardly extends the Convention to political groups. Political affiliations, as noted above, are insufficient to establish nationality. In application, the tag-along political (or social, economic, etc) character of a protected group is irrelevant.[110] The proper inquiry under the Convention is whether the group qualifies as a protected group, not whether it also possesses additional characteristics that fall outside the Convention.

C. Determining group membership

The composition of the group targeted for destruction is a critical inquiry that determines the very life and death of group members. This became painfully clear in the *Einsatzgruppen* case, which dealt with SS death squads in occupied territory during World War II. Although all 'Jews' were to be eliminated,

[n]o precise definition was furnished the Einsatz leaders as to those who fell within this fatal designation. Thus, when one of the Einsatzgruppen reached the Crimea, its leaders did not know what standards to apply in determining whether the Krimchaks they found there should be killed or not. Very little was known of these people.... It was rumoured, however, that somewhere along the arterial line which ran back into the dim past some Jewish blood had entered the strain of these strange Krimchaks. If this were so, should they be regarded as Jews and should they be shot? An inquiry went off to Berlin. In due time the reply came back that the Krimchaks were Jews and should be shot. They were shot.[111]

States and other international bodies also make determinations on genocide. The US State Department, for example, concluded in early 1994 that Rwandan Tutsi were an ethnic group and that genocide probably was being committed against them.[112] The UN General Assembly declared Serbian 'ethnic cleansing' in the

[107] *Krstic (TC)* [2001] ICTY ¶¶555–6.

[108] Official Records (6th Comm 1948) (SR128) 663–4.

[109] Drost 62 (1959).

[110] *Nahimana (TC)* [2003] ICTR ¶969 (association of ethnic Tutsi with political agenda and identity did not 'negate the genocidal animus' against Tutsis as an ethnic group).

[111] *Einsatzgruppen* [USMT 1948] 4 TWC 1, 415.

[112] S Murphy, 'Department of State Legal Analysis of 1994 Genocide in Rwanda' (2002) 96 AJIL 258, 259–60.

former Yugoslavia to be genocide.[113] In criminal adjudication, courts must ascertain the nature of the group that the perpetrator sought to destroy in order to determine whether it qualifies under the Convention. But how are such decisions best made?

One possibility is an *objective* determination of group status, where the court ascertains the definition of the group and criteria for membership and applies those criteria to the group attacked to see whether it qualifies. In the objective inquiry, neither the victim's, the perpetrator's, nor any third party's views are dispositive, though they are considered as evidence. Also relevant are expert testimony from anthropologists, historians and religious scholars, evidence from knowledgeable 'outsiders' (eg, former colonial rulers), testimony from legal scholars on the citizenship law of a particular nationality, and other similar sources.

The alternative is a *subjective* (and retrospective) inquiry into the criteria used by an accused to define the group targeted for genocide.[114] The perpetrator's view, once established, is dispositive on the group-defining criteria. Rather than seeking an anthropological understanding of the group and then inquiring whether he intended to destroy *that* collective 'as such', the subjective test accepts the group as defined by the perpetrator and aims to ascertain whether the group so-defined qualifies under the Convention.

The objective approach

The Security Council's expert panel that recommended establishing the ICTR saw no need 'to presume or posit the existence of a race or ethnicity itself as a scientifically objective fact'.[115] Nevertheless, early ICTR jurisprudence largely proceeded in this manner. In *Akayesu*, the tribunal grounded its decision in tangible indicia of group membership and an objective assessment of the group. Evidence credited by the tribunal included testimony on national identity cards (a holdover from former Belgian colonizers) that identified their holders as Hutu or Tutsi.[116] The court found that Tutsi witnesses testified credibly on their separate ethnic identity[117] and determined that former Belgian colonizers likewise distinguished them on ethnic grounds.[118] Based on 'facts brought to its attention during the trial',[119] the court determined that Tutsi were a distinct ethnic group 'identified as such by all'.[120] The objective standard applied in *Akayesu* was followed in *Kayishema*.[121]

113 'The Situation in Bosnia and Herzegovina' UNGA Res 47/121 (7 Apr 1993) UN Doc A/Res/47/121/Rev1.

114 The subjective test also applies in other contexts, as well *Cf Amanfi v Ashcroft* (2003) 328 F3d 719 (US Ct App (3rd Cir)) 730 (for asylum purposes, persecution for membership in a 'particular social group' includes the offender's perception of the victim's membership in that group).

115 Security Council Expert Report (27 May 1994) UN Doc A/1994/674 ¶159.

116 *Akayesu (TC)* [1998] ICTR ¶702.

117 ibid ¶122.

118 ibid ¶122 n 56.

119 ibid ¶702.

120 ibid.

121 *Kayishema (TC)* [1999] ICTR ¶¶522–6.

The objective theory appears rooted in earlier international cases interpreting minority protection treaties prior to World War II. In *Minorities in Upper Silesia*, Germany sought recognition of 'the unfettered right of an individual to declare according to his own conscience... that he himself does or does not belong to a racial, linguistic or religious minority'.[122] In opposition, Poland argued that the question was one 'of fact and not one of intention'.[123] The PCIJ sided with Poland, focusing on apparently conflicting treaty provisions,[124] though it did note that 'a subjective element' could be considered in resolving the objective determination.[125]

But the objective/subjective debate was alive even then. Judge Nyholm dissented, suggesting that there was little point to a 'rigid and objective definition of the idea of "minority" since the linguistic, religious and ethnical divisions cannot be disentangled'.[126] He also pointed out that persons could subjectively consider themselves part of a minority group for one purpose (religion) but not for another (education).[127]

As noted previously, the ICJ followed similar practice in *Nottebohm*, opting for an objective view of nationality that prevailed over the subjective views of the individual and the state concerned (at least for admissibility of diplomatic claims). Although *Nottebohm*'s utility has been criticized, the 'genuine link' concept that it embodied has been sustained.[128] The fact that the *Akayesu* tribunal adopted *Nottebohm*'s methodology in defining national groups may explain its search for objective indicia of ethnic collectives as well. The objective approach does not appear to have progressed much further, however. Most tribunals and other sources utilize a subjective approach, as did later decisions in the ICTR.[129]

The subjective approach

In *Jelisic*, an ICTY trial chamber rejected the objective approach:[130]

> Although the objective determination of a religious group still remains possible, to attempt to define a national, ethnical or racial group today using objective and scientifically irreproachable criteria would be a perilous exercise whose result would not necessarily correspond to the perception of the persons concerned by such categorization. Therefore, it is more appropriate to evaluate the status of a national, ethnical or religious group *from the view of those persons who wish to single that group out from the rest of the community.* (Emphasis added.)[131]

[122] *Minorities in Upper Silesia* [1928] PCIJ Rep Ser A No 15 (26 Apr) 5, 5.
[123] ibid 32.
[124] ibid 32–44.
[125] ibid 40–1.
[126] ibid 65 (Nyholm J dissenting).
[127] ibid.
[128] SM Schwebel, 'The treatment of human rights and of aliens in the International Court of Justice' in Lowe and Fitzmaurice 327, 336 (1996).
[129] *Musema (TC)* [2000] ICTR ¶161; *Rutaganda (TC)* [1999] ICTR ¶56.
[130] The court considered both *Akayesu* and *Kayishema*. *Jelisic (TC)* [1999] ICTY ¶61.
[131] ibid ¶70. The basis of the tribunal's suggestion that religious groups could be defined objectively, but that national, racial and ethnic groups could not, is unclear. It seems genuinely misplaced. As noted below, religious characteristics seem no less and no more immutable than those of nationality, ethnicity, or race.

The subjective approach recognizes that genocidaires stigmatize (and thus define) the victim groups that they intend to destroy. Stigmatization is targeting based on the accused's assessment of the group's characteristics (eg, dark skin, attending Synagogue, cultural traits, etc).[132] Although it applies to any human group,[133] it cannot be used to qualify otherwise excluded (eg, political or social) groups for protection under the Convention.[134] The inquiry applies 'on a case-by-case basis, taking into account both the relevant evidence proffered and the political and cultural context . . .'.[135]

The stigmatization discussed above must be 'positive' in character—meaning that it requires the perpetrator to identify and act upon the characteristics of the targeted group. Theoretically, it is possible to identify groups through so-called 'negative' stigmatization as well. In such cases, offenders identify the characteristics of their own national, ethnical, racial or religious groups and target 'others' that lack such characteristics.[136] The rejected individuals form a distinct group by virtue of their exclusion.[137] Negative stigmatization has been rejected by both the ICTY Appeals Chamber[138] and the ICJ,[139] however, as incompatible with the Genocide Convention itself.

Evaluating the subjective and objective approaches

The subjective and objective inquiries both contemplate case-by-case application.[140] The primary distinction between them is the reliance placed upon the offender's definition of the protected group. His definition is dispositive under the subjective approach, whereas it is only one of several factors objectively.

Viewed in isolation, neither approach is entirely satisfactory. The 'perilous exercise' of defining groups 'using objective and scientifically irreproachable criteria' does not necessarily lead to sensible results corresponding 'to the perceptions of the persons concerned by such categorization'.[141] Unless a genocidaire consults anthropologists or historians to develop criteria, the 'scientific' composition of a protected group may bear no resemblance to the group actually targeted. Scientific and historic evidence also is subject to competing expert testimony and clashes of scholarly opinion. The beliefs of former colonizers and knowledgeable 'outsiders' likewise are susceptible to identical criticisms of irrelevance (except where perpetrators themselves adopt or utilize such beliefs) and differences of opinion.

Reliance upon group members' self-identity is problematic in this context because in cases of genocide it is how the *perpetrator* defines the group that really

[132] ibid ¶71. [133] ibid ¶¶69–72.
[134] ibid ¶69; *Rutaganda (TC)* [1999] ICTR ¶56; *Musema (TC)* [2000] ICTR ¶162.
[135] *Rutaganda (TC)* [1999] ICTR ¶58. [136] ibid.
[137] *Krnojelac (AC)* [2003] ICTY ¶187 (ill treatment of 'non-Serb detainees because of their political or religious affiliation'); *Nahimana (TC)* [2003] ICTR ¶1071 ('discriminatory acts against all those who do not belong to a particular group'). [138] *Stakic (AC)* [2006] ICTY ¶¶16–28.
[139] *Application of Genocide Convention—Merits* [2007] ICJ 1 ¶¶193–6.
[140] ibid; *Akayesu (TC)* [1998] ICTR ¶¶122, 702 n 56. [141] *Jelisic (TC)* [1999] ICTY ¶70.

counts. In Nazi Germany, what mattered was how the Nazi government defined Jews, not whether the victim attended Synagogue, participated in the Jewish community, spoke Hebrew, etc.[142] Serbs, Muslims, and Rwandans determine the religion and ethnicity of a child based solely upon the religion and ethnicity of the father.[143] Jews do not.[144] Whether an individual sees himself as a member of a particular group thus is largely irrelevant to whether or not he ultimately is victimized as a member of the group.[145]

Evidence from victims also suffers from the practical drawback of being susceptible to loss during the genocide itself. If the genocide is particularly successful, there may be few or no survivors left to testify about the group identity. Those who remain justifiably may fear retaliation if they testify, whatever procedural measures exist to shield them.[146] If cultural genocide accompanies physical and biological genocide (and it often does),[147] documentary and historical records of the group's self-definition also may be destroyed.

In cases of genocide, individual victims have little say in whether they will be targeted as group members. Genocidaires subjectively define target groups for the purpose of destroying them. The best way to ascertain a group's contours therefore is to analyse the membership criteria adopted by those who sought to destroy it. This ensures congruity between the *actus reus* and *mens rea* of the crime. Genocide is punished, not based solely upon the underlying acts of murder, kidnapping, etc, but because of the *special intent* with which those acts are perpetrated (discussed in Chapter 3 below). The offender's *mens rea* against the group is critical—genocide addresses acts against protected groups *qua* groups. Without a subjective approach, the aims of the Convention are thwarted because the accused's acts and intentions, which it seeks to punish, will not necessarily correspond to the 'objective' contours of the group that international law seeks to protect.

This is not to suggest that the offender's definition of the group should be seen in a vacuum or taken as entirely dispositive. Taken to its logical extreme, the subjective test risks severing a fundamental link between the genocidaire's definition and the contours of the group as it existed in society before the genocide. At a minimum, there must be colourable evidence that the victim group had some recognized racial, national, ethnic or religious characteristics outside of the mind

142 The application of the Nuremberg Laws led to a complex formula to determine whether a person was a 'full Jew'. Ultimately, the question turned on whether one had three or more Jewish grandparents. Lesser categories of Jews included *Mischlinge* of the first (two Jewish grandparents) and second (one Jewish grandparent) degrees. Reich Citizenship Law: First Regulation arts 2, 5; Lemkin 75–8 (1944).

143 *Kayishema (TC)* [1999] ICTR ¶523 (Rwandans); Fisher (n 102) 114 (Serbs and Muslims).

144 Fisher (n 102) 114.

145 The group's internal criteria for membership certainly could be a characteristic that the genocidaire selects when defining the group for genocide, however.

146 *Cf* ICTR Statute arts 21, 22 (protections for victims and witnesses).

147 *Karadzic and Mladic—Rule 61* [1996] ICTY ¶¶94–5.

of the perpetrator. This is necessary to ensure that a perpetrator's conception bears *some* logical relation to the four categories set forth in the Convention.

Absent this requirement, a virtually unlimited number of protected groups would exist, depending solely upon an offender's creativity in defining membership criteria. An unbounded subjective test thus conflicts with the object and purpose of the Convention itself, where hard choices were made in reaching consensus on a restricted number of *enumerated* groups for protection.[148] But once a minimum connection exists to a genuine racial, ethnic, etc characteristic, the inquiry should focus solely upon the group as defined by the perpetrator:

> It would not be logically necessary to postulate the existence of objective and clear-cut distinctions among groups of people to prove that a particular group was stigmatized and targeted. In this sense, *the perception of differences is more important than the differences themselves*.... [T]he Genocide Convention can be implemented effectively only if courts recognize that the prosecution should not be expected to prove the unprovable. What matters is the targeting of the group in question, the intention to destroy the group in whole or in part and actual measures to carry this intention out.' (Emphasis added.)[149]

The subjective approach recognizes that groups are an esoteric concept. There is no genuinely 'scientific' or 'objective' conception of any group (though there are objective markers defining its existence for certain purposes). What the Convention drives at is not the protection of abstract notions of race, etc. Rather, it protects groups defined and targeted according to racial, etc *characteristics*.[150]

A genocidaire need not have any understanding that the groups he targets 'as such' are particularly ethnic, racial, religious or national in character. Jews, for example, might qualify as any or all of the four. It is enough that he defines the group based on 'Jewish-ness'. The 'group' thus is protected (or not) depending on the national, ethnic, racial or religious qualities of the criteria selected to target it.

This requires a retrospective analysis of the criteria utilized to define the group and an evaluation of whether those criteria are essentially racial, ethnic, etc in nature. If so, the group is protected. If not, the group is excluded. This objective 'backstop' prevents subjective notions from running rampant and divorcing the analysis from the groups actually enumerated in the Convention.

Any drawbacks associated with a primarily subjective approach to determining group status (tempered by a baseline of objectivity) are outweighed by the practical impossibility of defining groups in any other way. As shown above, efforts to define protected groups objectively have proved largely artificial, suffer

[148] As discussed in later chapters, the choices made by the drafters for the Convention do not *ipso facto* preclude a broader formulation covering political groups under customary international law.

[149] Sunga 112 (1997). See also *Krstic (TC)* [2001] ICTY ¶557 (tribunal 'identifies the relevant group by using as a criterion the stigmatization of the group, notably by the perpetrators of the crime, on the basis of its perceived national, ethnical, racial or religious characteristics.').

[150] *Application of Genocide Convention—Merits* [2007] ICJ 1 ¶193 (the group 'must have particular positive characteristics—national, ethnical, racial or religious—and not the lack of them.').

from serious analytical flaws, and in any event may bear no relation to the group ultimately targeted.

In practice, there often will be tangible markers reflecting the genocidaire's subjective understanding of the group. Subjective notions tend to become objectified (and thus more easily identifiable) over time. Historical and social perception 'gradually hardens and crystallizes into a real and factual opposition. It thus leads to an *objective contrast*.... It ultimately brings about the formation of two conflicting groups, one of them intent on destroying the other.'[151] The legitimacy of the subjective interpretation has gone largely unchallenged by states, suggesting that it 'has become part and parcel of international customary law'.[152]

151 SC Darfur Report (25 Jan 2005) ¶500.

152 ibid ¶501.

3

Fault Elements

Criminal offences require offenders not only to engage in specified prohibited conduct, but also that they do so with a particular state of mind (the personal fault element of the offence, also known as *mens rea*). As Professor Ashworth cogently puts it, '[t]he essence of the principle of *mens rea* is that criminal liability should be imposed only on persons who are sufficiently aware of what they are doing, and of the consequences it may have, that they fairly can be said to have chosen the behaviour and its consequences'.[1]

Under the American Model Penal Code (MPC), which is useful for present purposes, *mens rea* generally is divided into four types: purpose, knowledge, recklessness, and negligence.[2] 'Purpose' (also known as 'aim' or 'direct' intent) exists when the perpetrator has a positive subjective desire to engage in wrongful conduct or to have a wrongful result occur.[3] The wrongful consequences are both foreseen and desired.[4] Thus, if D places and detonates a bomb in V's car with the goal of causing V's death, D has acted with purpose.

'Knowledge' (also called 'indirect' intent) exists when the perpetrator possesses a subjective, practical certainty that a certain result will occur but has no positive desire to bring it about.[5] The wrongful consequences are virtually certain but not necessarily desired.[6] Assume now that D is aware that A is a passenger in V's car. D detonates the bomb with the goal of killing V and awareness that A almost certainly will die as well. D has acted with purpose toward V and knowledge toward A.[7]

'Recklessness' reflects the deliberate disregard of an objectively substantial and unjustifiable risk.[8] Although certain consequences are foreseen as a significant

[1] Ashworth, Principles 158 (2003).

[2] MPC s 2.02. In civil law, the first three correspond to *dolus directus*, *dolus indirectus* and *dolus eventualis*. JD Van der Vyver, 'Prosecution and Punishment of the Crime of Genocide' (1999) 23 Fordham ILJ 286, 306–7.

[3] MPC s 2.02(a).

[4] Van der Vyver (n 2) 307 (*dolus directus*).

[5] MPC s 2.02(b).

[6] Van der Vyver (n 2) 307 (*dolus indirectus*).

[7] Under English law, the term 'intent' covers both direct and indirect intent (purpose and knowledge). *Woollin* [1999] 1 AC 82 (UK HL) (intent exists where consequence is offender's aim or a virtual certainty from his conduct). This is similar to the general standard for *mens rea* in the ICC. ICC Statute art 30(2) (intent exists where offender means to engage in a course of conduct and either means to cause a consequence to occur or is aware that it will occur in the ordinary course of events).

[8] MPC s 2.02(c). The probability of the consequence occurring under the 'reckless' standard is lower than the 'virtual certainty' required by the 'knowledge' standard. Compare MPC s 2.02(c) with ibid s 2.02(b) and *Woollin* [1999] 1 AC 82 (UK HL).

possibility, the accused proceeds regardless.[9] If D detonates his car bomb in a public market, there is a substantial risk that bystanders will be killed in the explosion. D has acted with recklessness toward the bystanders.

The MPC reflects the 'advertent' formulation of recklessness. It includes an objective understanding of the nature of the risk (unjustified, unreasonable, substantial, etc) coupled with a subjective awareness of that risk and choice to disregard it.[10] Recklessness also can include so-called 'wilful blindness,' however, where an offender closes his mind and refuses to consider the risk at all (as opposed to assessing its merits and choosing to run it).[11]

The fourth category is criminal negligence. Culpability arises out of a gross deviation from the standard of care that a reasonable person would adopt in the same situation.[12] Offenders are criminally negligent when they objectively *should* be aware of a substantial and unjustifiable risk of harm but nevertheless genuinely (albeit unreasonably) fail to account for it.[13]

Despite its importance, mental state is rarely a simple matter to establish at trial.[14] This is particularly true in cases of genocide because direct evidence of genocidal intent is exceedingly rare.[15] In most cases, the accused's mental state must be inferred from other evidence presented.[16] Factors that the court will consider include, for example, the number of victims[17] and the methodology and pattern of the accused's prior conduct, statements and acts.[18] A 'general political doctrine that gave rise to the acts' is relevant, as is the 'repetition of destructive and discriminatory acts'.[19] Also germane are the scale and nature of the atrocities committed,[20] discriminatory targeting of the members or property

[9] Van der Vyver (n 2) 307 (*dolus eventualis*).

[10] MPC s 2.02(c); *Cunningham* [1957] 2 QB 396 (CA) (subjective awareness and disregard of an unjustified or unreasonable risk).

[11] *Satnam and Kewal* (1983) 78 Cr App R 149 (CA) (in the context of rape, closing one's mind to whether the victim genuinely consents).

[12] MPC s 2.02(d); *Adomako* [1995] 1 AC 171 (UK HL) (involuntary manslaughter charge against medical personnel following the death of a patient).

[13] Although reckless behaviour qualifies as negligent behaviour, the concepts are distinct. 'Recklessness involves an objective assessment of the *subjectively-perceived* risk. Negligence involves an objective assessment of an *objectively recognizable* risk.': Simester and Sullivan 150 (2003) (emphasis added).

[14] *Brdjanin (TC)* [2004] ICTY ¶970 (given comparative numbers of persons displaced versus persons subject to genocidal acts, the prosecution did not establish that genocidal intent to destroy—as opposed to intent only to displace—existed).

[15] An example of direct proof would be tangible documentation of a genocidal plan or policy, such as the Nazis' 'Final Solution' for Jews. *Eichmann (TC)* [1961] 36 ILR 5 (Isr Dist Ct) 230.

[16] *Akayesu (TC)* [1998] ICTR ¶523 (since 'intent is a mental factor which is difficult, even impossible to determine ... in the absence of a confession from the accused his intent can be inferred ....'). But intent may not be *presumed* by the court: *mens rea* is an essential element of the prosecutor's case. *Jelisic (TC)* [1999] ICTY ¶78. It must be the only reasonable inference from circumstantial evidence.

[17] B Bryant, 'The United States and the 1948 Genocide Convention' (1975) 16 Harvard ILJ 686, 693.

[18] *Jelisic (TC)* [1999] ICTY ¶73; *Kayishema (TC)* [1999] ICTR ¶¶531–9.

[19] *Karadzic and Mladic—Rule 61* [1996] ICTY ¶294.

[20] *Kayishema (TC)* [1999] ICTR ¶94.

of one group to the exclusion of others,[21] methodical or systematic planning or killing,[22] the weapons employed, and the extent of injury inflicted.[23] Acts amounting to cultural genocide[24] and other forms of conduct that violate (or which are perceived by offenders to violate) the 'very foundation of the group' also are relevant.[25] Serbian destruction of Muslim libraries and mosques, for example, served as evidence of genocidal intent against Muslims in the former Yugoslavia.[26]

The genocidaire's motives for engaging in the conduct are irrelevant, however.[27] If genocidal intent exists, it matters not whether that intent was fuelled by animus toward the protected group, by hopes of financial gain, by a personal grudge against individual group members, by ideological beliefs or indeed by any reason at all.[28] Motive certainly serves as further *evidence* of genocidal intent, however.[29]

There is no requirement of state involvement or of a widespread or organized plan of genocidal conduct. Both international criminal tribunals accept the theoretical possibility of a lone perpetrator.[30] A real world example is the case of Abba Kovner, a Holocaust survivor and former resistance fighter who unsuccessfully sought to poison the water supply in Hamburg with the goal of killing six million Germans.[31] But in most cases, it is 'very difficult in practice to provide proof of the genocidal intent of an individual if the crimes committed are not widespread [or organized]'.[32]

Note that the quantity and clarity of the evidence required to prove an accused's mental state is a separate question. How convinced the trier of fact need be that a certain type of *mens rea* existed depends to some extent on the nature of the case before the court. In criminal trials the evidence must establish all elements of the crime (including *mens rea*) beyond a reasonable doubt.[33] The standard is less clear in pre-trial proceedings[34] and in cases adjudicating state responsibility, although the ICJ recently held that 'claims against a State involving charges of exceptional gravity must be proved by evidence that is fully conclusive.... The Court requires that it be fully convinced that the allegations made in the proceedings, that the

[21] *Jelisic (TC)* [1999] ICTY ¶73. [22] *Kayishema (TC)* [1999] ICTR ¶94. [23] ibid.

[24] *Krstic (TC)* [2001] ICTY ¶480. [25] *Karadzic and Mladic—Rule 61* [1996] ICTY ¶94.

[26] ibid ¶95; *Krstic (TC)* [2001] ICTY ¶¶595–7 (attacks on 'cultural and religious property and symbols of the targeted group... may legitimately be considered as evidence of an intent to physically destroy the group.').

[27] *Jelisic (AC)* [2001] ICTY ¶49. This generally is the case in criminal law. J Horder, 'On the Irrelevance of Motive in Criminal Law' in Horder 173 (2000). [28] Drost 83–4 (1959).

[29] *Kayishema (TC)* [1999] ICTR ¶93. Motive and intent are not always distinct concepts, however. *Cf* FM Lawrence, 'The Case for a Federal Bias Crime Law' (1999) 16 Nat'l Black LJ 144, 156–7. [30] *Jelisic (TC)* [1999] ICTY ¶100; *Kayishema (TC)* [1999] ICTR ¶94.

[31] D Luban, 'A Theory of Crimes Against Humanity' (2004) 29 Yale JIL 85, 98 n 45.

[32] *Jelisic (TC)* [1999] ICTY ¶101. [33] *Kordic & Cerkez (AC)* [2004] ICTY ¶833.

[34] Compare *Al Bashir (Arrest Warrant—TC)* [2009] ICC 1 ¶¶147–223 with ibid (Usacka J dissenting) ¶¶7–14, 27–34, and 105 (debating the sufficiency of evidence required to issue an arrest warrant for genocide).

crime of genocide or the other acts enumerated in Article III have been committed, have been clearly established.'[35]

A. 'Special intent' and the Genocide Convention

It has been said that the *mens rea* characterizing genocide is the crime's primary distinguishing characteristic.[36] The Convention prohibits acts committed 'with intent to destroy, in whole or in part, a national, ethnical, racial or religious group, as such'.[37] Genocide quintessentially is a crime against collectives. *Mens rea* thus must extend to all or part of the protected *group*, as opposed to an individual or an institution of some kind. The intent must be to destroy the group itself—not just individual members.

Acts undertaken with the *purpose* of destroying the group certainly qualify. But what about acts committed with something less—the 'virtual certainty' formulation of indirect intent? Some commentators advocate such a knowledge-based formulation,[38] and the ILC's Draft Code implies that 'virtual certainty' is sufficient:

> The prohibited acts . . . are by their very nature conscious, intentional or volitional acts which an individual could not usually commit without *knowing* that certain consequences would result. These are not the type of acts that would normally occur by accident or even as a result of mere negligence. However, a general intent to commit one of the enumerated acts combined with a general awareness of the *probable* consequences of such an act . . . is not sufficient for the crime of genocide. (Emphasis added.)[39]

This theoretical possibility has been avoided in practice. The international criminal tribunals explicitly rejected a knowledge standard for genocide. In *Akayesu*, the Trial Chamber held that the offender is only culpable 'when he commits a [prohibited offence] with the clear intent to destroy, in whole or in part, a particular group'.[40] This strongly indicates purpose—it is unlikely that 'clear intent to destroy' reasonably equates to knowledge.

The ICTY was more explicit in *Jelisic* and held that the defendant 'could not be found guilty of genocide if he himself did not *share the goal* of destroying in part or in whole a group even if he knew that he was contributing to or thought his acts might be contributing to the partial or total destruction of a group' (emphasis added).[41] This legal standard appears intact after appeal,[42] even though the Appeals Chamber criticized and overruled the Trial Chamber's

[35] *Application of Genocide Convention—Merits* [2007] ICJ 1 ¶209.

[36] *Akayesu (TC)* [1998] ICTR ¶498.

[37] Genocide Convention art II.

[38] *Cf* AKA Greenawalt, 'Re-Thinking Genocidal Intent: The Case for a Knowledge-Based Interpretation' (1999) 99 Columbia LR 2259, 2288–92.

[39] [1996] Draft Code art 17 cmt 5. The Draft Code thus excludes criminal responsibility based upon recklessness or negligence. ibid.

[40] *Akayesu (TC)* [1998] ICTR ¶521.

[41] *Jelisic (TC)* [1999] ICTY ¶86.

[42] *Jelisic (AC)* [2001] ICTY ¶¶42–52.

determination of the evidence and decision to acquit the accused.[43] The *Krstic* Trial Chamber likewise adopted a purposeful standard for genocidal liability because it was 'not clear' whether a knowledge standard existed under customary international law.[44]

The application of this standard is complicated in practice. On appeal, the ICTY Appeals Chamber reversed the Trial Chamber's determination that General Krstic had acted with genocidal intent and substituted a conviction for aiding and abetting. The Appeals Chamber held (not unanimously) that Krstic's 'loan' of troops under his command, even at his own suggestion, to execute Muslim prisoners 'only establishes knowledge on the part of Krstic that genocide was being committed. It cannot establish intent to commit genocide'.[45]

Krstic's mere knowledge of the genocidal intent of others, even combined with the use of his own resources and personnel for genocidal purposes, thus failed to meet the 'stringent requirement of specific intent.'[46] In dissent, Judge Shahabuddeen noted that the line between knowledge of another's intent versus sharing that intent was 'a subtle one'[47] but opined that Krstic's authorization of the use of his troops was sufficient to deem him a co-perpetrator.[48]

Despite Judge Shahabuddeen's suggestion that his dissent turned on a different 'appreciation of the evidence',[49] the debate certainly implicates wider questions over the scope of genocidal intent. The majority position is that, whatever Krstic *knew* ultimately would happen to the Bosnian Muslims from the permissive use of his troops, this was insufficient (without more) to establish intent to destroy the group.[50] Judge Shahabuddeen, on the other hand, appears to implicitly recognize a broader understanding of intent, such that the authorization, combined with the knowledge (virtual certainty) of the genocidal scheme, would suffice.[51]

The majority view of the ICTY Appeals Chamber appears predominant in the ICJ as well. The matter was raised in the *Nuclear Weapons* case,[52] where a majority of the ICJ advised that despite their destructive power, the use of nuclear weapons did not per se establish genocidal intent.[53] This is so even though nuclear weapons are 'virtually certain' to cause the physical annihilation of the targeted population in the region where they are detonated. The ICJ's ruling thus implicitly rejects 'indirect' intent in favour of a purposeful formulation.

[43] ibid ¶¶53–72. But see ibid (Pocar J dissenting). Despite its reversal of the acquittal, the Appeals Chamber refused to remand the case, holding that justice would not be served by a new trial. ibid ¶¶72–7.

[44] *Krstic (TC)* [2001] ICTY ¶571.

[45] *Krstic (AC)* [2004] ICTY ¶104.

[46] ibid ¶134.

[47] ibid (Shahabuddeen J dissenting) ¶38.

[48] ibid ¶¶72–4.

[49] ibid ¶38.

[50] On the other hand, *ordering* an attack that leads to the massacre of a large number of victims will, without more, support an inference of genocidal intent. *Kamuhanda (AC)* [2005] ICTR ¶80.

[51] *Krstic (AC)* [2004] ICTY ¶95 (although genocidal intent is strictly formulated, 'stringency should not be overvalued.').

[52] *Nuclear Weapons* [1996] ICJ 227.

[53] ibid 240. This had long been the 'understanding' of the United States. MN Leich, 'Contemporary Practice of the United States Relating to International Law' (1986) 80 AJIL 612, 612–13.

The ICJ opinion was not unanimous, however. Judge Weeramantry advocated the broader form of intention in his dissenting opinion, which he felt better reflected the realities of a nuclear attack. 'Having regard to the ability of nuclear weapons to wipe out blocks of population ranging from hundreds of thousands to millions, there can be no doubt that the weapon targets, in whole or in part, the national group of the State at which it is directed.'[54] 'If the killing of human beings, in numbers ranging from a million to a billion, does not fall within the definition of genocide, one may well ask what will.'[55] This remains a minority position, however. The general rule that military force alone cannot establish genocidal intent was affirmed in later ICJ jurisprudence[56] and in domestic cases.[57]

The ICC Statute provides little additional guidance about the future application of a knowledge standard. Article 30 requires that, unless otherwise provided, the material elements of crimes within its jurisdiction must be 'committed with intent *and* knowledge' (emphasis added).[58] 'Intent' relates both to conduct and consequence and means: (i) that the offender 'means to engage in the conduct' and (ii) that he *either* means to cause the consequence to occur [MPC purpose] *or* is aware that it will occur in the ordinary course of events [MPC knowledge].[59] 'Knowledge' in the ICC relates to the circumstances in which an offence is committed or to the consequences of that offence. It means that the accused is aware either that a circumstance exists or that a consequence will occur in the ordinary course of events.[60]

At first blush, the ICC Statute appears broader than the majority position in *Nuclear Weapons* and decisions in the international criminal tribunals because intent can mean either purpose/aim or 'virtual certainty'. But Article 30 applies only where *mens rea* is not 'otherwise provided'.[61] Genocide is covered by Article 6, which incorporates verbatim Article II of the Genocide Convention. Article 6 arguably provides its own mental state because, like the Convention, it specifies prohibited acts committed 'with intent to destroy...a [protected] group'.[62] In contrast, the definitions of other crimes within the jurisdiction of the

[54] ibid 501 (Weeramantry J dissenting). [55] ibid 517.

[56] *Legality of Force—Provisional Measures* [1999] ICJ ¶35 ('the threat or use of [military] force against a State cannot in itself constitute an act of genocide within the meaning of...the Convention.'). But see ibid (Kreka J dissenting) (clarifying in dicta that extensive military force 'in particular if it is used against objects and means constituting conditions of normal life, can be conducive to "inflicting on the group conditions of life bringing about its physical destruction".') (Internal citation omitted). The ICTY declined to further investigate charges of unlawful conduct in NATO's bombing campaign, which included allegations of genocide: 'Final Report to the Prosecutor by the Committee Established to Review the NATO Bombing Campaign Against the Federal Republic of Yugoslavia' (2000) 39 ILM 1257 ¶¶2, 90–1.

[57] *Hipperson* [1996] CLY 1445 (QB) (dismissing appeal on criminal damage conviction and holding that destruction at nuclear weapons manufacturing facility were not justifiable efforts to prevent unlawful crimes and genocide). [58] ICC Statute art 30(1).

[59] ibid art 30(2). [60] ibid art 30(3). [61] ibid art 30(1). [62] ibid art 6.

ICC make no mention of *mens rea* within the criminalizing articles themselves.[63] Since Article 6 is more specific, Article 30 probably does not apply to genocide.[64] Given the ICC's strong protection of the rights of the accused,[65] the more stringent formulation is the most likely standard in that forum. This certainly appears to be the case in early ICC decisions at the pre-trial stage.[66]

B. *Mens rea* and human groups

Discriminatory targeting of group members

Genocidal acts manifest against members of the protected group, not in their individual capacities, but based upon the fact of group membership.[67] Individuals are a means to an end: a step further along the path of destroying the group.[68] 'Chosen as such... the victim of the crime of genocide is the group itself and not only the individual.'[69] The offence realizes 'an ulterior motive, which is to destroy... the group of which the individual is just one element.'[70]

The Draft Code specifies that a 'prohibited act must be committed against an individual *because of* his membership in a particular group *and* as an incremental step in the overall objective of destroying the protected group' (emphasis added).[71] Both international criminal tribunals adopted this formulation and require discriminatory targeting of group members to establish genocidal intent against the group.[72]

Discriminatory selection helps the court determine whether a particular attack really was directed at the larger group, rather than the individual. It ensures that victims are selected because of their group membership, rather than for personal (eg, revenge), financial (eg, murder for hire), or other reasons independent of the intent to destroy the group. Discriminatory targeting (unlike genocidal intent) can be presumed. '[A]n individual knowingly acting against the backdrop of widespread and systematic violence being committed against only one specific group could not reasonably deny that he chose his victims discriminatorily.'[73]

The degree of specificity with which a particular victim must be selected remains unclear. The inquiry must be made on a case-by-case basis. Nothing in the Draft Code or in the tribunal decisions requires detailed targeting

[63] Compare ibid art 6 (genocide) with ibid art 7 (crimes against humanity) and art 8 (war crimes).
[64] Elements of Crimes art 6.
[65] ICC Statute arts 20, 22–24, 64, and 66–67.
[66] *Al Bashir (Arrest Warrant—TC)* [2009] ICC 1 ¶¶139–61.
[67] *Kayishema (TC)* [1999] ICTR ¶97.
[68] [1996] Draft Code art 17 cmt 6.
[69] *Akayesu (TC)* [1998] ICTR ¶521.
[70] ibid ¶522.
[71] [1996] Draft Code art 17 cmt 6.
[72] *Akayesu (TC)* [1998] ICTR ¶521; *Jelisic (TC) [1999]* ICTY ¶67.
[73] *Jelisic (TC)* [1999] ICTY ¶73 (presumption on targeting) and ¶78 (cannot presume intent).

of specific or identified individuals, however. Nor should they. Genocide is defined in the inchoate mode and penalizes acts committed with a particular mental state, independent of the ultimate result. Genocidal intent does not (and should not) depend upon the fortuity of perpetrators having good information. If an attack is intended to destroy a protected group (*mens rea*) and a prohibited act is committed against one or more group members (*actus reus*), it suffices as genocide.

Consider the hypothetical mass murder of a busload of moderate Hutu and ethnic Tutsis at a roadblock in Rwanda in early 1994. Out of eighty victims, half are Tutsi and half Hutu. If the entire busload is slaughtered en masse, a prohibited act has taken place against members of a protected group with genocidal intent. There can be little doubt that the killing of the Tutsi passengers is genocide. There is no need to establish that the offender had specific knowledge that each of the forty Tutsi victims was, in fact, an ethnic Tutsi at the moment he killed them. He has committed a prohibited act against group members with the requisite intent, which is enough under the Convention.

This is nothing specific to international law or genocide. In a domestic case involving bombings, Lord Mustill noted that, in cases of such 'indiscriminate malice,' the

> intention is already aimed directly at the *class of potential victims* of which the actual victim forms part. The intent and the *actus reus* completed by the [offence] are joined from the start, even though the identity of the ultimate victim is not yet fixed.... No ancient fictions are needed to make these cases of murder.' (Emphasis added.)[74]

The UN Commission of Experts probably had similar considerations in mind when it opined that it would be an unreasonably high burden to require proof of an intent to destroy a protected group with respect to each individual killing in order to distinguish genocide from murder.[75]

Destroying groups 'as such'

To destroy a group 'as such' means to destroy it 'as a separate and distinct entity'.[76] 'An act of genocide constitutes not just an attack on an individual, but also a threat to the group with which the individual is identified. It is an offence against a core aspect of humanity—the very nature of collective human identities.'[77] Case law from the tribunals recognizes two ways in which a group can be destroyed. The first is destruction in terms of sheer size and homogeneous numerical composition (the 'quantitative' approach).[78] The second addresses the destruction of a key

[74] *Attorney General's Reference (No 3 of 1994)* [1998] AC 245 (UK HL) 261.
[75] Security Council Expert Report (27 May 1994) UN Doc A/1994/674 ¶167.
[76] *Jelisic (AC)* [2001] ICTY ¶¶79–80; [1996] Draft Code art 17 cmt 7.
[77] Abrams (n 151) 304.
[78] *Jelisic (TC)* [1999] ICTY ¶81.

part of the group, such as its leadership or other segments essential to its existence (the 'qualitative' approach).[79]

The quantitative approach

The accused need not intend to destroy a protected group in its entirety. It is sufficient to intend to destroy it 'in part'.[80] But when something less than absolute destruction is contemplated, does 'in part' refer to *any* part of the group (including individual members), to a majority of the group, to a certain percentage of the group in a given geographical area, etc?

The quantitative approach posits that victimization of a substantial part of the group[81] or a substantial number of its members[82] leads to the destruction of the group 'as such'. Group members are fungible under this approach—the focus is on sheer numbers or percentages. Most authorities indicate that 'in part' really means 'in *substantial* part'. The reading-in of 'substantial' arises out of the search for a practical way to distinguish genocide (a large-scale crime against a protected group) from ordinary 'hate' or 'bias' crimes (attacks on individuals because of their membership in that group).[83] The modifier is one way to distinguish matters of international concern and to reserve 'genocide' for large-scale atrocities.[84]

There is some debate over the meaning of 'substantial,' however. US genocide legislation[85] defines a 'substantial part' of a group as 'a part of a group of such numerical significance that the destruction or loss of that part would cause the destruction of the group as a viable entity within the nation of which the group is a part'.[86] This construction is unique and controversial, however, and even the US State Department recognizes that it is not the only realistic interpretation.[87] Both international criminal tribunals, for example, apply a 'substantial part' test without the concomitant 'viable entity' restriction, leaving the phrase open to broader understanding.[88] In either case, the method compares the number of

[79] ibid. For example, in the former Yugoslavia 'a substratum of the Bosnian Muslim population consisting of public officials, the well educated, and other leaders were targeted for annihilation.' Bassiouni and Manikas 530 (1996).

[80] Genocide Convention art II; [1996] Draft Code art 17 cmt 8 ('It is not necessary to achieve the complete annihilation of a group from every corner of the globe.').

[81] [1996] Draft Code art 17 cmt 8. [82] Robinson 63 (1960).

[83] Lawrence 9–10 (1999).

[84] *Krstic (AC)* [2004] ICTY ¶8 (genocide is 'a crime of massive proportions'). The ICC achieves this aim by imposing a contextual requirement, mandating that the genocidal attack either take place as part of an objective pattern of similar conduct against the group or that it be sufficient to destroy the group in and of itself. Elements of Crimes art 6.

[85] Proxmire Act (1988) 18 USC s 1091(a). [86] ibid s 1093(8).

[87] SP Murphy, 'Department of State Legal Analysis of 1994 Genocide in Rwanda' (2002) 96 AJIL 258, 260 ('The US position probably represents a maximum requirement….'); Sunga 114 (1997) (arguing against such a restrictive interpretation).

[88] *Krstic (AC)* [2004] ICTY ¶¶8–12; *Bagilishema* [2001] ICTR ¶64. The extent of destruction required often is linked to geographic considerations, which are discussed below.

intended victims to the overall group in order to ascertain whether the offender sought to destroy 'a quantitatively substantial part of the protected group'.[89]

In contrast to the 'substantial part' test, other authorities analyse the intent to destroy a *substantial number of members* of the protected group:

> Therefore, the intent to destroy a *multitude of persons* of the same group because of their belonging to this group, must be classified as Genocide even if those persons constitute only part of a group either within a country or within a region or within a single community, provided the number is substantial....[90] (Emphasis added.)

The international criminal tribunals built upon this formulation and interpreted 'in part' as encompassing the intent to destroy 'a considerable number of individuals who are part of that group'[91] or 'a reasonably substantial number relative to the total population of the group'.[92]

During the drafting process, one state offered a third interpretation and opined that 'in part' required intent to destroy the *entire* group but allowed that intent to be implemented in stages.[93] This view contributed to much controversy over ratification of the Convention in the US.[94] Putting aside its political impact on the American Congress, the viability of the interpretation is doubtful: it contradicts the plain text of the Convention and has been discredited.[95]

The two formulations of the quantitative approach discussed above might be called the 'percentage test' and the 'numeric test'. The concepts are similar but not coextensive. The percentage test compares the number of victims to the overall size of the group. The numeric test calculates whether the number of victims, in and of itself, is sufficiently large.

The numeric test is better suited to protecting large groups from genocide, while the percentage test works better for smaller populations. Thus, the intent to kill 10,000 Chinese in China probably suffices as intent to destroy a substantial number of victims, even if the figure is statistically insignificant compared to a national population exceeding one billion. On the other hand, the intent to kill three members of a tiny aboriginal tribe of a dozen people (25 per cent) probably is sufficient under the percentage test, whereas it hardly constitutes a 'multitude' or 'considerable number' of victims.

In practice, this often will be a distinction without a difference. The result in many cases will be identical: the 'part' of the group at issue will constitute both a significant number of victims and a significant percentage of the overall group. A UN investigatory study opined that both tests should be considered.[96] Both are utilized in the international criminal tribunals.[97]

[89] *Krstic (TC)* [2001] ICTY ¶586.
[90] Robinson 63 (1960).
[91] *Kayishema (TC)* [1999] ICTR ¶97.
[92] *Sikirica (TC)* [2001] ICTY ¶65.
[93] Official Records (6th Comm 1948) (SR73) 94–5 (Bel).
[94] LeBlanc 39–40 (1991).
[95] Robinson 63 (1960).
[96] Study (Second) on Genocide (2 Jul 1985) UN Doc E/CN4/Sub2/1985/6 ¶29.
[97] *Jelisic (TC)* [1999] ICTY n 111; *Kayishema (TC)* [1999] ICTR ¶96. The *Kayishema* court held, however, that destroying a group 'in part' required intent to 'destroy a considerable number of individuals', suggesting greater reliance on the numeric test. ibid.

Both formulations link to geographic considerations. Once the protected group is defined, each focuses upon the composition and size of the group within a particular geographical area.[98] The reliance on geography is somewhat problematic because the legal result changes depending on the scope of the area considered. Since the geographic line can be drawn in different places, identical facts could lead to different conclusions about whether genocidal intent existed. A dozen Muslims may constitute neither a 'substantial part' nor a 'substantial number' of Muslims in the world, in a particular nation, in a region, or even in many cities. It may well be a 'substantial part' or 'substantial number' of Muslims living in a small village or on a street. Genocidal *mens rea* thus to some extent depends upon how broadly 'part' of the group can be conceived.

Some states and commentators advocate a wide focus and argue that the intent must be to destroy the group in its entirety within the nation.[99] But this seems far too broad, effectively requiring intent against the full population of a state. This renders 'in part' superfluous, in violation of general rules of treaty and statutory construction.[100]

Case law from the international criminal tribunals reflects a better approach. The ICTY Appeals Chamber held that genocide could be perpetrated in an area as small as a municipality.[101] But the mere concentration of destruction in a limited geographical zone is not dispositive. What matters is the relation of the cluster of *intended* victims to the wider geographical understanding of the group. In *Sikirica*, the ICTY considered attacks on 1,000–1,400 Muslims and acquitted the accused of genocide, holding that '[t]his would represent between 2% and 2.8% of the Muslims in the Prijedor municipality and would hardly qualify as a "reasonably substantial" part of the Bosnian Muslim group in Prijedor'.[102] It also noted that 'the evidence does not establish that a substantial number of Bosnian Muslims or Bosnian Croats were victims',[103] which suggests a reliance on both the numerical and percentage tests. More recently, the ICJ held that the intent to destroy a 'group within a geographically limited area' could be sufficient but was careful to note that the enquiry is fact-specific and would depend on a number of considerations.[104]

The quantitative method probably has some ongoing application in determining genocidal intent, but it is not the only relevant inquiry.[105] The percentage test is better suited to protecting smaller collectives, whereas the numerical test is better for situations where large populations are victimized. Each is consistent with the object and purpose of the Genocide Convention to protect human groups

[98] Proxmire Act (1988) 18 USC s 1091(a); Robinson 63 (1960).

[99] Proxmire Act (1988) 18 USC s 1093(8); PB Perlman, 'The Genocide Convention' (1950) 30 Nebraska LR 1, 7.

[100] VCLT art 31(1); *Celebici (TC)* [1998] ICTY ¶161.

[101] *Krstic (AC)* [2004] ICTY ¶¶15, 18–22 (Bosnian Muslims of Srebrenica). See also *Jelisic (TC)* [1999] ICTY ¶83 ('international custom admits the characterization of genocide even when the exterminatory intent only extends to a limited geographic zone').

[102] *Sikirica (TC)* [2001] ICTY ¶72.

[103] ibid ¶75.

[104] *Application of Genocide Convention—Merits* [2007] ICJ 1 ¶¶200–1.

[105] ibid (considering quantitative figures 'along with other aspects of the evidence.').

from physical or biological destruction. Although the result in many instances will be the same, it is sensible and proper to infer genocidal intent if either test is satisfied.[106]

The qualitative approach

Qualitative analysis takes a different approach. It directly posits that group members have *unequal* worth for purposes of the survival of the group. *Per* Professor Bassiouni: genocide 'is sufficiently pliable to encompass not only the targeting of an entire group, as stated in the Convention, but also the targeting of certain segments of a given group, such as the Muslim elite or the Muslim women'.[107] The targeting of some group members is deemed more injurious because the loss of this 'part' of the group will contribute more significantly to its destruction.[108] The ICTY Appeals Chamber also has suggested that when 'a specific part of the group is emblematic of the overall group ... that may support a finding that the part qualifies as substantial ... '.[109]

To use a simple example, assume that a small aboriginal tribe is targeted for genocide. Five percent of the tribe are 'hunters' whose work produces almost all of the tribe's food. Under the qualitative approach, killing the hunters with the intent to destroy the tribe may constitute genocide even if killing 5 per cent of the tribe would not suffice numerically or percentage-wise. Without the food the hunters provide, the chances are much greater that the tribe as a whole will be destroyed.[110]

Qualitative genocide is not universally recognized[111] and presents some complications in application. An initial question arises as to the scope of qualitative destruction. Dicta from the *Jelisic* Trial Chamber and the ICTY Appeals Chamber in *Krstic* appears to move beyond physical and biological survival and into the group's economic, social and cultural preservation[112] or whether the targeted population was 'emblematic' of the overall group.[113]

These additional concepts were not included in the Genocide Convention and should not be considered in the analysis. If the qualitative approach is used at all,

[106] The issue is not susceptible to forward-looking mathematical resolution. LeBlanc 48 (1991) (noting that the issue can become 'a numbers game: Is a part or a substantial part of a group 1 out of 5, 5 out of 20, 1,001 out of 2,000, or 100,001 out of 200,000?'). Sensible judicial application must determine whether the quantitative test is satisfied in any particular case.

[107] MC Bassiouni, 'The Commission of Experts Established Pursuant to Security Council Resolution 780: Investigating Violations of International Humanitarian Law in the Former Yugoslavia' (1994) 5 Criminal LF 279, 323–4.

[108] Security Council Expert Report (27 May 1994) UN Doc A/1994/674 ¶94 (a focused attack on a specific segment of a protected group such as political, business, or intellectual leaders or military or law enforcement personnel 'may be a strong indication of genocide regardless of the numbers killed.').

[109] *Krstic (AC)* [2004] ICTY ¶12.

[110] ibid (attack on a segment of the group 'that is essential to its survival').

[111] Proxmire Act (1988) 18 USC s 1093(8) (only numeric loss destroys group as a 'viable entity').

[112] *Jelisic (TC)* [1999] ICTY ¶81.

[113] *Krstic (AC)* [2004] ICTY ¶12.

it should accord with the object and purpose of the Genocide Convention and focus upon the group's physical and biological existence. Attacks on academics, intellectuals, economic and religious leaders or 'emblematic' populations, in and of themselves, do not prove genocidal intent. There must be a link between the intent to destroy the 'essential' or 'emblematic' segment and the group's physical or biological viability.

Even when linked to the group's physical and biological existence, however, the qualitative approach retains a troubling premise. It presumes both that some human beings are (or were) inherently more valuable for the group's survival than others. It also presumes that a court can somehow make this determination. These assumptions are somewhat elitist and not even necessarily valid.

The notion of objectively-measurable worth may apply in certain clearly defined cases (as in the example of the aboriginal hunters, above). In general, however, it is fraught with practical complications. Group members hardly can be expected to accurately testify about the relative worth of their fellows *vis à vis* the survival of the group. Apart from distinguishing group members along functional lines and making assumptions about the value of those functions to the group, it is difficult, if not impossible, to develop sound criteria to judge the relative value of human beings.

The analysis elsewhere in *Krstic* comes closer to the mark by focusing upon what the Bosnian Serb forces knew or must have known would result from the killing of 7,500-plus military-aged Muslim men at Srebrenica.[114] The ICTY's focus in that case was properly directed to the perpetrator's intent. But even *Krstic* can be criticized somewhat for its lack of precision. As a matter of evidentiary law to establish that genocidal intent existed, the decision is sound. It certainly makes sense to look at what actually happened in Srebrenica to infer what the Bosnian Serbs intended for the region. But it should not be interpreted as requiring a qualitative attack to have any *actual* effect on the group itself. Nor does it mandate that the targeted segment of the group be valuable *in fact* to the group's physical or biological survival.[115]

A better approach restricts the qualitative analysis to the offender's subjective *beliefs* about the 'valuable' segments of the target group. This requires only an inquiry into the genocidaire's mental state, which is well within judicial competence. Framing the question in terms of what the perpetrator believed eliminates both the elitist tinge and results-focused bias.

The subjective version of the qualitative test is satisfied if, with the intent to destroy all or part of the group as such, an accused targeted specific group members with the *belief* that those victims had enhanced value to the physical or biological survival of the group (eg, that they were 'hunters,' medical doctors,

[114] ibid ¶¶19–21.

[115] ibid ¶8 (holding that accused must *intend* to destroy a part of the group 'significant enough to have an impact on the group as a whole'—not that his intent be objectively correct with respect to the group).

soldiers, etc). The focus is upon the *perpetrator's* understanding of the valuable segments of the group. Once the belief is proved, the accused is deemed to have targeted a 'substantial' part of the protected group.[116] There is no need to establish that his beliefs about the group (or its valuable segments) were in fact correct or that the qualitative targeting had any actual impact upon the group.

This formulation aligns best with the structure of the Convention, which penalizes acts committed with a certain mental state, rather than successful results from that conduct. It matters not whether the perpetrator was objectively correct about the value of the victims to the group. If he chose a segment in the *belief* that it had enhanced value, what matters is that a blameworthy choice was made in order to commit genocide, not that the choice was based upon good information or proved correct in hindsight. His attack on a certain segment of the protected group with the intent to destroy the group can and should be punished as genocide.

[116] ibid ¶12.

4

Human Groups and Genocide

A. Understanding human groups

Group existence is an inescapable consequence of modern life. 'As individuals, we are largely defined by our groups. Associations—whether voluntary or imposed—constitute inescapable elements of identity.'[1] Any study of 'protected' groups under the Genocide Convention thus begs the question of what constitutes a 'group' in the first place. Unfortunately, the question is impossible to answer definitively because there is no generally-accepted meaning. There are over 90 definitions of 'community' in the social sciences alone.[2]

Although difficult to define in the abstract, groups certainly possess common *characteristics*. These include matters like internal solidarity, a sense of belonging, and a common (and distinct) heritage and future destiny. But that only begins the inquiry. Such characteristics are only *markers* of 'groupness' and are themselves open-ended and susceptible to multiple interpretations. Even the most cogent understanding thus requires 'the ability to hold conflicting generalities in mind at the same time'.[3] Indeed, the characterization of others based on group status often is not even the product of conscious thought.[4]

Since groups are as infinitely varied as the individuals who comprise them, it helps to anchor the inquiry into a particular context. The analysis here, which by no means is the only method, focuses on two important questions. The first is: 'for what purpose is the group being defined?' The contours of the group change markedly depending on the answer. Whether one is 'Catholic', for example, differs depending on whether the inquiry is for the purposes of taking Communion at Mass, eligibility for education in parochial schools, entitlement to a divorce decree, religious discrimination in employment at a Jewish Synagogue, etc.

The second question is: 'who decides?' The identity of the decision maker often proves outcome-determinative, particularly when the decision maker has the power to impose a negative consequence or confer a positive benefit upon group members. This is true regardless of the actual source of the group's definition. Whatever misperceptions outsiders may have in defining a particular group, for example, it is

[1] Soifer 1 (1995). [2] ibid 3. [3] ibid 4.

[4] CE Feuss and JD Sosna, 'Courts are Warming to Claims of "Unconscious Bias"' (2007) 30 Nat'l LJ S2 (legal implications of social science data on unconscious biases and stereotypes).

important to recognize that group members often disagree *internally* on membership criteria.[5] Although these two questions hardly constitute an exhaustive definitional framework, the answers to these two questions nevertheless go a long way to facilitating a working definition of the group in a particular context.

Why human groups matter 'as such'

Social integration has been the hallmark of humanity for millennia. As Aristotle put it, 'Man is by nature a social being'.[6] Human groups continue to be an essential element of human existence:

> It is . . . a more or less common intuition that communality is a structure of existence. Not only is groupness an unfathomable fact of all of our lives, but it is also an unfathomable value. We are born into certain groups, others we choose, and still others choose us. Life not subject to the call of groupness is as difficult for us to imagine as life not subject to the individuating call of personhood or to the sociating call of sociality.[7]

But however self-evident this proposition may be, communicating this general consensus about the value of groups through legal terminology is a difficult prospect. There are many things about groups that are worth protecting through law. Identifying, selecting, and segregating those valuable components for legal protection can be equally slippery to defining groups in the first place. Value here has multiple dimensions. There are, for example, obvious practical interests in communal existence. Human survival has long depended on joint co-operation.[8] Group interests also facilitate necessary conditions for private dealings (eg, a contract is a private agreement interpreted and enforced through legal mechanisms established for all).[9]

But there is more at stake than simply facilitating day-to-day existence or maximizing survival over time. This includes the 'profound psychological and sociological importance . . . of associations, both as amplifiers of different viewpoints and as sources for our individual identities'.[10]

> [R]espect, and a range of other social goods that help define us, generally seem meaningful only in group contexts. Declare independence as vigorously as any of us may, we

[5] Jewish identity provides a good example. 'The *halachic* rules on matrilineal descent and on conversions have been contested since the 18th century by various streams of Conservative, Reformed or Progressive Judaism. The *halacha* itself accommodates diverse positions.' G Verdirame, 'The Genocide Definition in the Jurisprudence of the Ad Hoc Tribunals' (2000) 49 ICLQ 578, 588.

[6] Aristotle *Nicomachean Ethics* I viii 1097b (JAK Thompson trans Penguin 2004) 8–11.

[7] RR Garet, 'Communality and Existence: The Rights of Groups' (1983) 56 So Cal LR 1001, 1070.

[8] Survival even provides another mechanism for identity. 'Surely there was and still is strength in numbers. It must be added that there is also aid and comfort in identifying oneself by distinguishing the groups to which one belongs from groups of other people. . . . We are known by the company we keep; we do define our friends by identifying common enemies.': Soifer 35 (1995).

[9] Soifer 4–5 (1995).

[10] ibid 36.

cannot escape interdependence. The individuation of each woman and each man—perhaps an error bred in the bone, perhaps not—originates in others and cannot seem to elude their grasp. It is our numerous associations, our families, politics, ethnicities, religions, and so forth, that offer critical benchmarks for how others evaluate us—and thereby how we evaluate ourselves.[11]

Groups thus are more than pragmatic vehicles for imposing social controls or enabling individual freedoms. Some suggest that notions of personhood, communality, and sociality—corresponding to individuals, groups, and society—are *equally necessary* structures of human existence.[12] They provide the third leg of the stool of human existence, mediating between society and the individual, and thus are social goods in their own right.[13] The implication is that group rights are matters of intrinsic worth that must be protected in and of themselves. It is the application of legal principles—in particular, the protections achieved through criminal law—to these social goods that is the driving force behind the Genocide Convention.

The physical and biological destruction of human groups thus denies an 'ethical constituent of our humanity' which has 'unfathomable' value.[14] The Genocide Convention treats such destruction as a criminal act. It recognizes that people exist in groups, expresses that certain groups have the right to exist 'as such', and confirms that infringements of this right are an international crime of the highest order.[15]

The Convention reflects that not all human groups warrant equal treatment. At one level, this is only common sense. Despite the benefits of groups *in general*, there are obvious types of groups that do not elevate society as a whole. Parasitic groups—criminal organizations and such—which detract from the public weal are hardly worth protecting through law, even if they are highly valued by their members.[16] And apart from groups not worth protecting at all, there are other groups that, for one reason or another, have weaker claims to extended legal protection. However valuable they are to individual members, groups of bald people[17] and cat lovers[18] simply are not protected by law in the same way as racial and religious groups.

[11] ibid 82.

[12] Garet (n 7) 1001. 'Communality' means the intrinsic moral value of human groups: ibid.

[13] ibid 1001–2. [14] ibid 1002, 1070.

[15] Security Council Expert Report (27 May 1994) UN Doc A/1994/674 ¶88 ('The Convention was manifestly adopted for humanitarian and civilizing purposes. Its objectives are to safeguard the very existence of certain human groups and to affirm and emphasize the most elementary principles of humanity and morality.').

[16] It goes without saying that the human rights of *individuals* must be respected in all circumstances, whether or not those individuals belong to criminal organizations or other such parasitic groups. But there is no need to consider legal protection for *groups* organized around criminal or other harmful characteristics.

[17] GP Fletcher, 'The Storrs Lectures: Liberals and Romantics at War: the Problem of Collective Guilt' (2002) 111 Yale LJ 1499, 1523–4 (hypothetical murderer targeting victims based on hatred of baldness).

[18] *Brounstein v American Cat Fanciers Assn* (1993) 839 FSupp 1100 (US Dist Ct (NJ)) (claim against cat fancier association for revoking license as an 'all-breed' cat judge).

There certainly is a wider social context to the prohibition on genocide. Its legal conception is only one aspect of a multi-dimensional problem. The root causes of the crime are intensely complicated. The impulse to commit genocide is linked to complex psychological and sociological phenomena relating to prejudice, anthropological notions of belonging in certain collectives, and group violence.[19] It transforms neighbours into 'others' by way of a predictable course of conduct where the 'others' are defined, stigmatized, segregated, and ultimately destroyed.[20] Social perceptions of differences harden into 'an objective contrast... [between] two conflicting groups, one of them intent on destroying the other'.[21] At the end of the day, genocide unfolds as an intensely local phenomenon, with numerous intersecting forces operating simultaneously to influence both individual receptivity to commit the crime and the larger social constructs against which individual decisions are made.[22]

However important they are to a full understanding of genocide, the pervasive social complexities must be put aside here. For present purposes, the main issue is the substantive definition of the criminal offence, which requires a narrower focus on the legal issues involved. It also requires an understanding of the legal implications of human social groupings.

Legal conceptions of groups

The concept of a human 'group' in the abstract is unhelpful. As noted above, the relevant inquiries are the purpose for which the group is defined and the identity of the decision maker. *Legal* classifications of groups answer these questions within the framework of applicable law. The group is reduced through legal terminology to a technical description that establishes criteria for membership and provides rights and obligations as a consequence.[23]

Legal criteria in turn must be applied to specific factual circumstances. Judges in particular 'play active roles in establishing and legitimating criteria that define

[19] Study on Genocide (4 Jul 1978) UN Doc E/CN4/Sub2/416 ¶¶569–90. There is, for example, some evidence of economic crises preceding attacks. DM Amann, 'Group Mentality, Expressivism, and Genocide' (2002) 2 ICLR 93, 141.

[20] GH Stanton, 'The Eight Stages of Genocide' (1998) Genocide Watch (describing genocide as a process against groups that proceeds through classification, symbolization, dehumanization, organization, polarization, preparation and ultimately to extermination, followed by denial).

[21] SC Darfur Report (25 Jan 2005) UN Doc S/2005/60 ¶500.

[22] Straus 10–15, 17–40, 49–64 and 87–94 (2006) (impact of local and regional factors on genocide in Rwanda).

[23] *Cf* Soifer 70 (1995) ('the combination of language and legitimized violence that constitutes law reflects but also shapes social values...'). The broad underlying proposition applies to the legal construction of any aspect of group identity, extending even to such matters as when membership in a group constitutes a justification, excuse or mitigating circumstance in the commission of a criminal offence. E Milhizer, 'Group Status and Criminal Defences: Logical Relationship or Marriage of Convenience?' (2006) 71 Mo LR 547 (discussing claims of justification, excuse and mitigation for battered women, those with socially-disadvantaged backgrounds, and based upon theories of group culture).

involuntary groups'.[24] Misapplied, such classification can even be an overt tool of genocide. After World War II, for example, a number of Nazi judges and prosecutors were tried for perverting German security and high treason laws in order to destroy Jews and other groups.[25]

Legal conceptions require application and implementation, which poses practical difficulties when the defining characteristics are not readily apparent. This often leads to the imposition of some sort of 'objective' marker upon the group. The Nazis, for example, and even their anti-Semitic German predecessors, had tremendous difficulty in parsing out a coherent legal definition for the Jewish community or even in identifying its members. Years before the Final Solution was implemented, Jews were forced to wear arm bands or clothing labels bearing the Star of David.[26] This practice continued in the concentration camps, where triangular uniform patches specified the basis of confinement: yellow (Jews), pink (homosexual males), green (common criminals), purple (Jehovah's Witnesses), red (political prisoners), and black (Gypsies).[27] Later, in Rwanda, identity cards describing their holders as Tutsi or Hutu became overt proxies of life and death at checkpoints.

Political opponents can be overtly marked for destruction as well. In Cambodia, the Khmer Rouge required citizens living in the country's 'Eastern Zone' (adjacent to Vietnam) to wear blue and white checked headscarves (kromas) at all times. The scarves subsequently were utilized to relocate and ultimately destroy the people wearing them (who had been classified as political enemies of the new Khmer state).[28]

B. Responding to the limitations of the Convention

The Genocide Convention is a limited instrument that delineates a narrow offence against specified victim classes. The Convention does not apply to all cases of mass atrocity. Its failure to cover 'political' and 'social' groups, for example, has provoked much criticism.[29] Some judges and theorists alike have responded to such limitations by contorting the Convention's terms, sometimes beyond all sensible meaning. These efforts are jurisprudentially suspect and appear aimed at achieving a pre-ordained result of inclusion for a particular collective. Although such humanitarian motives are perhaps understandable, as discussed below, efforts to stretch existing definitions of protected groups to cover groups with very different characteristics are best avoided.

24 ibid 70. 25 *Justice* [USMT 1947] 3 TWC 1.

26 For a detailed account of the complexities faced by the Germans in creating a legal definition for Jews, see Hilberg 61–77 (2003).

27 'Chart showing markings for categories of prisoners, Dachau, Germany ca 1942.'

28 GH Stanton, 'Blue Scarves and Yellow Stars: Classification and Symbolization in the Cambodian Genocide' 1, 4 (1987). 29 Bassiouni, Conventions 245 (1997).

'Stability and permanence'

The plain text of the Convention denies protection to all human collectives except national, ethnical, racial and religious groups. But in *Akayesu*, the ICTR deviated from a strict textual analysis (and its own stated criteria for ethnic groups) to produce a murky determination that Rwandan Tutsi were a protected group under the Genocide Convention.

The tribunal found it 'particularly important to respect the intention of the drafters of the Genocide Convention, which according to the *travaux préparatoires*, was patently to ensure the protection of *any* stable and permanent group'. (Emphasis added.)[30] It determined that 'a common criterion in the four types of groups protected by the Genocide Convention is that membership in such groups would seem to be normally not challengeable by its members, who belong to it automatically, by birth, in a continuous and often irremediable manner'.[31] The tribunal thus found Tutsi ethnically stable and distinct in Rwanda despite sharing language, society and culture with Hutu that massacred them.[32]

The specific criteria for identifying such 'permanent and stable' groups are unclear. The tribunal suggested a case-by-case basis in light of the group's social, political and cultural context.[33] What remains uncertain from the decision is whether the ICTR merely offered additional criteria to interpret the *scope* of an existing group or recognized a broader conception of genocide covering all 'stable and permanent' groups.

The judgment can be read both ways. On one hand, the case is limited to its facts and the context of ethnic groups. It can be confined to Article 2 of the ICTR Statute, to Rwanda in 1994, and to the particular ethnic group of Tutsis. In this light, the tribunal simply adopted broader criteria (beyond generally-accepted characteristics of distinct language, society, and culture) to hold Tutsis distinctly 'ethnic' in Rwandan society under the ICTR Statute. Conversely, the case suggests a broader understanding of groups under the Convention itself, not just the ICTR Statute. Protected groups would be defined through the 'common criterion' of stability and permanence,[34] supposedly reflecting the 'manifest intent' of the drafters. Some commentators have suggested that this means that the Convention now covers all so-called 'institutional' groups.[35]

For a number of reasons, *Akayesu* is best confined to the more limited interpretation. The legal basis of the tribunal's decision is questionable. First, the tribunal

30 *Akayesu (TC)* [1998] ICTR ¶516. 31 ibid ¶511.

32 ibid ¶¶122, 124, 702 and n 56. For the contrary view, see T Sapru, 'Into the Heart of Darkness: The Case Against the Foray of the Security Council Into the Rwandan Crisis' (1997) 32 Texas ILJ 329, 343–4 (arguing that Tutsi are not a distinct ethnic group).

33 *Akayesu (TC)* [1998] ICTR ¶¶122, 702 and n 56. 34 ibid ¶511.

35 JD Van der Vyver, 'Prosecution and Punishment of the Crime of Genocide' (1999) 23 Fordham ILJ 286, 305. With little further analysis, the author summarily concludes that *Akayesu* justifies international protection of homosexuals and similar collectives from genocide. ibid 305–6.

departed widely from settled principles of treaty construction, relying solely upon the 'manifest intent' of the Convention's drafters.[36] But *travaux préparatoires* are hardly dispositive. Widely-accepted international law expressly prohibits their use in the first instance, limiting them to resolving manifestly absurd or conflicting treaty constructions and to confirming a plain-text interpretation.[37] Neither consideration was present in *Akayesu*. The Convention covers national, ethnic, racial and religious groups. The plain meaning is that only those four groups are covered.[38] If the 'manifest intent' was to cover *any* 'stable and permanent' group, the text easily could have reflected that. The tribunal's interpretation renders the restrictive enumeration superfluous, which further deviates from sensible principles of treaty construction.[39]

Second, reliance upon drafting records, whether or not otherwise appropriate, always is subject to criticism on grounds of selectivity in referencing source material to support a particular point. This is particularly true for instruments like the Convention, where fifty-seven participating states[40] expressed numerous views as they negotiated. There were close votes on many key provisions,[41] which hardly represents 'manifest' consensus on anything. Statements of meaning in the draft record are not binding; they merely indicate that a majority of the drafters ascribed to a certain interpretation.[42] The mere fact that a proposed text was accepted did not mean that the Committee also adopted the proponent's interpretation of that provision.[43]

Third, it is flatly wrong to suggest that 'voluntary' groups are never 'stable and permanent'.[44] Some groups covered by the Convention (which the court labelled 'stable and permanent') are themselves 'voluntary,' at least in part. The court's holding would exclude, for example, religious and national groups with flexible membership criteria that allowed entry and exit in respect of the group. Likewise where ethnicity can be altered through marriage and other social ceremonies.[45] Ironically, this would include Rwandan Tutsi—the very group the court aimed to protect. Hutus could become Tutsi through the ritual contract of *Ubuhake* and the transfer of cattle, which conveyed new social standing and ownership rights. And vice versa. Two leading Hutu extremists, one a leader of *Interahamwe* killing squads, had transferred from the Tutsi group to become Hutu.[46]

[36] *Akayesu (TC)* [1998] ICTR ¶516.

[37] VCLT arts 31–32.

[38] Note that this does not preclude a wider conception under customary international law. That question is addressed in Chapter 5. But as a matter of *treaty* interpretation, the court's heavy reliance on the *travaux* was misplaced.

[39] *Cf Celebici (TC)* [1998] ICTY ¶161 (applying plain meaning of treaty terms).

[40] Official Records (6th Comm 1948) xiv–xix.

[41] M Lippman, 'The Drafting of the 1948 Convention on the Prevention and Punishment of the Crime of Genocide' (1985) 3 BU ILJ 1 (detailing drafting history).

[42] Official Records (6th Comm 1948) (SR132) 700 (Chair).

[43] ibid 136–7 (US).

[44] *Akayesu (TC)* [1998] ICTR ¶511.

[45] This often turns on a legal question. *Cf Lovelace v Canada* (UNHRC 1981) ¶¶17–19 (Canadian legislation that deprived individual of rights and status as a Maliseet Indian for marrying a non-Indian violated the ICCPR).

[46] Verdirame (n 5) 589 n 51.

Moreover, this formulation also would *include* 'stable and permanent' groups that were never even considered for inclusion in the Convention. Groups of blue-eyed people,[47] Oxonians (established through the historical fact of attending Oxford University), one-armed men, and a myriad of other collectives derived from immutable criteria suddenly would fall within the Convention.

This cannot be. Neither permanence and stability nor inalienability of status are required by the Convention. And although the tribunal linked the concepts together, they are not the same. Voluntary membership in a group is separate from that group's stability and permanence in a given society. The ICTR conflated them and opined that individual choice was *ipso facto* inconsistent with stability and permanence. But 'choice' here is a misnomer. As discussed previously, for purposes of genocide, the relevant characteristics for membership in the target group are those selected by the genocidaire. Such criteria are equally immutable whether they are racial, national, ethnic, religious, political, etc in nature. It thus defies the reality of genocide to suggest that some groups are *inherently* stable and permanent and that others are not.

These issues are revisited further below in the context of evaluating a broader conception of genocide covering groups beyond the four enumerated categories. For now, *Akayesu* remains a well-meaning (but misguided) effort to expand the groups covered by the Convention to correspond to a new reality. The ICTR is not alone in such efforts, however.

'Auto-genocide'

Similar complexities arise when members of protected groups are destroyed by other group members. Some suggest that negative stigmatization directed internally creates a separate protected group *within* the protected group. It makes 'the case that genocide could be committed by perpetrators of the same ethnicity who justified their murders by an ideology which reclassified and labelled the victims, discriminating their collaborators and those to be saved as a new kind of people'.[48] Taken to its logical extreme, such internal stigmatization applies the Convention to cases of 'auto-genocide,' such as the Khmer Rouge destroying over 25 per cent of the 'national' group of Cambodians.[49]

Genocidaires need not belong to a different group,[50] although cases where victim and perpetrator are of the same group undoubtedly are rare.[51] Nevertheless,

[47] Professor Lawrence reminds us of the protagonist's nemesis in Poe's classic horror tale. *Cf* Lawrence 11 (1999) (victim's 'pale blue eye, with a film on it') citing EA Poe, *The Tell Tale Heart* (1895).

[48] Fein 20 (1993).

[49] ibid.

[50] Study (Second) on Genocide (1985) UN Doc E/CN4/Sub2/1985/6 37.

[51] Willing collaborators who facilitate genocide out of self-preservation, for financial gain, etc are equally responsible if they act with the requisite intent. Another example would be mass murder/suicide where a group deliberately self-destructs 'as such,' perhaps in the context of large scale cult activity such as that in Guyana's 'Jonestown' in late 1978 (900+ deaths in religious mass murder-suicide).

this over-broad application of negative stigmatization is problematic. It renders superfluous the treaty language 'as such' (an integral component of the offence). It also constructs the 'protected' sub-group after the fact based on the pattern of victimization, instead of subjectively assessing the perpetrator's targeting characteristics *a priori*.

Stigmatization in cases of auto-genocide in all probability is grounded in something other than the protected characteristics of nationality, ethnicity, religion or race. Although Khmers intentionally destroyed other Khmers, they did not aim to destroy Khmers 'as such'. Negatively stigmatized or not, the group targeted in Cambodia does not qualify as a 'national' group under the Convention.

Despite such theoretical problems, the statute of the mixed domestic/international tribunal adjudicating Khmer Rouge offences potentially contemplates auto-genocide, in that the commission left for the tribunal the question of whether the Khmer Rouge could be charged with genocide for atrocities against Khmers as a 'national' group.[52] This could create significant confusion in forthcoming trials, particularly where the atrocities at issue would constitute genocide under the Convention against indigenous Vietnamese and religious Muslims and Buddhists.[53] The broader formulation also may violate fundamental prohibitions on the prosecution of *ex post facto* offences.[54]

The text of the statute also appears to depart from the Convention in other ways. In particular, it provides that:

> The acts of genocide, which have no statute of limitations, mean any acts committed with the intent to destroy, in whole or in part, a national, ethnical, racial or religious group *such as*:
> —killing members of the group;
> —causing serious bodily or mental harm to members of the group;
> —deliberately inflicting on the group conditions of life calculated to bring about its physical destruction in whole or in part;
> —imposing measures intended to prevent births within the group;
> —forcibly transferring children from one group to another group.
> (Emphasis added.)[55]

The English version of the statute substitutes 'such as' for 'as such' in the Genocide Convention. On its face, the change renders the underlying acts illustrative instead of enumerative and significantly broadens the range of conduct that constitutes the crime. Below the surface, however, this amounts more to carelessness than overreaching. The divergence seems to reflect a translation error between the official French and English texts. The ending clause of the French

[52] ibid ¶65.

[53] Report of Experts on Cambodia (16 Mar 1999) UN Doc A/53/850 ¶¶63–4.

[54] *Hadzihasanovic (Interlocutory Appeal—AC)* [2003] ICTY ¶55 (prohibition on retroactive prosecution and punishment itself is a peremptory norm of customary international law); ICCPR arts 4(2), 15(1) (prohibition is non-derogable).

[55] Cambodian Genocide Law (10 Aug 2001) art 4.

version ('l'intention de détruire, en tout ou en partie, un groupe national, ethnique, racial ou religieux, *comme tel*') (emphasis added) translates directly to the English modifier 'as such'.[56]

As a general matter, international agreements authenticated in multiple languages are 'presumed to have the same meaning in each authentic text'.[57] Given a choice, the better interpretation is to read the Cambodian genocide law as being identical to the Genocide Convention that it incorporates by reference. Otherwise, the clause would substantially broaden the definition of the crime. Paradoxically, this would create a new offence with the identical label—simultaneously incorporating the Genocide Convention by reference and yet defining the substantive offence differently.[58] Such a confusing result is best avoided, particularly in light of the Vienna Convention's admonition to adopt 'the meaning which best reconciles the texts, having regard to the object and purpose of the treaty . . .'.[59]

'Creative' interpretations

Redefining the existing terminology

The limits of the Convention arose again in criminal proceedings against former Chilean dictator Augusto Pinochet in the domestic courts of Spain. The Spanish Criminal Code defines genocide as an offence against 'a national, ethnic, racial or religious group'.[60] But only two months after the ICTR's judgment in *Akayesu*, Spain's Audencia Nacional engaged in a similar 'creative' analysis that likewise defied both the plain text of the Convention and Spanish law. Specifically, the court held that 'national' was a social (as opposed to legal) concept that included political and social groups.

Genocide, said the court, was to be 'understood in social terms, without any need for a specific criminal law definition'.[61] The victim group at issue included Chilean citizens and residents 'differentiated' for extermination. It encompassed 'citizens opposed to the military regime of 11 September, contrary to the understanding of national identity, of the national value, embraced by the new rulers . . .'.[62] The court held that offences against this differentiated group constituted genocide even though the Convention expressly excluded political groups.[63] 'National' groups also would include AIDS patients, the elderly and all

[56] Loi sur la création des chambres extraordinaires, avec inclusion d'amendements, promulguée le 27 octobre 2004 (NS/RKM/1004/006).

[57] VCLT art 33(3).

[58] Cambodian Genocide Law (10 Aug 2001) art 4.

[59] VCLT art 33(4).

[60] Penal Code (Spain) Law No 10/1995 art 607(1). The original Spanish definition, which substituted 'social' for 'racial', was later aligned to mirror the groups in the Convention. Brody and Ratner 101–2 (2000).

[61] *Pinochet: Spanish Jurisdiction* [Audencia Nacional 1998] in Brody and Ratner 95, 100 (2000).

[62] ibid 102.

[63] ibid 103.

foreigners living in a country, provided that they were sufficiently 'differentiated' for attack.[64]

The decision is problematic in several respects. The court overtly substituted social constructs for legal precepts,[65] which certainly implicates (if not violates) the principles of legality in this criminal extradition proceeding.[66] The decision also stretches 'nationality' beyond all sensible boundaries. As defined by the court, a 'national' group is simply an efficient proxy for *any* 'differentiated' group targeted for genocide. This interpretation eviscerates the independent meaning conveyed by the term in the Convention and should be disregarded as beyond the scope of legitimate interpretation of that treaty and its terms. The higher courts of Spain recognized the problematic nature of the decision and in a later case held that political groups were not a 'national' group under Spanish law on genocide.[67]

Broadening the victim groups

Proposals aimed at broadening the existing group categories appear in academic literature as well, particularly in connection with efforts to broaden protected categories to include other victim groups:

> For the purpose of the Hutu-directed genocide campaign in Rwanda, a Tutsi—for the purpose of extermination—was often a moderate Hutu, a Hutu married to a Tutsi, the children of such a union, a Hutu Democrat, and more. Clearly, the conduct of those who planned and/or executed these mass murders is still within the reach of the Convention....[68]

Such expansive constructions are not unique to the crime of genocide. Offences in other contexts have been broadened to include 'ancillary' targets as well. The Apartheid Convention, for example, provided that apartheid also encompassed the '[p]ersecution of organizations and persons, by depriving them of fundamental rights and freedoms, because they oppose apartheid'.[69] It certainly is an understandable temptation to seek to protect non-enumerated groups by expanding the protected group to include all persons victimized as part and parcel of the same attack. But there is a vast difference between specifically providing for such expanded forms of protection in an international instrument and creatively reading it into the Convention. The latter is problematic for several reasons.

64 ibid 103. Indigenous foreigners would be covered regardless as a separate 'national' group (eg, 'non-Chileans in Chile').

65 ibid 101–2.

66 As detailed in Chapter 5, the British Home Office rejected genocide as a basis of extradition, perhaps troubled by the Spanish court's interpretation but electing to address that concern indirectly through the prism of double criminality.

67 *Scilingo* [2005] (Sup Ct Spain) ¶III(A)(6).

68 WP Nagan and VF Rodin, 'Racism, Genocide, and Mass Murder: Toward a Legal Theory About Group Deprivation' (2004) 17 Nat'l Black LJ 33, 186–7 n 186.

69 Apartheid Convention art 2(f).

First, it rests on a legal fiction—for example, that 'non-ethnic' Tutsis can be treated as 'ethnic' Tutsis for purposes of genocide. This mis-states what is really happening in such cases. Hutu were not attacked on the basis of Tutsi ethnicity. They were attacked for their political beliefs *about* Tutsis (eg, opposing a policy of extermination). The fiction both distorts the definition of ethnicity and fails to identify the existence of a separate attack on a political group.

Second, it transforms genocide into a results-based crime. There is no requisite link between the *group* and the perpetrator's mental state and no obvious way to distinguish members of the group. As with auto-genocide, it upsets the structure of the Convention to define the targeted 'ethnic' group after the fact instead of examining whether the accused actually targeted persons based on ethnic characteristics in the first place.

Third, and more problematic still, is the absence of any logical stopping point in defining the group. Pure subjectivity, as noted in Chapter 3, is unworkable in practice. Although all distinctions for purposes of genocide are in the end arbitrary, larger, pre-existing social structures provide a context that allows those arbitrary characteristics to be agreed upon by perpetrators and subsequently imposed upon the group. In Rwanda, for example, there were clear social and historic demarcations between ethnic Tutsis and Hutus. Tutsis were identified and targeted, among other things, based on national identity cards identifying them as Tutsi, regardless of other personal characteristics they may have possessed. However arbitrary this may seem to outsiders, the distinction made sense in context to Hutu extremists because identity cards were a legitimate characteristic of ethnicity in Rwanda in 1994.

But what if a perpetrator aimed to destroy the group of ethnic Tutsi in Rwanda but defined that group in a completely ridiculous way—something as ludicrous as individuals who purchased American-made cigarettes in 1993, for example. This definition (fairly characterized as 'nuts') has no connection *whatsoever* to 'ethnic' characteristics or to other aspects of daily living in Rwanda pre-1994. Even if an accused had intent to destroy 'Tutsi' 'as such' and killed purchasers of American cigarettes in furtherance of that intent, this is not genocide against Tutsis. The defining characteristic of the targeted group is not covered by the Convention. Despite a proffered aim of destroying all Tutsis, what he really sought to destroy was the group of purchasers of American cigarettes in 1993. Although some more-traditionally defined Tutsis were caught in his net, there remains a disconnect between his intentions and his actions *vis à vis* the Convention. It would be equally problematic if 'Tutsi' were defined to include both ethnic Tutsi and the 'friends' and 'supporters' massacred alongside them. The latter are not genuinely 'ethnic' characteristics and thus cannot bring these victims within the contours of a protected ethnic group under the Convention.

That said, there is some intuitive appeal to considering attacks on non-enumerated groups within the same overall framework. A more analytically sound argument would be to analyse attacks on Hutu as aiding and abetting the genocide against Tutsis.[70] As noted previously, aiding and abetting is intentionally assisting another in committing a certain offence with knowledge of a substantial likelihood that the offence would be committed.[71] If a criminal cuts alarm wires to facilitate a bank robbery, he commits an offence of property damage but also aids and abets the bank robbery.[72] Likewise, if he kills political opponents in order to eliminate those who would oppose the genocide against Tutsis, he commits direct crimes against the political victims (extermination, persecution, etc) and very likely the separate offence of aiding and abetting the acts of genocide against Tutsi.

The secondary offence certainly brings Hutu victims closer to the genocide itself. But it is an incomplete solution, at best. A conviction for merely aiding and abetting understates both the perpetrator's *mens rea* and his conduct. It reflects only that he aimed to *assist* destruction by others, not that he himself aimed to destroy a separate political group. It also fails to demonstrate that he committed serious offences against the person. Aiding and abetting alone puts a perpetrator of the serious physical violence inherent in political genocide on equal footing with the profiteer who sold jeeps to extremists to help them mobilize against protected groups. It also fails to denote the targeting of the larger group of politically-moderate Hutu itself as a separate victim of reprehensible criminal conduct.

C. Departing from the Convention

The inherent historical and textual limitations of the Genocide Convention have evoked creative interpretations of treaty language and the collectives that the language represents. Although the means are intellectually suspect, the goal (protecting additional human groups) is not. The analysis reveals a problem with the Convention itself—that without 'help' it is unable to respond to modern circumstances that seem to cry out for its application.

Semantic legerdemain clearly is not the answer. The better solution is to determine whether there is a more logically sound way to achieve the broader aim. This first entails sorting out the various theoretical justifications for including some groups in the Convention, while excluding others. It then requires an analysis of whether those theoretical grounds might apply equally to political groups, such that protecting them under the same basic structure may be warranted.

There is considerable debate over the question. Professor Schabas suggests, for example, that there is no logical stopping point beyond the existing structure of

[70] This argument does not appear to have been advanced in the international criminal tribunals.

[71] *Tadic (Merits—AC)* [1999] ICTY ¶229.

[72] If he intends for the robbery to be committed, he also might be guilty as a co-perpetrator of a joint criminal enterprise.

the Convention. 'Fundamentally, the problem with including political groups is the difficulty in providing a rational basis for such a measure. If political groups are to be included, why not the disabled, or other groups based on arbitrary criteria. Logically, the definition ought to be expanded to cover all episodes of mass killing.'[73]

This merits discussion. Why *not* cover all 'arbitrary' groups under the concept of genocide? Since perpetrators can define and destroy virtually all human groups in equally arbitrary ways, what justifies covering some but not others? Put another way, since the characteristics selected to define the group are always arbitrary and imposed by others, why should that commonality in means of selection not also justify equal measures of protection?

All 'arbitrary' groups

One answer to the question of under-inclusiveness is simply to cover all groups. Some states do this already via the 'broad form' conception of genocide reflected in some domestic legislation.[74] The French Penal Code provides an example:

> Genocide occurs where, in the enforcement of a concerted plan aimed at the partial or total destruction of a national, ethnic, racial or religious group, *or of a group determined by any other arbitrary criterion*, one of the following actions are committed or caused to be committed against members of that group....[75] (Emphasis added.)

One might suggest that such equal treatment is justified. Why not protect groups based on 'idiosyncratic hatreds that might be just as virulent as racial hatred [and other covered grounds]...?'[76] Whatever the group, the conduct is a serious infringement of human life, bodily and family integrity, etc. Why is it too large a burden simply to prohibit physical and biological destruction of all arbitrarily-formed groups?

The answer rests with the nature of genocide itself. The rights to life, bodily integrity, etc of individual group members are protected already. Genocide is a special crime that protects the *separate* physical and biological existence of the *group*. The premise underlying the 'broad form' definition is that *all* human groups—however defined—have equal rights to exist 'as such'. It fails to separate the wheat from the chaff. It protects Blacks, Catholics, bald people, cat lovers, one-armed men, Oxonians, etc to precisely the same degree. Despite vast social and legal differences between these groups, they are treated identically

[73] Schabas 132 (2009). [74] This formulation is detailed in Chapter 5.

[75] Code Penal (France) art 211–1. Similar sentiments appear in the ICC Statute's 'modernized' definition of persecution. ICC Statute art 7(1)(h) ('Persecution against any identifiable group or collectivity on...or other grounds that are universally recognized as impermissible under international law').

[76] GP Fletcher, 'The Storrs Lectures: Liberals and Romantics at War: the Problem of Collective Guilt' (2002) 111 Yale LJ 1499, 1523.

across all categories in the context of arguably the most serious crime known to humanity.

This premise is troubling. Even if the underlying grounds for protecting human groups are similar *in general*, it does not necessarily follow that the theory *applies* identically in all contexts. Professor Brownlie reminds us of the important distinction between theory and reality:

> The rights and claims of groups with their own cultural histories and identities are in principle the same—they must be. It is the problems of implementation of principles and standards which vary, simply because the facts will vary. The point can be expressed by saying that the problems of the Lapps, the Inuit, Australian Aboriginals, the Welsh, the Quebecois, the Armenians, the Palestinians, and so forth, are the same in principle but different in practice. This association of categories is not generally accepted, and the separation of categories is one reason for the hesitant approach to the definition of... [groups].[77]

The law should reflect distinctions that everyone recognizes in ordinary life. The extraction of legal consequences from the factual characteristics of group identity likewise must account for context and the group's actual existence in the society or geographic area affected. Without such recognition, the distinctions become meaningless, creating an untenable analytical conflict with other aspects of law that recognize and provide a specific form of legal protection for those distinctions. Undoubtedly aware of these issues, the international community made the judgment in 1948 that only four *enumerated* groups would be covered by genocide.

The question now becomes whether the underlying justifications for protecting the four groups in the Convention are *sui generis* to those categories or might apply more broadly to other types of groups as well. This presumes, of course, that the categories are explainable by something other than political compromise at the dawn of the Cold War.[78] If uniform grounds exist, they should explain both the *inclusion* of all four enumerated groups and justify the *exclusion* of all other groups. Any theory that cannot account for both lacks full coherence and therefore fails as a reason to leave the present structure of the Convention untouched. This does not mean that—as an historical matter—justifications which do not fully account for inclusion and exclusion are irrelevant or that they played no part in the drafting of the Convention. Rather, it means that satisfying that particular criterion is not a *sine qua non* of determining whether other groups might be legitimately covered by the concept.

The aim here is to take a fresh approach to delineating the grounds *underlying* the Convention's existing groupings. This is important because debate continues

[77] Ian Brownlie, 'The Rights of Peoples in Modern International Law' in Crawford 1, 16 (1988).

[78] The history of the Genocide Convention was covered briefly in Chapter 1 and is discussed in greater detail in Chapter 5.

over whether the Convention's existing grouping is so unique that it essentially renders the current listing untouchable.[79] As one commentator put it:

> Despite criticism that the enumeration of protected groups in the Convention is limited and restrictive, the final result is coherent [and] . . . aims at protecting groups that were defined, prior to the Second World War, as 'national minorities', 'races' and 'religious groups.' A more contemporary usage seems to prefer 'ethnic' groups. But these are really all efforts to describe a singular reality. Applied with a mix of common sense and intuition, the definition appears to work. . . . Diluting the definition, either by formal amendment of its terms or by extravagant interpretation of the existing text, risks trivializing the horror of the real crime when it is committed.[80]

The analysis of commonalities among the Convention's existing groups thus helps to inform the legitimacy of the larger question of whether political collectives are sufficiently similar to *potentially* justify protecting them in a similar way.

Criteria justifying inclusion in groups

When something other than all 'arbitrary groups' are covered, there should be a reasonable basis for saying yes to some groups and no to others. A number of proposals have been offered to explain the groupings in the Convention, many of which will now be considered here. The fact that various aspects of group identity are parsed out for analysis here does not mean that they are isolated factors in practice, however. The groups enumerated in the Convention are complex, multidimensional structures, and there is much overlap among the various justifications offered for their inclusion in the treaty.

Historical justifications and pragmatic needs

One explanation is purely pragmatic: that there simply was a greater *need* to protect certain groups as historically-victimized collectives. There is some merit to this. Racial and religious groups were the targets of the most extreme examples of genocide in the 20th century—chief among them the Nazi Holocaust against Jews and the Ottoman genocide against Armenians. The former unquestionably was in the mind of the drafters (and the rest of the world watching) as the Convention was negotiated in the late 1940s.

But pragmatic needs are not a sufficient explanation. There were massive 20th century atrocities against political groups as well. Millions had been slaughtered in Germany, in the Soviet Union and elsewhere before the Genocide Convention was finalized. Political groups were deliberately *removed* from the Convention

[79] Schabas 131 (2009) ('There is a danger that a search for autonomous meaning for each of the four terms will weaken the overarching sense of the enumeration as a whole . . . Deconstructing the enumeration risks distorting the sense that belongs to the four terms, taken as a whole.').

[80] Schabas 132–3 (2009).

despite forewarning that they were the most likely targets of future genocides.[81] This caution proved lamentably prescient: the four decades after World War II witnessed far greater destruction of political collectives than of other types of groups.[82]

Neither historic victimization nor likely future exigencies can fully explain the distinctions embodied in the Convention.[83] The distinctions between enumerated groups and other groups therefore must derive from matters more theoretical than pragmatic. Historic vulnerability and future needs certainly are sensible factors in *choosing* among groups to cover. But they are not sufficient in and of themselves to explain the groups ultimately selected for inclusion in the Convention.

Involuntary groupings

'Involuntary' associations are 'an inartful designation for the groups we are born into and which we may not be able to leave even if we want to'.[84] Some suggest that the groups covered by the Convention have in common that they are *all* involuntary groups. Political groups, in contrast, supposedly were not readily identifiable, lacked 'stable, permanent and clear-cut characteristics', and were not 'inevitable and homogenous grouping[s]' because they derived from the will of the members and not 'factors independent of that will'.[85]

But permanence, stability, inevitability, etc cannot sufficiently explain the groups protected in the Convention because not all of the groups in the Convention are drawn from wholly immutable characteristics. Nationality and religion are freely alienable and have been for some time.[86] Indeed, the UDHR, adopted on the heels of the Genocide Convention, affirms the right to alter both nationality and religion,[87] although some states disagreed[88] (and continue to disagree)[89] with respect to religion. As noted previously, in some cases ethnicity can be cast off by adopting the social, cultural and linguistic characteristics of another group.

[81] Official Records 723 (6th Comm 1948) UN Doc A/C6/SR219 (Fr).

[82] B Harff and TR Gurr, 'Toward Empirical Theory of Genocides and Politicides: Identification and Measurement of Cases Since 1945' (1988) 32 ILQ 359, 368 (politicides outnumbering genocides by more than four to one).

[83] *Cf* Nagan and Rodin (n 68) 195 ('the legal definition of genocide does not account for a good deal of "historical" genocide').

[84] Soifer 128 n 6 (1995).

[85] Study (Second) on Genocide (2 Jul 1985) UN Doc E/CN4/Sub2/1985/6 ¶35. But see Schabas 153 (2009) (disputing validity and utility of stability and permanence paradigm).

[86] This was recognized even during the drafting of the Convention. Official Records (6th Comm 1948) (SR69) 60 (UK).

[87] UDHR arts 15, 18.

[88] 'Memorandum Submitted by the Kingdom of Saudi Arabia to International Organizations on Human Rights and their Implementation within its Territory' (15 Jun 1970) No 10/6/10/J6/1350; DG Littman, 'Universal Human Rights & Human Rights in Islam' (1999) 45 Midstream 2.

[89] 'Cairo Declaration on Human Rights in Islam' (5 Aug 1990) UN Doc A/CONF157/PC/62/Add18.

Racial characteristics, perhaps most immutable of all, increasingly can be altered through surgical and technological advances.[90] More importantly, however, even 'immutable' racial characteristics are inherently linked to social constructs and thus change when the social context changes. Consider the racial transformation of a Harvard professor based simply on geography:

I am an African American... but in parts of Africa, I am white. To do fieldwork as a medical anthropologist in Senegal, she says, 'I take a plane to France, a seven- to eight-hour ride. My race changes as I cross the Atlantic. There, I say, '*Je suis noire*', and they say, 'Oh, okay—*métisse*—you are mixed.' Then I fly another six to seven hours to Senegal, and I am white. In the space of a day, I can change from African American, to *métisse*, to *tubaab* [Wolof for 'white/European']. This is not a joke, or something to laugh at, or to take lightly. It is the kind of social recognition that even two-year-olds who can barely speak understand. '*Tubaab*', they say when they greet me.[91]

Apart from the shifting social dimensions, it is worth pointing out that the Convention also excludes many groups that are *more* immutable than some of the enumerated groups. Age-based groups, for example, can be defined irrefutably based upon date of birth. Such criteria are used already to establish legal obligations and benefits.[92] Groups also can be established based on definitive scientific evidence—HIV status,[93] for example, or the presence of certain genetic diseases (eg, cystic fibrosis) from birth onward. They also can be based upon physical disabilities (paralysis, blindness, etc).[94] Despite the fact that these groups are not 'voluntary' and are highly 'stable and permanent,' they have no protection under the Convention.

This is not to suggest that immutability is irrelevant to social constructs, group understanding, or questions of individual identity. It is important to

[90] Griffin (1962) (narrative of white reporter who medically altered his skin colour in order to experience first-hand the racial segregation laws governing southern Blacks in the United States during the late 1950s).

[91] 'Race in a Genetic World' (2008) 110 Harvard Magazine 62.

[92] Children are an age based group. *Cf* CRC arts 1 (age of 'child'), 38 (minimum age for military service), and 37(a) (maximum penalty for criminal offence based on age). Age also determines eligibility for pension, health care, and other benefits to retirees and elder members of society. These are instances of age used as a proxy for a legal classification of entitlement. Such criteria could easily be misused to identify and target a group for purposes of genocide-like crimes.

[93] *Cf* 'International Guidelines on HIV/AIDS and Human Rights' UNCHR Res 1997/33 (11 Apr 1997) UN Doc E/CN4/1997/150 Guideline Nos 4 ('States should review and reform criminal laws and correctional systems to ensure that they are consistent with international human rights obligations and are not misused in the context of HIV/AIDS or targeted against vulnerable groups' and 5 ('States should enact or strengthen antidiscrimination and other protective laws that protect vulnerable groups, people living with HIV/AIDS and people with disabilities from discrimination in both the public and private sectors....').

[94] Convention and Optional Protocol on the Rights of Persons with Disabilities (13 Dec 2006) UN Doc A/61/611 art 5(2) ('States Parties shall prohibit all discrimination on the basis of disability and guarantee to persons with disabilities equal and effective legal protection against discrimination on all grounds.'); 'Declaration on the Rights of Disabled Persons' UNGA Res 3447 (XXX) (9 Dec 1975) UN Doc A/10034 art 4 ('Disabled persons have the same civil and political rights as other human beings....').

remain mindful of the narrow context in which group identity is addressed here. Whatever the technical possibilities, if plotted on a continuum of individual characteristics, it is obvious that some aspects of group identity simply are harder to change than others. It is much easier, for example, to file legal papers to alter nationality or to change personal religious practices than to alter the results of ethnic heritage or the biological markers of DNA and skin pigmentation.

That said, the operative question here is not whether personal characteristics are immutable for all purposes, or even for most purposes. As noted previously,[95] it is critical to identify the purpose for which group characteristics are defined, as well as who gets to define them. In the narrow context of genocide, the many broader social questions of immutability are overridden by the nefarious intentions of the genocidaire. The fact is that *all* genocides are based upon involuntary association. The victim has no choice on whether the perpetrator decides he will be targeted as a member of the victim group. Notions of the immutability or involuntariness of membership thus fail to explain fully either the groupings in the Convention or the exclusion of other groups from its protections.

Reconstitution after attack

Although involuntary association cannot fully explain the groups covered by the Convention, there nevertheless remains an intuitive pull toward providing greater protection for groups that simply are what they are, without any sense of voluntary choice among members. It seems *worse*, somehow, to injure someone based upon an aspect of their personhood that was imposed upon them by the fortuity of birth and heredity, rather than personal choice.

A major reason for this is that it is harder for such groups to reconstitute themselves after a genocidal attack. Race, certainly, is the most important category in this regard. If all Blacks in a state are killed, it will be extremely difficult for that group to reformulate. This is hardly hypothetical. The Nazis clearly aimed to eliminate Jews forever as a European group—even if Germany lost the war, there would be too few Jews left to 'threaten' Germany in the future.[96] Likewise in Rwanda, where 800,000 dead amounted to 10 per cent of the general population but some 75 per cent of minority Tutsi.[97]

Racial groups have the strongest link to continuity through procreation and heredity. But even these highly immutable characteristics are problematic as a basis for defining groups because they are present in varying degrees among group members and are subject to dilution over time. Procreation with other races decreases the 'pure' content of a particular race—one-half, one quarter, etc

95 See Chapter 4 (A).

96 R Lemkin, 'Genocide as a Crime Under International Law' (1947) 41 AJIL 145, 147 (Nazi efforts 'to *change permanently* the population balance in occupied Europe in their favour') (emphasis added).

97 P Verwimp, 'Death and survival during the 1994 genocide in Rwanda' (2004) 58 Population Studies 233.

downward through succeeding generations. At what point is one no longer 'Jewish,' 'Native American,' 'Black', etc?

On one hand, racial 'characteristics' are impossible to shed entirely. Scientific advances in DNA testing can determine heredity dating back hundreds of years, if not longer.[98] On the other hand, scientific research indicates that human beings are much more alike than not, sharing over 99.9 per cent of their DNA.[99] Paradoxically, genetic variation is greater within a given race than among different races.[100] When it comes to groups, 'scientific' composition thus is far less important than social understanding:

> [G]enetically homogeneous populations do not exist and traits are not discontinuous between populations; therefore, a population can only be described in terms of relative frequencies of various traits. Clear-cut categories do not exist. The particular traits which have generally been chosen to characterize races have been criticized as having little biological significance.... These observations and others have led some, but not all, scientists to conclude that racial classifications are for the most part socio-political, rather than biological, in nature.[101]

The answer requires subjective determinations and line drawing. Groups typically have their own internal membership criteria, which may or may not change over time. It also can be framed as a legal query in cases involving family relationships,[102] the application of criminal laws,[103] and the like. Courts have long grappled with this issue. *Hudgins v Wright*[104] involved a suit for freedom in 1806 by three generations of slaves on grounds of white ancestry. Virginia law presumed that Blacks were slaves but that Whites and Indians were free. The burden of proof shifted depending on the court's determination of race. The chancellor examined the petitioners' appearance at trial and found them to be sufficiently 'white' to place the burden of proof on the purported owner, who was unable to rebut the presumption.[105] On appeal, Justice Tucker offered 'guidance' for future cases:

> Nature has stampt upon the African and his descendants two characteristic marks, besides the difference of complexion, which often remain visible long after the characteristic distinction of colour either disappears or becomes doubtful; a flat nose and woolly head of hair. The latter of these characteristics disappears the last of all: and so strong

[98] E Beckenhauer, 'Redefining Race: Can Genetic Testing Provide Biological Proof of Indian Ethnicity' (2003) 56 Stan LR 161, 180–190 (DNA testing to determine tribal ancestry).

[99] ibid 175.

[100] ibid.

[101] *St Francis College v Al-Khazraji* (1987) 481 US 604 (US Sup Ct) 610 n 4.

[102] *Ferrall v Ferrall* (1910) 69 SE 60 (Sup Ct NC) 61–2 (under an anti-miscegenation statute that voided marriages between whites and persons 'of negro or Indian blood to the third generation inclusive' (someone 1/8 Black or Indian) the court held that the wife was legally white unless her great-grandfather was a 'full negro'—a 'negro of pure African blood.').

[103] *Vialpando v State* (1982) 640 P2d 77 (Sup Ct Wyo) 80 ('one-eighth Indian blood is not a "substantial amount of Indian blood" to classify appellant as an Indian' for purposes of subjecting his criminal offences to tribal jurisdiction).

[104] *Hudgins v Wright* (1806) 11 Va (1 Hen & M) 134 (Sup Ct App Va).

[105] ibid 1.

an ingredient in the African constitution is this latter character, that it predominates uniformly where the party is in equal degree descended from parents of different complexions, whether white or Indians; giving to the jet black lank hair of the Indian a degree of flexure, which never fails to betray that the party distinguished by it, cannot trace his lineage purely from the race of native Americans.[106]

In one sense, little has changed since 1806. Whether the markers of group identity are DNA polymorphisms or stereotyped judgments about physical appearance, the result always depends upon the *selection of criteria* marking the contours of the group and the *application of those criteria* to individuals. In cases of genocide, it is the *genocidaire* who determines whether a victim is part of the group or has been 'diluted' out.[107] Whatever the answer is sociologically, anthropologically, according to the group's internal criteria, etc, when it comes to genocide, a person is no longer 'Jewish' when the perpetrator says that he is no longer Jewish.

But although choices about which groups to protect are justified to some extent by the ability of a group to reconstitute after an attack, this cannot fully explain the groups covered in the Convention. Groups under the Convention exist principally in one of *two* ways: what they 'are' or what they 'believe'. The latter prolong their institutional existence by indoctrinating new group members into their belief system—either by 'converting' non-members or by handing down beliefs to the next generation through procreation and education in the ways of the group. Although the scope of permissible assimilation and integration varies from group to group, as a general matter ethnical, national, and religious groups are all better able than racial groups to reconstitute themselves after an attack.

As noted previously, ethnic Hutus and Tutsis could switch ethnicity via marriage and other social ceremonies in Rwanda.[108] Religious and national groups—protected equally under the Convention—are even more easily reconstituted. The grouping in the Convention thus appears to depend on factors other than a particular group's ability to reconstitute itself after attack.

Institutional existence and legal personality

On a practical level, some groups are easier to identify than others. This depends to some extent on the group's recognized existence independent of its individual members. As groups become larger and move toward institutional existence, they tend to play larger roles (for good or ill) and have heightened impact upon society. Not all groups that technically could be formulated based upon the arbitrary whim of the genocidaire also have a separate institutional identity of some kind.

[106] ibid 5.

[107] *Cf* Reich Citizenship Law: First Regulation (individual fate turned on Nazi test for 'full' Jew, and Jews of 'second' and 'third' degrees, based on number of Jewish grandparents).

[108] Verdirame (n 5) 589 n 51.

The 'perennial' debate is, of course, whether groups have identity in and of themselves, separate from their members.[109] It seems inescapable that some 'groups' are simply two or more individuals sharing a common characteristic and that others are something more.[110] All four groups in the Convention meet this latter criterion, but not exclusively. Although the characteristic is uniform among the enumerated groups, it also is present in other groups. Political organizations, for example, have long been viewed as having interests separate from the aggregated desires of their members:

> The party, regarded as an entity, as a piece of mechanism, is not necessarily identifiable with the totality of its members, and still less so with the class to which these belong. The party is created as a means to secure an end. Having, however, become an end in itself, endowed with aims and interests of its own, it undergoes detachment... from the class which it represents. In a party, it is far from obvious that the interests of the masses which have combined to form the party will coincide with the interests of the bureaucracy in which the party become[s] personified.... By a universally applicable social law, every organ of the collectivity, brought into existence through the need for division of labour, creates for itself, as soon as it becomes consolidated, interest peculiar to itself. The existence of these special interests involves a necessary conflict with the interests of the collectivity.[111]

Institutional identity to some degree is connected with the existence of separate legal personality. In the *Reparations* case, the ICJ framed the operative inquiry as whether the UN possessed 'rights which it is entitled to ask [its Members] to respect' and held that the UN had independent legal capacity as an organization[112] The ICJ applied similar criteria five years later in *Nottebohm*, determining that nationality—another social grouping with legal consequences—required 'a legal bond having its basis [in] a social fact of attachment, a genuine connection of existence, interests, and sentiments, together with the existence of *reciprocal rights and duties*.' (Emphasis added.)[113]

Similar issues arose 25 years later in connection with claims that the various tribes and emirates dwelling in the Western Sahara region of Africa formed a distinct legal entity. While acknowledging the 'somewhat special context' of its prior jurisprudence, the ICJ held that its *Reparations* jurisprudence 'expresses the essential test where a group, whether composed of States, of tribes or of individuals,

[109] Professor Dan-Cohen, for example, compares the 'holistic' view (organizations are more than a 'description of individuals and their inter-relations' for purposes of 'legal personhood as the bearer of rights and duties') with the 'atomistic' view (the 'normative status of any collective entity is identical with the normative status of the individuals that compose it'): Dan-Cohen 15 (1986).

[110] In the context of domestic policy on bias crimes, for example, Professor Lawrence notes the distinctions between prejudice driven by 'rather odd peccadillo[s]' and 'group antipathy that has a social context.' Lawrence 11–12 (1999).

[111] Michels 389 (1915).

[112] *Reparations* [1949] ICJ 174, 178.

[113] *Nottebohm* [1955] ICJ 4, 23 (standing of state to assert diplomatic claim for expropriation of individual's property).

is claimed to be a legal entity distinct from its members.'[114] Despite some commonalities, the group lacked reciprocal legal connections and therefore had no legal personality 'distinct from the several emirates and tribes which composed it'.[115]

The fact that the groups enumerated in the Convention *can* have a separate legal existence does not mean that they *must* have one to qualify. Although legal capacity may be a helpful proxy for defining a group, it is not the only method of doing so. There is a difference, for example, between targeting racial Blacks in Birmingham, Alabama and targeting members of the Birmingham NAACP. The Convention is not limited to the latter. A theory justifying the enumerated groups based upon their capacity for legal personality also fails to account for the many excluded social groups that have clear legal personality—trade unions being probably the best example. Legal personality thus cannot fully explain the groupings in the Genocide Convention (although it may provide useful evidence of group membership).

Separate from the issue of legal personality, even wider concepts of 'institutionalism' fail to explain the categories in the Convention. '[G]roup membership is constructed by society and changes with society.'[116] 'Institutional' groups protected under the Convention can disappear and change as the circumstances around them change. National identity, for example, can shift rapidly. The shift from 'Yugoslavia' to Serbia-Montenegro, Bosnia-Herzegovina and Croatia in the early 1990s is a good example.[117] Religious philosophies can be equally short-lived, particularly those involving smaller groups, splinter organizations departing from a more mainstream religion, cults, and the like.

But all nations, religions, political movements, etc have to start someplace. Historical examples of breakaway groups developing a separate institutional character are the birth of Protestantism during the Reformation and the inception of the United States with the Declaration of Independence. The premise of the Genocide Convention is that certain groups—emergent or otherwise—have value. There is nothing in the Convention that restricts its protections to 'institutional' groups.

The common denominator: a rights-based approach

As noted previously, Professor Schabas argues that there is no legitimate basis for moving beyond the groupings in the Convention.[118] He asserts that historical

[114] *Western Sahara* [1975] ICJ 12 ¶148. [115] ibid ¶149.

[116] DM Amann, 'Group Mentality, Expressivism, and Genocide' (2002) 2 ICLR 93, 135.

[117] There are legal prerequisites for statehood under international law. *Cf* Restatement (Third) of Foreign Relations s 201 (defined territory, permanent population, government and capacity to conduct international relations). The usage here is broader and would cover emergent national identity even when the formal requisites are not met.

[118] Schabas 131 (2009) ('There is a danger that a search for autonomous meaning for each of the four terms will weaken the overarching sense of the enumeration as a whole... Deconstructing the enumeration risks distorting the sense that belongs to the four terms, taken as a whole.').

justifications continue to provide a uniform basis justifying only the four enumerated categories. 'Despite criticism that the enumeration of protected groups in the Convention is limited and restrictive, the final result is coherent [and] ... aims at protecting groups that were defined, prior to the Second World War, as "national minorities", "races" and "religious groups".'[119] Schabas thus advocates an 'holistic' approach that avoids swapping the forest for the trees,[120] positing that the groups covered by the Convention are largely synonymous concepts that 'not only overlap ... [but] also help to define each other, operating much as four corner posts that delimit an area within which a myriad of groups covered by the Convention find protection.'[121]

If the groups in the Convention were indeed different faces of a coherent whole, Schabas might be correct to suggest that no logical stopping point exists beyond that grouping.[122] But despite the merits of this well-considered view, the historical evidence hardly seems to *compel* this sole conclusion.[123] Participating states initially voted 29 in favour[124] to 13 against[125] to retain political groups, with 9 abstentions.[126] It was only toward the very end of the drafting process that the issue was revisited. Although political groups subsequently were deleted, this was expressly described as a 'conciliatory' measure to ensure ratification, rather than a legalistic concession that political groups somehow were analytically incongruent.[127] It is equally possible that the reasons for covering only groups amounting to 'national minorities' in the original Convention were based far more on pragmatic needs than on theoretical grounds compelling this 'holistic' approach.

The greater difficulty is with the underlying premise[128] that internal coherence among 'national minorities' necessarily *precludes* the application of genocide

[119] Schabas 132 (2009). See also *Krstic (TC)* [2001] ICTY ¶556 (referring to writings of Professor Schabas and opining that the Convention 'was designed more to describe a single phenomenon, roughly corresponding to what was recognized, before the second world war, as "national minorities", rather than to refer to several distinct prototypes of human groups.').

[120] Schabas 131 (2009).

[121] ibid 129 and 133 (groups included 'are really all efforts to describe a singular reality. Applied with a mix of common sense and intuition, the definition seems to work.').

[122] ibid 646 (concluding 'that the definition of genocide is not an unfortunate drafting compromise but rather a logical and coherent attempt to address a particular phenomenon of human rights violation, the threat to the existence of what we would now call "ethnic" groups and what the drafters conceived of essentially as "national minorities"').

[123] The drafting process of the Convention is detailed in Chapter 5.

[124] Netherlands, New Zealand, Norway, Panama, Paraguay, Philippines, Saudi Arabia, Siam, Sweden, Syria, Turkey, UK, USA, Yemen, Australia, Bolivia, Burma, Canada, Chile, China, Cuba, Denmark, Ecuador, El Salvador, France, Haiti, Iceland, India and Luxembourg. ibid (SR75) 115.

[125] Poland, Ukrainian SSR, Union of South Africa, USSR, Uruguay, Venezuela, Argentina, Belgium, Brazil, Belorussian SSR, Czechoslovakia, Dominican Republic and Iran: ibid.

[126] Nicaragua, Pakistan, Peru, Yugoslavia, Afghanistan, Egypt, Ethiopia, Greece and Lebanon. ibid. Political groups appeared in further drafts of the Convention even as of late November 1948. Draft Resolutions and draft convention on genocide proposed by the Drafting Committee (23 Nov 1948) UN Doc A/C6/289 art II.

[127] Official Records (6th Comm 1948) (SR128) 661–2 (US).

[128] Schabas 129–32 (2009).

to other collectives. This is not to say that the existing groups do not overlap or mutually reinforce one another. They are, and they do. But with due respect to minds that differ, a coherence theory cannot preclude all future expansion of the concept of genocide because the groups reflected in the Convention are *not* internally coherent in a way that renders the current listing untouchable.

There is an implicit schism in the Convention between groups based principally upon what they *are* and groups based upon what they *believe*. Racial and ethnic groups fall largely into the former category, while religious groups fall into the latter. National groups have characteristics of both—nationality based upon locus of birth and parental lineage (what one is) and grounded in beliefs (the freedom to change nationality by seeking citizenship elsewhere and adopting the beliefs—the oath and obligations of citizenship—of that state).[129]

The concepts can be harmonized through the Convention's implicit presumption that certain groups *are* what they *believe*. Certain shared beliefs form so much of the core identity of members that they drive the reality of the group's existence—for group members and everyone else. Put another way, there are certain aspects of identity that no one should have to give up in order to avoid physical and/or biological destruction, religion being one and nationality (as a belief system) being another. This is especially true when one considers that group identity inevitably is a social, rather than scientific, question.[130]

This idea is not necessarily limited to the context of genocide. Similar protections of inherent value through some form of individual right to group identity appear elsewhere in international law. In *Ward*,[131] for example, the Supreme Court of Canada noted that the protections for a 'particular social group' in refugee law include 'groups whose members voluntarily associate for reasons so fundamental to their human dignity that they should not be forced to forsake the association' and 'groups associated by a former voluntary status, unalterable due to its historical permanence' as well as 'groups defined by an innate or unchangeable characteristic'.

The context of genocide is different, to be sure: victims of genocide typically are labelled by persecutors and targeted for destruction with no say in the matter.[132]

[129] Certain formalities are required in order to demonstrate that beliefs accompanying the election of citizenship are genuine, as opposed to a matter of convenience. *Nottebohm* [1955] ICJ 4, 23 (requiring 'a *legal bond*... [and] a genuine connection of existence, interests, and sentiments, together with the existence of reciprocal rights and duties.').

[130] *St Francis College v Al-Khazraji* (1987) 481 US 604 (US Sup Ct) 610 n 4 (criticizing 'common popular understanding that there are three major human races—Caucasoid, Mongoloid, and Negroid' as 'arbitrary and of little use in understanding the variability of human beings' and noting that 'racial classifications are for the most part socio-political, rather than biological, in nature.').

[131] *Ward v Canada* [1993] 2 SCR 689 (Can Sup Ct) ¶87 (LaForest J).

[132] A possible exception would be a situation akin to the Spanish Inquisition, where some victims chose the death, torture, etc that would accompany continued membership in the to-be-destroyed Jewish group rather than renounce their faith and convert to Christianity. AS Greene, 'The Pledge of Allegiance Problem' (1995) 64 Fordham LR 451, 476 n 118 ('Jews were forced to convert, flee or die').

The group label constitutes an 'innate or unchangeable characteristic', at least insofar as the perpetrator is concerned, and thus is more than a mere voluntary association. Nevertheless, a limited analogy to refugee law is helpful as a useful recognition that certain types of group beliefs and associations are fundamental to human life.[133]

The concept is not necessarily limited to beliefs or desired associations that are acted upon or otherwise manifested. It is true that the genocidal criteria used to identify 'belief' groups often will be evidence of members exercising (or being perceived to exercise) certain rights (eg, cultural ceremonies, worship, taking a citizenship oath, voting, etc). But not always. There are many examples in Indonesian anti-communist attacks, purges in Stalinist Russia, atrocities in Equatorial Guinea and mass murders by the Khmer Rouge of entire families being massacred as a form of collective guilt through political association.[134]

The group's 'scientific' reality apart from its social context is irrelevant for purposes of genocide. It is the offender's definition of what the group 'is' or 'believes' that delineates the contours of the victimized group. If he aims to destroy Catholics, his view of what the group 'is' (a target) will derive from his subjective understanding of the objective manifestations of the group's beliefs (attending Mass on Sunday, owning a Rosary, being baptized in a Catholic church, etc). To paraphrase Kierkegaard, the perpetrator labels the group in order to destroy it.[135]

But there is no requirement that genocidaires draw upon sensible characteristics in the selection of groups for destruction. 'Perpetrators inconsistently, if not irrationally, establish group membership criteria.'[136] This is because groups essentially are social constructs—'"imagined" entities entirely dependent on variable and contingent perceptions....'[137] There typically is a method to the madness, however. Selection usually derives from the larger set of prejudicial beliefs of the perpetrators. Thus, as Nazi ideology was based on notions of 'superior' and 'inferior' races determined by birth, the Nazis defined 'Jews' based on heredity (the number of Jewish grandparents).[138] The class warfare implicit in Khmer Rouge ideology[139] likewise illustrates the selection of intellectuals, city dwellers and similar groups for destruction in Cambodia. Arbitrary or not, rational or

133 The ICTY has recognized that concepts from international refugee law are not directly applicable to international criminal law. *Kupreskic (TC)* [2000] ICTY ¶589.

134 Kuper, Prevention 127 (1985); GH Stanton, 'Blue Scarves and Yellow Stars: Classification and Symbolization in the Cambodian Genocide' (1987) 1, 5.

135 The actual quote is 'Once you label me, you negate me.'

136 TW Simon, 'Defining Genocide' (1996) Wis ILJ 243, 245.

137 Verdirame (n 5) 592.

138 Reich Citizenship Law: First Regulation.

139 Constitution of Democratic Kampuchea (5 Jan 1976) c 1 art 1 ('The State of Kampuchea is a State of the people, workers, peasants and all other Kampuchean labourers'), c 5 art 3 ('This new [State] culture is absolutely opposed to the corrupt, reactionary culture of the various oppressive classes and that of colonialism and imperialism in Kampuchea'), c 5 art 5 (providing legislative representation for peasants, 'labourers and working people' and the revolutionary army only), and c 7 art 10 ('Dangerous activities in opposition to the people's State must be condemned to the high-

not, for purposes of genocide, the only criteria that matter are those selected by the perpetrators.

There is no need to prove that an offender aimed to destroy the 'objective' or 'scientific' or 'real' group as it actually existed in society. It is enough that he used discriminatory means (racial characteristics, religious characteristics, etc) to create his own definition of the group and that he implemented that definition through genocide.[140] The offence thus does not require proof that a victim actually is racially 'Black,' ethnically 'Tutsi,' religiously 'Jewish', etc in the larger sense. It is enough that the criteria used to form and apply the perpetrator's beliefs were racial, religious, etc in character and that the victim—selected as a means to the larger end of destroying the group—possessed those characteristics.[141]

Genocide thus criminalizes infringements upon what amount to essentially *theoretical* groups—not groups as they actually exist in society. There often will be substantial commonality between the targeted group and the actual group, but co-incidence is not required. Groups at issue in cases of genocide always are *sui generis* for that purpose, whatever its commonalities with similar groups created for other ends (eg, marriage in the Catholic Church, voting in the Connecticut Republican primary, membership in the Black Law Students Association, etc).

For the purposes of punishing genocide, what matters is a perpetrator acting on intentions to destroy a group formed on the basis of enumerated racial, national, etc characteristics. The relevant inquiry is to take the group targeted and to ascertain whether the basis of that targeting was essentially racial, ethnic, etc in nature. If so, it constitutes genocide. This type of inquiry—a retrospective analysis of an offender's mental state at the time he acted—is part and parcel of every criminal trial, in every legal system, where *mens rea* is an element of the offence. Courts are far better suited to perform this type of legal analysis than they are at identifying and applying abstract notions of group identity, which in any event may not correlate at all with the group actually targeted. In practice, the same methodology applies to *any* group targeted for destruction via genocide.

This brings us to the unifying feature explaining the groups enumerated in the Convention. Genocide is an attack on the rights of individuals either to exist in community with others or to practise certain belief systems in community with others. For legal purposes, it is convenient analytically to characterize genocide as an attack on 'protected groups.' But in application such groups exist only in the

est degree. Other cases are subject to constructive re-education in the framework of the State's or people's organizations').

140 *Application of Genocide Convention—Merits* [2007] ICJ 1 ¶193 ('the essence of [genocidal] intent is to destroy the protected group, in whole or in part, as such. It is a group which must have particular positive characteristics—national, ethnical, racial or religious—and not the lack of them.').

141 Acts based on incorrect beliefs about whether victims possess the target characteristics as *individuals* are likely to constitute attempts.

minds of the genocidaires who create and utilize them for that specific purpose. The 'theoretical' group protected under the Convention is nothing more than a means to an end. It is a symbol—manifest evidence that there has been an attack on a fundamental aspect of the social order (the individual's right to engage in certain forms of communal existence).

At the deepest level, 'protected groups' under the Convention are abstract proxies for individual rights to certain forms of collective existence that cannot be infringed through physical and biological destruction. The legal prohibition on harming a 'protected group' essentially preserves the *individual* rights to exist or to practise certain belief systems in community with others. It is the attack on those individual legal rights, which are necessary for and incidental to group existence, that endangers the 'real' or 'objective' or 'scientific' group as it exists in society. The 'real' group is protected by using international law to prohibit attacks that seriously infringe the individual's rights to belong to such groups in the first place.

In the overall structure of international human rights law, the protection of the individual is paramount. This reflects an underlying philosophy 'that group rights would be taken care of automatically as the result of the protection of the rights of individuals'.[142] Group rights typically are *inferred* from the collective nature of certain individual rights.[143] The four groups in the Convention all derive from the exercise of other human rights that are both important *and* of a collective nature; rights that make sense in application largely (albeit not exclusively) in group settings.

It matters not whether these collective rights are exercised in practice. Genocidaires commit their offences based on arbitrary criteria—not based upon what group members actually do. A limit based on certain visible forms of engagement with, or participation in the group is unwarranted and would dictate different levels of protection for those who keep their religion, nationality, politics, etc private versus those who express them publicly. This makes little sense because the injury to the *right* at stake is the same. The Convention protects the theoretical application of the legal right—the *ability to exercise* it if the individual so chooses—not the actual exercise of group participation.[144]

Applying the common denominator to political groups

As discussed above, the Genocide Convention is a rights-implementing instrument that protects important individual rights of a collective character that are clearly recognized under international law. We now must consider whether other groups that are not covered nevertheless have similar characteristics to those of

[142] Ian Brownlie, 'The Rights of Peoples in Modern International Law' in Crawford 1, 2 (1988).

[143] B Mawhinney, 'Canadian Practice in International Law' (1993) Can YBIL 343, 345 ('The classic individual rights and freedoms in most international human rights instruments possess a 'collective rights' element as well.').

[144] *Cf* UNHCR Refugee Handbook ¶81 (noting that even if political opinions have not become public 'it may be reasonable to assume that [the] opinions will sooner or later find expression and that the applicant will, as a result, come into conflict with the authorities.').

the enumerated groups. The more similar the rights at stake, the more viable the candidacy of a currently-excluded group for similar protection 'as such' will be.

It is not necessary to generate a definitive listing of all groups that possess similar theoretical 'qualities' to the groups included in the Convention. Many potential candidates exist. Apart from political groups, proposals for inclusion at one time or another have included 'economic' groups[145] (presumably including trade unions[146] and professional groups),[147] as well as groups based on disability,[148] sexual orientation,[149] and other types of social groups.[150] Historically, some of

145 'USA: Amendments to the draft convention on genocide (E/794)' (4 Oct 1948) UN Doc A/C6/214 art 2. The US withdrew the proposal without ever defining the group: Official Records (6th Comm 1948) (SR75) 115 (US).

146 ICESCR art 6 (right to work), art 8 (protecting trade unions).

147 Lawyers, for example, are an easily identified class derived from the historical facts of admission to practice or bar membership. Per fictional anarchist Dick the Butcher: 'The first thing we do, let's kill all the lawyers.' Shakespeare act 4 sc 2 (1591). The actual proposal on economic groups evoked concern over 'the absurd result that certain professions, when threatened by economic measures which were required in the interest of the country, might invoke the convention to protect their own interests'. Official Records (6th Comm 1948) (SR74) (Neth).

148 Convention and Optional Protocol on the Rights of Persons with Disabilities (13 Dec 06) UN Doc A/61/611 art 1 (covering 'those who have long-term physical, mental, intellectual or sensory impairments which in interaction with various barriers may hinder their full and effective participation in society on an equal basis with others'); 'Declaration on the Rights of Disabled Persons' UNGA Res 3447 (XXX) (9 Dec 1975) UN Doc A/10034 art 1 ('The term "disabled person" means any person unable to secure by himself or herself... the necessities of a normal individual and/or social life, as a result of deficiency... in his or her physical or mental capabilities'); *Pinochet: Spanish Jurisdiction* [Audencia Nacional 1998] in Brody and Ratner 95, 103 (2000) ('Aids patients, as a differentiated group'). The Nazis euthanized 'defective' Germans in order to 'improve' the Aryan race. Helen Fein, 'Genocide, Terror, Life Integrity and War Crimes: The Case for Discrimination' in Andreopoulos 95, 104 (1994). And in what now could be characterized as biological genocide against the mentally disabled, in the mid-1920s the US Supreme Court authorized sterilization of mental defectives, spurring Justice Holmes's infamous aside that 'three generations of imbeciles are enough'. *Buck v Bell* (1927) 274 US 200 (US Sup Ct) 207 ('[T]he public welfare may call upon the best citizens for their lives. It would be strange if it could not call upon those who already sap the strength of the State for these lesser sacrifices... in order to prevent our being swamped with incompetence. It is better for all the world, if instead of waiting to execute degenerate offspring for crime, or to let them starve for their imbecility, society can prevent those who are manifestly unfit from continuing their kind.').

149 AT Feindel, 'Reconciling Sexual Orientation: Creating A Definition of Genocide That Includes Sexual Orientation' (2005) 13 Michigan JIL 97 (arguing that definition of genocide should be included to cover homosexuals); JD Van der Vyver, 'Prosecution and Punishment of the Crime of Genocide' (1999) 23 Fordham ILJ 286, 305–6 (advocating protection of homosexuals as 'institutional' group); AM Gilbert and ED Marchand, 'Splitting the Atom or Splitting Hairs—The Hate Crimes Prevention Act of 1999' (1999) 30 Saint Mary's LJ 931, 964–8 (advocating inclusion of sexual orientation in domestic hate crimes legislation). It was Nazi policy to exterminate male homosexuals . Study (Second) on Genocide (2 Jul 1985) UN Doc E/CN4/Sub2/1985/6 ¶30. Recent efforts in the human rights community have focused on identifying protections for such groups under international law. *Cf* Yogyakarta Principles (March 2007) pmbl (discussing human rights violations perpetrated, inter alia, because victims 'are or are perceived to be transsexual, transgender or intersex or belong to social groups identified in particular societies by sexual orientation or gender identity'). International consensus on this issue appears unlikely to emerge any time soon. 'Gender,' for example, was defined in the ICC Statute as 'the two sexes, male and female, in the context of society' for the express purpose of excluding homosexuals from the penumbra of persecution as a crime against humanity: ICC Statute art 7(3); Boot 522 (2002).

150 Lemkin's earliest proposals in 1933 covered 'social' groups: R Lemkin, 'Genocide as a Crime Under International Law' (15 Jan 1948) UN Bull 70–1 ('racial, religious or social collectivity').

these groups even have been subject to destruction 'as such'—perhaps best exemplified by Nazi programmes that led to the deaths of some 200,000 disabled individuals[151] and tens of thousands of homosexuals.[152]

That said, the question of protecting these other groups requires a detailed analysis that is outside the scope of the present effort. For a variety of reasons (detailed below), this work focuses on political groups. This focus should not be taken as implying that the analytical framework outlined herein cannot be applied to other types of human groups, however.

D. Political groups and political genocide

As an historical matter, political groups were included in the first General Assembly resolution on genocide and initially appeared in all three drafts of the Genocide Convention. They were removed from the final version of the Convention as part of a political compromise designed to ensure the widest possible participation in the Convention.[153] Apart from the historical point—that they were clearly recognized as an important group and very nearly were included in the Convention in 1948—this work focuses on the protection of political groups for four primary reasons:

1. Political rights are important rights that have a similar (albeit not identical) level of international acceptance and recognition;
2. on a theoretical level, political rights correspond closely to the rights underlying the groups included in the Convention in terms of how such rights are implemented and protected, particularly in respect of religion;
3. because national, racial, ethnic and religious characteristics are so often used as a proxy for political identity, in practice political groups often overlap significantly with the enumerated group categories; and
4. there have been many historic examples of political genocide.

The rights at issue

Some rights are meaningful only where there is an opportunity to exercise them in community with others. All four groups in the Convention are characterized

Certain social groups have been subjected to genocidal massacres. Stalin, for example, liquidated 6.5 million Kulak peasants as a class from 1930–39: DM Amann, 'Under Destruction' (2000) 3 Green Bag 369, 369 n 3.

[151] AR Ford, 'A Race Apart: Genocide and the Protection of Disabled Persons Under International Law' (2009) Review of Disability Studies 15, 15–16.

[152] AT Feindel, 'Reconciling Sexual Orientation: Creating a Definition of Genocide that Includes Sexual Orientation' (2005) 13 Michigan JIL 197, 204.

[153] The history of the Genocide Convention was covered briefly in Chapter 1 and is discussed in greater detail in Chapter 5.

by rights that have (or which at least must accommodate) a public dimension—the right to publicly *exist* as a member of a certain race, ethnicity, or nation, or the right to *believe and practise* religious tenets or principles of national philosophy.

Political rights have a similar character. The core set of political rights[154] appears to include, at a minimum, the right to hold opinions,[155] freedom of political association and assembly,[156] freedom to express political opinion,[157] rights to participate in government,[158] and freedom from unlawful discrimination[159] based on political opinion.[160] These rights are reflected nearly uniformly across all of the major international human rights instruments—the UDHR, the ICCPR, the ECHR, the ACHR and the AfCHR.[161]

The scope, sources, and implementation of each of these various 'political' rights are vast topics in and of themselves. For now, however, it suffices to note that the rights in question are: (i) necessary and incidental to the formation, transmission and implementation of political beliefs; (ii) fully meaningful only when there is the opportunity to exercise them in community with others; and (iii) important human rights that are nearly universally recognized as protected under international law.

[154] Meron notes that the terminology in the field varies and suggests that the terms 'human rights', 'freedoms', 'fundamental human rights', 'fundamental freedoms', 'rights and freedoms' and 'human rights and freedoms' are for the most part interchangeable. Meron, *Law Making* 178 (1986). This writing accepts that proposition and makes no attempt to distinguish finer subtleties.

[155] ECHR art 10(1), UDHR art 19, ICCPR art 19(1), ACHR art 13, and AfCHR art 9 (right to hold opinions). This concept includes positive beliefs as well as criticism and opposition of the government and ruling political parties. *Bahamonde v Equatorial Guinea* (UNHRC 1993) ¶9.4.

[156] ECHR art 11, UDHR art 20, ICCPR art 22, ACHR art 16, and AfCHR art 10 (freedom of association) and ECHR art 11, UDHR art 20, ICCPR art 21, ACHR art 15, AfCHR art 11 (freedom of assembly).

[157] ECHR art 10(1), UDHR art 19, ICCPR art 19(2), ACHR art 13(1), and AfCHR art 9 (freedom of expression).

[158] UDHR art 21, ICCPR art 25, ACHR art 23, and AfCHR art 13 (right to participate in government). The opportunity to be elected means that 'citizens should have the opportunity to join, or organize, their own political parties'. S Joseph, 'Rights of Political Participation' in Harris and Joseph 535, 550 (1995).

[159] 'Discrimination' here does not mean choice or differentiation. It is used in the negative sense and means 'any distinction, exclusion, restriction or preference which is based on any [prohibited] ground... which has the purpose or effect of nullifying or impairing the recognition, enjoyment or exercise by all persons, on an equal footing, of all rights and freedoms.' CCPR General Comment No 18 (10 Nov 1989) ¶7. Excluded are temporary measures such as affirmative action that differentiate but which are aimed at achieving rather than preventing equality. WA McKean, 'The Meaning of Discrimination in International and Municipal Law' (1970) 44 BYBIL 177, 180–1.

[160] ECHR art 14, UDHR art 2, ICCPR arts 2(1), 26, ACHR arts 1, 24, and AfCHR art 2 (political opinion as prohibited basis of discrimination). This is not a guarantee of equality, but rather a prohibition on impermissible grounds of distinction. Lord Lester of Herne Hill QC and S Joseph, 'Obligations of Non-Discrimination' in Harris and Joseph 563, 565 (1995).

[161] As of 2010, 165 states are parties to the ICCPR: Multilateral Treaties Deposited with the Secretary-General: ICCPR (11 Jan 2010). The UDHR has been held to reflect fundamental obligations under the UN Charter. *Filartiga v Pena-Irala* (1980) 630 F2d 876 (US Ct App (2d Cir)) 882–3. The UDHR, ICCPR, ECHR and AmCHR have all have been cited as evidence of customary international law. *Siderman de Blake v Republic of Argentina* (1992) 965 F2d 699 (US Ct App (9th Cir)) 716 n 15.

It is not necessary here to analyse the specifics of freedom of expression, freedom of assembly, etc or to detail the manner in which they are exercised. What is important is that a genocidaire can pervert the actual or potential exercise of these rights (or his perception thereof) into objective indicia defining the political group that he aims to destroy. It is the ability to define and destroy groups using the underlying rights themselves (in all their multiplicitous forms) that is characteristic of political genocide.

'Political' rights have little practical value unless they can be facilitated and acted upon in groups. 'Representative democracy in any populous unit of governance is unimaginable without the ability of citizens to band together in promoting among the electorate candidates who espouse their political views.'[162] They certainly include the opportunity to be elected to public office, which necessarily means that 'citizens should have the opportunity to join, or organize, their own political parties'.[163]

The linkage with groups is implicit within any political system—even those premised upon the *absence* of participation, such as authoritarian or totalitarian regimes that give rise to 'opposition' groups of political non-adherents. Regardless of the philosophy at issue, it is a *sine qua non* of political freedom to engage political issues and advocate a political viewpoint (be it democracy, communism, theocracy, etc) in concert with others.[164] This necessarily includes freedom from discrimination based upon criticism and opposition of the government and ruling political parties.[165]

Genocide (and political genocide) focuses upon physical and biological destruction of the group in question. Their occurrence always entails a violation of the most fundamental rights of the person—*ipso facto* transgressing protected rights to life,[166] to bodily and mental integrity,[167] etc. In this sense neither genocide nor political genocide could ever be considered legitimate conduct. But it is important not to overstate the point, because it is not the violation of the *individual* rights alone that warrants treatment as genocide.

Genocide involves a *two-fold* rights violation—the underlying rights of the individual *and* the group's right to exist 'as such'. 'Group' rights are upheld by prohibiting genocidal attacks on individual rights of a communal nature—rights to physically and biologically exist while holding certain beliefs in

[162] *Democratic Party v Jones* (2000) 530 US 567 (US Sup Ct) 574.

[163] S Joseph, 'Rights of Political Participation' in Harris and Joseph 535, 550 (1995).

[164] *Cf* B Mawhinney, 'Canadian Practice in International Law' (1993) Can YBIL 343, 345 (per the Legal Bureau of the Canadian Ministry of External Affairs, although 'freedom of association is granted to individuals, it is largely meaningless unless exercised in association with others for political . . . purposes.').

[165] *Bahamonde v Equatorial Guinea* (UNHRC 1993) ¶9.4. Such claims also provide grounds for asylum. UNHCR Refugee Handbook ¶80 ('opinions not tolerated by the authorities, which are critical of their policies or methods . . . .').

[166] UDHR art 3, ICCPR art 6, ECHR art 2, ACHR art 4, and AfCHR art 4.

[167] UDHR art 5, ICCPR art 7, ECHR art 3, ACHR art 5, and AfCHR art 5.

community with others. It is the infringement of this second 'group' right that distinguishes genocide from other serious injuries to the life and well-being of individuals.

It would be incomplete to posit simply that individuals have certain collective rights and that a perpetrator violated them. Mere violation, by itself, is not enough. Where compelling reasons exist, there are many instances where infringements on the rights giving rise to groups protected under the Convention are perfectly acceptable.[168] Apart from the strength and nature of the right itself, the manner in which it is violated is critical. Genocide is a specific offence dealing with both a particular *method* and *degree* of infringement.

As discussed above, the Convention is not inherently holistic, and there are important distinctions in the underlying communal rights it protects. The underlying rights that give rise to protected groups are not treated equally elsewhere in international law. The general prohibition on racial and religious discrimination, for example, is a non-derogable *jus cogens* obligation.[169] Not so for national groups. Discriminatory infringements based on nationality are permissible in some contexts. For example, Koreans permanently resident in Japan were lawfully denied the right to vote,[170] even though political participation is guaranteed under the ICCPR and nationality is a prohibited basis of discrimination.[171] But denying the voting rights of racial or religious groups in the same manner would be prohibited.[172]

The rights of political groups raise similar issues. Not all forms of political discrimination constitute persecution, for example, either in asylum proceedings[173] or criminal law.[174] Discrimination on reasonable and objective political considerations is permitted in hiring for certain key government posts, for example.[175]

To some extent, the importance of a particular right under international law is reflected in the ease with which it is dispensed with in times of exigency.[176]

168 *Cf Employment Division v Smith* (1990) 494 US 872 (US Sup Ct) (upholding denial of state unemployment benefits to members of Native American Church who lost their jobs as drug counsellors for ingesting peyote during a religious ritual); *Reynolds v United States* (1878) 98 US 145 (US Sup Ct) (upholding bigamy as a criminal offence despite the interference with religious freedom).

169 Lerner 30 (2003). Ethnicity often equated to race and 'racial' in the UN Charter and probably includes what are known as ethnic groups today. *Namibia* [1971] ICJ 16, 57 ¶130.

170 *X v Japan* (1996) 6 Asian YBIL 221 (Fukui Dist Ct) 223 (denying Koreans who were permanent residents of Japan the right to vote).

171 ICCPR arts 2(1), 26.

172 *Cf* Voting Rights Act (1965) 42 USC s 1973 (prohibiting discrimination on racial and religious grounds in voting).

173 UNHCR Refugee Handbook ¶¶54, 80–6.

174 ICC Statute art 7(2)(g) ('intentional and severe deprivation of fundamental rights').

175 Joseph (n 163) 550.

176 CCPR General Comment No 18 'Non-Discrimination' (10 Nov 1989) ¶11 (limitations on derogation recognize 'the peremptory nature of some fundamental rights ensured in treaty form in the Covenant.'). A corollary is that derogation is impermissible where it entails a breach of other obligations of international treaty or customary law. CCPR General Comment No 29 'States of Emergency' (31 Aug 2001) ¶9.

National emergencies provide convenient excuses to deny human rights,[177] and non-derogability is evidence of its fundamental nature.[178] For that reason, derogation is 'of an exceptional and temporary nature and may only last as long as the life of the nation concerned is threatened'.[179] It is further subject to principles of necessity and proportionality.[180]

Certain rights are non-derogable regardless of circumstances.[181] These include rights to life, recognition as a person before the law, freedom of thought, conscience and religion, as well as the prohibitions on torture and cruel, inhuman or degrading punishment or treatment, slavery and servitude, imprisonment for economic reasons, and retroactive criminal laws.[182] The political freedoms discussed above are not among these non-derogable rights.[183] Likewise, although certain discriminatory grounds are prohibited as grounds for derogation,[184] nationality and political opinion are not among them.

The conclusion from this disparity is that it is not the nature of the right alone that merits treating an infringement as genocide. Groups need not derive from rights that are fundamental and non-derogable. All four groups in the Convention certainly are based on characteristics[185] drawn from *important* rights—some of which are *fundamental* rights that are universally recognized as protected under international law. It is the character and degree of the *infringement* of important rights, combined with their important nature, which determines the proper response.[186] When important communal rights are infringed through serious personal violence, the violation may warrant treatment as genocide.

Any theory of political genocide must follow the path laid out for genocide under the Convention. If a social democrat is illegally prohibited from voting, his rights to political participation have been infringed. If he is murdered because he votes for the 'wrong' party, his right to life has been infringed *and* his rights to political participation have been infringed in an extreme manner. If all social democrats in the state are rounded up and shot with the intent to destroy them as a political group, there has been a violation of the individuals' rights to life, to

[177] J Oraa, 'The Protection of Human Rights in Emergency Situations under Customary International Law' in Goodwin-Gill and Talmon 413 (1999).

[178] Morris and Scharf, The ICTR 138–9 (1998).

[179] CCPR General Comment No 5 'Derogation of Rights' (31 Jul 1981) ¶3.

[180] Expert Report on Protecting Human Rights (7 Feb 2005) UN Doc E/CN4/2005/103 ¶9.

[181] ICCPR art 4(2).

[182] ICCPR arts 6 (life), 16 (personhood), 18 (thought, conscience and religion), 7 (torture), 8(1)–(2) (slavery), 11 (debtor's imprisonment), and 15 (retroactive offences).

[183] ICCPR art 4, ECHR art 15, and ACHR art 27. The ACHR allows derogation of the right to hold political opinions but does not allow derogation of rights to participate in government under art 23 ibid.

[184] ICCPR art 4 ('discrimination solely on the ground of race, colour, sex, language, religion or social origin.').

[185] *Application of Genocide Convention—Merits* [2007] ICJ 1 ¶193 (groups with 'particular positive characteristics—national, ethnical, racial or religious').

[186] *Cf* Restatement (Third) of Foreign Relations s 702 ('consistent pattern of gross violations of internationally recognized human rights' violates international law) (emphasis added).

participate in state politics, *and* rights to engage in political participation and beliefs in concert with others. It is the latter that is characteristic of considering political genocide. Such severe infringements ultimately destroy the rights themselves.[187]

The analogy of politics to other groups

As discussed previously, the inherent permanence and stability of a group (as derived through the exercise of the right in question) are not sufficient to explain the groups included in the Convention. The ability to save oneself from genocide by denouncing group status (foregoing exercise of the right) does not mitigate the existence of the crime. The Convention represents a judgment that, even if an overt opportunity to exit the group is theoretically possible (unlikely for race) and actually made available,[188] no one should be forced to choose between physical/biological destruction and his religious, national, ethnic or racial identity.[189]

The rights of political groups share many characteristics with those of national groups. As noted previously, the concept of nationality is linked to some measure of exercising reciprocal rights and duties under law, which in turn define the contours of the national group itself. Political identity is similar to—and can be wholly or partially coextensive with—national identity. This is reflected in some measure through identical treatment of national and political characteristics in other areas of international criminal law.[190] Rights of similar importance, infringed in the identical way, thus may warrant equal treatment in respect of genocide as well.

Similar considerations apply to rights protecting political opinion and participation, which are exercised largely through assembly and activity in political groups. As discussed above, political rights are widely-recognized, important rights of a collective nature. Much like religious groups, political groups derive from a combination of identifiable beliefs and the right to engage in practices grounded in those beliefs (here—advancing the belief system through voting, publicly expressing and explaining viewpoints, publicly associating with like-minded people, etc). As with religion, political philosophy or opinion presupposes that the belief system—the defining characteristic of the group—can be transmitted in some way to others. Yet the right to hold collective

[187] CCPR General Comment No 10 'Freedom of Opinion' (29 Jun 1983) ¶4.

[188] For example, during the Spanish Inquisition (which arguably had genocidal characteristics) Jews could save themselves by renouncing their religion and embracing Christianity. AS Greene, 'The Pledge of Allegiance Problem' (1995) 64 Fordham LR 451, 476 n 118 ('Jews were forced to convert, flee or die').

[189] Lawrence 19 (1999) (it is 'outrageous' 'to suggest that a Jew or Catholic might just choose to avoid discrimination by giving up her religion.').

[190] ICC Statute art 7(1)(h) (persecution inter alia against national and political groups).

political beliefs means little if it comes at the expense of physical and biological destruction.

For many, political beliefs are equally core aspects of human existence. Indeed, in some cases religion and political identity are factually inseparable. States (and their citizens) have the right to choose their own social, political, economic and cultural structures and to implement those choices through legal mechanisms.[191] A commitment to respecting the 'rule of law' is a pre-eminent international value and a defining purpose of the UN as an institution.[192] It ranks equally with the preservation of peace, respect for human rights, and the evolution of social progress and freedom—all of which are facilitated (at least in part) through *legal* institutions.[193] The commitment to 'international social justice' implicit in the UN system 'is increasingly thought to constitute the very essence of public international law in the second half of the 20th century.'[194]

It is the belief of many that the 'rule of law' incepts equally well with a higher power as it does with a political philosophy.[195] The primary sources of theocratic law (and the political institutions they support) are religious texts, which are adopted in daily life as a further aspect of the religious belief system.[196] Some religious institutions (eg, the Vatican) have personality similar to that of states on the world stage (representation at the UN, sending and receiving ambassadors, etc). Similar considerations apply to the theocratic 'government in exile' of the fourteenth Dalai Lama of Tibet.

In theocratic societies, the extensive permeation between religious, political and national rights and identity makes it all but impossible to analytically segregate the various groups characterized by these rights from one another.[197] The lines are unclear even in more secular societies, where religious institutions may operate within the existing political structure and provide varying degrees of governmental and legal functions. Nigerian Muslims in twelve Shariah states, for example, are subject to strict Shariah law applied through a separate legal

[191] *Nicaragua* [1986] ICJ 14 ¶263.

[192] UN Charter pmbl ¶3 ('to establish conditions under which justice and respect for the obligations arising from treaties and other sources of international law can be maintained.').

[193] ibid.

[194] O Kimminich, (1984) 'History of the Law of Nations Since World War II' in Bernhardt 849, 850–1 (1993).

[195] Compare G Sawer, 'The Western Concept of Law' in II David 14 (1973) and I Szabo, 'The Socialist Conception of law' in II David 49 (1973) (linking legal theory with political philosophy) with H Afchar, 'The Muslim Concept of Law' in II David 84 (1973), JDM Derrett and TK Krishnamurthy, 'The Hindu Conception of Law' in II David 107 (1973) and Hoenig (1993) (linking legal philosophies with religious convictions).

[196] *Cf* Malekian 4–7, 28–30 (1994) (noting that Islamic law—international and domestic—relies principally upon the *Qur'an*, the *Sunnah* and Orthodox practices of the early *Caliphs*).

[197] VN Dadrian, 'Genocide as a Problem of National and International Law: The World War I Armenian Case and its Contemporary Legal Ramifications' 14 Yale JIL 221, 230 (1989) ('Although Islam is a religious creed, it is also a way of life for its followers, transcending the boundaries of faith to permeate the social and political fabric of a nation.').

system.[198] Even modern England has a theocratic tinge because its monarch presides over the Church of England and is the nation's chief 'defender of the faith'.[199] State churches also exist in Norway, Denmark, Greece, Liechtenstein, Monaco and other modern European states.[200]

To complicate matters further, governments can migrate between theocratic and secular structures, or even different forms of theocracy, over time. The nation of Nepal, for example, recently deposed its Hindu king in favour of a secular government.[201] And after the overthrow of Saddam Hussein, Iraq experienced many years of escalating bloodshed between Sunni and Shiite Muslims. Although the violent conflict between these two Islamic sects is historic and long standing[202]—within Iraq and elsewhere—the political character of the recent violence is evident, as the two sides fought for control over Iraq's political and economic destiny.

Intersections with protected groups

There is much interplay between political power and the rights characterizing national, ethnic, religious and racial groups. In many cases, it is difficult to ascertain whether targeting is premised on these characteristics, on political characteristics, or both. If a perpetrator believes that 'all Russians are Communists' and aims to destroy all Russian Communists in his state, is this political genocide or genocide against a protected group? Likewise with respect to racial groups in Cambodia, where minority Vietnamese were targeted by the Khmer Rouge as 'enemies' of the state.[203] Attacks on citizens of a theocratic state could qualify simultaneously as attacks on a religious group, a national group or a political group.

The inevitable consequence of this permeation is that '[m]ost genocide has at least some political tinge...'.[204] Some even suggest that the Convention's distinctions are impossible to maintain in practice:

> The strength of political factors and the inextricable weaving of political considerations in so many genocides against racial, ethnic and religious groups, demonstrate

198 J Walberg, 'The Conflict of Muslim and Secular Law in Nigeria' (2004) 12 ILSA Quarterly 4, 4–6 (mandatory death sentence by stoning—reversed on appeal—for adultery applied to a Nigerian Muslim woman who bore a child out of wedlock).

199 R Hirschl, 'The Theocratic Challenge to Constitution Drafting in Post-Conflict States' (2008) 49 W&M LR 1179, 1192–3 ('In England, the monarch is "Supreme Governor" of the Church of England and "Defender of the Faith." ').

200 Josh Goodman, 'Divine Judgment: Judicial Review of Religious Legal Systems in India and Israel' (2009) Hastings ICLR 477, 478 n 6.

201 S Taylor, 'Nepal's deposed king leaves palace for last time' USA Today (11 Jun 2008).

202 WP Nagan and VF Rodin, 'Racism, Genocide, and Mass Murder: Toward a Legal Theory About Group Deprivation' (2004) 17 Nat'l Black LJ 33, 176.

203 Kuper, Prevention 130–5 (1985).

204 Study (Second) on Genocide (2 Jul 1985) UN Doc E/CN4/Sub2/1985/6 ¶36.

> the impossibility of separating the racial, ethnic and religious from the political, as seemingly required by the Genocide Convention with its exclusion of political groups from its scope.... In the context of the present discussion of ideology, there is the further absurdity of this artificial separation in the fact that political ideologies of dehumanization may have great relevance for genocide against ethnic, racial and religious groups.[205]

As discussed previously, the fact that there often are political overtones to genocides committed against enumerated groups[206] does not preclude the application of the Convention. It is sufficient to have an attack based partially on an enumerated characteristic. If an offender attacks Russian Communists with the aim to destroy all Russian Communists, the attack on the 'national' characteristic of 'Russians' suffices for purposes of genocide.

The absence of political groups from the Convention complicates things considerably, however, when the basis of targeting is unclear. Perpetrators can defend their actions by claiming that any attack which *might* have occurred (which of course is denied) was done on political grounds and therefore could not constitute genocide in any event. This certainly was the position the Paraguayan government took with respect to crimes against indigenous Ache Indians who interfered with the extraction of natural resources.[207] Proscribing political genocide would end the need for this sort of enquiry and eliminate this defence—specious as it is.

This is not to suggest that inter-group permeation is *limited* to political groups. Certain insular sub-groups can result from a social structure that further classifies them but which is driven in some way by enumerated group characteristics. Caste-based discrimination has occurred against Dalits ('untouchables') in Hindu-dominated societies in India, Bangladesh, India and Nepal, against eta ('extreme filth') in Japan, and against similar birth-based social classes in Pakistan and Sri Lanka.[208] Although the sub-groups derive from social status established at birth, it is clear that the social structure itself is inextricably intertwined with dominant religious practices and beliefs.[209] Genocidal attacks on such groups raise complications similar to those identified above, in terms of whether the group was a religious group, a social group, an economic group, etc.

[205] Kuper, Political Use 93–4 (1981).

[206] Nagan and Rodin (n 68) 213 (political underpinnings of the 1994 Rwandan Genocide).

[207] J Gordon, 'When Intent Makes all the Difference in the World: Economic Sanctions on Iraq and the Accusation of Genocide' (2002) 5 Yale HRDLJ 57, 76.

[208] Prevention of Discrimination and Protection of Indigenous Peoples and Minorities: 'Working paper by [RKW Gooneskere] on the topic of discrimination based on work and descent, submitted pursuant to Sub-Commission Resolution 2000/4' (14 Jun 2001) UN Doc E/CN4/Sub2/2001/16.

[209] ibid ¶15 ('Hindu society recognizes a caste hierarchy of four classes or varnas: Brahmins (priests and scholars); Kshathriyas (rulers and soldiers); Vaishyas (merchants and farmers); and Sudras (servant class)'); ¶¶43–4 (similar structures in Muslim society in Northern Pakistan).

Pragmatic needs

As an historical matter, no group excluded from the Convention has been victimized to the same extent as political groups.[210] Since limited resources are best applied where they are needed most, this factor weighs in favour of focusing—at least for the time being—on political groups. A revised conception of genocide is hardly a new idea. It was contemplated even when the Convention was finalized that the exclusion of political groups could be revisited if later circumstances so warranted.[211]

Engaging with the question of protecting political groups in no way suggests that all other groups are less worthy of protection.[212] Sometimes serious problems must be addressed in stages. Even if the theoretical justifications weighed in favour of treating all human groups equally (which they do not), as a policy matter it simply makes sense to focus first where the greatest need already exists. To be sure, there are examples of genocidal acts against certain social groups (eg, Kulak peasants in the former Soviet Union). But there have been many more instances of political genocide.

In particular, practical considerations favour moving groups that theoretically *could* be targeted (but which have never been) to the very bottom of the list. There are no known examples of 'Oxonicide' or 'baldicide' or 'one-armed-man-icide' or 'feline-aficionado-icide'. Progress with respect to political groups, which clearly need additional protection under international law, should not be held hostage to a debate over whether other groups might also qualify. Such qualification is a separate question, and resolving the viability of all other groups should not be a condition precedent to addressing the far larger problem of political genocide.

E. Political genocide

As discussed above, there are many solid reasons to apply the concept of genocide to political groups. As is the case with any group, however, it is nearly impossible to develop an exhaustive definition of political groups *a priori* for purposes of genocide. There simply are too many variables in application. That said, it is helpful to delineate some of the major characteristics of political groups and how political genocide may be perpetrated against them.

210 *Cf* Kuper, Prevention 127 (1985) (anti-communist attacks in Indonesia, purges in Stalinist Russia, atrocities in Equatorial Guinea and mass murders by the Khmer Rouge of entire families based upon political association.).

211 Official Records (6th Comm) (SR72) 81 (Venez).

212 The failure to cover gender, sexual orientation and disability as grounds of protection in the Convention for the Elimination of All Forms of Racial Discrimination, for example, hardly constitutes incitement to discriminate on these grounds. Schabas 164–5 (2009).

Defining political groups

As discussed above, the core set of political rights includes matters such as 'freedom of political association, freedom of political opinion, the existence of a free press, the holding of free elections periodically, [and] transparency and accountability in the process of government'.[213] A political group therefore can be defined by the characteristic of exercising (or having the option to exercise, or being perceived to exercise) any right under international law that guarantees political beliefs or participation.

There is some intuitive link between the rights of 'peoples' and political groups. But although the concept of 'self-determination' drips with political overtones, overall the analogy is unhelpful in the context of genocide. The concept of a 'people' is far broader than that of groups under the Convention. A UNESCO study group concluded that the concept could include 'a group of individual human beings who enjoy some or all of the following common features: (a) a common historical tradition; (b) racial or ethnic identity; (c) cultural homogeneity; (d) linguistic unity; (e) religious or ideological affinity; (f) territorial connection; and (g) common economic life', as well as a certain (albeit undetermined) critical mass of size, the collective will to be identified as 'a people', and institutions or other means of expressing their group characteristics.[214] This broad description is rendered even more imprecise by context dependency, as the definition of 'a people' varies depending on the rights at stake and the objectives of defining the collective.[215]

A 'people' under international law possesses the characteristics of *many* groups simultaneously. Some of these (eg, religion, ethnicity) are covered by the Convention. Others (cultural heritage, linguistic identity, identity with tribal or ancestral lands) are not. 'Groups include peoples... [but] not every group can claim the rights of a people'[216] in such matters as development, access to natural resources and the like.[217] Historical links to anti-colonialism complicate matters even further,[218] and overall the concept is not helpful here.

As discussed previously, in cases of genocide, there will be a specific definition of the group for that purpose, provided by the genocidaire. The group targeted almost certainly will be abundantly clear from the circumstances—identified by

[213] C Beyani, 'The Legal Premises for the International Protection of Human Rights' in Goodwin-Gill and Talmon 26 (1999).

[214] United Nations Educational, Scientific and Cultural Organization 'International Meeting of Experts on Further Study of the Concept of the Rights of Peoples' (22 Feb 1990) UN Doc SHS-89/CONF602/7 ¶22.

[215] ibid ¶23.

[216] Lerner (2003) 35.

[217] *Cf* 'Permanent Sovereignty over Natural Resources' (14 Dec 1962) UNGA Res 1803 (XVII).

[218] 'Declaration on the Inadmissibility of Intervention in the Domestic Affairs of States and the Protection of Their Independence and Sovereignty' UNGA Res 2131 (XX) (21 Dec 1965) UN Doc A/6014.

the offender's targeting of group members based upon their collective political beliefs and activities. Although a single individual can be the victim of genocide, it is important to remember that—for purposes of this crime—he is a representative victim on behalf of the group. The serious wrong done to him on account of his group membership is the wrong to the larger political group made manifest.

As noted above, abstract and conceptual notions of political groups must be structured through legal terminology in order to be useful for present purposes. Ultimately, this requires the political rights characterizing political groups to be analysed and evaluated against the factual circumstances of the genocidal attack. Fortunately, there is an ample existing base upon which to build for this purpose. In delineating criteria for the legal characteristics of political groups, there are many useful analogies to draw upon from other contexts.

The US Supreme Court acknowledged that the question is not always easy, opining in a voting rights case that political groups were less discernible than racial groups in part because '[p]olitical affiliation is not an immutable characteristic'.[219] Two dissenting justices, however, pointed out that the task is hardly insurmountable. Whenever a political group claimed injury, the 'evidence must at least imply that the defendants themselves sat down, identified the relevant groups, and set out to concentrate the vote of one and dilute that of the others. If a plaintiff has the evidence, a court can figure out what was going on.'[220] Similar points were raised during the drafting of the Convention, with some observing that the Nazis had identified and destroyed Communists and that the Allies had identified the Nazi party for the purpose of outlawing it.[221]

The same is true in other contexts, such as the ICC. In prosecutions for the crime against humanity of persecution, for example, political groups must be delineated to ascertain whether the offence was committed 'against any identifiable group or collectivity on political…grounds'.[222] The participation or tacit approval of 'political organization' can be a constituent element of the crime against humanity of forced disappearance.[223] The locus of where 'political rights' are exercised even impacts eligibility to serve on the Court as a judge.[224]

Additional analogies appear in human rights cases involving discrimination based on political opinion,[225] as well as in the interpretive restrictions on the

[219] *Vieth v Jubelirer* (2004) 541 US 267 (US Sup Ct) 287.

[220] ibid 347 n 2 (Souter and Ginsberg JJ dissenting).

[221] Official Records (6th Comm 1948) (SR74) 101 (US).

[222] ICC Statute art 7(1)(h). Persecution is discussed in greater detail in Chapter 6.

[223] ICC Statute art 7(2)(i) (enforced disappearance 'of persons by, or with the authorization, support or acquiescence of, a State or political organization….').

[224] ICC Statute art 36(7) ('A person who, for the purposes of membership of the Court, could be regarded as a national of more than one State shall be deemed to be a national of the State in which that person *ordinarily exercises civil and political rights*.') (emphasis added).

[225] *Ireland v United Kingdom* (1 Oct 1972) ECHR Case No A/5310/71 (detention without trial and failure to charge under ECHR arts 5 and 6 must be considered in conjunction with claim for discrimination on grounds of political opinion).

application of international criminal law in the ICC.[226] In refugee law, political opinion can form the basis of an asylum claim.[227] The exception to extradition for 'political' offences is long-standing,[228] and political opinion is subject to legal obligations even in business and economic contexts.[229]

This is not to suggest that jurisprudence from these (or other) fields is dispositive. As noted previously, groups defined for purposes of genocide always are *sui generis*. The determination of the contours of the targeted political group will require a case-by-case analysis of the characteristics selected and applied by the political genocidaire within the larger social context of the group's existence. But this is no more and no less than what courts are required to do already with respect to enumerated groups.

The first steps in the genocidal process always are classification (perpetrators identifying the relevant characteristics of group members) and symbolization (forcing group members to display indicia of those selected characteristics (eg, the Star of David)).[230] The contours of the targeted group become increasingly clear as it progresses through various genocidal stages (symbolization, dehumanization, preparation, etc) toward physical and biological destruction. It thus should be no more difficult in practice for a court to identify the contours of a political group than any of the groups already enumerated in the Convention.[231]

Defining political genocide

Political genocide is defined herein as conduct against a political group that would constitute genocide if committed against a racial, national, ethnic or religious group. It is any of the acts listed in Articles II(a)–(e) in the Genocide Convention committed with intent to destroy, in whole or in part, a political group 'as such'. The determination of whether a genocidaire has targeted a political group requires analysis of whether the criteria used by the perpetrator to define

[226] ICC Statute art 21(3) ('The application and interpretation of law [in the ICC]...must be consistent with internationally recognized human rights, and be without any adverse distinction founded on grounds such as...political or other opinion....').

[227] *Cf* Refugee Convention art 33(1) (prohibiting expulsion where the life or freedom of the applicant is threatened on account *inter alia* of political opinion); Extradition Act 2003 ss 13, 81 (same).

[228] *Cf Quinn v Robinson* (1986) 783 F2d 776 (US Ct App (9th Cir)) 793–814 (detailing historical development of various legal tests for application of the exception and ascertaining whether a crime is essentially political in nature).

[229] *Cf* Convention for the Protection of Individuals with Respect to Automatic Processing of Personal Data (28 Jan 1981) Eur TS No 108 art 6 ('Personal data revealing racial origin, political opinions or religious or other beliefs...may not be processed automatically unless domestic law provides appropriate safeguards').

[230] GH Stanton, 'The Eight Stages of Genocide' (1998).

[231] Although the analysis here is retrospective and focuses upon prosecution and punishment, similar considerations would apply in identifying groups in emergent or pre-emergent political genocides for purposes of prevention.

the group are essentially political in character. This definition incorporates in full all other existing law on genocide. The only difference is its application to attacks on political groups in addition to national, ethnic, religious and racial groups.

Political genocide is an equally narrow concept to genocide under the Convention. Political groups would receive the same protection as enumerated groups under the Convention—no more, no less. What should be clear is that the concept would not cover all malignant efforts toward political hegemony. If, for example, a ruling party eliminates political opposition by jailing members of an opposition group, deporting them, restricting their civil liberties, or eliminating their rights of political participation, this alone would not constitute political genocide. Even assassination, torture, and other crimes against political opponents alone would not suffice, even if these crimes were perpetrated to achieve political supremacy and/or ultimately lead to the disbanding or dissolution of the political group to which the individuals belonged.

Genocide—and political genocide—fundamentally are crimes against *groups*. Not only is the intent to destroy the group 'as such' paramount, that intent must be focused upon the group's physical and biological existence. Conduct constitutes 'political genocide' only when there is an enumerated act (killing, physical or mental harm, sterilization, removing children, etc) committed against a group member with intent to *physically or biologically destroy* the political *group* 'as such'.

As outlined here, it should be clear that the concept of political genocide hardly constitutes a panacea for malfeasance against political opponents. There can be little doubt that the type of conduct outlined above violates many fundamental human rights. It also constitutes an international crime—notably persecution—provided that the discrimination is severe enough and the chapeau elements of crimes against humanity can be established. But it is not political genocide unless serious physical or biological violence is perpetrated against group members with specific intent to destroy all or part of the political group to which they belong.

Targeting physical or biological destruction based upon the characteristics of group members exercising or possessing (or of being perceived to exercise or possess) any of the political rights discussed above certainly would qualify.[232] The social science literature suggests that such violence often is grounded in the hierarchical position of political groups relative to those that would destroy them.[233]

[232] Genocides often 'occur during governmental upheaval or transitions of power.' Fein, *Human Wrongs* 137 (2007).

[233] B Harff and TR Gurr, 'Toward Empirical Theory of Genocides and Politicides: Identification and Measurement of Cases Since 1945' (1988) 32 ILQ 359, 360 (detailing various forms of 'politicide' and defining political groups 'primarily in terms of their hierarchical position or political opposition to the regime and dominant groups.'). Although useful, caution should be exercised in drawing upon social science materials, in that genocide often is defined differently sociologically than it is for legal purposes under the Convention. ibid (defining genocide as 'the promotion and execution of policies by a state or its agents which result in the deaths of a substantial portion of a group.').

'Retributive' attacks, for example, are perpetrated against previously-dominant political groups that have fallen out of power. 'Repressive' and 'revolutionary' attacks are opposite sides of the same coin: the former involving destruction of political groups to preserve existing power (eg, Hitler's and Stalin's numerous political purges) and the latter to alter the status quo and impose a new ideology (eg, Mao's cultural revolution in China).[234]

As noted previously, there certainly will be instances where political and other aspects of identity overlap. 'Repressive' political destruction involves a presumption that an otherwise distinct group (which may be, but is not necessarily, a protected group under the Convention) possesses uniform political characteristics that merit its destruction. An example would be the Khmer Rouge's destruction of indigenous Muslim Cham, Buddhists, and Christians in Cambodia as ipso facto political enemies of the new regime.[235]

As with enumerated groups, a prosecution for political genocide will turn on a case-by-case analysis in light of the offender's mental state and the social context in which he acted. This retrospective analysis of the perpetrator's intentions at the time of his crime is part and parcel of nearly every criminal trial where *mens rea* is an issue. It is a framework with which all criminal courts are eminently familiar and therefore poses no special challenges in application.[236]

[234] ibid 363, 368–70.

[235] ibid; GH Stanton, 'Blue Scarves and Yellow Stars: Classification and Symbolization in the Cambodian Genocide' (1987) 1, 3–5. In such cases, cumulative convictions may be warranted for the separate offences of genocide and political genocide. Cumulative convictions are discussed in Chapter 6.

[236] As noted previously, classification and symbolization are always the first steps toward targeting and destroying any group. The need for perpetrators to define and mark the group in order to commit the crime necessarily also facilitates group identification for the forward-looking purpose of protecting it from physical and biological destruction.

5

Political Genocide and Customary International Law

A. Customary international law and international crimes

Now that political genocide has been defined, it is necessary to address whether, as some suggest, political genocide is prohibited *already* as a stand-alone crime by virtue of post-Convention developments in customary international law. This requires a detailed empirical analysis of state practice and *opinio juris* on genocide and political genocide.

It is helpful to anchor this analysis with a preliminary discussion of the methods by which legal rules become binding precepts of international law. The substantive content of international criminal law is created in the same manner as other international regulations. Article 38(1) of the ICJ Statute, which 'is generally regarded as a complete statement of the sources of international law',[1] provides that:

> The Court, whose function is to decide in accordance with international law such disputes as are submitted to it, shall apply:
>
> a. international conventions, whether general or particular, establishing rules expressly recognized by the contesting states;
>
> b. international custom, as evidence of a general practice accepted as law;
>
> c. the general principles of law recognized by civilized nations;
>
> d. subject to the provisions of Article 59 [providing that decisions are binding only on parties], judicial decisions and the teachings of the most highly qualified publicists of the various nations, as subsidiary means for the determination of the rules of law.[2]

Binding international law can arise through any of the sources noted in Article 38(1)(a)–(c). A prohibition on political genocide arising under customary international law thus is no less obligatory than one arising via a treaty.[3]

[1] Brownlie 3 (1998). [2] ICJ Statute art 38(1).

[3] A study group of the International Law Commission reached a consensus that all three sources had identical status. MJ Matheson, 'The Fifty-Eighth Session of the International Law Commission' (2007) 101 AJIL 407, 424 ('All members of the study group agreed that there was no hierarchical distinction between the main sources of international law—treaties, custom, and general principles of law recognized by all systems.').

Despite some unique aspects, human rights law fits 'within the theory and discipline of public international law'.[4] So does international criminal law.[5] Both are equally subject to the formal requirements of rule making on the international plane. Chief among these is the axiom that customary international law derives from tacit agreement among states on legal principles.[6] The rule in question is made explicit, at least in theory, by state practice in conformity with it. Total agreement is not necessary but 'substantial, virtual uniformity or consistency of state practice' is, at least for states impacted by the rule.[7]

State practice certainly includes the external diplomatic and legal relations among states on the international plane. But it also includes internal domestic legislation and judicial decisions, as well as government memoranda and pronouncements in legislative and similar bodies.[8] The practices of some international organizations also are relevant. Although not itself state practice,[9] it can *evidence* state practice if views expressed elsewhere by states are reflected therein or if the materials are subsequently adopted by states. State practice on genocide includes practice with respect to the Convention itself and other instruments replicating it, decisions interpreting those instruments by national and international courts, formal positions taken in international contexts, and a myriad of other matters.

There is extensive state practice on *genocide*. But this does not necessarily translate to state practice on *political* genocide or the question of whether political groups are entitled to similar protection under international criminal law. As a whole, the international community has declined virtually every opportunity even to consider the issue.[10] A UN Special Rapporteur recommended revising the Convention to include political groups, but the suggestion was ignored.[11] More recently, the issue was deemed too controversial for ICC negotiations.[12]

The lack of state practice is not surprising. States often refrain from taking positions on human rights issues or violations unless their own interests or nationals

[4] Meron, *Humanitarian Norms* 101 (1989).

[5] The ICC Statute, for example, specifies a similar hierarchy of evidentiary sources applicable in that forum ICC Statute art 21(1). This reflects the general view that the sources of international criminal law mirror the traditional sources of international law reflected in the ICJ Statute. Cassese, ICL 26 (2003).

[6] *Lotus* [1927] PCIJ Ser A (No 10) 3 (7 Sep) 18.

[7] Villiger 43 (1997).

[8] B Simma and AL Paulus, 'Responsibility of Individuals for Human Rights Abuses in Internal Conflicts: A Positivist View' (1999) 93 AJIL 302, 306.

[9] Villiger 17 (1997).

[10] State reticence in dealing with political genocide certainly raises practical concerns in connection with any suggestion that a broader offence *should* be adopted. The focus here is on the substantive offence, which puts these issues outside the scope of this work. They are addressed briefly, however, in the concluding remarks.

[11] Study (Second) on Genocide (2 Jul 1985) UN Doc E/CN4/Sub2/1985/6 ¶30.

[12] ICC Ad Hoc Committee Report (6 Sep 1995) UN Doc A/50/22 ¶¶60–1; ICC Preparatory Committee Report (13 Sep 1996) UN Doc A/51/22 ¶59.

are affected.[13] Unfortunately, this thins the field of available practice and *opinio juris*. Given the limited sources available, a wide view of what constitutes 'state practice' will be utilized here. Where multiple interpretations are legitimately possible,[14] they are indulged in favour of treating the matter as state practice.[15] Villiger's summary is useful: 'State practice includes any act, articulation or other behaviour of a State, as long as the behaviour in question discloses the State's conscious attitude with respect to recognition of the rule.'[16] This broad view of state practice is adopted here, albeit with the caution that in international law—as in much of life—words may be far less demonstrative of genuine commitment to a principle than deeds in support of it.[17]

The practice in question must be 'accepted as law'—undertaken with a sense of legal obligation.[18] The ICJ's classic statement on *opinio juris* is worth quoting in full:

> [T]wo conditions must be fulfilled. Not only must the acts concerned amount to a settled practice, but they must also be such, or be carried out in such a way, as to be evidence of a belief that this practice is rendered obligatory by the existence of a rule of law requiring it. The need for such a belief, i.e., the existence of a subjective element, is implicit in the very notion of the *opinio juris sive necessitatis*. The States concerned must therefore feel that they are conforming to what amounts to a legal obligation. The frequency, or even habitual character of the acts is not in itself enough. There are many international acts, e.g., in the field of ceremonial and protocol, which are performed almost invariably, but which are motivated only by considerations of courtesy, convenience or tradition, and not by any sense of legal duty.[19]

This decision has been criticized on grounds of circularity—that law exists when states subjectively believe that law exists—and there is much theoretical uncertainty on *opinio juris*.[20] The uncertainty reflects deeper concerns about

[13] C Beyani, 'The Legal Premises for the International Protection of Human Rights' in Goodwin-Gill and Talmon 32 (1999).

[14] For example, there is much debate on verbal position statements. Some claim that only *actions*—not statements—are state 'practice', while others argue that 'verbal acts' are sufficient. *Cf* Villiger 17–28 (1997).

[15] Meron, *Humanitarian Norms* 94 (1989) ('rights which are most crucial to the protection of human dignity of an universally accepted values of humanity, and whose violation triggers broad condemnation by the international community, will require a lesser amount of confirmatory evidence.').

[16] Villiger 16 (1997).

[17] As Judge Simma puts it, the caution in using such practice is 'that it is grown like a flower in a hot-house and that it is anything but sure that such creatures will survive in the much rougher climate of actual state practice'. Simma 216 (1993).

[18] *Cf* Restatement (Third) of Foreign Relations s 102(2) ('Customary international law results from a general and consistent practice of states which is followed by them from a sense of legal obligation.').

[19] *North Sea Continental Shelf* [1969] ICJ 3 ¶77.

[20] HHG Post, 'The Role of State Practice in the Formation of Customary International Humanitarian Law' in Dekker and Post 129, 136–8 (2003).

Article 38(1)(b) itself,[21] and the evidence,[22] nature,[23] and requirements[24] of *opinio juris* are much debated. There is no need to engage that controversy here. It is enough for present purposes to consider *opinio juris* in the broadest sense—to scrutinize state conduct to ascertain whether it was engaged in with a genuine recognition of legal significance.

As with most subjective intentions, *opinio juris* can be inferred from objective circumstances,[25] although it must be clearly premised on conduct amounting to an acknowledgement of legal consequences. Practices adopted for moral reasons or out of political expediency do not create enforceable rules of international law.[26] Without more, conduct reasonably susceptible to multiple interpretations also does not evidence *opinio juris*.

Under certain circumstances, the *failure* to object can make legal rules binding upon the non-objecting state.[27] Silence is taken as consent when the state could have made its objections known and refrained from voicing them under circumstances when other states would expect an objection.[28] The rule's domestic analogy is quasi-contract, where legal obligations arise from a synthesis of the failure to communicate when expected to do so and others' reasonable reliance on that silence.[29]

This is significant for human rights law. Sometimes what states do *not* claim matters more than that which they do. States accused of international crimes and other bad behaviour typically refute the allegations without denouncing the legal principle involved. They rarely claim the right to engage in the conduct, usually responding instead that it never happened, it was unauthorized, or that it fell short of the requisite standard.[30] Paradoxically, this is state practice favouring the prohibition. Defending conduct on the basis that a rule was not violated or

[21] GG Fitzmaurice, 'Some Problems Regarding the Formal Sources of International Law' [1958] Symbolae Verzijil 153, 174 (although international custom 'is an undoubted formal source of international law,' 'head (b) in Article 38 is notoriously defective').

[22] RY Jennings, 'What is International Law and How Do We Tell It When We See It?' (1981) 37 Schweitzerisches Jahrbuch für Internationales Recht 59, 67 ('There also is a disquieting side to [the] ferment in the law. There are so now many vehicles for the expression of *opinio juris*... that it is increasingly difficult to say with any conviction what is *lege lata* and what is *lege ferenda*.').

[23] Professor Byers suggests that *opinio juris* is a transformative lever that shifts international 'power into obligation' in order to 'maximize the interests of most if not all States by creating rules which protect and promote their common interests.': Byers 18–19, 120–4 (1999).

[24] *Cf* M Mendelson, 'The International Court of Justice and the Sources' in Lowe and Fitzmaurice 70 (1996) (noting that the ICJ's case law on *opinio juris* 'has not been uniformly helpful. Its pronouncements are somewhat inconsistent on whether the subjective element consists of belief or consent.').

[25] Restatement (Third) of Foreign Relations s 102 cmt c.

[26] *Flores v Southern Peru Copper Corp* (2003) 406 F3d 65 (US Ct App (2d Cir)) 80.

[27] *Nuclear Weapons* [1996] ICJ 227 ¶67.

[28] Restatement (Third) of Foreign Relations s 102 cmt b (inferring approval from state acquiescence in another state's conduct that affects its rights).

[29] Restatement (Second) of Contracts s 69 (1981).

[30] *Filartiga v Pena-Irala* (1980) 630 F2d 876 (US Ct App (2d Cir)) 884.

was subject to exceptions[31] (as opposed to claiming no rule exists) is *opinio juris* reinforcing the precept.[32]

Evidentiary sources

As noted previously, there is much practice on genocide, but far less on *political* genocide. This has analytic consequences. The cogency of any study necessarily depends upon the availability of underlying data. An absence of data means either: (i) that data simply does not exist; or (ii) that data exists but has gone unrecognized. To some extent, this dilemma is inevitable. The hazards of definitively establishing the *absence* of practice on a particular matter—proving the negative—are obvious.

The most that can be done is to define the universe of materials for review and to balance comprehensiveness against diminishing returns when the study fails to yield the information sought. The methodology herein involves a review of the *most likely* evidentiary sources of state practice either for or against a legal norm prohibiting political genocide. These include the following:

- Historical materials on genocide (early General Assembly resolutions, drafts of the Convention, *travaux préparatoires*, and the like);
- Case law from domestic courts and international tribunals (including the ICJ, the ICTY and ICTR, the ICC, mixed or hybrid tribunals, human rights bodies like the ECHR, etc);
- Domestic legislation and/or regulatory materials on genocide and related matters;
- Treaty practice—the text of relevant treaties, as well as state participation and related practice (reservations, objections, etc);
- Legal materials reflecting state practice in international contexts (drafting committees, UN voting records, and the like) ;
- UN materials and reports (the work of Special Rapporteurs, investigatory bodies, expert panels, the ILC, etc);
- Yearbooks, digests, and the like reflecting state practice (AJIL, BYBIL, Asian YBIL, Whiteman, etc); and
- Academic writings discussing state practice and similar issues.

This is not an exhaustive list.[33] It is possible that additional practice exists that has not been reviewed. On the other hand, an important inference can be drawn

[31] States 'invariably deny responsibility' by claiming that victims were domestic criminals, that the perpetrators were terrorists or other non-government officials, or (more rarely) suggesting that 'regrettable excesses' occurred while denying that the 'excesses' were condoned or part of state policy. Kuper, *Prevention* 145–6 (1985).

[32] *Nicaragua* [1986] ICJ 14 ¶186.

[33] Obviously, some evidentiary sources (diplomatic papers expressing clear positions on legal issues) are more valuable than others (abstaining from a vote at a multilateral conference). Where appropriate, the weight of a particular source is noted when discussing its content.

from the absence of readily-available evidence. The more important and accepted a norm is, the more state practice in compliance with that norm should make itself apparent. From a legal perspective, there is no need to establish the *absence* of practice. The burden of proof rests with the advocate of the norm. The default position is that no rule exists.

The starting position on the legal rule is important here because the review of many of the sources above yielded no results. The bulk of available evidence of state practice on political genocide concentrates principally in two areas—historic treaty materials on the Convention and domestic legal materials on genocide (legislation and case law). Additional discussion of these two sources is warranted before analysing the applicable evidence.

Treaties and related materials

The Genocide Convention is a multilateral treaty that is properly analysed under the interpretive principles codified in the Vienna Convention on the Law of Treaties. Treaties must be interpreted in good faith according to the *ordinary meaning* of their text in light of their object and purpose.[34] Side agreements and instruments provide guidance on ambiguous treaty provisions, as do any subsequent interpretations or course of conduct between the parties.[35] The interpreting body should account for any rules of international law that govern the relationship between the parties[36] and will apply special meanings to terms if the parties so intended.[37]

The VCLT allows supplementary recourse to *travaux préparatoires* in one of two situations.[38] First, the drafting history can confirm a textual analysis.[39] Second the *travaux* are useful if a textual interpretation is ambiguous or leads to a manifestly absurd or unreasonable result.[40] The drafting records of the Genocide Convention[41] have been drawn upon to help interpret the meaning of the prohibition on genocide.[42] But '[r]ecourse to the *travaux préparatoires* must always be undertaken with caution and prudence'.[43] Vagueness in the treaty, for example, often is mirrored in the *travaux*.[44] Context also matters. The Convention was a compromise negotiated among fifty-seven states,[45] with close votes on a number

[34] VCLT art 31(1); Sinclair 119–26, 130–5 (1984).

[35] VCLT art 31(2)-(3); Sinclair 127–30, 135–8 (1984). An ICTY Trial Chamber held case law from the ICTR and national courts to be 'subsequent practice grounded on the Convention.' *Jelisic (TC)* [1999] ICTY ¶61 (using VCLT to interpret an identical provision of the ICTY Statute).

[36] VCLT art 31(2)-(3).

[37] ibid art 31(4); Sinclair 126–7 (1984).

[38] This 'ensure[s] that the supplementary means do not constitute an alternative, autonomous method of interpretation divorced from the general rule.': Sinclair 116 (1984).

[39] VCLT art 32.

[40] ibid.

[41] Official Records (6th Comm 1948) (SR61–110, SR128–134).

[42] *Krstic (AC)* [2004] ICTY ¶52 (Shahabuddeen J dissenting) (the *travaux* of the Convention 'have been and will be consulted with profit.').

[43] Sinclair 142 (1984).

[44] ibid.

[45] Official Records (6th Comm 1948) xiv–xix.

of key provisions.[46] Given the divergent views expressed, conclusions drawn from the original drafting records are open to critique on the basis of selectivity in referencing source material.

In any event, statements of meaning are not necessarily dispositive interpretations that exclude other views. They indicate merely that a majority of the drafting committee ascribed to a certain interpretation.[47] Even when proposals were adopted, the drafters did 'not necessarily adopt the interpretation given by [the proposal's] author'.[48] With these caveats in mind, the *travaux préparatoires* of the Convention and related historical documents provide a useful opportunity to study early state practice on political genocide. The inclusion of political groups proved to be one of the most controversial issues throughout the drafting process.

Domestic law

Domestic legislation and judicial decisions constitute state practice.[49] They also can evidence principles of law generally accepted among nations.[50] But this does not mean that domestic law is imported 'lock, stock and barrel' into international jurisprudence.[51] Whether common law or civil law in origin, each precept must be evaluated and modified to suit the international context. Disagreement within a domestic body can reflect a lack of consensus about the precept's content and/or application,[52] which lessens its evidentiary weight. Even when domestic law is clear, the international context may require divergent interpretation even of identical language.[53] In that sense, 'internationalized' rules of domestic law become *sui generis* to the forum to which they are exported.[54]

The *nature* of the rules complicates the analysis. US law, for example, provides a civil forum for aliens to prosecute tort claims for violations of international law or treaties of the United States.[55] This includes torts based upon international crimes.[56] But the claim itself is civil, with concomitant differences in burden

46 M Lippman, 'The Drafting of the 1948 Convention on the Prevention and Punishment of the Crime of Genocide' (1985) 3 BU ILJ 1.

47 Official Records (6th Comm 1948) (SR132) 700 (Chair).

48 ibid (SR77) 136–7 (US).

49 Simma (n 8) 306.

50 ICJ Statute art 38(1)(c); *Norman (Judicial Independence—AC)* [2004] SC-SL ¶¶27–36 (citing US law on judicial independence).

51 *Milosevic (Motion to Acquit—TC)* [2004] ICTY ¶7 (Sep Op Robinson J).

52 Compare *Roper v Simmons* (2005) 125 S Ct 1183 (US Sup Ct) 1184 (drawing inter alia upon international law to ascertain whether execution of offenders aged 18 and under when they committed their crimes violated 8th Amendment prohibition on cruel and unusual punishment in US Constitution) with ibid 1206 (O'Connor J dissenting) (conceding relevance of international law to 8th Amendment jurisprudence but disagreeing with result) with ibid 1217 (Scalia and Thomas JJ dissenting) (rejecting relevance of international law to 8th Amendment cases).

53 *Stakic (TC)* [2003] ICTY ¶413.

54 *Milosevic (Motion to Acquit—TC)* [2004] ICTY ¶7 (Sep Op Robinson J).

55 Alien Tort Claims Act (1789) 28 USC s 1350.

56 *Kadic v Karadzic* (1995) 70 F3d 232 (US Ct App (2d Cir)) (tort case against Serb leaders in former Yugoslavia for genocide and other offences).

of proof, procedural guarantees and the like. International crimes also are construed in domestic courts in the context of extradition proceedings, which are quasi-criminal procedures that facilitate inter-state enforcement of criminal norms.[57]

Particularly where novel issues are raised[58] or little other authority exists (as with political genocide), domestic law may provide useful guidance on the legal principles at issue as well as the practice of that state. But there is a clear difference between criminal punishment and other forms of legal adjudication.[59] Domestic materials must be evaluated with their original context firmly in mind.

B. State practice on genocide and political genocide

Resolutions and voting practices in multilateral drafting conventions can evidence customary international law.[60] The analysis of state practice on political genocide begins here with an historic review of international materials on genocide and the drafting of the Genocide Convention. The inclusion of political groups was hotly contested almost from the start, with states taking divergent positions on legal, political and pragmatic grounds. These merit detailed analysis, as the question has not since received the concentrated attention of many states.

Historic records on the Genocide Convention

General Assembly Resolution 96(I)

General Assembly Resolution 96(I) in December 1946 was the UN's first official pronouncement on genocide:

> Genocide is a denial of the right of existence of entire human groups, as homicide is the denial of the right to live of individual human beings; such denial of the right of existence shocks the conscience of mankind, results in great losses to humanity in the form of cultural and other contributions represented by these human groups, and is contrary to moral law and to the spirit and aims of the United Nations.
>
> Many instances of such crimes of genocide have occurred when racial, religious, *political, and other groups* have been destroyed, entirely or in part.
>
> The punishment of the crime of genocide is a matter of international concern.

[57] *Demjanjuk v Petrovsky* (1985) 776 F2d 571, 581–3 (US Ct App (6th Cir)) (analysing universal jurisdiction over genocide under customary international law).

[58] *Cf Beanal v Freeport-McMoran* (1999) 197 F3d 161, 165–8 (US Ct App (5th Cir)) ('cultural' genocide not recognized under customary international law).

[59] *In re Yamashita* (1946) 328 US 1 (US Sup Ct) 39 (Murphy J dissenting) ('The difference between arbitrating property rights and charging an individual with a crime against the law of nations is too obvious to require elaboration.').

[60] *Fisheries Jurisdiction* [1974] ICJ 3 ¶¶56–8, 74 (conference resolutions on the law of the sea).

The General Assembly, therefore, *affirms* that genocide is a crime under international law which the civilized world condemns, and for the commission of which principals and accomplices—whether private individuals, public officials or statesmen, and whether the crime is committed on religious, racial, political or any other grounds—are punishable.... (Emphasis added.)[61]

The text of the resolution

The use of the word 'affirms' implies a belief that genocide was already a crime. What the General Assembly understood to be included in the concept is unclear, however. Whether the concept applies to all groups or to a restrictive number of 'other groups' is unclear. The first paragraph overtly references political groups as victims, along with racial, religious and 'other groups.' And although genocide clearly involves the *destruction* of groups, the resolution is silent on the methods of that destruction. Little else can be gleaned from the text.

Nevertheless, some argue that Resolution 96(I) is the key that unlocks a wider conception of political genocide.[62] The claim is that, since the resolution explicitly mentioned political groups, a larger conception must exist under customary international law. Since so much is placed on this resolution, it makes sense to consider the legal implications of General Assembly resolutions before discussing the specifics of Resolution 96(I).

The legal effect of General Assembly resolutions

General Assembly resolutions are not among the sources reflected in the ICJ Statute. The General Assembly is not a legislature and has no direct power to create binding international law:

[T]he General Assembly has no power of decision—as distinguished from recommendation—imposing itself with binding force upon the substantive action of the Member States, its Resolutions have no binding force.... [and a] State is not bound to comply with any specific Resolution recommending it to undertake or to abstain from any particular legislative or administrative action.[63]

Nevertheless, there has been some suggestion that *all* General Assembly resolutions have some legal effect.[64] The question is one of degree. Judge Lauterpacht, for example, distinguished resolutions addressed to internal UN matters from those constituting recommendations to member states. Internal directives have 'legal validity and effect'.[65] Recommendations are not binding directly but create '*some* legal obligation which, however rudimentary, elastic and imperfect, is nevertheless a legal obligation and constitutes a measure of supervision'.[66] They

[61] UNGA Res 96 (I) (11 Dec 1946) UN Doc A/BUR/50.

[62] *Cf* B Van Schaak, 'The Crime of Political Genocide: Repairing the Genocide Convention's Blind Spot' (1997) 106 Yale LJ 2259, 2280–2.

[63] *Voting Procedure* [1955] ICJ 67, 118 (Lauterpacht J).

[64] ibid.

[65] ibid.

[66] ibid 118–19 (emphasis in original).

cannot simply be ignored: '[t]he state in question, while not bound to accept the recommendation, is bound to give it due consideration in good faith' and to articulate its reasons for disagreeing with it.[67]

This view is not universally credited, and for good reason. Judge Lauterpacht offers no guidance on about how much deference is required, the legal standard under which to review it, or any details on the resolutions impact other (potentially conflicting) legal obligations. 'Due consideration in good faith' creates no workable or even cognizable legal standard and is unhelpful in assessing the 'legal' obligation purportedly imposed.

A better view is that the 'obligation' is procedural—that under the UN Charter states must participate in the General Assembly's *processes* in good faith. But this simply reiterates long-standing duties of *pacta sunt servanda*—that participants in any treaty regime (of which the UN Charter is one) must discharge their obligations in good faith.[68] The notion that General Assembly resolutions impose a 'rudimentary' legal obligation was implicitly rejected eleven years later in the *South-West Africa Cases*, where the ICJ held that non-internal resolutions have a political, not a legal, character. 'The persuasive force of Assembly resolutions can indeed be very considerable, but this is a different thing. It operates on the political not the legal level: it does not make these resolutions binding in law.'[69]

Despite their political character, General Assembly resolutions can serve as *evidence* of binding rules of customary international law.[70] '[W]ith all due caution *opinio juris* can be deduced from Assembly resolutions when a State's acceptance of the resolution may be understood as an acceptance of the validity of the rule or set of rules declared by the resolution by themselves.'[71] This applies to international crimes and genocide.[72] But the legal rule itself comes from outside the General Assembly. The resolution may codify or reflect consensus on international custom but does not itself *create* binding law.[73]

Resolutions also can support the subsequent development of binding international law.[74] Certain aspects of the Universal Declaration on Human Rights,[75] for example, have hardened into customary international law.[76] General Assembly

[67] ibid 119. [68] VCLT art 26. [69] *SW Africa* [1966] ICJ 1, 50–1.

[70] Higgins 22 (1994) ('With the development of international organizations, the votes and views of States have come to have legal significance as evidence of customary law....').

[71] *Nicaragua* [1986] ICJ 14, 99–100 (considering Friendly Relations Declaration).

[72] *Justice* [USMT 1947] 3 TWC 1, 983 ('The General Assembly is not an international legislature, but it is the most authoritative organ in existence for the interpretation of world opinion. Its recognition of genocide as an international crime is persuasive evidence of the fact.').

[73] General Assembly resolutions are not 'a short cut to ascertaining international practice in its entirety on a matter—practice in the larger world arena is still the relevant canvas, although UN resolutions are a part of the picture. Resolutions cannot be a substitute for ascertaining custom....' Higgins 28 (1994).

[74] Higgins 27 (1994) (resolutions as 'first step in the process of law creation.').

[75] UNGA Res 217-A (III) (10 Dec 1948) UN Doc A/810.

[76] Meron, *Humanitarian Norms* 82–4 (1989).

resolutions thus 'play a significant role in creating norms'[77] that can later crystallize into binding obligations (assuming state practice supporting the norm with *opinio juris*). But again, these resolutions simply *mirror* a legal obligation existing elsewhere—they do not *impose* the obligation.

The history of Resolution 96(I)

Resolution 96(I) began with a joint proposal on genocide by Cuba, India and Panama that covered 'national, racial, ethnic and religious groups'.[78] This initial proposal did not include political groups. The General Assembly referred the proposal to the sixth committee,[79] which considered it over four meetings.[80] Political groups and often groups covered by genocide were not discussed.

Textual amendments were submitted by the UK, India, France and the USSR.[81] Saudi Arabia proposed a draft protocol defining the offence,[82] and additional written comments came from France and Chile.[83] None of these mentioned political groups or the categories of groups to be covered by the offence. The sixth committee then referred the interim draft resolution to a subcommittee (comprised of members from Chile, Cuba, France, India, Panama, Poland, Saudi Arabia, the UK, the USSR, and the US), which met twice and reported back to the full committee.[84]

No discussion of the groups covered by the offence is reflected in the committee's report. But the subcommittee did modify the initial submission and for the first time added political groups. How it happened is unknown. There is no indication about whether the legal implications were discussed at all. Records of the subcommittee's discussions were not maintained, but the issue did not appear contentious at the time. The subcommittee approved its report and draft resolution unanimously.[85] The full committee likewise adopted the report and draft resolution without dissent.[86] The General Assembly in turn unanimously adopted the draft as Resolution 96(I), again without change or debate.[87]

Analysis and conclusions

It is ironic that the conflagration about to erupt over political genocide was sparked by this most inauspicious of beginnings. The inclusion of political groups later proved to be one of the most contentious debates on genocide. But at the

[77] Higgins 28 (1994).

[78] 'Draft Resolution relating to the crime of genocide proposed by the delegations of Cuba, India and Panama' (2 Nov 1946) UN Doc A/BUR50. Ironically, the definition subsequently travelled through three resolutions, three drafting conferences, and three draft conventions before returning to a final version that covered exactly these four groups.

[79] 'Prevention and Punishment of Genocide: Historical Summary (2 Nov 1946–20 Jan 1948)' (26 Jan 1948) UN Doc E/621 4.

[80] Official Records (6th Comm 1946) 101–4, 111–13, 113–19 and 172–4.

[81] ibid 242–3. [82] ibid 243–4. [83] ibid 244.

[84] 'Draft report and resolution adopted by Sub-Committee 3 relating to the crime of genocide' (6 Dec 1946) UN Doc A/C6/120. [85] Official Records (6th Comm 1946) 172.

[86] ibid 174. [87] UN GAOR (Verbatim Record 23 Oct–16 Dec 1946) 1134–5.

outset, the drafting of the resolution specifying their inclusion was uneventful. *How* political groups came to be so-included, and whether the future implications were foreseen at the time, remains a mystery.

The historical record also provides little guidance about the legal character of genocide in 1946. This is not surprising. Less than two years after the Resolution was adopted, the Convention's drafters could not even agree on whether genocide was a crime already under international law.[88] The ambiguity over the legal effect of Resolution 96(I) was reflected two years later in the Convention itself. The preamble states that the drafters of the Convention 'considered' Resolution 96(I) but provides no further guidance.[89]

Whatever the prior legality of genocide, the Convention itself unquestionably specified in late 1948 that genocide was an international crime:

Article I

The Contracting Parties confirm that genocide, whether committed in time of peace or in time of war, is a crime under international law which they undertake to prevent and to punish.

Article I did not resolve the issue of whether genocide was an offence pre-Convention. The use of the word 'confirm' seems to point to a pre-existing offence. Others suggest that Article I 'was retained mainly to evade the issue whether or not genocide already was a crime recognized by international law [at the time of drafting].'[90] The ICJ also failed to answer the question. It cited Resolution 96(I) in early jurisprudence on genocide[91] and in later cases[92] but has not clarified its legal significance.

All in all, the resolution reflects neither consistent state practice nor any sense of *opinio juris*. This is not surprising, as the concept itself was in flux at the time. 'Genocide' in Resolution 96(I) did not necessarily have the same meaning as it did in late 1948 or does today. Use of the term was largely *descriptive* at Nuremberg, as it appeared in the indictment[93] and the prosecutors' closing arguments.[94] Likewise with cases under CC10.[95] Even where legal content was recognized, genocide was seen as a *type* of crime against humanity, not a separate crime.[96]

Genocide also had much broader theoretical underpinnings in 1946. Just two years earlier, Lemkin's groundbreaking treatise identified eight different types of genocide: political, social, cultural, economic, biological, physical, religious, and moral.[97] Any or all of these could have been contemplated in Resolution 96(I),

[88] Official Records (6th Comm 1948) 49 (Dom Rep) (arguing in favour) and 50 (US) (arguing against).
[89] Genocide Convention pmbl.
[90] Drost 77 (1959).
[91] *Reservations* [1951] ICJ 15, 23.
[92] *Application of Genocide Convention—Prov Measures I* [1993] ICJ 3, 23.
[93] *IMT Indictment* (1946) 1 IMT Proceedings 43–4.
[94] (1946) 19 IMT Proceedings 497, 498, 509, 515, and 531.
[95] *Justice* [USMT 1947] 3 TWC 1, 983; *RuSHA* [USMT 1948] 4 TWC 599, 609, 626.
[96] ibid.
[97] Lemkin 79–90 (1944).

which was adopted simultaneously with the Nuremberg Principles.[98] The records are ambiguous, and no evidence supports the view that the core meaning of genocide was settled when it was adopted.

It puts too much weight on Resolution 96(I) to suggest that it inherently recognizes a broader offence of political genocide under customary international law. Judge Higgins rightly cautions against 'examining only part of the picture' by focusing on the text of a resolution and ignoring its wider setting. Any analysis must account for the complex debate and exchange of views among states, draft proposals, and other 'decision making that may or may not imply a legal view upon a particular issue.'[99] Many of these wider issues are reflected in the drafting records of the Genocide Convention itself.

The drafting of the Convention

The reference to political groups in Resolution 96(I) carried over to the first draft of the Genocide Convention.

The Secretary General's draft

The initial drafting of a convention on genocide was tasked to the UN's Economic and Social Council (Ec/Soc Council). At the Council's request, the Secretary General agreed to facilitate discussions by preparing a draft convention.[100] The Secretary General was to work with experts on international and criminal law, the Committee on the Progressive Development and Codification of International Law, and the Commission on Human Rights. The draft then would be made available for government commentary before the Ec/Soc Council began work.[101]

The original version of the Secretariat Draft was authored by the Division of Human Rights and modified by three experts, one of whom was Raphael Lemkin.[102] The Committee on the Progressive Development declined to comment in the absence of input from member states.[103] The Secretariat Draft subsequently was sent back to the General Assembly for transmission to member states.[104]

The Secretary General drafted a broad document meant 'to embrace all points likely to be adopted' in subsequent negotiations. '[T]he Secretary General did not intend to recommend one political solution rather than another, but wished to offer a basis for full discussion and bring out all the points deserving of notice.'[105] The resolution of these issues was expressly recognized as a 'political question.'[106]

[98] UNGA Res 95 (I) (11 Dec 1946) UN Doc A/64/Add1. [99] Higgins 24 (1994).

[100] 'Crime of Genocide' EC/SOC Res 47(IV) (28 Mar 1947) UN Doc E/325.

[101] 'Comments on the Draft Convention' (26 Jun 1947) UN Doc E/447 14–15.

[102] 'Prevention and Punishment of Genocide: Historical Summary (2 Nov 1946–20 Jan 1948)' (26 Jan 1948) UN Doc E/621 19.

[103] 'Opinion of the Committee on the Progressive Development of International Law and Its Codification' (17 Jun 1947) UN Doc E/447 65.

[104] 'Genocide' (6 Aug 1947) EC/SOC Res 77(V). [105] ibid 16. [106] ibid.

The draft convention added national and linguistic groups to the racial, religious, and political categories referenced in Resolution 96(I) but dropped the illustrative reference to 'other groups.'[107] The Secretary-General recognized, however, that the enumeration was 'not exhaustive' and that the groups covered was 'the first general question which will have to be settled.'[108]

Disagreement over the inclusion of political groups was evident. All three experts took different positions. Professor Lemkin voiced doubts, suggesting that political groups were not permanent and lacked the characteristics of other groups.[109] He also made the practical argument that the Convention 'should not run the risk of failure by introducing ideas on which the world is deeply divided'.[110] In contrast, Professor de Vabres claimed that 'genocide was an odious crime, regardless of the group which fell victim to it....'[111] Professor Pella felt the inclusion of political groups was a political decision for the Assembly.[112] He also offered a value judgment on political groups, however, suggesting that the concept should exclude 'political groups with Nazi or Fascist tendencies, for those are the very groups which in the past were guilty of committing or instigating the crime of genocide'.[113]

The draft was forwarded initially to the Sixth Committee, which recommended direct reference to the Council.[114] It was transmitted through General Assembly Resolution 180(II), which prompted the Council to begin work even without government commentary on the Secretary General's draft.[115]

The Secretary General's draft offers little evidence of state practice on political groups. It was largely a product of international lawyers who disagreed among themselves. It also was drafted as a broad text that deliberately left the harder decisions to later efforts. More significant, perhaps, is the view that the decision on what groups to include was political—as opposed to legal or theoretical—in nature. This suggests the absence of any legal or codificatory character to the drafting effort.

The Economic and Social Council / Ad Hoc Draft

The 'political' nature of what groups to include was reflected again in the terms of reference to the Ec/Soc Council. It fell 'essentially within the competence of governments' to decide: '[w]hat human groups should be protected? Should all human groups, whether racial, national, linguistic, religious or political, be protected or only some of them?'[116]

107 ibid. 108 ibid. 109 ibid 22. 110 ibid. 111 ibid. 112 ibid.
113 ibid.
114 'Prevention and Punishment of Genocide: Historical Summary (2 Nov 1946–20 Jan 1948)' (26 Jan 1948) UN Doc E/621 26–37.
115 UNGA Res 180 (II) (21 Nov 1947) UN Doc A/519.
116 'Terms of reference given to the Council by General Assembly Resolution 180(II)—Note by Secretary General' (3 Feb 1948) Official Records (Ec/Soc 6th Sess 1948) 123, 125 (Annex) UN Doc E/622.

The terms of reference were augmented by written comments from governments on the Secretary General's draft, which arrived over a period of four months (some even after work started on the second draft of the Convention). Eleven states provided comments—India, Haiti, Philippines, Venezuela, US, France, Denmark, UK, Norway, Netherlands, Luxembourg, and Siam.[117] Comments also arrived from four NGOs, one of which proposed 'that the words "political" groups be omitted... in order that the acceptance of the Convention may not be delayed by differences of opinion as to the definition of political groups.'[118]

Several states commented on the groups that should be covered. The US suggested that linguistic groups were redundant of other categories and could be excluded. It also advocated retaining political groups 'on the understanding that genocide as to such groups is confined to physical destruction'.[119] Other states offered textual alterations, none of which sought the exclusion of political groups. France suggested changing the text to cover 'nationality, race, religion or opinion'[120] with the understanding that 'opinion' included 'political opinion'.[121] Siam approved the existing categories but proposed adding 'ideological' groups 'in order to extend the protection under the Convention not only to religion but to other philosophical belief or principles which may be professed by some group of human beings as well'. It is unclear whether Siam was aiming at atheistic and non-theistic groups or political philosophy. Following internal discussion by the Ec/Soc Council's social committee,[122] the Council referred drafting to an ad hoc subcommittee of representatives from seven nations: China, France, Lebanon, Poland, the US, the USSR and Venezuela.[123]

A variety of positions on political groups were taken during the twenty-eight negotiating sessions.[124] The USSR submitted an early proposal arguing that genocide was 'organically bound up with Fascism-Nazism and other similar race

[117] Prevention and Punishment of Genocide—Comments by Governments on the Draft Convention Prepared by the Secretariat—Communications from Non-Governmental Organizations (30 Jan 1948) UN Doc E/623 (India, Haiti, Philippines, Venezuela, USA, France and Denmark); 'France: Draft Convention on Genocide' (5 Feb 1948) UN Doc E/623/Add1 (France); Prevention and Punishment of Genocide—Comments by Governments on the Draft Convention Prepared by the Secretariat (19 Apr 1948) UN Doc E/623/Add2 (UK and Norway); Prevention and Punishment of Genocide—Comments by Governments on the Draft Convention Prepared by the Secretariat (19 Apr 1948) UN Doc E/623/Add3 (Netherlands); Prevention and Punishment of Genocide—Comments by Governments on the Draft Convention Prepared by the Secretariat (19 Apr 1948) UN Doc E/623/Add4 (Luxembourg and Siam).

[118] 'Consultative Council of Jewish Organizations' (24 Jul 1947) UN Doc E/C2/49 1. Other comments were provided by the World Jewish Congress (8 Aug 1947) UN Doc E/C2/52, the Commission of Churches on International Affairs (31 Oct 1947) UN Doc E/C2/63, and the World Federation of United Nations Organizations (12 Nov 1947) UN Doc E/C2/64.

[119] UN Doc E/623 (n 117) 11. The Secretariat's draft included cultural genocide as well.

[120] UN Doc E/623/Add1 (n 117) 1.

[121] Summary Records (Ad Hoc Comm 1948) (SR4) 9 (Fr).

[122] Report of the Social Committee (23 Feb 1948) UN Doc E/690.

[123] EC/SOC Res 117(VI) 'Genocide' (3 Mar 1948) UN Doc E/734. The committee was instructed to account for both the Secretariat Draft and drafts and government commentary. ibid.

[124] Summary Records (Ad Hoc Comm 1948) (SR1-SR28).

"theories" which preach racial and national hatred, the domination of so-called "higher" races and the extermination of so-called "lower" races.'[125] This position is hardly surprising when seen in context. In the late 1940s, it is impossible to think that the Soviet Union could sanction a treaty that covered political groups without putting its own *recent* crimes directly into issue. Upon the eve of its entry into World War II, Russian soldiers massacred 4,000 Polish political prisoners at Lemborg.[126] Another 15,000 Polish officers and intellectuals were shot *en masse* in the Katyn Forest because the Soviets believed that they would oppose efforts to 'Communize' Poland.[127] Earlier examples included 10 million deaths during the liquidation of Kukak peasant classes and the deliberate organization of widespread famine in Ukraine in 1932–33.

Jurisdictional measures precluded inquiry into Soviet crimes at Nuremberg. As discussed below,[128] the so-called 'Berlin Protocol' linked the tribunal's jurisdiction inextricably to Germany's aggressive war. During the drafting of the Convention, the Soviets attempted to establish that the 'scientific' definition of genocide required an 'organic link' between genocide and Nazism/fascism. This definition likewise would put Soviet practices beyond the realm of inquiry. Although no other state adopted the theory, the Soviets maintained it consistently throughout the drafting process and even into the General Assembly session where the final draft of the Convention was adopted.

Poland opposed the inclusion of political groups on the grounds that (unlike the other three categories) such groups had no firm historical basis or stable form.[129] Venezuela opposed political groups on pragmatic grounds. It expressed concerns that opposition political groups would abuse the Convention and that states would not participate in a treaty that stopped them from suppressing insurgencies.[130]

In contrast, France sought to broaden the Convention to cover 'nationality, race, religion or opinion'.[131] 'Opinion' included political opinion and other types of opinion (such as intellectual opinion) guaranteed by the Declaration of Human Rights of Man in 1789.[132] France's proposed coverage of opinion was limited to physical genocide based on the opinions of group members,[133] but the proposals were rejected. Thereafter, France focused on supporting political groups, as did the US.[134] They were joined by Lebanon, which recognized dissimilarities within

[125] 'Basic Principles of a Convention on Genocide Submitted by the Delegation of the Union of Soviet Socialist Republics' (7 Apr 1948) UN Doc E/AC25/7.

[126] J Turley, 'Transformative Justice and the Ethos of Nuremberg' (2000) 33 Loy LA LR 655, 667 n 57.

[127] SW Becker, 'Maintaining Secret Government Dossiers on the First Amendment Activities of American Citizens: the Law Enforcement Exception to the Privacy Act' (2000) 50 DePaul LR 675, 740 n 438.

[128] See Chapter 6.

[129] Summary Records (Ad Hoc Comm 1948) (SR4) 10–11 (Pol).

[130] ibid 12 (Ven); ibid (SR13) 2 (Ven).

[131] UN Doc E/623/Add1 (n 117) 1.

[132] Summary Records (Ad Hoc Comm 1948) (SR4) 9–10 (Fr).

[133] ibid 11 (Fr).

[134] ibid 11 (US).

the categories but argued that political groups should be covered as the most likely victims of future genocides.[135]

China's vote became the most decisive. It initially expressed doubts about political groups, suggesting that they lacked homogeneity and posed difficulties in application.[136] China later changed position and even offered a proposed text including them.[137] The reasons for the shift are unclear. Nevertheless, its changed stance was crucial because China cast the deciding vote. Political groups were retained by a margin of 4 in favour (US, France, Lebanon, and China) to 3 against (Venezuela, USSR, and Poland).[138]

As a unified document, the Ad Hoc Draft was adopted 5–1 in favour (USSR against) with 1 abstention (Poland).[139] The committee reported back to the full Ec/Soc Council in mid-May 1948, summarizing its work and providing a second draft convention.[140] Its report noted the division over political groups as well as unanimous agreement on national, racial and religious groups.[141] Linguistic groups were dropped entirely.

State positions taken in the Ad Hoc Committee were affirmed in the full Ec/Soc Council. The USSR, Poland and Venezuela restated their opposition, with Venezuela adding that political groups could be protected instead through other human rights mechanisms.[142] Brazil joined them.[143] The US and France retained their arguments in favour.[144] Surprisingly, the Council never actually voted on the Ad Hoc draft; it simply was transferred to the General Assembly as it stood.[145]

The evidence is contradictory on whether the work of the Ec/Soc Council or the Ad Hoc Committee constitutes state practice undertaken with *opinio juris*. As noted previously, the Secretary General's terms of reference framed the difficult questions on groups as political—not legal—matters. The Danish representative reiterated that position during the Ec/Soc Council's final debates, claiming that the issues 'on which it had not been possible to reach unanimous agreement in the *ad hoc* Committee were predominantly of a political character....'[146]

On the other hand, there clearly was an analogue between the drafting of the Convention and other work on the codification of legal principles arising out of Nuremberg. A formal comparison of the two efforts placed genocide within the wider rubric of customary international law and crimes against humanity.

> It may be said that a convention on genocide, without weakening the condemnation of crimes against humanity under international common law, which is valid for all members

[135] ibid 13 (Leb). [136] ibid (SR3) 5 (China).

[137] 'Draft Articles for the Inclusion in the Convention on Genocide Proposed by the Delegation of China' (16 April 1948) UN Doc E/AC25/9 art I.

[138] Summary Records (Ad Hoc Comm 1948) (SR13) 4. [139] ibid (SR26).

[140] Ec/Soc Report on Genocide (26 May 1948) UN Doc E/794. [141] ibid 5–6.

[142] Official Records (Ec/Soc 7th Sess 1948) (SR218) 705 (Ven) and 712 (Pol); ibid (SR219) 721 (USSR). [143] ibid (SR218) 719 (Brazil).

[144] ibid (SR219) 723 (Fr) and 725 (US). [145] ibid 728–9.

[146] ibid (SR218) 717 (Den).

of the international community, *will organize a practical system for the punishment of the crime of genocide* which will be implemented by the States that have ratified the convention. It will not be the first time that a convention has been concluded on a matter on which rules of common law already exist. Common law retains its full force for the States which have not signed the convention, but the States parties to the Convention *define and develop the rules of common law* in order to secure certain practical results. (Emphasis added.)[147]

Matters are confused further because the same comparison suggests an element of innovation (as opposed to codification or clarification) in the Convention. It conceived of genocide as a separate offence that was not linked to aggressive war in the way that crimes against humanity were at Nuremberg. This would ensure that genocide could be punished in peace as well as war.[148] This latter position is bolstered by the Ad Hoc Committee's rejection of French efforts to characterize genocide as a type of a crime against humanity.[149]

What emerges from the Ec/Soc records are wide differences of opinion on the legitimacy and wisdom of retaining political groups. Equally diverse is the question of the legal character of the drafting process. It is unclear whether the drafters even saw themselves as making legal—as opposed to political—decisions. And if the decisions had a legal character, less clear still is whether they were codifying pre-existing customary law on genocide, codifying and defining a type of crime against humanity, or innovating and creating a new offence through the treaty process. It is difficult to draw strong conclusions about the overall character of the Ec/Soc effort. Its value as state practice undertaken with *opinio juris* thus is questionable.

The final draft of the Convention

The UN's Sixth (Legal) Committee drafted the final text of the Genocide Convention. Many matters resolved in the Ad Hoc Committee were raised again on a wider scale. France re-introduced its proposals to link genocide to crimes against humanity and to modify it to cover groups organized based on 'opinions.'[150] The Soviets sought again to characterize genocide as 'organically bound up with fascism-Nazism and other similar race theories which preach national and racial hatred, the domination of the so-called higher races and the extermination of the so-called lower races'.[151]

[147] Relations Between the Convention on Genocide on the one hand and the Formulation of the Nurnberg Principles and the Preparation of a Draft Code of Offences Against Peace and Security on the Other—Note by the Secretariat (2 Apr 1948) UN Doc E/AC25/3 7. [148] ibid 6–7.

[149] Ec/Soc Report on Genocide (26 May 1948) UN Doc E/794 4–5.

[150] France: Draft convention on genocide (1 Oct 1948) UN Doc A/C6/211 art 1 ('The crime against humanity known as genocide is an attack on the life of a human group or of an individual as a member of such group, particularly by reason of his nationality, race, religion or opinions.').

[151] 'USSR: Amendments to the draft convention on genocide (E/794)' (4 Oct 1948) UN Doc A/C6/215/Rev1.

Numerous objections, which fell generally into three camps, were raised to including political groups. The Soviets felt that political groups were incompatible with the so-called 'scientific' definition of genocide.[152] Other nations claimed that political groups were difficult to identify and lacked the stability inherent in other categories.[153] The third was a pragmatic view that including political groups would reduce participation in the treaty.[154]

The arguments favouring retention of political groups were equally varied. Cuba's representative pointed out that political opinion could be used as a pretext to destroy racial and religious groups.[155] Ecuador's representative agreed,[156] noting also that there were significant differences between genocide and maintaining public order, that frivolous allegations could be made with any penal provision, and that it was incumbent on courts to ascertain the difference.[157] The US argued that political groups could be identified, pointing out that the Nazis identified and destroyed Communists and that the Allies identified the Nazi party for the purpose of outlawing it.[158]

The Sixth Committee initially voted 29 in favour[159] to 13 against[160] to retain political groups, with 9 abstentions.[161] This provision went unchanged for much of the remaining work on the Convention, and political groups appeared in further drafts of the Convention even as of late November 1948.[162] Toward the end of the process, however, the US shifted its position. Although it felt that political groups should be included as a matter of principle 'in a conciliatory spirit and in order to avoid the possibility that the application of the convention to political groups might prevent certain countries from acceding to it... [the US supported deleting] the provisions relating to political groups.'[163] Despite this key concession, the Soviet bloc[164] mysteriously abstained from the final vote deleting

152 Official Records (6th Comm 1948) (SR64) 14 (USSR).

153 ibid (SR69) 58 (Venez) (summarizing positions of states).

154 ibid (SR65) 21 (Venez) (arguing that many 'States would not accept such limitations to their right to suppress internal disturbances.'); ibid (SR69) 58 (Sweden) (noting that the value of the Convention was linked to the number of ratifications and that the less controversial definition would facilitate that goal).

155 ibid (SR65) 23 (Cuba).

156 ibid (SR74) 100 (Ecuador).

157 ibid 101 (Ecuador).

158 ibid (SR74) 101 (US).

159 Netherlands, New Zealand, Norway, Panama, Paraguay, Philippines, Saudi Arabia, Siam, Sweden, Syria, Turkey, UK, USA, Yemen, Australia, Bolivia, Burma, Canada, Chile, China, Cuba, Denmark, Ecuador, El Salvador, France, Haiti, Iceland, India, and Luxembourg. ibid (SR75) 115.

160 Poland, Ukrainian SSR, Union of South Africa, USSR, Uruguay, Venezuela, Argentina, Belgium, Brazil, Belorussian SSR, Czechoslovakia, Dominican Republic, and Iran. ibid.

161 Nicaragua, Pakistan, Peru, Yugoslavia, Afghanistan, Egypt, Ethiopia, Greece, and Lebanon. ibid.

162 Draft Resolutions and draft convention on genocide proposed by the Drafting Committee (23 Nov 1948) UN Doc A/C6/289 art II.

163 Official Records (6th Comm 1948) (SR128) 661–2 (US).

164 The precise degree of Soviet influence on the drafting process is debated. *Cf* Schabas 160 (2009) (noting variety in voting patterns and suggesting that removal of political groups was not 'some Soviet machination.').

political groups,[165] which was approved 22 in favour[166] to 6 against,[167] with 12 abstentions.[168]

The basis for the Soviet abstention is unclear in the records but may be connected to subsequent proceedings on Article VI, which at that point contained no reference to an international tribunal. On its face, the US concession on political groups was meant to ensure wider participation in the treaty.[169] It also may have been a bargaining chip elsewhere. After the vote on political groups, the US immediately proposed reconsideration of Article VI, suggesting that an international tribunal might be more palatable now that political groups were removed from the Convention.[170] Following debate and vigorous opposition from the Soviet bloc, Article VI was amended to refer to a not-yet-existing international criminal court.[171]

The final vote on the draft General Assembly Resolution and final text of the Convention[172] was approved 30 in favour to 0 against.[173] Eight states abstained.[174] Only the UK representative explained his abstention, attributing it solely to constitutional issues in Parliament.[175] It is likely that the Soviet bloc persisted in its dissatisfaction with amended Article VI.

The draft resolution and final text of the Convention were then transmitted to the General Assembly. Further debate in that body was spurred largely by the USSR, which proposed amendments to add cultural genocide and to link genocide to Nazi/Fascist ideology. It also sought to delete the reference to an international criminal court in Article VI.[176] The Soviet proposals were rejected, and a separate amendment by Venezuela[177] was withdrawn.[178] None of the proposed amendments or debate in the General Assembly addressed political groups or other collectives covered by the Convention.[179] The Convention subsequently was unanimously approved, with even the USSR voting in favour.[180]

[165] ibid (SR128) 663–4.

[166] Union of South Africa, UK, USA, Uruguay, Venezuela, Afghanistan, Argentina, Australia, Belgium, Brazil, Canada, Denmark, Dominican Republic, Egypt, Greece, India, Iran, Mexico, Pakistan, Peru, and Syria. ibid.

[167] Burma, Chile, China, Ecuador, Netherlands, and Philippines. ibid.

[168] USSR, Yugoslavia, Belorussian SSR, Cuba, Czechoslovakia, France, Luxembourg, New Zealand, Norway, Poland, Sweden, and Ukrainian SSR. ibid.

[169] ibid (SR133) 704 (US).

[170] ibid (SR129) 669 (US).

[171] ibid (SR130) 684.

[172] ibid (SR132) 701.

[173] Burma, Canada, Chile, China, Columbia, Cuba, Denmark, Dominican Republic, Egypt, France, Greece, India, Luxembourg, Mexico, Netherlands, New Zealand, Norway, Peru, Siam, Sweden, Syria, USA, Uruguay, Venezuela, Afghanistan, Argentina, Australia, Belgium, Bolivia, and Brazil. ibid.

[174] Belorussian SSR, Czechoslovakia, Poland, Ukrainian SSR, Union of South Africa, USSR, UK, and Yugoslavia. ibid.

[175] ibid (SR132) 701–2 (UK).

[176] 'Union of Soviet Socialist Republics: amendments to the draft convention on the prevention and punishment of genocide proposed by the Sixth Committee' (5 Dec 1948) UN Doc A/760.

[177] UN Doc A/770.

[178] 69 Journal of the General Assembly (10 Dec 1948) 5–6.

[179] ibid.

[180] UNGA Res 260-A (III) (9 Dec 1948) UN Doc A/810; 69 Journal of the General Assembly (10 Dec 1948) 6 (adopted 56–0, 2 absences—Costa Rica and El Salvador).

As with the two prior drafts, no clear consensus emerges on whether the drafting of the Convention was a legal or a political exercise. As noted above, numerous positions were advanced on all sides. Deeper questions involving its intersection with pre-existing law went unresolved. For example, most states opposed all efforts to link the Convention to the Nuremberg proceedings and crimes against humanity.[181] A smaller number expressed the contrary view.[182] The view of many was that a convention was required to make any pre-existing norm against genocide legally enforceable.[183]

There was undeniable pressure to finish quickly. 'Having regard to the troubled state of the world, it was essential that the convention be adopted as soon as possible, before the memory of the barbarous crimes which had been committed faded from the minds of men.'[184] At the end of the day, it appears that the Sixth Committee tacitly adopted the suggestion of the Iranian representative, which was to conclude a Convention on which agreement was possible and to postpone the more difficult issues for a later time.[185]

Conclusions on the drafting records

In the final analysis, it is important to understand the debate over political groups in its wider context. Initial drafts of the Convention included provisions on cultural genocide and mandatory jurisdiction before an international penal body. It is easy to understand the reticence toward including political groups when state officials could be prosecuted in an international forum for destroying the 'culture' of a political group—confiscating and destroying copies of Mein Kampf among Neo-Nazis, for example. The fact that broad liability either was present or lurking in the immediate background goes a long way to explaining the reluctance to covering political groups.

It is fair to characterize the exclusion of political groups as a negotiated political compromise, rather than a theoretical determination that they were unsuitable. This impacts the legal significance of the exclusion. Practices adopted for political expediency (as opposed to legal obligation) do not create enforceable rules of customary international law.[186] There is no evidence

[181] Official Records (6th Comm 1948) (SR109) 489 (Venezuela), 490 (US), 490–1 (Uruguay), 491 (Egypt), 491 (Cuba), 91 (Peru), 492 (UK), 492–3 (Iran), 492 (Ecuador), 494 (Brazil), 495–6 (Lebanon), 496 (Dominican Republic), and 496 (El Salvador).

[182] ibid (SR109) 492 (Syria), 494 (Greece), 497 (Czechoslovakia), and 501–3 (France).

[183] *Cf* (SR67) 40 (UK) (noting that Article I of the Ad Hoc Draft 'reaffirm[ed] in a legislative text, in a written convention, the existence of a crime already known in international law....'); ibid (SR74) 104 (USSR) (noting that if Resolution 96(I) had settled the matter, there would be no need to spend two years drafting a convention); ibid (SR74) 107 (Iran) (purpose of Resolution 96(I) was 'not to give a definition of genocide, but to denounce the extermination of human groups, political as well as national, racial or religious.').

[184] ibid (SR63) 5 (US).

[185] ibid (SR66) 31 (Iran).

[186] *Flores v Southern Peru Copper Corp* (2003) 406 F3d 65 (US Ct App (2d Cir)) 80.

of consensus either *for* or *against* political genocide as a matter of *lex lata* in 1948. The Secretary-General overtly presented the choice of which groups to include as a political matter, which seems consistent with the overall drafting process.

But even if the decision to exclude political groups did constitute state practice in 1948, it cannot be so-taken today. Much has changed in the past 60 years. It would be folly to suggest that states are locked into historic positions taken while negotiating the genocide treaty. The actual *practice* in the intervening years for the vast majority of states is in the opposite direction—even for those states that initially supported the inclusion of political groups. What states *wanted* or *hoped for* in the Convention is far less important than what states *actually did* in their subsequent practice *inter se*. As shown below, few states today actually 'live' the convictions of the view that political groups are protected 'as such' from genocide.

Domestic legislation on genocide

Domestic legislation on genocide can evidence state practice if undertaken with *opinio juris*.[187] But the motives for enactment must be considered carefully. As noted previously, the Genocide Convention obligates states party to make genocide an offence under domestic law. Accordingly, domestic legislation on genocide implements a treaty obligation, which renders legislative enactments less clear as recognitions of *separate* international obligations. Where legislation broadens the text of the Convention, however, two things are possible. Either the expanded view is purely a matter of domestic province, or the practice represents belief in a wider *international* obligation.

For the purpose of comprehensively analysing state practice, domestic legislation from 84 states was reviewed in order to ascertain whether groups beyond the four categories enumerated in the Convention are covered. These laws are summarized in Table I of Appendix A. The legislative practice of the 84 states whose statutory provisions were available for review reveals the following:

- 11 states overtly recognize political groups in their domestic legislation on genocide;[188]
- 9 states recognize a 'broad form' conception of genocide (groups based on 'any arbitrary criterion');[189] and

[187] Simma (n 8) 306.

[188] Bangladesh, Cambodia, Columbia, Costa Rica, Côte d'Ivoire, Ecuador, Ethiopia, Lithuania, Panama, Poland, and Slovenia. Appendix A, Table I.

[189] Belarus, Burkina Faso, Canada, Congo (DR), Estonia, Finland, France, Latvia, and Romania. See Appendix A, Table I. This broad definition links to early critiques of the Convention. Drost 125 (1959) ('genocide in its most serious form is the deliberate destruction of physical life of individual human beings by reason of their membership in *any human collectivity* as such.') (Emphasis added.)

- 64 states adopt the definition embodied in the Convention and protect only racial, ethnic, religious and national groups.[190]

Statistically, the states covering political genocide are far outnumbered by those that do not. States overtly recognizing political groups form approximately 13 per cent of the sample pool. When the seven 'broad form' states are added (approximately 11 per cent), the total approximates 24 per cent—nevertheless a significant minority. The remaining 76 per cent follow the definition in the Convention. Almost all major powers fall into the latter category. Only one of the five permanent members of the Security Council (France) falls within the 24 per cent minority grouping. Canada and France are the only major western powers to cover political groups. The remaining states that cover political groups tend to be smaller, developing nations in South America, Eastern Europe and Asia.

The lack of uniformity and consensus indicates that state legislative practice is insufficient to demonstrate a legal norm against political genocide. But there is a clear minority view that political groups can be identified and protected. The lack of geographic cohesion among states taking the minority position indicates that this view does not constitute any sort of regional custom. It may, however, be evidence of an emergent legal norm that has yet to achieve a critical mass of international consensus.

Domestic case law

Decisions from municipal courts can constitute state practice.[191] Such pronouncements do not directly bind states but can evidence custom and general principles as applied by state organs.[192] The character of the decision must be taken into account, and not all domestic law has international application.[193] Historically, domestic courts have provided an important forum for the prosecution of genocide. The earliest criminal trials for genocide took place in domestic courts in Poland,[194] and the Convention itself contemplated domestic enforcement.[195] There have been several domestic prosecutions for genocide[196]

[190] Appendix A, Table I. [191] Simma (n 8) 306. [192] ibid 307.

[193] *Cf Erdemovic (AC)* [1997] ICTY ¶2 (Cassese J dissenting) ('notions, legal constructs and terms of art upheld in international law... cannot be mechanically imported into international criminal proceedings.'); *United States v Noriega* (1990) 746 FSupp 1506 (US Dist Ct (SD Fla)) 1525–8 (presumption against extra-territorial application of domestic criminal laws).

[194] *Greiser* [1946] 13 LRTWC 70 (Pol Sup Nat'l Trib); *Goeth* [1947] 7 LRTWC 1 (Pol Sup Nat'l Trib); *Hoess* [1947] 7 LRTWC 11 (Pol Sup Nat'l Trib).

[195] Genocide Convention arts V-VI. The international prosecution mentioned in the Convention legally was a dead letter at the time, as no such forum yet existed. ibid art VI.

[196] Related jurisprudence on genocide creating civil liability in tort, *Kadic v Karadzic* (1995) 70 F3d 232 (US Ct App (2d Cir)), or adjudicating inter-state obligations, *Application of Genocide Convention—Jurisdiction* [1996] ICJ 595, is not discussed here.

involving Nazi atrocities[197] and the genocides in Rwanda[198] and the former Yugoslavia.[199]

For present purposes, the more important cases are instances where domestic and regional courts applied a broader conception of genocide during a criminal trial. Cases involving Bangladesh, Cambodia, Equatorial Guinea, Romania, Estonia, Ethiopia, and Spain, as well as a proceeding in the IACHR, stand out in this regard. To the extent that these cases legitimately recognize and apply a broader definition of genocide that covers political groups, such jurisprudence could evidence relevant state practice on political genocide under customary international law.

Note that prosecution need not be 'successful' in order to establish state practice. Provided that the legal principle underlying the trial is clear and applied through legitimate adjudicative mechanisms, it suffices as state practice undertaken with the requisite *opinio juris*, even if a particular case results in acquittal.

Bangladesh-India-Pakistan

In the early 1970s, East Pakistan (now Bangladesh) broke ties with West Pakistan in order to establish a separate state. Over one million Bengalis were killed during the ensuing nine-month military conflict.[200] The conflict ended when India intervened militarily and captured 93,000 Pakistani soldiers in East Pakistan.[201] Most POWs were returned pursuant to the Indo-Pakistani Agreement of August 1973.[202] But 195 Pakistanis who were the object of genocide charges in Bangladesh were not released. Bangladesh sought to prosecute the alleged offenders under a special law that covered genocide and other offences.[203] The definition of genocide was broader than the Convention in two respects. It rendered the prohibited acts illustrative, rather than enumerative. More importantly, it added 'political groups' as a protected category.[204]

[197] *Demjanjuk (SC)* [1993] Crim App No 347/88 (Isr Sup Ct) (reversing conviction due to new evidence calling into question accused's identity as concentration camp guard nicknamed 'Ivan the Terrible' at the former Treblinka concentration camp); *Eichmann (AC)* [1961] 36 ILR 277 (Isr Sup Ct) (affirming conviction and death sentence for genocide against a key architect of Nazi 'Final Solution' for Jews in Europe).

[198] *Munyeshyaka* [1998] 1 YB-IHRL 598 (Fr Ct Cass) (reinstating genocide charges in France). See also MA Drumbl, 'Law and Atrocity: Settling Accounts in Rwanda' (2005) 31 Ohio NU LR 41 (genocide in Rwandan domestic courts and gacaca tribal systems).

[199] *Jorgic (TC)* [1997] 2 StE 8/96 (Ger Dist Ct) (guilty on 11 counts of genocide in former Yugoslavia); *Jorgic (AC)* [1999] 2 BvR 1290/99 (Ger Fed Const Ct) (merging 11 genocide convictions into a single count but affirming life sentence). Additional cases are detailed in WA Schabas, 'National Courts Finally Begin to Prosecute Genocide—the "Crime of Crimes"' (2003) 1 Oxford JICJ 39.

[200] R Jahan, 'The Bengalis of East Pakistan' in Porter 256, 257 (1982).

[201] HS Levie, 'Legal Aspects of the Continued Detention of the Pakistani Prisoners of War by India' (1973) 67 AJIL 512, 514.

[202] HS Levie, 'Indo-Pakistani Agreement' (1974) 68 AJIL 95, 96–7.

[203] Bangladesh International Crimes (Tribunals) Act (19 Jul 1973) art 1(2).

[204] ibid art 3(2)(c): 'Genocide: meaning and including any of the following acts committed with intent to destroy, in whole or in part, a national, ethnic, racial, religious or political group, such as....'

The allegations of genocide, at least against a religious group, appear well-founded. One author notes 'a strong prima facie case that the crime of genocide was committed against the group comprising the Hindu population of East Bengal.'[205] Pakistan subsequently instituted ICJ proceedings against India, seeking the immediate release of its citizens. Its request for preliminary relief was denied.[206] In late 1973, Pakistan discontinued the ICJ proceedings and agreed to try the alleged offenders domestically,[207] although by all accounts trials never took place.

Less clear is the position of the parties on Bangladesh's intentions to try offenders for genocide against political groups. It does not appear that the substantive definition in Bangladesh's statute was raised in the ICJ. The fact that India held the POWs for later extradition to Bangladesh for trial could reflect tacit support by India of the decision to include political groups as a category, assuming that extradition requires double-criminality by both the requesting and requested states. An equally plausible explanation, however, is that India believed the attacks, which concentrated on East Bengali Hindus, were aimed at a religious group 'as such'.[208] The fact that Pakistan may have identified Hindus as political opponents does not alter the religious focus of the targeting, which would be sufficient to establish responsibility under the Convention.

The evidence is inconclusive. The position of Bangladesh is known, but that of India and Pakistan is not. Pakistan's failure to raise the substantive content of the Bangladeshi law in preliminary proceedings hardly constitutes assent to its validity, particularly where the case was discontinued so quickly. Likewise, India could have detained the POWs on grounds of genocide against Hindus—a religious group under the Convention. The most that can be said is that Bangladesh took the view that political groups are protected, which appears unaltered today.[209]

Cambodia

A domestic trial in 1979 against two former Khmer Rouge leaders in Cambodia also involved charges of genocide. Over 2 million died during the four years that Pol Pot held power.[210] Some of these atrocities clearly involve genocide under the Convention. There is significant evidence that the Khmer Rouge targeted Muslim Chams, indigenous Vietnamese and other minority groups as well as

205 Kuper, *Political Use* 79–80 (1985).

206 *Pakistani POWs* [1973] ICJ 1.

207 Levie, *Agreement* (n 202) 96 n 12.

208 One also might speculate that India also could have been motivated by political retribution. During the drafting of the Convention 25 years earlier, Pakistan accused India of genocide against Muslims during the partition of East and West Pakistan from India. Official Records (6th Comm 1948) (SR 63) 10–11 (Pak). India vigorously denied the charges. ibid (SR64) 15–16 (Ind).

209 See Appendix A, Table I.

210 Study (Second) on Genocide (2 Jul 1985) UN Doc E/CN4/Sub2/1985/6 ¶ 24 n 17.

Buddhist monks,[211] all of whom qualify as national, ethnic or religious groups under the Convention. Nevertheless, the vast majority of killings took place on political and social grounds in an effort to eliminate intellectuals and other similar classes in favour of a new society of peasant workers.[212]

The 1979 trial took place *in absentia* under a special law that charged the former leaders with acts of genocide, which were defined as:

> planned massacres of groups of innocent people; expulsion of inhabitants of cities and villages in order to concentrate them and force them to do hard labour in conditions leading to their physical and mental destruction; wiping out religion; destroying political, cultural and social structures and family and social relations.[213]

Pol Pot and Ieng Sary were both found guilty of genocide.[214] The verdict was more symbolic than substantive, as neither accused was in custody. In any event, the definition of 'genocide' at issue bore little resemblance to the Convention. Rather, it seems the term was used as a proxy for mass murder and the intentional destruction of the nation's economic and cultural life. As state practice on an expanded concept of genocide, the judgment and Decree Law No 1 offer little value.

More authoritative is the position Cambodia recently took in its 1999 proposal on what ultimately became the joint UN-Cambodia special tribunal on other Khmer Rouge offences.[215] Cambodia's initial proposal sought to enlarge the enumeration of protected groups within the concept of genocide to include: 'wealth, level of education, sociological environment (urban/rural), *allegiance to a political system or regime* (old people/new people), social class or social category (merchant, civil servant, etc)' (emphasis added).[216] The proposal was dropped in favour of covering only the groups in the Convention[217] out of concern that the broader proposal would violate the principles of legality.[218]

Equatorial Guinea

In 1979, deposed tyrant Francisco Macias was tried by a domestic court in Equatorial Guinea for offences against political opponents and others throughout

[211] Report of Experts on Cambodia (16 Mar 1999) UN Doc A/53/850 ¶¶63–4. The Commission left for the tribunal whether the Khmer Rouge could be charged with genocide for atrocities against Khmers as a 'national' group. ibid ¶65.

[212] *Cf* Constitution of Democratic Kampuchea (5 Jan 1976) c 1 art 1 ('The State of Kampuchea is a State of the people, workers, peasants and all other Kampuchean labourers'), c 5 art 3 ('This new [State] culture is absolutely opposed to the corrupt, reactionary culture of the various oppressive classes and that of colonialism and imperialism in Kampuchea'), c 5 art 5 (providing legislative representation for peasants, 'labourers and working people' and the revolutionary army only) and c 7 art 10 ('Dangerous activities in opposition to the people's State must be condemned to the highest degree. Other cases are subject to constructive re-education in the framework of the State's or people's organizations').

[213] Decree Law No 1 (Cambodia) (15 Jul 1979) in De Nike 45 (2000).

[214] *Verdict of the Phnom Penh Revolutionary Tribunal* (Aug 1979).

[215] This was detailed in Chapter 4 in connection with 'auto-genocide'.

[216] Schabas 166 (2009).

[217] Cambodian Genocide Law (10 Aug 2001).

[218] Schabas 166–7 (2009).

his brutal 10-year regime. Although Equatorial Guinea never ratified the Genocide Convention, the indictment included charges of genocide. Proceedings were observed and reported on by a representative of the International Commission of Jurists.[219] There was some question over whether the charge embodied genocide under the Convention or a formulation imported from the Spanish Penal Code, which technically had been repealed upon independence in 1968. At the time, Article 137 bis of the Spanish Penal Code substituted 'social' groups for 'racial' groups in the Convention, which arguably is much broader.[220] Macias was found guilty of genocide and other crimes and was executed five hours later.[221]

The value of the Macias trial as state practice on a broader formation of genocide is thin. Not only is the applicable law unclear, the international observer concluded that the specific *mens rea* of genocide had not been proved, which means that a conviction ought not to have entered for genocide irrespective of the groups covered.[222] Dr Artucio also noted numerous procedural irregularities, not the least of which was the failure of defence counsel to make certain important legal arguments (albeit under unpopular and difficult circumstances).[223] Under the circumstances, the Macias trial cannot be taken as legitimate state practice supporting political genocide.

Romania

Domestic trials on genocide also transpired after the fall of the brutal Communist regime in Romania in 1989. Former President Nicolae Ceausescu and his wife, Deputy Prime Minister Elena Ceausescu, were tried 48 hours after the five-day revolution succeeded. Charges of genocide were premised upon 60,000 killings during Ceausescu's dictatorship.[224] Not surprisingly under the circumstances, the Ceausescus were convicted of genocide (as well as undermining the state and national economy). They were executed two days later.[225] Other associates and family members also were charged (and convicted) of genocide. These charges addressed the government's brutal and lethal response to the revolution[226] as well as historical conduct perpetrated during the Ceausescu regime.[227]

Massacres during the Ceausescu regime clearly were driven by political ideology and imposed to eliminate political opposition. The trials thus raise the spectre of political genocide as a legitimate separate offence. Controlling Romanian law appears to support such charges. It defined genocide as a prohibited act (murder, etc) committed 'for the purpose of completely or partially destroying *a collectivity* or a national, ethnic, racial, or religious group...' (emphasis added).[228]

219 Artucio i–iii (1979). 220 ibid 27–30. 221 ibid 54–5. 222 ibid 31–2.
223 ibid 29, 55–9.
224 A Nitoiu, 'Accountability for State-Sponsored Human Rights Abuses in Eastern Europe and the Soviet Union' (1992) 12 BC Third World LJ 241, 254 n 66. 225 ibid 254–5.
226 A Neier, 'Peaceful Transitions to Constitutional Democracy' (1998) 19 Cardozo LR 1953, 1978. 227 Nitoiu (n 224) 255–7.
228 Romanian Socialist Republic Penal Code (1976) Special Part art 356.

The distinct references to 'collectivity' were enumerated again for each prohibited act as well.[229] The text implies a definition of genocide covering groups under the Convention as well as a separate 'collectivity,' which presumably includes political groups.

The chief difficulty in relying upon the Romanian prosecutions of the Ceausescus is the unmistakable character of those proceedings as 'show' trials. In five short days, the Ceausescus went from ruling Romania to the firing squad. Their trial started within two days of the revolution's success—hardly time for gun barrels (let alone tempers) to cool. Related trials of associates and other family members are equally suspect.[230] The rush to judgment, together with the absence of procedural mechanisms guaranteeing a fair trial,[231] suggests that the trials were more political retribution than legitimate exercises of legal process. Under the circumstances, even if the applicable legal principles supported a broader conception of political genocide, the procedural irregularities weigh against relying on the Romanian trials as legitimate state practice.

Estonia

Estonia defines genocide as a type of crime against humanity involving 'deliberate acts whose aim it is to fully or partially eradicate a group, based on national, ethnic, racial or religious distinction, *which is resisting an occupation regime, or any other social group*...' (emphasis added).[232] There have been some Estonian prosecutions involving attacks on resistance groups and deportations during World War II. These trials achieved mixed results. Proceedings were complicated by the facts that the offences dated back to the 1940s and many accused were in their 80s and 90s at trial.[233] Apart from pragmatic difficulties, there was jurisprudential confusion over both the substantive offences being applied and the identity of the 'group' at issue.

The Estonian conception of genocide has a strong analogy to the French conception of crimes against humanity. The French definition ensures that crimes against humanity covered members of the French Resistance, who might otherwise have been excluded.[234] The Estonian language covering a group 'resisting an occupation regime' is remarkably similar, and in many trials no distinction was drawn between crimes against humanity and genocide.[235]

[229] ibid art 356(a)–(e). [230] Nitoiu (n 224) 255–7.

[231] *Cf* ICC Statute art 67 (rights of the accused).

[232] Estonian Criminal Code (2001) art 61(1).

[233] L Malksoo, 'Soviet Genocide? Communist Mass Deportations in the Baltic States and International Law' (2001) 14 Leiden JIL 757, 773–80.

[234] *Barbie* (1985) 78 ILR 125 (Fr Ct Cass) 136 ('Jews and members of the Resistance persecuted in a systematic manner in the name of State practicing a policy of ideological supremacy, the former by reason of their membership of a racial or religious community, the latter by reason of their opposition to that policy, can equally be the victims of crimes against humanity').

[235] Malksoo (n 233) 780.

It also is clear that many cases involved deportations of Jews and other groups that are protected under the Convention.[236] If a targeted group qualified as both a political group as well as a religious, etc group, the political characteristic is not dispositive to the analysis. The fact that a protected group has additional characteristics is irrelevant.[237] It remains genocide whether Estonian Jews were targeted because they were Jews or because Jews were identified with a political ideology resisting the Nazi puppet government. The few successful convictions for genocide thus can be supported equally based on the victims' classification in enumerated groups.

Likewise with later cases involving Soviet-era repression. In a 2000 decision, the Estonian Supreme Court indicated that 'a group initiating resistance against an occupying regime as noted in [s 61] of the Estonian Criminal Code, is a feature of an offence of genocide, not a crime against humanity'.[238] There was significant confusion over which crime the defendant had been convicted of, however, as well as the role of Nuremberg precedent and international law. The jurisprudence in Estonia was sufficiently confusing to prompt Estonian lawmakers subsequently to revise the Estonian Criminal Code to more clearly distinguish between the two offences.[239]

The judicial confusion over the relevant legislation, together with sketchy evidence of specific intent against the target groups, indicates that the offences are best 'understood as convictions of "crimes against humanity," and not of "genocide."'[240] For these reasons, the Estonian jurisprudence cannot be relied upon as clear state practice in support of a separate offence of political genocide.

Ethiopia

Domestic trials in Ethiopia may demonstrate the ongoing application of political genocide as a separate offence. Trials began in the mid-1990s for thousands charged with atrocities in the 'Red Terror' of the brutal Mengistu regime that ruled for 17 years.[241] Ethiopian law has covered political groups in its domestic formulation on genocide since 1957.[242] But it is not clear that Ethiopian prosecutors have availed themselves of the opportunity to prosecute offenders for political genocide. In November 1993, perhaps motivated by Ethiopia's ratification of the ICCPR five months earlier, Ethiopian prosecutors took the position that they would only prosecute members of the deposed regime 'under those

[236] ibid 773–80.

[237] *Nahimana (TC)* [2003] ICTR ¶969 (association of Tutsi with political opponents could not 'negate the genocidal animus' against Tutsis as an ethnic group).

[238] *Paulov Judgment* [2000] Case No 3-1-1-31-00 (Sup Ct Estonia) ¶5.

[239] ibid ¶A6.

[240] Malksoo (n 233) 780.

[241] JV Mayfield, 'The prosecution of War Crimes and Respect for Human Rights: Ethiopia's Balancing Act' (1995) 9 Emory ILR 553, 558–62, 567.

[242] Penal Code of the Empire of Ethiopia of 1957 art 281.

rules of international humanitarian law which are beyond any doubt part of customary law'.[243]

On its face, this would seem to exclude cases of political genocide charged as a separate offence. Later jurisprudence from the Ethiopian Federal Court clarified that the Ethiopian law on genocide was in harmony with international law on genocide because it was no less broad and thus complied with the minimum requirements of the Genocide Convention.[244] Ultimately, twenty-five out of fifty-five former government officials were convicted of atrocities, including genocide perpetrated against opposition political groups.[245]

The trials to date were not limited to attacks on political opponents. Ethnic Amhara, for example, were targeted as hostile to the ruling regime.[246] This makes the value of the trials less significant as state practice on political genocide. The trials are problematic in other respects as well. Legitimate concerns exist about excessive pre-trial detention without charge, trials in absentia and infringements upon the right to counsel and the ability to prepare a defence.[247] Such concerns do not here warrant a total disregard of the Ethiopian jurisprudence (as was the case with Romania, discussed above). Nevertheless, it does give the practice less weight than proceedings conducted with the full panoply of fair trial rights.

The IACHR (Diaz v Columbia)

Decisions from human rights tribunals like the Inter-American Court of Human Rights (IACHR) are not state practice per se. But they are persuasive authorities on the content of state practice and customary international law. Political genocide was presented squarely in the *Diaz* case, where the petitioners alleged genocide against them as a political group.[248] The case was not a criminal trial, but rather a civil claim against Columbia for violations of human rights under the ACHR. It merits discussion as one of the few judicial decisions overtly dealing with political genocide.

The court considered that Resolution 96(I) included political groups. It noted, however, that subsequent instruments (the Genocide Convention, the ICTY Statute and the like) excluded them.[249] The court held that political genocide was not separately prohibited under customary international law. Although the claim presented

> a situation which shares many characteristics with the occurrence of genocide and might be understood in common parlance to constitute genocide...the facts alleged do not

[243] Mayfield (n 241) 572.

[244] *Hailemariam Judgment* [2007] Crim File No 1/87 (Fed High Ct Ethiopia) ¶¶H1–H2.

[245] FK Tiba, 'The Mengistu Genocide Trial in Ethiopia' (2007) 5 JICJ 513, 519–20.

[246] A Botha, 'Genocide perpetrators to die' News24 (12 Oct 2004) (death sentences and prison term for genocide against ethnic minority).

[247] Mayfield (n 241) 575–92; Amnesty International 'Human rights trials and delayed justice' (29 Jul 1996) AI Index AFR 25/011/1996.

[248] *Diaz* [IACHR 1997] OEA/SerL/V/II95 ¶23.

[249] ibid ¶24.

tend to establish, as a matter of law, that this case falls within the current definition of genocide provided by international law.[250]

The decision was brief but significant. The IACHR ruled against the broader conception almost out of hand—disposing of the issue in a few short paragraphs. The case related to admissibility, not substance, which suggests that not even a prima facie case of political genocide was cognizable. Shortly thereafter, however, Spain's Audencia Nacional reached precisely the opposite conclusion.

Spain (Pinochet)

As discussed previously, the Spanish Audencia Nacional expressly recognized political genocide in *Pinochet*. Despite the deliberate exclusion of political groups in the Convention, the court held that 'silence is not perforce equivalent to exclusion. Whatever intent the drafters of the text may have had, the Convention takes on life by virtue of the successive signatures and accessions to the treaty....'[251] The court expressly justified its broad holding under the Genocide Convention, even if technically it was interpreting the Spanish Criminal Code in the context of extradition.[252]

The Audencia Nacional's decision can be taken as state practice in support of political genocide. The decision clearly articulated a belief that limiting the Genocide Convention to its strict text 'would be unreasonable in the logic of the system'.[253] The court demonstrated *opinio juris* by holding that an *international* prohibition on genocide required the result.

That said, whether or not it is wise to protect all 'differentiated' groups, the Audencia Nacional's methodology is highly suspect. The decision appears result-driven and more a product of wishful thinking about what international law should require than a cogent analysis of the Convention's meaning under customary international law. Whatever the authority of the decision within the Spanish legal system, it has little interpretive value for purposes of international law, although it does constitute state practice with *opinio juris* for Spain.

No other state has approved of the methodology underlying the case or the result in the decision. Indeed, the available evidence of state practice in response is that the proposition was rejected. The British government refused to extradite on the genocide charges as articulated by the Audencia Nacional:[254]

Senator Pinochet is also charged, under Spanish law, with genocide, and the CPS advised, on behalf of the Spanish Government, that murder is also disclosed by the request. The Secretary of State does not consider that the contents of the extradition request satis-

[250] ibid ¶25.

[251] *Pinochet: Spanish Jurisdiction* [Audencia Nacional 1998] in Brody and Ratner 95, 103 (2000).

[252] ibid 103.

[253] ibid.

[254] Extradition was authorized on torture charges, however. *Ex Parte Pinochet (Pinochet III)* [1999] 2 WLR 827 (UK HL).

fied the definition of an extradition crime under section 2 of the Act in respect of these offences, and has therefore not included them in the authority to proceed.[255]

The Home Office's response can be taken in one of two ways. The first is overt state practice rejecting political genocide as incompatible with controlling international law. The second is a more limited decision on grounds of double criminality in the extradition context. On the whole, the better view is to limit Britain's response to double criminality. The alternative requires inferring wider implications from a decision equally justified on narrower grounds. It also seems that such a pronouncement, which would impact any number of states with a broader understanding of genocide (including France and Canada) would be stated more clearly, if it truly was the British intention to take a position against the recognition of political genocide in this context.

In any event, higher courts in Spain later rejected the proposition that political groups fall within the concept of genocide under Spanish law. In the *Scilingo* appeal—which involved the conviction in Spain of an Argentinian naval officer for violations of international criminal law in Argentina—the Spanish Supreme Court held that political groups were not covered by the Genocide Convention, noting the near unanimity of doctrine on the subject.[256]

Ratification of the Genocide Convention

International agreements constitute state practice and contribute to the development of customary international law.[257] This requires evidence of *opinio juris* in the drafting and ratification process—that the treaty embodies or declares all or part of a separate obligation of customary international law.[258] *Opinio juris* can be extracted not only from the treaty text, drafting records, and the object and purpose of the instrument, but also from the positions taken by states as they formally recognize their treaty obligations.[259] At ratification, states often go 'on the record' with respect to treaty obligations. They also comment on practice by other states. This has legal implications not only for the operation of the treaty between states,[260] but also on whether the position in question is legally compatible with the object and purpose of the treaty.[261]

Relevant state practice in connection with the ratification of the Genocide Convention is thin. Most reservations to the Convention involved Article IX, which provided compulsory jurisdiction in the ICJ for disputes between state parties over the treaty. In 1951, the ICJ held that such reservations were compatible

[255] United Kingdom Home Secretary: Response of Her Majesty's Government Regarding the Spanish Extradition Request (9 Dec 1998) ¶14.
[256] *Scilingo* [2005] (Sup Ct Spain) ¶III(A)(6).
[257] *North Sea Continental Shelf* [1969] ICJ 3, 28–9, 37–43.
[258] M Akehurst, 'Custom as a Source of International Law' (1976) 47 BYBIL 1, 49–53.
[259] ibid 49–50.
[260] VCLT arts 20 (reservations), 21 (legal effect of reservations).
[261] *Reservations* [1951] ICJ 15.

with the 'object and purpose' of the Convention.[262] A number of states made reservations to Article IX,[263] though some have withdrawn them in recent years.[264]

Only the US ratified with detailed reservations and understandings. Its so-called 'sovereignty package' included one declaration,[265] two reservations,[266] and five understandings.[267] It was the only party to ratify with an interpretation (Understandings 1, 2 and 4) of Article II on the definition of genocide.[268] Several states objected to US Reservation 2 (that 'nothing in the Convention requires or authorizes legislation or other action by the United States of America prohibited by the Constitution of the United States as interpreted by the United States').[269] These objections were premised on either VCLT Article 27 (that US law did not excuse non-compliance with international obligations),[270] confusion about the US position,[271] or both.[272]

No state objected to the US 'interpretation' of Article II, however. The American understandings took a narrow view of the substantive definition of genocide. They provided that 'intent' meant 'specific intent' to destroy (eg, 'purpose'), that 'part' of a group meant 'substantial part,' that 'mental harm' required *permanent* impairment of mental faculties, and that armed conflict alone could not establish genocidal intent.[273] Although some of these understandings were rejected in later applications of the Convention,[274] many were adopted and applied elsewhere.[275]

[262] ibid 15.

[263] Multilateral Treaties Deposited with the Secretary-General: Genocide Convention (11 Jan 2010) (Algeria, Argentina, Bahrain, Bangladesh, China, India, Malaysia, Montenegro, Morocco, Philippines, Serbia, Singapore, US, Venezuela, Vietnam, and Yemen).

[264] ibid (Albania, Belarus, Bulgaria, Czech Republic, Hungary, Mongolia, Poland, Romania, Russian Federation, Rwanda, Spain, Slovakia, and Ukraine). Serbia and Montenegro added reservations to Article IX. ibid.

[265] The declaration required the President to delay ratification until Congress enacted the corresponding enabling legislation. MN Leich, 'Contemporary Practice of the United States Relating to International Law' (1986) 80 AJIL 612, 613.

[266] The first reservation matched that of many other states and rejected mandatory ICJ jurisdiction under Article IX. The second was more contentious, in that it specified that US obligations under the Convention were secondary to its obligations under the Constitution of the United States (as interpreted by the US). ibid 612.

[267] The understandings provided that: (1) the 'intent to destroy, in whole or in part' in Article II meant the intent to destroy in substantial part; (2) 'mental harm' under Article II(b) meant permanent mental injury resulting from physical bodily intrusion; (3) that extradition would only be granted in accord with the 'double criminality' principle and that the US retained jurisdiction over acts by US nationals; (4) that military force, in and of itself, was insufficient to constitute genocide; and (5) that the US would only participate in an international penal tribunal upon entry into another treaty specifically for that purpose. ibid 612–13.

[268] Multilateral Treaties Deposited with the Secretary-General: Genocide Convention (11 Jan 2010).

[269] ibid (US).

[270] ibid (Denmark, Finland, Greece, Ireland, Norway, Spain, and Sweden).

[271] ibid (Italy and UK).

[272] ibid (Estonia and Netherlands).

[273] ibid (US).

[274] *Stakic (TC)* [2003] ICTY ¶516 and *Musema (TC)* [2000] ICTR ¶157 (mental injury need not be permanent or irremediable) and Elements of Crimes art 6(b) (same in ICC).

[275] *Krstic (AC)* [2004] ICTY ¶¶8–12 ('substantial part' of group); ibid ¶104 (requiring 'specific intent' or 'purpose' to destroy the group); *Nuclear Weapons* [1996] ICJ 227, 240 (requiring specific intent and holding armed conflict alone insufficient to establish genocidal intent).

The lack of opposition is significant. Reservations offending *jus cogens* obligations are incompatible with the object and purpose of a human rights treaty.[276] Presumably another state would have objected if the US reservations altered the core aspects of Article II. This suggests some malleability and room for interpretation of the terms in the Convention itself. Whether this extends to the groups covered is uncertain, however.

No state offered a *wider* view of genocide upon ratification. Consequently, there has been no opportunity for direct response on whether broader provisions are consistent with the object and purpose of the Convention (or with international custom crystallized around the Article II definition). But the issue was presented implicitly in connection with the ratification of the ICC Statute, which required states to enact domestic legislation expressly covering genocide and other ICC offences. As noted previously, the legislation from some states that are now parties to the ICC is broader and covers political groups, which have drawn no objections in that context.[277]

Although hardly dispositive, the lack of objection to an overt practice by twenty states has some significance. It suggests that a broader view of genocide is consistent with the definition of genocide under the treaty, which in turn embodies customary international law on the offence. Put another way, there is no suggestion of any conflict between treaty obligations or obligations *erga omnes*[278] on genocide and the use of domestic law to cast a wider net of protection for political groups.

C. Synthesis and conclusions

State practice

Before a legal norm against political genocide is recognized in state practice, 'the definition of the core norm claiming customary law status and preferably the contours of the norm [must be] widely accepted.'[279] Professor Meron suggests a framework relying upon '[e]mpiric studies of state practice' that analyse: first, the degree to which the articulation of the norm is accepted elsewhere (as recognized by repetition in other instruments); and second, confirmation of that right in national practice, subject to legitimate domestic restrictions on the right.[280] That framework is useful here in comparing genocide to political genocide.

[276] CCPR General Comment No 24 'Reservations Upon Ratification or Accession' (4 Nov 1994) ¶8.

[277] Multilateral Treaties Deposited with the Secretary-General: ICC Statute (11 Jan 2010).

[278] The primary distinction with *obligations erga omnes* is one of standing to assert a violation, as opposed to hierarchy; the relevant inquiry is to whom legal obligations flow. M Matheson, 'Current Development: The Fifty-Eighth Session of the International Law Commission' 101 AJIL 407, 425.

[279] Meron, *Humanitarian Norms* 93 (1989).

[280] ibid 94.

State practice on the Genocide Convention

There are 141 states party to the Genocide Convention.[281] All of these states support, at a minimum, the core definition of the crime in Article II and the protection of racial, national, religious and ethnic groups. There are 51 states not party to the Genocide Convention.[282] Of these, 36 have signed the ICC treaty, 26 of whom also have ratified.[283] (Absent information to the contrary, these 36 states are presumed to support only the four groups covered in the Genocide Convention, as mirrored in the ICC). This leaves only 15 of 192 UN member states[284] that overtly support neither the Convention nor the ICC Statute and have no state practice at all in connection with genocide.

The vast majority of states treat genocide as a crime by way of treaty obligations (either the Convention or the ICC). But those treaty obligations of the 141 states party and 36 ICC participants are mirrored in *separate* obligations prohibiting genocide under customary international law.[285] These other obligations are peremptory norms of *jus cogens*.[286] States can no longer deviate from the substantive obligations imposed by Article II, even though the Convention itself contemplated derogation. The prohibition is absolute in all circumstances—genocide by one party never justifies a response in kind, for example.[287] These customary obligations extend *erga omnes* (to all nations), beyond the reciprocal rights and duties imposed by treaty relationships in respect of the Convention and the ICC.[288]

Groups enumerated in the Convention—racial, ethnic, national and religious—thus are protected from physical and biological destruction on dual grounds, both as a matter of treaty law among 177 states[289] and as a matter of customary international law binding on *all* states. In many respects, the latter obligations have been more important. Apart from its norm-setting contributions and a handful of cases in the ICJ, the Convention has seen little implementing activity in and of itself. In contrast, the customary norms that the Convention represents provided the basis for international prosecutions in the ICTY and ICTR, both of which apply customary international law.[290] The focus

281 Appendix A, Table IV. 282 Appendix A, Table III. 283 ibid.

284 Multilateral Treaties Deposited with the Secretary-General: UN Charter (11 Jan 2010).

285 *Reservations* [1951] ICJ 15, 23 (The 'principles underlying [the Convention] are recognized by civilized nations as binding on States, even without any conventional obligations.').

286 *Barcelona Traction* [1970] ICJ 3, 32; *Application of Genocide Convention—Prov Measures II* [1993] ICJ 325, 440 (Lauterpacht J) ('the prohibition on genocide has long been regarded as one of the few undoubted examples of *jus cogens*').

287 *Application of Genocide Convention—Counter-Claims* [1997] ICJ 243 ¶35.

288 *Application of Genocide Convention—Jurisdiction* [1996] ICJ 595 ¶¶31–2; *Barcelona Traction* [1970] ICJ 3, 32.

289 141 Convention states, plus 36 ICC-only states.

290 *Blaskic (AC)* [2004] ICTY ¶141; Secretary General ICTY Report (3 May 1993) UN Doc S/25704 ¶9 (rules that 'are beyond any doubt part of customary law').

on international custom ensures 'that the problem of adherence of some but not all states to specific conventions does not arise.'[291]

There is almost no state practice that could be regarded as *inconsistent* with the Genocide Convention.[292] A small minority (eight states) deviate somewhat in their domestic legislation. Four states (Bolivia, Nicaragua, Paraguay, and Lithuania) exclude the term corresponding directly to racial groups.[293] Four others (Brazil, Costa Rica, Guatemala, and Liechtenstein) exclude that for ethnic groups.[294] Nicaragua's law also does not mirror the Convention's reference to national groups.[295]

The mere absence of specific terms in domestic legislation does not necessarily suggest state practice in support of a narrower definition that excludes certain groups, however. First, although the wording of texts authenticated in different languages is presumed to have the identical meaning,[296] this alone does not preclude states from using different terminology locally to implement international obligations and accomplish the same goal. Inherent difficulties in ensuring accurate translation—particularly in order to convey complex legal concepts—complicate matters further.[297]

The more likely explanation for the absence of all four groups is that some states conceive of ethnic and racial (and perhaps national) characteristics as legally interchangeable. This view has some legal support in other contexts[298] and is the best reading of the omitted language in context. The only other conclusion would be that deviating states are in breach of their obligations under the Convention, which is hardly compelled by the evidence. Genocide is a *jus cogens* norm[299] to which states cannot claim persistent objector status, even if the other requirements of the persistent objector principle were established.[300] This makes

[291] *Jelisic (TC)* [1999] ICTY ¶61 n 74. *Cf* Sierra Leone Statute art 20(3) (recognizing ICTY and ICTR decisions as persuasive authority).

[292] Obviously, committing genocide is inconsistent with the Convention. There certainly have been instances of that since it came into effect. Inconsistent practice here means disagreement with the contours of the legal obligation (as opposed to decisions to *violate* obligations that are clear).

[293] Appendix A, Table I. [294] Ibid. Liechtenstein substitutes 'a people.'. ibid.

[295] Compare Penal Code (Nicaragua) bk 2 tit 14 art 549 ('un grupo étnico o religioso') with Genocide Convention–Spanish Text art II ('un grupo nacional, étnico, racial, o religioso').

[296] VCLT art 33(3).

[297] *Cf* D Nersessian, 'The Contours of Genocidal Intent: Troubling Jurisprudence from the International Criminal Tribunals' (2002) 37 Texas ILJ 231, 268–75 (2002) (discussing translation issues and meaning of Article II(a) in the context of jurisprudence from the international criminal tribunals and English, Spanish, and French texts of the Genocide Convention).

[298] UNHCR Refugee Handbook ¶68 (race includes 'all kinds of ethnic groups that are referred to as 'races' in common usage. Frequently it will also entail membership of a specific social group of common descent forming a minority within a larger population.') and ¶74 (nationality 'is not to be understood only as 'citizenship.' It refers also to membership of an ethnic or linguistic group and may occasionally overlap with the term "race." ').

[299] *Application of Genocide Convention—Prov Measures II* [1993] ICJ 325, 440.

[300] Hillier 74 (1998) (status requires objection during early stages of rule formation and consistent practice thereafter supporting the objection).

little sense, however, particularly given the equally plausible alternate view that is available to explain the alternative terminology.

State practice on political genocide

The Convention itself is limited to the four enumerated groups. But are the obligations under customary international law likewise so limited? There certainly are cases where customary law develops beyond the textual framework of treaties. This was the case with violations of Common Article III of the Geneva Conventions, which the ICTY determined to have evolved into an international crime.[301] So, too, with the Convention. The treaty contemplated an initial period of effectiveness, allowed states to denounce it, and provided that it would cease operation if a certain number of states withdrew.[302] None of these provisions is consistent with the understanding of genocide today as a *jus cogens* prohibition.[303] The Convention also has since evolved beyond its initial bases of national and territorial jurisdiction to universal enforcement.[304]

The question thus becomes: has international law developed a separate criminal prohibition on political genocide that applies irrespective of the Convention framework? The evidence of state practice discussed above indicates that it has not. The foregoing analysis reveals that the offence simply is not reflected in the practice of most states. The *Asylum* case describes what is *not* sufficient under international law:

> The facts . . . disclose so much uncertainty and contradiction, so much fluctuation and discrepancy in the exercise of . . . [the rule] and in the official views expressed on various occasions, and the practice has been so much influenced by considerations of political expediency in the various cases, that it is not possible to discern in all this any constant or uniform usage, accepted as law, with regard to the alleged rule.[305]

Even under the *broad* view of state practice adopted herein, virtually all case law, domestic legislation and other applicable practice point away from international recognition of a norm prohibiting political genocide as a separate offence. The issue usually is rejected when presented squarely. As noted previously, Great Britain could have recognized Spain's broader conception but declined. The IACHR directly considered the matter but determined that no such offence exists under customary international law.

[301] *Tadic (Jurisdiction—AC)* [1995] ICTY ¶¶128–37.

[302] Genocide Convention arts XIV–XV.

[303] VCLT art 64 (emergent peremptory norms render void inconsistent provisions of existing treaties).

[304] *Eichmann (TC)* [1961] 36 ILR 5 (Isr Dist Ct) 10; Restatement (Third) of Foreign Relations s 404 n 1. This evolution is ongoing. For example, in December 2007 the US amended its genocide law to cover aliens and stateless persons as well as other persons brought into or found in the US, even where the offence itself occurred abroad. Genocide Accountability Act of 2007 s 2.

[305] *Asylum* [1950] ICJ 266, 277.

Spain's Audencia Nacional recognized the concept indirectly by stretching the concept of a 'national' group to cover political victims. Its framework would apply genocide to any 'differentiated' group, much like the 'broad form' domestic legislation discussed above. Although the court genuinely seemed to believe that its position was supported by the Genocide Convention, it remains the lone authority for that view. In any event, the proposition was rejected by a higher Spanish court, which expressly determined that political groups were not covered under this concept.[306]

At most, there may be an *emergent* norm against political genocide 'as such' that some states are beginning to recognize. But there is no majority consensus among states (as represented in their practice) recognizing a separate crime now existing that protects political groups 'as such'. It is not enough for the right at issue to be fundamental and worth upholding on a moral basis. Customary international law derives from agreement established through state practice.[307] Overt consensus on international crimes is critical because (absent treaty language) it is the only way to provide fair notice that the specific conduct in question is criminal. Political genocide simply is not supported as a matter of state practice.

Opinio juris

At most, state practice reveals an emergent norm against political genocide. But practice alone—even a uniform majority practice—is insufficient. There must be a clear link between the practice and legal significance.[308] Here, there is no evidence at all suggesting that the states which criminalize political genocide as a matter of domestic law did so with the requisite *opinio juris*. The absence of documented consensus that the broader domestic formulation is *required* by supervening international obligations is fatal to any claim that political genocide is prohibited today under customary international law.

That said, no state has objected to the broader formulations either, although this alone hardly constitutes *opinio juris* in support of the rule. As noted previously, under some circumstances the failure to object can make a precept binding.[309] But silence equals consent only when a state could have made its views known and failed to do so under circumstances where other states would rely upon the failure to object.[310] No such expectation is warranted here. International law typically

[306] *Scilingo* [2005] (Sup Ct Spain) ¶III(A)(6). [307] VCLT art 53.

[308] *North Sea Continental Shelf* [1969] ICJ 3 ¶76 (The 'acts concerned... [must] evidence... a belief that this practice is rendered obligatory by the existence of a rule of law requiring it.... The States concerned must therefore feel that they are conforming to... a legal obligation. The frequency, or even habitual character of the acts is not in itself enough.').

[309] *Nuclear Weapons* [1996] ICJ 227 ¶67.

[310] Restatement (Third) of Foreign Relations s 102 cmt b (inferring approval when a state acquiesces in another state's acts that affect its rights).

sets *minimum* standards for human rights.[311] States may exceed those minima if they wish. The broader domestic conception of genocide is equally explained as an instance of states voluntarily surpassing the baseline in domestic laws.[312] The absence of international objection simply is of no consequence where the matter is one of domestic province only.

There also have been states with broader conceptions of genocide that later narrowed their laws to mirror the Convention (Portugal[313] and Spain).[314] There is no evidence that any other state objected or raised concerns about these revisions. This is further evidence that the wider formulation is an optional feature of *domestic* law—not an international obligation.

D. Political genocide and the principles of legality

There is no sound basis for recognizing political genocide as a separate offence as a matter of international *lex lata*. The minority practice recognizing the offence is equally justified as a matter of domestic province. Since there is almost no overt practice in support of the proposed norm, the only way to recognize the offence would be to draw a questionable inference from lofty aspirational language in international texts. This would be folly. That there are strong moral, theoretical and even pragmatic justifications for preventing political genocide is of no moment. To indulge the inference is to violate fundamental principles of legality.

The driving force behind the 'long and honourable pedigree' of the legality principles is fundamental fairness to the accused.[315] As applied to acts that were not officially prohibited prior to their commission, *ex post facto* laws are unfair for a number of reasons, including that:

They arbitrarily change the legal consequences and significance of the act after the fact;

They violate the principle that conduct not otherwise prohibited at the time of commission is permissible; and

They punish an accused who had no prior notice of the law and no ability to modify his conduct to comply with it.[316]

[311] *Nicaragua* [1986] ICJ 14 ¶218 ('minimum yardstick' of behaviour); C Beyani, 'The Legal Premises for the International Protection of Human Rights' in Goodwin-Gill and Talmon 22–3 (1999).

[312] Amnesty International takes this view: 'International Criminal Court: The failure of states to enact effective implementing legislation' (1 Sep 2004) AI Index IOR 40/019/2004 6.

[313] Appendix A, Table I.

[314] *Pinochet: Spanish Jurisdiction* [Audencia Nacional 1998] in Brody and Ratner 95, 101–2. The Audencia Nacional clearly disfavoured the preceding legislative activity.

[315] Glueck 74–5 (1946).

[316] ibid 75–84 (discussing issues in context of Nuremberg trials).

The legality principles also prohibit after-the-fact aggravation of the degree of the offence, increased sentences for identical conduct, and alterations of evidentiary rules designed to make it easier to convict.[317]

One cannot simply create a new crime from whole cloth and hold individuals criminally responsible for it. Even the most cogent policy and theoretical arguments must be segregated from the legitimacy of the legal proscription. 'The elements of the formation of rules of general international law—international custom—are not some esoteric invention; rather they provide criteria by which the actual expectations and commitments of States can be tested. International law is about the real policies and commitments of governments, it is not about the incantations of secular or religious morality.'[318]

This is not to suggest that international crimes must derive from treaties. Custom is *not* a disfavoured method of creating law.[319] Indeed, custom is the principal legal method in a number of domestic systems, separate from judicial decision-making and legislative and regulatory law.[320] Some states even define domestic crimes by reference to customary international law.[321]

So too for international crimes. Offences under customary international law are no less criminal.[322] Individuals have been criminally prosecuted for violating the law of nations for centuries.[323] Customary international law was applied at the Nuremberg and Tokyo trials and in cases under CC10, and the nearly universal acceptance of the decisions of those tribunals demonstrates *opinio juris* on the legitimacy of that jurisprudence.[324] Early proposals for an international criminal court presumed that the law would continue to progress in this fashion and did not even address substantive offences in the court's enabling documents.[325]

And yet, even without a recognized norm against political genocide in state practice, there is almost an intuitive sense that somehow there *should be*. There is some difficulty in reconciling the absence of state practice and *opinio juris*

[317] *Wright v CA* (1995) 5 Asian YBIL 265 (Philippines) 266.

[318] I Brownlie, 'The Rights of Peoples in Modern International Law' in Crawford 1, 14–15 (1988).

[319] Hillier 64 (1998) (treaties and international custom are equally authoritative methods).

[320] III David 97 (1973).

[321] *Cf* Crimes Against Humanity and War Crimes Act: Offences Within Canada SC 2000 c 24 s 4(3) (acts that 'constitute a crime against humanity according to customary international law or conventional international law or by virtue of its being criminal according to the general principles of law recognized by the community of nations.'); *US v Smith* (1820) 18 US (5 Wheat) 153 (US Sup Ct) 162 (piracy as domestic offence defined by reference to law of nations was not too vague to enforce).

[322] *Tadic (Jurisdiction—AC)* [1995] ICTY ¶¶128–37.

[323] *Respublica v De Longchamps* (1784) 1 Dall 111 (Pa) 116 (convicting offender for threatening bodily injury to the Secretary of the French Legation—an offence against diplomats under the law of nations which, 'in its full effect, is part of the law of this State').

[324] Simma (n 8) 311. See also ICCPR art 15(2) (contemplating offences that are 'criminal according to the general principles of law recognized by the community of nations.').

[325] Draft Statute for an International Criminal Court (1952) UN Doc A/2136 (Annex) art 2 ('The Court shall apply international law, including international criminal law, and where appropriate, national law') and Draft Statute for an International Criminal Court (1954) UN Doc A/2645 (Annex) art 2 (same).

with the clear fact that the conduct involved in political genocide is hardly tolerated by international law. As discussed in Chapter 4, certain well-established 'political' rights make sense only when exercised in a community, and there is much state practice supporting the protection of those rights. Added to this is the fact that the offences constituting political genocide are among the most serious in criminal law. The underlying acts of murder, rape, causing serious bodily and mental injury, kidnapping, etc all violate 'elementary considerations of humanity'.[326] The strength and communal nature of the political rights affected, together with the serious character of the infringement, certainly come very close to the grounds justifying the inclusion of all four enumerated groups.

It also is clear that no state can legitimately claim a *right* to commit political genocide. In this sense, states probably do refrain from the practice (or deny responsibility for it) out of a sense of legal obligation. Since the underlying conduct is illegal in any case, and since no state can claim the right to engage in it, why does that not prove the existence of political genocide by inference? There is an understandable human impulse to respond to vicious atrocities by *assuming* 'that noble humanitarian purposes that deserve recognition as the positive law of the international community have in fact been recognized as such by states'.[327] Given limited state practice in the area, the tendency has been to utilize the heinousness of the act in question as a proxy for more traditional criteria in order to extract 'a positive norm of customary law' from 'a moral principle of humanity'.[328]

The reliance on broad generalities—'elementary considerations of humanity'—often yields jurisprudence far more expansive than the narrower factual and legal inquiry before the court necessarily dictates. For example, the ICTY Appeals Chamber went beyond the precise issue of whether violations of common Article III of the Geneva Conventions warranted treatment as a separate offence under customary international law. It held that

> elementary considerations of humanity and common sense make it preposterous that the use by States of weapons prohibited in armed conflicts between themselves be allowed when States try to put down rebellion by their own nationals on their own territory. What is inhumane, and consequently proscribed, in international wars, cannot but be inhumane and inadmissible in civil strife.[329]

326 *Cf Corfu Channel* [1949] ICJ 4, 22 (legal obligation to warn of a nautical minefield arose from 'certain general and well recognized principles, namely: elementary considerations of humanity, even more exacting in peace than in war…'); *Nicaragua* [1986] ICJ 14 ¶¶218–20 (reaffirming *Corfu Channel* and holding that 'elementary considerations of humanity' apply regardless of conventional obligations and reservations).

327 T Meron, 'The Geneva Conventions as Customary Law' (1987) 81 AJIL 348, 361.

328 ibid.

329 *Tadic (Jurisdiction—AC)* [1995] ICTY ¶119. Similar considerations motivated the Audencia Nacional: *Pinochet: Spanish Jurisdiction* [Audencia Nacional 1998] in Brody and Ratner 95, 103 (2000).

Neither treaties nor customary international law are static institutions. Treaties are 'living instrument[s]' that 'must be interpreted in the light of present-day conditions'.[330] And the application of custom always requires 'an element of innovation'.[331] Nevertheless, there are limits to what can (and should) be achieved through these mechanisms. However desirable expansive humanitarian protections are, the analytic approach to international crimes should be more guarded. Each precept must be examined on its own. The humanitarian context—often inspired by the 'object and purpose' of international treaties that offer a springboard for the development of custom—perhaps does warrant a broad view of what constitutes state practice with *opinio juris*. But it does not justify widening those requirements beyond all recognized meaning. International law is a system fundamentally premised on consent—if not of all states, than at least of the majority affected by the rule.

Whatever its propriety in other areas of the law, inferring broad legal protections in the context of international criminal law conflicts directly with other *equally important* international values. Chief among these are limitations imposed by the prohibition on *ex post facto* criminal laws, which preclude the recognition of a separate offence of political genocide by inference.

Despite their rhetorical (and even intuitive) appeal, the 'elementary considerations of humanity' are thin support from which to derive a substantive *criminal offence* of the highest magnitude. Customary international law arises from state practice that is all but unequivocal. An inference of legal obligation is warranted only when it is the sole reasonable conclusion to be drawn from the conduct.[332] Here, outside the minority of states that cover political groups in domestic formulations, there is no overt state practice protecting political groups from genocide *qua* groups. Violations of the right to physical and biological existence, family integrity, etc are criminal acts—no question. But there is no consensus that violation of the separate existence of *political groups* is a crime, independent of the violations of the underlying rights of group members.

The burden of proving a customary rule rests with the party claiming that it is obligatory.[333] That burden cannot be discharged here because it is not the *only* conclusion to be drawn from state practice. The basis of illegality is equivocal. The decision not to engage in political genocide could arise from a recognition that political groups have a right to exist 'as such'. It also could arise simply because political genocide necessarily involves serious underlying conduct that itself constitutes a criminal infringement of fundamental human rights. These other acts are sufficient to impose a legal barrier without the need to recognize a

[330] *Soering v United Kingdom* (1989) ECHR Ser A No 161 ¶102.
[331] Simma (n 8) 313.
[332] *North Sea Continental Shelf* [1969] ICJ 3 ¶¶76–7.
[333] *Asylum* [1950] ICJ 266.

wider prohibition on the destruction of political groups 'as such'. Where doubt exists, it is resolved against liability.[334]

To infer a *separate* 'group' right from the prohibition, even a criminal prohibition, on infringements against individuals is a large step. Genocide is a more serious offence than any of its underlying acts alone.[335] Fair notice requires the specific conduct at issue to be clearly prohibited (with a defined punishment) *before* the offender acts. Offences cannot be extended or created by analogy.[336] For customary offences, it is state practice, together with *opinio juris*, that provides the clear statement of criminality.[337]

Under these circumstances, convicting a perpetrator today of the separate (and more serious) offence of political genocide, which presumably warrants heavier punishment, would violate both heads of the legality principles—*nullum crimen* (no offence) *nulla poena* (no punishment) *sine lege* (without prior law). The prohibition on retroactive criminal prosecution and punishment itself is a peremptory norm of customary international law.[338] It is a fundamental right that cannot be derogated.[339] As matter of *lex lata*, great need and the moral high ground justify such an offence no more than do wishful thinking or speculation.

This closes the inquiry on political genocide under customary international law. Even under the most generous understandings of state practice and *opinio juris*, there is insufficient evidence to support the existence of a separate international crime. When the international community wanted to protect group rights, it did so overtly through the Genocide Convention. Political groups, for whatever reason, justified or unjustified, good judgment or bad, were not included. The fact that custom has crystallized around the norms in the treaty to protect the four enumerated groups is of no moment. Political groups were excluded then and they are excluded now, unless and until the international community chooses specifically to recognize and protect them.

There is an important corollary to the preceding analysis, however. Although customary international law does not *recognize* political genocide as a separate offence, it does not *preclude* the creation of a broader offence, either. The Convention itself supports this conclusion—it defines genocide expressly for

[334] *Kayishema (TC)* [1999] ICTR ¶103 (court must interpret law in manner most favourable to accused).

[335] As discussed in Chapter 6, assuming equal underlying conduct, it also is a more serious offence than the other 'core' international crimes of war crimes and crimes against humanity.

[336] *Cf* ICC Statute art 22(2).

[337] On a deeper level, the doctrine also serves the aims of deterrence—which aims to keep offenders from engaging in certain conduct by threatening them with criminal punishment for engaging in it. The underlying predicate of rational choice requires them to know where the line is in the first place and to understand clearly the consequences for transgression. The theories justifying criminal punishment are detailed in Chapter 7.

[338] *Hadzihasanovic (Interlocutory Appeal—AC)* [2003] ICTY ¶55; Meron, *Humanitarian Norms* 96 (1989).

[339] *Cf* ICCPR arts 4(2), 15; ECHR arts 7, 15.

the purposes of that treaty.[340] Likewise in the various instruments adopting the Convention's definition.[341] There is nothing in the traditional understanding of genocide that is legally *inconsistent* with states recognizing a broader formulation of genocide that protects political groups 'as such,' either in their domestic laws or through international efforts.[342]

This is the question that is considered next.

[340] Genocide Convention art II ('In the present Convention, genocide means....').

[341] ICTR Statute ('genocide as defined in paragraph 2 of this Article....'); ICTY Statute art 4 ('genocide as defined in paragraph 2 of this article....'); ICC Statute art 6 ('[f]or the purposes of this statute, "genocide" means...').

[342] As noted above, a clear minority of states (some 24 percent of the survey population) already protect political groups from genocide as a matter of domestic law.

6

The Role of Other International Crimes

A. Introduction

Before determining whether *creating* a separate offence of political genocide under positive international law is warranted, it is useful first to analyse other international crimes that implicate similar interests. Some diplomats[1] and academics[2] claim, for example, that political groups are protected already through other provisions of international law; namely, the concept of crimes against humanity.

It is true that crimes against humanity can operate to prohibit violence committed on a massive scale and to protect individuals from serious discrimination based upon their membership in protected groups. But the simple fact that there may be some overlap does not necessarily mean that such offences sufficiently respond to political genocide. The question turns more precisely on the contours of crimes against humanity and a more robust comparative analysis with genocide as defined in the Convention.

B. Crimes against humanity

All civilized nations protect a baseline of human dignity by criminalizing serious offences against person and property. Many domestic and international crimes thus 'are in some sense or other offences against "humanity".'[3] But there is a distinction between normative ideals and the substantive composition of a criminal offence that has changed significantly over time. Since a variety of legal conceptions of crimes against humanity exist, it is helpful to anchor the analysis of these crimes with a brief history of their origins.

Historical antecedents

The Nuremberg trials following World War II were the first instances of 'crimes against humanity' being defined and applied in an international instrument

[1] ICC Ad Hoc Committee Report (6 Sep 1995) UN Doc A/50/22 ¶61.

[2] Schabas 171 (2009); FS Benavides-Vanegas, 'The Elimination of Political Groups under International Law and the Constitution of Political Claims' (2003) 15 Florida JIL 575, 579, 612–13.

[3] E Schwelb, 'Crimes Against Humanity' (1946) 23 BYBIL 178, 196–7.

providing criminal sanctions.[4] But notions of 'humanity' as a barrier imposing some form of legal constraint appeared many years earlier, both in connection with the slave trade[5] and in certain treaties regulating warfare. In 1868, the St Petersburg Declaration provided that military science and weaponry should yield in some cases to the 'laws of humanity.'[6] Later, the 'Martens clause' of the Hague Conventions grounded baseline protection for individuals in 'the usages established among civilized peoples, from the *laws of humanity*, and the dictates of the public conscience'.[7] The Martens clause set the stage for the first international efforts to hold individuals criminally responsible for violating the 'laws of humanity.'

Germany and World War I

Soon after hostilities ended in World War I, the victorious Allies convened an investigative body to determine whether the defeated parties could be held legally accountable for their conduct during the war, as well as for starting the war itself. An international Commission on Responsibility found legal violations warranting *individual* responsibility and punishment:

The war was carried on by the central empires, together with their allies, Turkey and Bulgaria, by barbarous or illegitimate methods in violation of the established laws and customs of war and the elementary *laws of humanity*.

* * *

All persons belonging to enemy countries, however high their position may have been, without distinction of rank, including Chiefs of States, who have been guilty of offenses against the laws and customs of war *or the laws of humanity*, are liable to criminal prosecution.[8]

Separate from war crimes and *jus ad bellum*, the Commission also found that individual criminal responsibility was warranted for violations of the 'laws of humanity', even to the extent of abrogating then sacrosanct notions of sovereign

[4] IMT Charter art 6(c). A slightly modified definition applied in proceedings against Japanese war criminals. IMTFE Charter art 5(c).

[5] Clark 77 n 7 (2001). Slavery is now a crime against humanity in its own right. ICC Statute art 7(1)(c).

[6] Declaration Renouncing the Use, in Time of War, of Explosive Projectiles Under 400 Grammes Weight (11 Dec 1868) art 31 (declaring certain explosive and incendiary projectiles 'contrary to the laws of humanity' and setting forth an agreement to adopt later instruments 'in view of future improvements which science may effect in the armament of troops, in order to maintain the principles which they have established, and to conciliate the necessities of war with the laws of humanity.').

[7] [1907] Hague Convention IV pmbl ¶8 and [1899] Hague Convention II pmbl ¶9 (emphasis added). The 1907 treaty was meant to replace the 1899 convention, but 18 states party to the 1899 treaty did not join it. Roberts and Guelff 44 (1989) (Argentina, Bulgaria, Chile, Columbia, Ecuador, Greece, Honduras, Italy, Korea, Montenegro, Paraguay, Persia, Peru, Serbia, Spain, Turkey, Uruguay, and Venezuela).

[8] Commission on the Responsibility of the Authors of the War and on the Enforcement of Penalties, Report Presented to the Preliminary Peace Conference (29 Mar 1919) (1920) 14 AJIL 95, 115, 117 (emphasis added).

immunity.[9] The Commission proposed an international tribunal but fell short on substance, suggesting a vague mandate of applying 'the principles of the law of nations as they result from the usages established among civilized peoples ... the laws of humanity and ... the dictates of public conscience'.[10]

In an interesting juxtaposition to its position later at Nuremberg, the American delegation dissented from the Commission's report, in part because of the references to 'laws of humanity.'[11] The United States distinguished legality from morality, arguing that

> legal offenses were justiciable and liable to trial and punishment by appropriate tribunals, but that moral offenses, however iniquitous and infamous and however terrible in their results, were beyond the reach of judicial procedure, and subject only to moral sanctions.[12]

The US delegation also questioned the matter on the basis of legality, noting that 'the laws and principles of humanity are not certain, varying with time, place, and circumstance, and according, it may be, to the conscience of the individual judge. There is no fixed and universal standard of humanity.'[13] Unlike the laws and customs of war, which were codified in legal texts and state practice, the laws of humanity were impermissibly vague, rendering them unfit for criminal sanction.[14]

Despite the misgivings of the United States, the Treaty of Versailles singled out Kaiser Wilhelm II for trial before an international court, charging him with 'a supreme offense against international morality and the sanctity of treaties'.[15] Procedural substance was sparse: the tribunal would 'be guarded by the highest motives of international policy, with a view to vindicating the solemn objectives of international undertakings and the validity of international morality'.[16]

But international trials were not to be. The Kaiser fled to the Netherlands at the end of the war.[17] Extradition subsequently was refused on several grounds, including the lack of dual criminality (the charged offences were not recognized under Dutch law), the absence of any treaty obligation to extradite for such conduct, and because the Netherlands determined that the crimes were subject to the 'political offense' exception.[18] Thereafter, growing Allied concerns about the rise of Bolshevism and the potential return of the German monarchy led to a compromise where Germany would try its own war criminals before the German *Reichsgericht* (Supreme Court) in Leipzig.[19]

From the viewpoint of international justice, the Leipzig trials were an utter failure. Of nearly 4,500 alleged war criminals the Allies sought to try, Germany

[9] ibid 116–17. [10] ibid 122.

[11] ibid 128. The American delegation also opposed criminal proceedings against heads of state. ibid 144. [12] ibid 128.

[13] ibid. [14] ibid 134. [15] Treaty of Versailles (28 Jun 1919) art 227.

[16] ibid. Another provision contemplated the trial of other German offenders for violations of the 'laws and customs of war.' ibid art 228. [17] Marrus 11–12 (1997).

[18] Taylor 16 (1992). [19] ibid 12.

agreed to try only forty-five. Of these, only twelve were actually tried and six convicted.[20] Punishment was light—the longest sentence was four years' imprisonment for two U-boat officers who ordered the shooting of survivors of a torpedoed hospital ship.[21] Those convictions later were annulled during a closed session of the *Reichsgericht* based upon 'new' evidence.[22]

The Ottoman Empire and the Armenians

Separate from war crimes against opposing belligerents, early efforts to punish crimes against humanity emerged in response to atrocities by the crumbling Ottoman Empire against indigenous Armenians during World War I.[23] Following the armistice of Mudros, the successor Turkish government agreed to court martial those responsible for Armenian massacres, causing many 'Young Turk' leaders to flee.[24] Domestic prosecution initially looked promising. In April 1919, an Ottoman court convened in Constantinople to try offences against Armenians. Two former Turkish officials were found guilty of acting 'against humanity and civilization' for deporting, robbing and murdering Armenians.[25] But when one was sentenced to death and hanged, political enemies of the new regime made him 'a national martyr and turned his funeral into a patriotic protest against abject submission to the Allies'.[26]

The prosecution of twenty other high level officials continued with increasing nationalist opposition. Trials often were held in absentia, leading to verdicts 'more symbolic than practical'.[27] Other prisoners were freed without charge. After yet another regime change, any remaining prospect of Turkish justice for Armenians expired when the new government arrested four officials from the Constantinople tribunal for allegedly contravening proper judicial procedures.[28]

As with Germany, there were some early efforts toward international prosecution. British, French and Russian diplomats declared jointly in 1915 that:

> In view of these *crimes of Turkey against humanity* and civilization, the Allied governments announce publicly to the Sublime Porte that they will hold personally responsible

[20] ibid.

[21] Bring 14–15 (2001). This contrasts sharply with Germany's prosecutorial efforts after World War II, where some 6,500 offenders were convicted in domestic proceedings from 1945–1985. ibid 22.

[22] Willis 146 (1982). For more details on the Leipzig trials, and the systematic withdrawal of Belgium, France and Great Britain from the process as their farcical character became apparent, see Taylor 16–18 (1992).

[23] For details on the Armenian genocide, see VN Dadrian, 'The Armenian Genocide and the Legal and Political Issues in the Failure to Prevent or Punish the Crime' (1998) 29 UWLA LR 43.

[24] Willis 154 (1982).

[25] ibid; Hirsh 43–4 n 28 (2003).

[26] Willis 154–5 (1982).

[27] ibid 156.

[28] For details on domestic trials in Turkey, see VN Dadrian, 'The Turkish Military Tribunal's Prosecution of the Authors of the Armenian Genocide: Four Major Court-Martial Series' (1997) 11 Holocaust and Genocide Studies 28.

[for] these crimes all members of the Ottoman Government and those of their agents who are implicated in such massacres.[29]

This was a significant development because it recognized that atrocities by the Ottoman Empire against its *own citizens* were criminal acts independent of the notion of war crimes against adversaries.[30] After the war, the Treaty of Sevres contemplated an international tribunal created by the League of Nations:

The Turkish Government undertakes to hand over to the Allied Powers the persons whose surrender may be required by the latter as being responsible for the massacres committed during the continuance of the state of war on territory which formed part of the Turkish Empire on August 1, 1914.

The Allied Powers reserve to themselves the right to designate the tribunal which shall try the persons so accused....[31]

Despite an early impetus toward international punishment of atrocities against non-combatants,[32] the Treaty of Sevres was never ratified. Allied willpower eroded soon after the war ended, and various Allied states subsequently divorced themselves from the issue.[33] Great Britain's efforts were impeded by a confluence of prisoner escapes, growing Turkish nationalism, and difficulty obtaining evidence.[34] The Treaty of Lausanne,[35] which replaced the Treaty of Sevres, provided amnesty and omitted all references to war crimes and massacres.[36]

The inability of the Allies (and Turkey itself) to sufficiently respond to massacres of Armenians (who went unrepresented in Allied councils) had serious consequences. Armenian radicals exacted violent retribution and assassinated a number of Turkish officials in the early 1920s.[37] Worse still, it may have encouraged future crimes against humanity on a much larger scale. Adolf Hitler clearly believed that he would never account for Nazi atrocities:

I have sent to the East only my Death's Head units, with the order to kill without pity or mercy all men, women and children of the Polish race and language. Only in such a way

[29] William G. Sharp Letter to Bryan, 28 May 1915, reprinted in Willis 26 (1982) (emphasis added).

[30] Clark 77 (2001). Historical precedent was not entirely lacking. In 1474, two years before war broke out, Baron Peter von Hagenbach was stripped of his knighthood and executed for improperly administering foreign territory under his control by oppressing the populace and committing crimes against the 'laws of God and Man' (including murder, rape, pillage, and perjury). Paust 622 (2000).

[31] Treaty of Sevres (10 Aug 1920) art 230.

[32] *Cf* Schwelb (n 3) 180–3 (discussing diplomatic commission's conclusion that the 'Central Empires together with their allies, Turkey and Bulgaria [had employed] barbarous or illegitimate methods in violation of the established laws and customs of war and the elementary laws of humanity').

[33] Willis 158–61 (1982).

[34] Other Allies, including the United States, France, and Italy, refused to cooperate in providing documentary evidence (scant as it was) and in arresting suspects, let alone actually supporting international prosecution. ibid 158, 162.

[35] Treaty of Lausanne (24 Jul 1923) arts 119–20.

[36] Willis 161–3 (1982); Cassese, ICL 67–8 (2003).

[37] Willis 163 (1982).

will we win the vital space we need. Who still talks nowadays about the extermination of the Armenians?[38]

The international community also proved unable to grapple with serious international crimes on a prospective basis. Raphael Lemkin later introduced a proposal to the League of Nations to criminalize the destruction of religious, racial and social groups.[39] He proposed two international crimes:

Whosoever, out of hatred towards a racial, religious or social collectivity, or with a view to the extermination thereof, undertakes a punishable action against the life, bodily integrity, liberty, dignity or economic existence of a person belonging to such a collectivity, is liable for the crime of *barbarity*....

Whosoever, either out of hatred towards a racial, religious or social collectivity, or with a view to the extermination thereof, destroys its cultural or artistic works, will be liable for the crime of *vandalism*... (emphasis added).[40]

Lemkin's proposal was rejected.

The serious consequences of both these retrospective and prospective failures were not lost on the Nuremberg prosecutors who found themselves grappling with atrocities perpetrated on a far greater scale. American prosecutor, Robert Jackson specifically referenced Leipzig during his opening statement, noting the 'futility of leaving adjudication to the vanquished'.[41] And Sir Hartley Shawcross, Great Britain's Chief prosecutor at Nuremberg, recalled Lemkin's proposal in light of the decision by the International Military Tribunal at Nuremberg to limit its temporal jurisdiction solely to offences committed after World War II began in September 1939.[42] Shawcross noted that, had Lemkin's overture been accepted in 1933, the Allies could have tried the Nazis for all of their crimes against humanity, whether or not committed in conjunction with Germany's aggressive war.[43]

Nevertheless, these developments played an important role in setting the stage for international tribunals after World War II, as the Allies sought to avoid repeating mistakes made twenty-five years earlier.[44]

The Nuremberg trials

In October 1943, the Allied leaders issued a joint Declaration on German Atrocities in response to 'evidence of atrocities, massacres and cold-blooded mass executions....'[45] The Declaration warned that offenders would be 'sent back to

[38] R Perlman, 'The Genocide Convention' (1950) 30 Nebraska LR 1, 5.

[39] R Lemkin, 'Genocide as a Crime Under International Law' (1947) 41 AJIL 145, 146; R Lemkin, 'Genocide' (1946) 15 Am Scholar 229.

[40] Lemkin, *Genocide as a Crime* (n 39) 146.

[41] Marrus 12 (1997).

[42] 41 Journal of the United Nations 52 (1946).

[43] ibid.

[44] Willis 174 (1982).

[45] Moscow Declaration 308–11. What 'atrocities' included is uncertain. The Declaration referenced the execution of Polish officers, hostages and peasants as examples but did not note Germany's treatment of its own Jewish citizens or Nazi concentration camps.

the countries in which their abominable deeds were done in order that they may be judged and punished according to the laws of these liberated countries....'[46] The Allies never specified the role of international law, instead promising prosecution under the domestic law of the *locus* of the crimes. But they left an opening for future trials under international law by providing that '[t]he above declaration is without prejudice to the case of the major criminals whose offences have no particular geographical localization and who will be punished by the joint decision of the Governments of the Allies'.[47]

Soon after the war ended, the Moscow Declaration crystallized into the London Agreement,[48] which specified that an international military tribunal (IMT), located in Nuremberg, Germany, would try high-level Nazis whose crimes had no particular location.[49] Lower-level offenders were returned to the places where they committed their crimes for trial by national or military courts.[50]

The IMT Charter provided jurisdiction over four offences: (i) conspiracy to wage aggressive war; (ii) crimes against peace; (iii) crimes against humanity; and (iv) war crimes.[51] It addressed atrocities against civilians in two ways. In occupied territories, they were war crimes.[52] All other civilian populations (including Germany's own) were covered by crimes against humanity.[53] The definition of crimes against humanity in the IMT Charter thus was quite close conceptually to the less-novel concept of war crimes, the key difference being the nationality of the victims.[54]

The IMT Charter designated two categories of crimes against humanity. The 'murder-type' encompassed mass atrocities against civilians, while the 'persecution-type' covered extreme forms of discrimination against civilians and military personnel:

> *6(c) Crimes Against Humanity*: Namely, murder, extermination, enslavement, deportation, and other inhumane acts committed against any civilian population, before or during the war, or persecutions on political, racial or religious grounds in execution of or in connection with any crime within the jurisdiction of the Tribunal, whether or not in violation of the domestic law of the country where perpetrated.[55]

The IMT Charter resulted from arduous negotiation between the former Allies at the outset of the Cold War.[56] This certainly was the case with crimes

[46] ibid. [47] ibid.

[48] London Agreement 280. Nineteen other states subsequently acceded to the Agreement. ibid n 1 (Australia, Belgium, Czechoslovakia, Denmark, Ethiopia, Greece, Haiti, Honduras, India, Luxembourg, the Netherlands, New Zealand, Norway, Panama, Paraguay, Poland, Uruguay, Venezuela, and Yugoslavia). Parallel prosecutions were undertaken against Japanese war criminals. IMTFE Charter; *Araki* [IMTFE 1946] 101–3 IMTFE Proceedings 48413–858.

[49] IMT Charter art 1. [50] ibid arts 4, 6. [51] ibid art 6.

[52] ibid art 6(b) ('civilian population of or in occupied territory').

[53] ibid art 6(c) ('any civilian population'). [54] Bassiouni, CAH 558–9 (1999).

[55] IMT Charter art 6(c).

[56] For details on the political wrangling, see R Overy, 'The Nuremberg Trials: International law in the Making' in Sands 1 (2003). The authors of the IMT Charter served in other capacities

against humanity. Article 6(c) alone went through some 20 drafts before it was finalized[57] and was amended even further by the 'Berlin Protocol' to rectify a discrepancy between the Russian and French/English texts.[58] The French/English texts placed a semi-colon between 'war' and 'or,' whereas the Russian text carried a comma in the same place.[59] With the support of the Allied prosecutors, the French/English texts were revised to match the Russian text.[60] As revised, crimes against humanity fell within the IMT's jurisdiction only if there was a nexus with war crimes or crimes against peace.[61] The IMT thus could take jurisdiction only over crimes against humanity committed after World War II began in September 1939.[62]

Political (and practical) considerations no doubt intertwined deeply with the IMT's mandate, and the textual revision and subsequent restrictive interpretation may have been a concession to *realpolitik*.[63] But taking the politicized climate as a given, the Berlin Protocol and the IMT's restrictive reading of its charter also had important legal consequences. Professor Bassiouni, for example, suggests that the restrictions actually strengthened the legitimacy of the IMT proceedings under the principles of legality.[64]

Nuremberg (and its progeny) ostensibly were efforts to apply *pre-existing* norms of customary international law, rather than to legislate prospectively.[65] The IMT expressly determined that '[t]he Charter [was] not an arbitrary exercise of power on the part of the victorious nations, but... [was] the expression of international

thereafter as prosecutors and judges, raising some question 'about the impartiality and fairness of the subsequent legal process.': Bassiouni, CAH 19 n 46 (1999). IMT Charter art 6(a)–(c).

57 For a discussion of the drafting of art 6(c), see Bassiouni, CAH 19–32, 37–40 (1999).

58 Berlin Protocol (6 Oct 1945) 1 IMT Proceedings 17.

59 IMT Charter art 6(c).

60 Protocol Rectifying Discrepancy in Text of Charter (6 Oct 1945) 1 IMT Proceedings 17–18.

61 ibid.

62 *Göring* [IMT 1946] 1 IMT Proceedings 171, 254–5 ('The Tribunal therefore cannot make a general declaration that the acts before 1939 were Crimes Against Humanity within the meaning of the Charter.').

63 The Soviets could have been charged with crimes against humanity for Stalin's political purges during the previous 25 years (which involved estimated deaths of 20–66 million). Kuper, *Genocide—Political Use* 97, 141–8 (1981). The link to wartime activities precluded inquiry into prior Soviet practice. Some argue, albeit less persuasively, that the United States also was vulnerable to such allegations. A Clapham, 'Issues of complexity, complicity, and complementarity' in Sands 31, 42–3 (2003) (noting potential application to 'Jim Crow' discrimination laws governing Blacks in the southern United States).

64 Bassiouni, CAH 29–30 (1999) ('The change from semicolon to the comma... avoid[ed] the criticism that Article 6(c) crimes were entirely new to international law... [The] trade-off was intended to strengthen the validity of the crime in light of the requirement of the "principles of legality".'). Legality commonly is referenced by the Latin maxim *nullum crimen sine lege, nulla poena sine lege*—no crime or punishment without pre-existing law covering the offence and its sanction. For a discussion of retrospective application and legal certainty, see Emerson and Ashworth 281–92 (2001).

65 R Clark, 'Crimes Against Humanity and the Rome Statute of the International Criminal Court' in Polti 79 n 19 (2001) ('The most convincing explanation of the legal status of crimes against humanity in 1945–46 was as general principles of law').

law existing at the time of its creation; and to that extent [was] itself a contribution to international law'.[66]

The IMT Charter cannot be evaluated in a retrospective legal vacuum, and it is naive to suggest that political retribution played no part. But the influence of political considerations upon the drafting process is best left to historical interpretation. What is known is that defence counsel raised legality arguments unsuccessfully at trial.[67] In this sense, any debate over legality today amounts to a retrospective critique of one aspect of the IMT judgment.[68] Although some suggest that the IMT reached the wrong conclusion,[69] its judgment has been recognized time and again in national and international courts,[70] and there is little doubt on the legitimacy of crimes against humanity today.[71]

Twenty-three high-level Nazi officials were indicted for trial before the IMT. One committed suicide before trial, three were acquitted, and nineteen were convicted, of whom twelve were sentenced to death by hanging and seven imprisoned. Göring escaped the hangman's noose only by committing suicide before execution.[72]

Nuremberg thus marked the beginning of a trend toward the international criminalization of atrocities separately from war crimes and *jus in bello*. The IMT Charter was followed by Control Council Law No 10 [CC10], which provided uniform standards for additional trials of Nazi war criminals within the four Allied occupation zones.[73] Unlike the IMT Charter, CC10 did not establish specific tribunals, but rather left it to occupation zone commanders to create appropriate mechanisms.[74] Participation in the scheme varied. Crimes against

[66] *Göring* [IMT 1946] 1 IMT Proceedings 171, 218. See also *High Command* [USMT 1948] 10 TWC 3, 487 (IMT Charter expressed 'international law existing at the time of its creation' and did not extend 'the international common law... to add any new element of criminality....') and 510 ('For a defendant to be held criminally responsible, there must be a breach of some moral obligation fixed by international law, a personal act voluntarily done with knowledge of its inherent criminality under international law.').

[67] Motion Adopted by all Defence Counsel (19 Nov 1945) 1 IMT Proceedings 168.

[68] The legitimacy of crimes against humanity was only one of a host of legal issues at Nuremberg, and perhaps not even the most important one. Schwelb (n 3) 207 (crimes against humanity were 'subsidiary or accessory to the traditional types of war crimes.'). Only two defendants, Streicher and Von Schirach, were convicted exclusively of crimes against humanity. Marrus 258–61 (1997).

[69] For a criticism of Nuremberg on legality grounds (as well as lack of defence access to evidence and improper separation of powers), see O Kranzbuhler, 'Nuremberg Eighteen Years Afterwards' (1965) 14 DePaul LR 333, 336 (commentary by former defence counsel for Nuremberg defendant Admiral Donitz).

[70] Bassiouni, CAH 562–5 (1999).

[71] *Cf* ICTY Statute art 5, ICTR Statute art 3, ICC Statute art 7. Chapter 5 discusses the legality principles in considerably more detail.

[72] Marrus 258–61 (1997).

[73] CC10 technically was national legislation for Germany adopted through the Allies' supreme legislative authority following Germany's unconditional surrender, rather than an international instrument per se. Bassiouni, CAH 33 (1999). Nevertheless, CC10's relation to the IMT and international law is readily apparent, and its progeny are more than a series of decisions under domestic law.

[74] Trials in the American Zone took place under special military regulations. Military Government Ordinance No 7 (18 Oct 1946), as modified by Military Government Ordinance No 11 (17 Feb 1947) in Taylor 286–93 (1949).

humanity played a part in all twelve American trials under CC10,[75] but not in prosecutions by the other Allies.[76] CC10 defined crimes against humanity as:

> *Atrocities and offences, including but not limited to* murder, extermination, enslavement, deportation, *imprisonment, torture, rape*, and other inhumane acts committed against any civilian population, or persecutions on political, racial or religious grounds whether or not in violation of the domestic laws of the country where perpetrated.[77]

CC10 included additional punishable offences and designated them illustrative rather than exhaustive. It also deleted the textual nexus to the war that had restricted the IMT's jurisdiction. Twelve American trials addressed Nazi atrocities including:

- cruel (and often deadly) medical experiments performed on inmates at concentration camps;[78]
- perversion of the legal processes by the German justice ministry and judicial officials;[79]
- dedicated death squads carrying out massacres of Jews and Gypsies in occupied territories;[80]
- administration of concentration camps;[81]
- slave labour;[82]
- hostage-taking and reprisals against civilians in occupied territories;[83]
- development of German race policy;[84]
- decision making of the German High Command and other German Ministries, particularly German race policy in occupied territories;[85] and
- unlawful labour and economic practices by German industrialists.[86]

CC10 made important contributions to the development of crimes against humanity but did not successfully implement its full mandate. In theory, crimes against humanity were offences 'against international law even when committed by nationals of one country against their fellow nationals or against those of other nations irrespective of belligerent status'.[87] In practice, indictments covering

[75] 185 defendants were tried by the United States, resulting in 150 convictions and 24 death sentences: Bring 22 (2001); Taylor 69, 118–19 (1949) (summarizing indictments and outcomes). For details, see M Lippman, 'The Other Nuremberg: American Prosecutions of Nazi War Criminals in Occupied Germany' (1992) 3 Indiana ICLR 1.

[76] British trials, for example, took place under a special military order that limited trials to war crimes. See Royal Warrant 0160/2498 (14 Jun 1945) in Taylor 254–7 (1949). See also Schwelb (n 3) 221–2 (discussing Royal Warrant).

[77] CC10 art II(1)(c) (emphasis added distinguishing CC10 from art 6(c) of the IMT Charter).

[78] *Medical* [USMT 1947] 1 TWC 1.

[79] *Justice* [USMT 1947] 3 TWC 1.

[80] *Einsatzgruppen* [USMT 1948] 4 TWC 1.

[81] *Concentration Camp* [USMT 1947] 5 TWC 195.

[82] *Milch* [USMT 1947] 2 TWC 773.

[83] *Hostages* [USMT 1948] 11 TWC 759.

[84] *RuSHA* [USMT 1948] 4 TWC 599.

[85] *High Command* [USMT 1948] 10 TWC 3; *Ministries* [USMT 1949] 12 TWC 3.

[86] *IG Farben* [USMT 1948] 12 TWC 1; *Krupp* [USMT 1947] 9 TWC 1; *Flick* [USMT 1947] 6 TWC 3.

[87] Taylor 65 (1949).

conduct before the war typically were dismissed as being outside the tribunal's jurisdiction.[88] Tribunals that recognized the broader temporal authority did so only in *dicta*.[89] The issue of whether Germans were liable for offences committed solely against other Germans was likewise avoided.[90]

After Nuremberg, there was little doubt that crimes against humanity, as defined in the IMT Charter, were international offences. The more expansive views expressed in CC10 and the IMTFE Charter[91] (covering atrocities committed in the Pacific Theatre) were more questionable. Apart from the statutory texts, the only support for the broader definition of crimes against humanity appeared as *obiter dicta*. At least one tribunal overtly rejected a broader understanding.[92]

Perhaps in light of the absence of clarity, the International Law Commission avoided the issue altogether when, at the behest of the UN General Assembly, it drafted the so-called 'Nuremberg Principles'. The Principles codified the more restrictive definition of the IMT Charter.[93] This less controversial definition subsequently was reflected in a unanimously-adopted General Assembly resolution,[94] which later was characterized as reflecting customary international law.[95] The viability of the broader conceptions under CC10 and the IMTFE Charter thus remained for later resolution in domestic courts[96] and subsequent international tribunals.[97]

Crimes against humanity: the modern understanding

Apart from the IMT Charter, crimes against humanity were not embodied in any multilateral treaty until the advent of the ICC.[98] When it became desirable to prosecute the offence, the definition was modified to fit the circumstances. This led to slightly different versions in the international criminal tribunals and

[88] *Flick* [USMT 1947] 6 TWC 3, 25–6 (dismissing charges against German industrialists).

[89] *Justice* [USMT 1947] 3 TWC 1, 39–41 (discussing the issue in a case where the acts charged were committed in concert with Germany's war) and *Einsatzgruppen* [USMT 1948] 4 TWC 1, 499 (same, but in the context of an indictment covering 1941–43).

[90] *Cf Medical* [USMT 1947] 1 TWC 1, 196–8 (declining to address euthanasia programmes against German citizens because euthanasia of 'non-German nationals' was sufficient to support convictions for war crimes and crimes against humanity).

[91] IMTFE Charter art 5(c). Article 5(c) eliminated all references to civilians, specified who could be punished (major criminals), and removed religion as a basis for persecution. ibid. The distinctions had little practical effect. No Tokyo defendant was convicted of crimes against humanity as a stand-alone offence, though some were convicted of acts constituting crimes against humanity within the rubric of war crimes. *Araki* [IMTFE 1946] ¶¶101–3 IMTFE Proceedings 48413; Paust 632 (1999) (summarizing dispositions).

[92] *Flick* [USMT 1947] 6 TWC 3, 25–6.

[93] Nuremberg Principles art 6(c) (2 Aug 1950) 2 YB-ILC 374.

[94] UNGA Res 95 (I) (11 Dec 1946) UN Doc A/64/Add-1.

[95] Secretary General ICTY Report (3 May 1993) UN Doc S/25704 ¶35.

[96] *Cf Finta* (1994) 1 SCR 701 (Can Sup Ct) (domestic case in Canada); *Barbie* (1985) 78 ILR 125 (Fr Ct Cass) and *Touvier* (1995) 100 ILR 338 (Fr Ct Cass) (domestic cases in France); *Eichmann (TC)* [1961] 36 ILR 5 (Isr Dist Ct) ¶1 and *Enigster* [Isr Dist Ct 1951] 18 ILR 542 (domestic cases in Israel). See also Bassiouni, CAH 543–55 (1999) (collecting other domestic cases).

[97] *Tadic (TC)—Merits* [1997] ICTY ¶623.

[98] MP Scharf, 'Justice versus Peace' in Sewall and Kaysen 185 (2000).

an ICC text that incorporated aspects of both, in addition to language from other international instruments.[99] Since no single text can claim authoritative precedence, it is essential to remain mindful of the source originating the prosecution and the precise definition of the crime at issue when considering the application of case law from one jurisdictional context in another.

ICTY and ICTR decisions are perhaps most useful because both tribunals have been careful to explain context-specific distinctions between their respective statutes and customary international law. The ICTY Appeals Chamber described five essential elements of all crimes against humanity under customary international law:

1. There must be an attack;
2. The attack must be directed against a civilian population;
3. The attack must be widespread or systematic;
4. The offender's individual conduct must form part of the attack; and
5. The offender must know that his acts are part of widespread or systematic attack on the civilian population.[100]

The ICC Statute is similar. It defines crimes against humanity as certain prohibited acts 'committed as part of a widespread or systematic attack directed against any civilian population, with knowledge of the attack'.[101] The first three elements comprise the so-called 'chapeau'[102] elements, or requisite contextual backdrop, against which all crimes against humanity must be committed. The fourth sets forth the specific conduct prohibited within that larger context. The fifth specifies *mens rea*—which applies to both the chapeau and the specific conduct at issue.

The attack

While not overtly specified at Nuremberg,[103] the modern view of crimes against humanity requires the background context of a wider attack.[104] This 'attack'

[99] The drafting of the ICC Statute involved analysing crimes against humanity in the IMT Charter, CC10, the IMTFE Charter, the 1954 and 1996 Draft Codes, the ICTY and the ICTR (all of which differed) and 'picking and choosing parts that delegates preferred to keep or discard, and also adding heretofore un-enumerated components to the definition'. KD Askin, 'Crimes Within the Jurisdiction of the International Criminal Court' (1999) 10 Crim LF 33, 41–2. Significant differences over 'vague and, in many respects, contradictory' precedents were put aside in the ICC Statute, which does not limit 'in any way existing or developing rules of international law for [other] purposes....'. Lee, *Making of the ICC* 90 (1999); ICC Statute art 10.

[100] *Kunarac (AC)* [2002] ICTY ¶85. Unlike the ICTR and ICC statutes, the ICTY Statute does not specify 'widespread or systematic' acts, but the ICTY still recognizes these criteria as mandatory under customary international law. ibid.

[101] ICC Statute art 7(1).

[102] Translated literally, the term means 'hat'. In this context, 'chapeau' refers to the overarching special circumstances against which the offence is committed, which can amount to one or more substantive elements of the offence itself. It is the commission of such ordinary offences (murder, rape, etc) within this larger forbidden context that gives them the character of crimes against humanity: K Ambos and S Wirth, (2001) 'Commentary' in 2 Klip and Suiter 704 (2001).

[103] IMT Charter art 6(c). But see Clark (n 65) 89 ('the requirement... that the 'inhumane acts' be 'committed against any civilian population' carried with it a notion of scale (and even organization) inconsistent with random acts.').

[104] ICC Statute art 7(1).

provides an analytical threshold separating matters of domestic province from those of international concern. It excludes isolated offences that are not part of a wider pattern of similar organized activity.[105] Except in the ICTR, the attack itself need not be discriminatory in nature.[106]

The ICC Statute defines an 'attack' as a 'course of conduct involving the multiple commission of [prohibited acts] . . . pursuant to or *in furtherance of a State or organizational policy* to commit such an attack.' (Emphasis added.)[107] 'Multiple' is undefined but certainly suggests more than one event, or perhaps a single prolonged course of conduct.[108] The requirement of planning or policy derives from French jurisprudence. In *Barbie*,[109] the Court de Cassation (Criminal Chamber) defined crimes against humanity as

> inhumane acts and persecution committed in a systematic manner in the name of a State practicing a *policy of ideological supremacy*, not only against persons by reason of their membership of a racial or religious community, but also against the opponents of that policy, whatever the form of their opposition. (Emphasis added.)[110]

A similar definition appeared later in the French *Code Penal*[111] and the domestic law of other states.[112] The policy in question must 'actively promote or encourage' the

[105] Lee, *The ICC* 58 (2001).

[106] *Akayesu (AC)* [2001] ICTR ¶469. The suggestion that *all* crimes against humanity require discrimination derives from questionable domestic case law, rather than international jurisprudence. *Cf Finta* (1994) 1 SCR 701 (Can Sup Ct) ¶76 (requiring 'that the inhumane acts were based on discrimination against or the persecution of an identifiable group of people'). For a blistering critique, see I Cotler, 'Case Comment: Regina v. Finta' (1996) 90 AJIL 460.

[107] ICC Statute art 7(2)(a). [108] Askin (n 99) 40.

[109] *Barbie* (1985) 78 ILR 125 (Fr Ct Cass). *Barbie* was decided under French Law No 64–1326 (26 Dec 1964), which provided that 'Crimes against humanity, as defined in the United Nations Resolution of 13 February 1946 which takes note of the definition of crimes against humanity contained in the Charter of the International Military Tribunal of 8 August 1945, are by their nature not subject to statutory limitation of prosecution.' There was no substance apart from the reference to the IMT Charter. *Barbie* itself has been criticized as an overt misinterpretation of the IMT Charter: LS Wexler, 'Prosecutions for Crimes Against Humanity in French Municipal Law: International Implications' (1998) 91 ASILPROC 270, 271–2.

[110] *Barbie* (1985) 78 ILR 125 (Fr Ct Cass) 136–7. See also *Touvier* (1995) 100 ILR 338 (Fr Ct Cass) (reversing the dismissal of an indictment against a French administrator for deporting and persecuting Jews; although Touvier did not share Nazi ideology per se, he knew that he was implementing German race policy, which was sufficient).

[111] Code Penal (France) art 212–1 [1] ('Deportation, enslavement, or the large-scale and systematic practice of summary executions or of kidnappings followed by the disappearance of the victims, torture, or other inhumane acts, when inspired by political, philosophic, racial or religious motives and organized in the execution of a prearranged plan against a group in the civilian population . . . .'). The French definition ensured that crimes against humanity covered members of the French Resistance, who otherwise might not have been subject to the offence. *Barbie* (1985) 78 ILR 125 (Fr Ct Cass) 136 ('Jews and members of the Resistance persecuted in a systematic manner in the name of State practicing a policy of ideological supremacy, the former by reason of their membership of a racial or religious community, the latter by reason of their opposition to that policy, can equally be the victims of crimes against humanity').

[112] *Cf Finta* (1994) 1 SCR 701 (Can Sup Ct) 813 ('the cruel and terrible actions which are essential elements of the offence . . . [must be] undertaken in pursuance of a policy of discrimination or persecution of an identifiable group or race.').

attack and can be implemented overtly or even (in exceptional cases) by omission.[113] This requirement limits the offence to an *organized* series of similar acts, which further separates crimes against humanity from a domestic crime wave.[114] The additional requirements of planning or organizational policy are not required under customary international law,[115] however. The jurisdictional threshold thus is higher in the ICC and any domestic jurisdictions that specify the additional requirements.

'Attack' here is not co-extensive with the jurisdictional specifications of the IMT Charter. In particular, the original nexus between crimes against humanity and the waging of aggressive war[116] is no longer required under customary international law.[117] The concept encompasses *any* mistreatment of the civilian population.[118] Although armed force often will be present, it is not required.[119] This distinguishes the chapeau of crimes against humanity from that of war crimes,[120] although some overlap between them is inevitable.[121]

The civilian population

The second chapeau element requires the attack to be directed against a 'civilian population'. The modern view that *all* crimes against humanity are limited only to civilians represents something of a contraction since World War II. The IMT Charter and CC10 only restricted murder-type crimes against humanity to the 'civilian population', not the persecution-type.[122] The concept of persecution thus applied to military personnel as victims, even if other crimes against humanity did not.[123] The IMTFE Charter was even more expansive and had no restriction to civilians at all.[124] Nevertheless, the modern ICTY and ICTR

[113] It may not be inferred *solely* from inaction, however. Elements of Crimes art 7 n 6.

[114] Lee, *The ICC* 64 (2001).

[115] *Kunarac (AC)* [2002] ICTY ¶98 ('nothing in the [ICTY] Statute or in customary international law... required proof of... a plan or policy to commit these crimes.').

[116] IMT Charter art 6(c).

[117] *Tadic (Jurisdiction—AC)* [1995] ICTY ¶¶140–1. This represents an evolution of customary international law since Nuremberg, because the Nuremberg Principles did reflect the restrictive link. See Nuremberg Principle art 6(c) (2 Aug 1950) 2 YB-ILC 374. Despite the absence of a *required* nexus, the ICTY Statute nevertheless contained such a jurisdictional limitation. ICTY Statute art 5 (the 'Tribunal shall have the power to prosecute... crimes [against humanity] when committed in armed conflict, whether international or internal in character....').

[118] *Kunarac (AC)* [2002] ICTY ¶86. *Cf* Geneva Protocol I art 49 (providing that, in the context of war crimes, the term 'attack' refers to offensive or defensive 'acts of violence against the adversary.').

[119] Elements of Crimes art 7; Clark (n 65) 91.

[120] Lee, *The ICC* 74 (2001); *Tadic (AC)—Merits* [1999] ICTY ¶251 ('the "attack on the civilian population" and "the armed conflict" must be separate notions, although of course under Article 5 of the Statute the attack on "any civilian population" may be part of an 'armed conflict'....').

[121] Military attacks on civilians also constitute war crimes. ICC Statute arts 8(2)(b)(i) and 8(e)(i) ('intentionally directing attacks against the civilian population as such or against individual civilians not taking direct part in hostilities....'); 8(e)(viii) (displacing a civilian population for reasons other than its own safety or military imperative).

[122] IMT Charter art 6(c); CC10 art II(1)(c).

[123] This probably was intended to cover captured Russian and Polish soldiers persecuted in Nazi concentration camps.

[124] IMTFE Charter art 5(c).

statutes limit *all* crimes against humanity (both the 'murder' and 'persecution' types) to civilian populations,[125] as does the ICC Statute.[126]

The notion of a 'civilian population', which is a contextual element of all crimes against humanity[127] and some war crimes,[128] has strong links to international humanitarian law reflected in the Geneva Conventions. Although related, Geneva law applies to crimes against humanity only by analogy.[129] The four Geneva Conventions classify 'protected persons' under each treaty. The first covers wounded and sick in the field, together with religious and medical personnel.[130] The second protects the sick and wounded at sea and shipwrecked combatants.[131] The third covers prisoners of war.[132] Civilians in occupied territories are protected under the fourth.[133]

None of the four original Geneva treaties defines 'civilian' or 'civilian population', even though such terms appear throughout.[134] The phrase 'civilian population' was initially defined in the first optional protocol to the Geneva Conventions.[135] Article 50 delineates it by exclusion and default, such that 'civilians' are individuals who are *not* members of armed forces,[136] militias or volunteer corps,[137] organized resistance movements,[138] or groups within occupied territories that spontaneously take up arms.[139] It thus covers persons accompanying military units that are not part of them, as well as the crews of merchant marine vessels and civil aircraft of parties to the conflict.[140] When in doubt, victims are classified as civilians.[141] Article 50 is largely viewed as reflecting customary international law.[142]

125 ICTY statute art 5; ICTR Statute art 3.

126 ICC Statute art 7. The ICC's more restrictive articulation does not alter the viability of the broader Nuremberg definition under customary international law, however. Cassese, ICL 64, 354 (2003) (arguing that military personnel are still covered by persecution).

127 ICC Statute art 7.

128 ibid arts 8(2)(b)(i) and 8(2)(e)(i) (prohibiting 'intentionally directing attacks against the civilian population as such or against individual civilians not taking direct part in hostilities'); 8(2)(b)(viii) (prohibiting occupying power from transferring its own 'civilian population' into occupied territory); and 8(2)(e)(viii) (prohibiting displacement of a civilian population for reasons other than their own safety or military necessity).

129 *Tadic (TC)—Merits* [1997] ICTY ¶639.

130 Geneva Convention I arts 12–13.

131 Geneva Convention II arts 12–13.

132 Geneva Convention III art 4.

133 Geneva Convention IV art 4.

134 *Cf* Geneva Convention I art 18; Geneva Convention III art 23; and Geneva Convention IV arts 49, 55, 57, and 63(a).

135 Geneva Protocol I art 9.

136 ibid art 50(1) (excluding armed forces, as defined in Article 43 of the same instrument and in Geneva Convention III art 4(1)).

137 ibid (excluding militias or volunteer corps, as defined in Geneva Convention III art 4(2)).

138 ibid (excluding organized resistance movements, as defined in Geneva Convention III art 4(3)).

139 ibid (excluding residents of occupied territories who spontaneously take up arms, as defined in Geneva Convention III art 4(6)).

140 Geneva Convention III arts 4(4) and 4(5) (listing classifications not excluded from the definition of 'civilian' by Geneva Protocol I art 50(1)).

141 *Kunarac (TC)* [2001] ICTY ¶¶426, 435; Geneva Protocol I art 50(1). Note that the perpetrator's status is irrelevant—a member of the victim group can be liable for offences committed against other members of his group. *Enigster* [1951] 18 ILR 542 (Isr Dist Ct) (addressing crimes against fellow inmates at a Nazi concentration camp).

142 *Kordic & Cerkez (AC)* [2004] ICTY ¶97.

Logically, the civilian population comprises 'all persons who are civilians.'[143] The entire population need not be victimized, however.[144] Rather, the provision addresses collective violence and excludes isolated acts that may constitute war crimes or domestic offences not 'ris[ing] to the level of crimes against humanity.'[145] The population need not be homogeneous—it qualifies even if it includes non-civilians, provided that it is 'predominantly civilian'.[146]

Ultimately, the question requires a case-by-case determination.[147] The inquiry focuses on practical circumstances and includes victims who are 'not combatants' at the time of the offence.[148] This departs from the strict exclusionary criteria in Geneva law and permits civilian classification for some resistance fighters, even those *actively* engaged in a resistance movement, as well as individuals who at one time bore arms.[149] This includes former 'belligerents *hors de combat* who have laid down their weapons, either because they are wounded or because they have been captured'.[150] Armed individuals protecting their homes and families qualify as civilians, as do police and civil defence personnel.[151] There is no geographic link, either; refugees are covered as well.

Widespread or systematic

The third chapeau element requires the attack to be widespread *or* systematic in nature. Some domestic legislation specifies widespread *and* systematic,[152] but

143 ibid art 50(2). 144 *Tadic (TC)—Merits* [1997] ICTY ¶644.

145 ibid. This is somewhat redundant in light of the 'widespread or systematic' requirement (discussed below).

146 *Galic (TC)* [2003] ICTY ¶143. Individual members of the armed forces do not lose combatant status and become 'civilians' simply because they are not armed or in combat at the time the crimes are committed. *Blaskic (AC)* [2004] ICTY ¶114. As noted above, military status is important because it determines whether Geneva Conventions I–III or Geneva Convention IV will apply.

147 *Brdjanin (TC)* [2004] ICTY ¶134. Factors include the method and means of attack, the number and status of the victims, the nature of the offences during the attack, and the degree of resistance offered: ibid.

148 Secretary General ICTY Report (3 May 1993) UN Doc S/25704 ¶78; Geneva Protocol I art 1(2) (distinguishing 'combatants' from 'civilians'); *Akayesu (TC)* [1998] ICTR ¶582 ('[m]embers of the civilian population are people who are not taking any active part in the hostilities....'). Although *Akayesu* referenced Common Article 3 of the Geneva Conventions (which provides baseline humanitarian protection independent of the international or national character of the armed conflict) rather than Article 50 of Geneva Protocol I, the underlying concept is similar.

149 *Tadic (Merits—TC)* [1997] ICTY ¶643; *Barbie* (1985) 78 ILR 125 (Fr Ct Cass) 140 (members of French resistance). It excludes resistance movements effectively operating as military units, however: *Blaskic (AC)* [2004] ICTY ¶113 (evaluating criteria such as the existence of an organized command structure, the wearing of fixed signs recognizable at a distance, carrying arms openly, and the like).

150 Cassese, ICC 375 (2002); *Akayesu (TC)* [1998] ICTR ¶582. Early authority for this expanded view appears in the *High Command* case, where the tribunal held Germany's policy of inspiring mob violence against downed Allied fliers to be a crime against humanity. K Brand, 'Commentary' (1949) 15 LRTWC 1, 138.

151 Security Council Expert Report (27 May 1994) UN Doc A/1994/674 ¶78 ('"Civilian population" is used...in contradistinction to combatants or members of armed forces...the distinction between improvised self defence and actual military defence may be subtle, but none the less important.').

152 *Cf* Code Penal (France) art 212–1[1] ('large-scale *and* systematic practice') (emphasis added).

customary international law does not. 'Widespread' references the scale of the attack or the multitude of victims (or both)[153] but also includes 'the singular effect of an inhumane act of extraordinary magnitude'.[154] 'Systematic' addresses the organizational quality of the attack and the deliberate recurrence of similar criminal conduct.[155]

These alternate descriptors have different aims. 'Widespread' conveys an objective threshold of volume or scale, whereas 'systematic' is more qualitative and covers acts committed with deliberation or planning.[156] Although the characteristics are disjunctive, the ICC statute appears to require something close to *both* criteria because it defines an 'attack' as a '*course of conduct* involving the *multiple commission* of [prohibited acts] . . . pursuant to or in furtherance of a State or organizational policy to commit such an attack.' (Emphasis added.)[157] Unless 'widespread' was limited to geography, it is doubtful that a 'course of conduct' involving 'multiple' acts in furtherance of a 'plan or policy' would not be both widespread *and* systematic. In this sense, the analytic distinction between the concepts probably is not as clear in practice as the ICC's text implies.[158]

Prohibited acts

Crimes against humanity are ordinary criminal acts committed within a wider criminal context. The prohibited act in question (murder, rape, mistreatment, etc) must form part of the larger attack on the civilian population. Isolated offences are not crimes against humanity.[159] But as long as it is part and parcel of the wider attack, even a single prohibited act will suffice.[160]

There is significant geographic and temporal flexibility in determining whether a particular offence forms part of the larger attack. It includes offences committed before and after the main attack and even crimes occurring in a different region, as long as they cannot reasonably be characterized as isolated events.[161] The underlying conduct amounting to crimes against humanity under customary

153 *Kamuhanda (TC)* [2004] ICTR ¶¶664–5.

154 *Kordic & Cerkez (TC)* [2001] ICTY ¶179.

155 *Brdjanin (TC)* [2004] ICTY ¶135; *Kamuhanda (TC)* [2004] ICTR ¶¶664–5.

156 Clark (n 65) 91.

157 ICC Statute art 7(2)(a). The existence of a plan or policy also is useful as an evidentiary matter to establish that a given attack was widespread or systematic. *Kunarac (AC)* [2002] ICTY ¶98.

158 Clark (n 65) 91 ('something very close to widespread *and* systematic appears to be required by the very definition of "attack".').

159 *Tadic (Indictment—TC)* [1995] ICTY ¶11; Cassese, ICC 357 (2002) ('isolated or sporadic misbehaviour, however heinous and revolting, cannot be regarded as a crime against humanity.').

160 *Kunarac (AC)* [2002] ICTY ¶96; Cassese, ICC 360 (2002).

161 *Kunarac (AC)* [2002] ICTY ¶100; *Semanza (TC)* [2003] ICTR ¶330 ('The victim(s) of the enumerated act need not necessarily share geographic or other defining features with the civilian population that forms the primary target of the underlying attack, but such characteristics may be used to demonstrate that the enumerated act forms part of the attack.').

international law, which is identical in the ICTY and ICTR Statutes,[162] appears to have been drawn verbatim from CC10.[163] The listing of prohibited acts was expanded significantly in the ICC Statute,[164] which also widened the types of groups covered by persecution.[165] At present, the authoritative list (derived from the ICC Statute[166] and jurisprudence from the international criminal tribunals) appears to include:

- Murder;[167]
- Extermination;[168]
- Enslavement;[169]
- Deportation or forcible transfer;[170]
- Imprisonment or severe deprivation of liberty;[171]

[162] ICTR Statute art 3 and ICTY Statute art 5 (including murder, extermination, enslavement, deportation, imprisonment, torture, rape, persecutions on political, racial and religious grounds, and other inhumane acts).

[163] CC10 art II(1)(c).

[164] ICC Statute art 7(1) (adding forcible transfer, sexual violence (sexual offences besides rape), enforced disappearance and apartheid). The expansion appears to derive from the ILC's Draft Code of Offences Against the Peace and Security of Mankind, which had expanded upon prior articulations of crimes against humanity. [1996] Draft Code art 18. Whether this represents a genuine enlargement of prohibited conduct is debatable—the conduct at issue probably qualified already as a form of 'other inhumane acts'). It does reflect more specific labelling of that conduct, however.

[165] ICC Statute art 7(1)(h) (adding nationality, ethnicity, culture, gender and a provision covering discrimination 'universally recognized as impermissible under international law.').

[166] The ICC Statute is useful to consider here, not only because it is the key international forum for the enforcement of international criminal law (at least prospectively), but also because it represents some consensus on state practice. *Tadic (AC)—Merits* [1999] ICTY ¶¶221–5. Nevertheless, the ICC treaty was never intended to codify or further develop international law beyond its own jurisdiction. It is not conclusive on international criminal law, and its provisions must be considered in that context. ICC Preparatory Committee Report (13 Sep 1996) UN Doc A/51/22 ¶59 (purposes of the ICC Statute).

[167] *Akayesu (TC)* [1998] ICTR ¶589; ICC Statute art 7(1)(a) and corresponding Elements of Crimes (that accused killed or caused the death of members of the protected population).

[168] ICC Statute arts 7(1)(b), 7(2)(b) and corresponding Elements of Crimes ('mass killing') and Clark (n 65) 83 ('core meaning' is 'multiple killings'). Extermination requires: (i) acts contributing to the killing of a large number of individuals; and (ii) intent to kill or inflict serious injury, with 'reasonable knowledge that such act or omission is likely to cause death' or intent 'to participate in the elimination of a number of individuals, in the knowledge that his action is part of a vast murderous enterprise in which a large number of individuals are systematically marked for killing or killed.': *Vasiljevic (TC)* [2002] ICTY ¶229.

[169] *Kunarac (AC)* [2002] ICTY ¶¶116–24; ICC Statute arts 7(1)(c), 7(2)(c) and corresponding Elements of Crimes (exercising 'any or all of the powers attaching to the right of ownership over one or more persons') and Clark (n 65) 83 (concept includes *de facto* or *de jure* exercise of power over another).

[170] *Brdjanin (TC)* [2004] ICTY ¶540 ('forced displacement of individuals from the area in which they are lawfully present without grounds permitted under international law,' either beyond the state's borders (deportation) or within the state (displacement)); ICC Statute arts 7(1)(d), 7(2) (d) and corresponding Elements of Crimes (forcibly displacing persons 'by expulsion or other coercive acts'). This includes so-called ethnic cleansing. Clark (n 65) 84.

[171] *Kordic & Cerkez (TC)* [2001] ICTY ¶¶302–3 ('arbitrary imprisonment . . . the deprivation of liberty of the individual without due process of law. . . .'); ICC Statute art 7(1)(e) and corresponding Elements of Crimes ('severely deprived one or more persons of physical liberty.').

- Torture;[172]
- Sexual violence (including rape,[173] sexual slavery,[174] enforced prostitution,[175] forced pregnancy,[176] enforced sterilization,[177] and other acts of 'comparable gravity');
- Persecution;[178]
- Enforced Disappearance;[179]
- Apartheid;[180] and
- Other inhumane acts of similar character and gravity.[181]

The mens rea *of crimes against humanity*

The *mens rea* of all crimes against humanity is the intent to commit a prohibited act coupled with knowledge of the broader criminal context (chapeau) in which the act is committed.[182] In order to capture opening salvos, it also suffices to

[172] *Kunarac (AC)* [2002] ICTY ¶¶142–56; ICC Statute arts 7(1)(f), (2)(e) and corresponding Elements of Crimes ('inflicting severe physical or mental pain or suffering' upon persons 'in the custody or under the control of the perpetrator' which 'was not inherent in or incidental to . . . lawful sanctions'). This is broader than the Convention on Torture, which also requires 'the consent or acquiescence of a public official or other person acting in an official capacity.' Convention Against Torture art 1(1) (10 Dec 1984) 1465 UNTS 85.

[173] *Akayesu (TC)* [1998] ICTR ¶¶596–8; ICC Statute art 7(1)(g) and corresponding Elements of Crimes (requiring penetration of victim's person under forcible or coercive circumstances). But see *Kunarac (AC)* [2002] ICTY ¶¶129–30 (overruling inconsistent case law and holding that force or the threat of force is *not* required).

[174] ICC Statute art 7(1)(g) and corresponding Elements of Crimes (exercising 'powers attaching to the rights of ownership over one or more persons' combined with causing 'such person or persons to engage in one or more acts of a sexual nature.').

[175] ICC Statute art 7(1)(g) and corresponding Elements of Crimes (causing victims to engage in 'acts of a sexual nature' under forcible or coercive circumstances in order 'to obtain pecuniary or other advantage.').

[176] ICC Statute arts 7(1)(g), 7(2)(f) and corresponding Elements of Crimes (confining 'one or more women forcibly made pregnant, with the intent of affecting the ethnic composition of any population or carrying out other grave violations of international law.').

[177] ICC Statute art 7(1)(g) and corresponding Elements of Crimes (depriving victims 'of biological reproductive capacity' without medical necessity or the genuine consent of the victim).

[178] ICC Statute arts 7(1)(h), 7(2)(a), 7(2)(g) and corresponding Elements of Crimes (depriving 'one or more persons of fundamental rights' by reason of the victim's identity with a group or collectivity, including without limitation, groups defined on 'political, racial, national, ethnic, cultural, religious, gender . . . or other grounds that are universally recognized as impermissible under international law.').

[179] ICC Statute arts 7(1)(i), 7(2)(i) and corresponding Elements of Crimes (arresting, detaining or abducting one or more persons and refusing to acknowledge or provide information about same).

[180] ICC Statute art 7(1)(j) and corresponding Elements of Crimes ('inhumane acts . . . committed in the context of an institutionalized regime of systematic oppression and domination by one racial group over any other racial group or groups . . . .'). This definition is narrower than the definition provided in the Apartheid Convention. Apartheid Convention arts I-II.

[181] ICC Statute art 7(1)(k) and corresponding Elements of Crimes ('great suffering, or serious injury to body or mental or physical health.'); *Kupreskic (TC)* [2000] ICTY ¶¶563–4 (offence provides 'a residual category, as it was felt to be undesirable for this category to be exhaustively enumerated . . . .' and covers 'a set of basic rights appertaining to human beings, the infringement of which may amount, depending on the accompanying circumstances, to a crime against humanity . . . .').

[182] *Tadic—Merits (TC)* [1997] ICTY ¶¶656–9; *Kupreskic (TC)* [2000] ICTY ¶556.

intend certain conduct to become part of a broader attack.[183] *Knowledge* does not necessarily imply *support*. The opportunist who takes advantage of a wider attack, for whatever reason, is equally guilty as one who participates to further it.[184] His motives are irrelevant,[185] as is whether his acts are directed against the targeted population overall or against individual victims.[186] He need not have precise details of the attack or all of its characteristics;[187] it is sufficient to know that 'there is an attack on the civilian population and that his acts comprise part of that attack'.[188] 'Knowledge' here thus extends beyond 'virtual certainty'.[189] It certainly includes actual knowledge (which typically is inferred from the circumstances).[190] But it also covers so-called advertent recklessness, where the accused deliberately disregards a known risk relative to the broader attack.[191]

Various occupation courts following World War II appeared willing to *presume* knowledge of the broader criminal context.[192] In contrast, modern practice requires proof of this element at trial.[193] The latter is preferable. It is the perpetrator's awareness of the overarching context in which his crimes are committed that transforms his conduct from a domestic offence into a serious international crime.[194] The requirement of knowledge of the chapeau distinguishes the substantive elements of the crime from the procedural question of the court's power to exercise jurisdiction over such offences.[195] The circumstances

[183] Elements of Crimes art 7; Lee, *The ICC* 61 (2001).

[184] *Blaskic (TC)* [2000] ICTY ¶¶254–7.

[185] *Tadic (AC)—Merits* [1999] ICTY ¶272.

[186] *Kunarac (AC)* [2002] ICTY ¶103.

[187] Elements of Crimes art 7.

[188] *Kunarac (AC)* [2002] ICTY ¶102, quoting *Kunarac (TC)* [2001] ICTY ¶434.

[189] *Cf* MPC s 2.02(2)(b).

[190] *Kunarac (AC)* [2002] ICTY ¶102 (sufficiency of actual knowledge); *Celebici (TC)* [1998] ICTY ¶386 (setting forth criteria to draw an inference of knowledge).

[191] MPC s 2.02(2)(c) ('consciously disregards a substantial and unjustifiable risk that the material element exists....'); *Kunarac (TC)* [2001] ICTY ¶434 (D must 'at least take the risk that his act is part of the attack') and ¶435 (D 'must have known or considered the possibility that the victim of his crime was a civilian.').

[192] *Justice* [USMT 1947] 3 TWC 1, 977–8 (D 'knew or should have known ... that he was guilty of participation in a nationally organized system of injustice and persecution'); *Ministries* [USMT 1949] 12 TWC 3, 339 (although knowledge of Hitler's aggressive war was 'an essential element of guilt under count one of the indictment, a very different situation arises with respect to [war crimes or crimes against humanity].'). But see *IG Farben* [USMT 1948] 7 TWC 1, 1113 (refusing to impute military-style knowledge of an illegal plan for the general rearmament of Germany to civilian industrialists).

[193] *Celebici (TC)* [1998] ICTY ¶386. But see Askin (n 99) 43 (disputing knowledge requirement and arguing that 'has no foundation in the fifty-three year legislative history and customary usage of crimes against humanity').

[194] In the ICC, similar considerations apply to war crimes. Offenders must be aware of the factual circumstances of the armed conflict but need not formulate any understanding of its legal character as an 'armed conflict' (internal or international) as defined in international law. Elements of Crimes art 8 intro ¶3.

[195] Compare *Finta* (1994) 1 SCR 701 (Can Sup Ct) ¶98 (arguing that chapeau elements were substantive components of crimes against humanity) with ibid ¶291 (LaForest J dissenting) (arguing that chapeau were merely 'additional circumstances ... in terms of the international system to justify extraterritorial jurisdiction ....').

in which crimes against humanity are committed thus are intricately related to the substance of the offence itself. As discussed below, the line of demarcation is entirely different for genocide, which becomes an international matter based solely upon the genocidaire's specific intent against the group and conduct against group members.

C. Persecution

Of the two basic types of crimes against humanity, the persecution-type depends far more upon the offender's mental state than the murder-type. Persecution is a more specific offence because it requires the additional element of intent to discriminate on prohibited grounds.[196] It is this heightened *mens rea* that fundamentally characterizes the crime of persecution; no other crime against humanity need be committed on discriminatory grounds.[197] This brings persecution closest analytically to the crime of genocide, which likewise is characterized by its specific intent.

Persecution was charged and proven at Nuremberg, although specific details were lacking. The IMT concluded that 'persecution of the Jews at the hands of the Nazi Government has been proved in the greatest detail before the Tribunal. It is a record of consistent and systematic inhumanity on the greatest scale'.[198] Persecution played no role in the Tokyo trials,[199] although it was an issue in several trials under CC10.[200]

The ICTY classifies persecution as an 'umbrella' crime whose 'unique character is derived from a requirement of a specific discriminatory intent'.[201] Its elements were discussed at length in *Krnojelac*, which synthesized three key decisions on

[196] In contrast, '[a]any form of inhumanity for any purpose or caused by reason of any prompting falls under the definition of the first part....' Drost 188 (1959).*Göring* [IMT 1946] 1 IMT Proceedings 171, 247.

[197] *Tadic (Merits—AC)* [1999] ICTY ¶305. This is notwithstanding the ICTR Statute, which requires *all* crimes against humanity within ICTR jurisdiction to be committed on discriminatory grounds: ICTR Statute art 3. As noted previously, the ICTR's limitation is jurisdictional and does not reflect customary international law.

[198] *Göring* [IMT 1946] 1 IMT Proceedings 171, 247. A more specific case involved Nazi propagandist Jules Streicher. ibid 302–4 (finding defendant guilty of incitement to 'murder and extermination at the time when Jews... were being killed under the most horrible conditions' constituted persecution).

[199] O Swaak-Goldman, 'Persecution' in 1 McDonald and Goldman 249 (2000).

[200] *Cf Justice* [USMT 1947] 3 TWC 1, 64.

[201] *Banovic (TC)* [2003] ICTY ¶¶38, 41 (internal quotations omitted). See also Ratner and Abrams 61 (1997) ('[c]ertain acts are so heinous and destructive of a person's humanity that they per se are crimes. Others are crimes because the perpetrator acts against the victim based on political, racial or religious grounds and attacks humanity through some of the most basic groups into which it is organized.').

the offence.[202] In addition to the chapeau characteristic of all crimes against humanity, persecution is a culpable act or omission that:

1. Discriminates in fact and which denies or infringes upon a fundamental right laid down in international customary or treaty law (*actus reus*); and
2. Was carried out deliberately with the intention to discriminate on one of the listed grounds... (*mens rea*).[203]

The ICC Statute is similar:

> Persecution against any identifiable group or collectivity on political, racial, national, ethnic, cultural, religious, gender...or other grounds that are universally recognized as impermissible under international law, in connection with any act referred to in this paragraph or any crime within the jurisdiction of the Court.[204]

Actus reus of persecution

Persecution covers particularly grave or harmful conduct that deprives fundamental rights guaranteed under *international* law.[205] Although a course of conduct usually is involved, a single act can suffice.[206] Acts constituting other crimes against humanity (murder, rape, etc) certainly can qualify,[207] as do unlawful detention,[208] denial of medical care,[209] deportation or forcible transfer,[210] terrorizing civilians,[211] and war crimes.[212]

Conduct not qualifying as a 'murder-type' crime against humanity must be of equivalent gravity in order to constitute persecution. 'This test will only be met by gross or blatant denials of fundamental human rights... [when] examined in their context and with consideration of their cumulative effect.'[213] Put another way, such conduct violates 'fundamental freedoms to which every individual is entitled without distinction,' as embodied in international instruments like the UN Charter and the ICCPR.[214] The underlying conduct need not even be otherwise criminal.[215] The essence of persecution is unlawful discrimination, rather

[202] *Tadic (Merits—TC)* [1997] ICTY ¶15; *Kupreskic (TC)* [2000] ICTY ¶¶567–627; *Kordic and Cerkez (TC)* [2001] ICTY ¶¶89, 195.

[203] *Krnojelac (TC)* [2002] ICTY ¶431 and n 1290.

[204] ICC Statute art 7(1)(h).

[205] Elements of Crimes art 7(1)(h); Lee, *The ICC* 96 (2001).

[206] *Simic (TC)* [2003] ICTY ¶50.

[207] *Kupreskic (TC)* [2000] ICTY ¶¶600, 615.

[208] *Blaskic (TC)* [2000] ICTY ¶234.

[209] *Brdjanin (TC)* [2004] ICTY ¶¶1046–48.

[210] ibid.

[211] *Obrenovic (TC)* [2003] ICTY ¶36.

[212] Swaak-Goldman (n 199) 255.

[213] *Vasiljevic (TC)* [2002] ICTY ¶¶247, 434. See also *Banovic (TC)* [2003] ICTY ¶42 (conduct 'of the utmost gravity').

[214] [1996] Draft Code art 18 cmt 9; UN Charter arts 1, 55 and ICCPR art 2.

[215] [1996] Draft Code art 18 cmt 9; *Krnojelac (AC)* [2003] ICTY ¶¶5–6 (Shahabuddeen J) (opining that the *persecution* must arise to the same level of gravity as other crimes against humanity and noting that non-criminal acts like closing bank accounts and denying educational and work opportunities—which would never possess equivalent inherent gravity to criminal acts like

than the underlying conduct per se.[216] The seriousness of the conduct and its cumulative effect upon the victims are the determining factors.[217]

Persecutory acts need not be physical in nature. While personal violence certainly qualifies, severe discrimination in economic,[218] social[219] or judicial affairs,[220] or with respect to property,[221] also can suffice. Persecution extends beyond denying the *equal enjoyment* of rights allowed to others. There must be a genuine deprivation of the right itself, although serious discrimination in equality may well work a rights deprivation in practice.[222]

The ICTY and ICTR statutes, like the IMT Charter and CC10, limited persecution to political, racial, and religious groups.[223] The categories were 'modernized'[224] in the ICC and expanded to include national, ethnic, cultural and gender groups, together with a 'catch-all' provision covering 'grounds that are universally recognized as impermissible under international law'.[225] The ICC, however, requires persecution to be committed in conjunction with another crime against humanity or one of the other offences within the ICC's jurisdiction.[226] In this sense, the ICC Statute reflects a narrower definition of persecution than that available under customary international law.[227]

murder and assault—nevertheless could amount to persecution when committed with discriminatory intent).

[216] *Barbie* (1985) 78 ILR 125 (Fr Ct Cass) 143 ('the discrimination itself makes the act inhumane' and a crime against humanity).

[217] Compare *Simic (TC)* [2003] ICTY ¶¶53–6 (by itself, forcible occupation was not of equivalent gravity), ¶¶67–9 (interrogations and forcing victims to sign false statements were not acts of equivalent gravity) with *Krnojelac (AC)* [2003] ICTY ¶199 (forced labour was of equivalent gravity) and *Banovic (TC)* [2003] ICTY ¶¶41–2 ('confinement in inhumane conditions, harassment, humiliation and psychological abuse' were of equivalent gravity).

[218] *Brdjanin (TC)* [2004] ICTY ¶¶1032–41 (deprivation of livelihood and participation in certain professions*); Eichmann (TC)* [1961] 36 ILR 5 (Isr Dist Ct) ¶¶56, 130 (same).

[219] *Tadic (TC)—Merits* [1997] ICTY ¶708 (inciting hatred and violence against the victim group); *Eichmann (TC)* [1961] 36 ILR 5 (Isr Dist Ct) ¶¶56, 130 (denial of participation in the cultural life of a state). Whether 'hate speech' constitutes persecution is an open question. Compare *Nahimana (TC)* [2003] ICTR ¶¶1072, 1078 (hate speech constitutes persecution, which is broader than direct and public incitement) with *Kordic & Cerkez (TC)* [2001] ICTY ¶209 (short of incitement, encouraging or promoting hatred of a group does not constitute persecution). The intersection of hate speech and countervailing rights of free expression are significant issues in and of themselves. For an analysis of opposing viewpoints on these issues, compare Lawrence 80–110 (1999) with Jacobs and Potter 111–30 (1998).

[220] *Brdjanin (TC)* [2004] ICTY ¶¶1044–5 (denial of judicial process); *Justice* [USMT 1947] 3 TWC 1 (perversion of legal process and law of high treason).

[221] *Obrenovic (TC)* [2003] ICTY ¶37. The property offence must be linked to the victim's well-being, however. *Eichmann (TC)* [1961] 36 ILR 5 (Isr Dist Ct) ¶204 (determining that crimes against humanity include plunder of property where 'the plunder is only part of a general process' of violence); *Flick* [USMT 1947] 6 TWC 3, 26 (finding that acts against industrial property would not constitute crimes against humanity but that acts against personal property that negatively impacted health and welfare would).

[222] Swaak-Goldman (n 199) 253.

[223] IMT Charter art 6(c); CC10 art II(1)(c); ICTY Statute art 5; ICTR Statute art 3.

[224] Lee, *The ICC* 95 (2001).

[225] ICC Statute art 7(1)(h).

[226] ibid.

[227] *Kupreskic (TC)* [2000] ICTY ¶581 (finding that 'article 7(1)(h) is not consonant with customary international law' and refusing to adopt a similar limitation in the ICTY).

Persecution also is a *results-based* crime.[228] There must be an actual discriminatory *effect* upon the victims.[229] This differentiates the *actus reus* of persecution from that of other crimes against humanity.[230] There has been some confusion over this requirement in the international criminal tribunals, however, apparently stemming from a failure to analytically segregate mistakes of fact by the accused from the composition of groups in the first instance.[231]

For a variety of reasons, the superior method of defining a group's membership is to adopt the genocidaire's subjective understanding of the group's defining characteristics.[232] But once those subjective criteria are discerned, they become objectively dispositive in determining whether a member of the group has been victimized.[233] Offences involving groups and their members typically involve a *shared* agreement by perpetrators about what characteristics group members possess. In Nazi Germany, for example, membership in the group of 'Jews' was determined based on birth and the number of Jewish grandparents. These criteria represent the objective manifestation of the Nazis' subjective determination of what constituted a 'Jew'.[234] But once such criteria are established, any erroneous subsequent belief as to whether a particular victim possesses those group characteristics should be treated as a mistake of fact.

Assume, for example, that D defines the political group, communists as anyone who registers as a communist on the voting rolls. The registration characteristic is dispositive: if someone registers, he is a communist, if not, he is outside the group. D attacks and seriously injures V, believing (incorrectly) that V had registered as a communist. In fact, V had never so registered and actually was a Social Democrat. D thus is factually mistaken about whether V is a communist.

[228] *Krnojelac (TC)* [2002] ICTY ¶431; *Ruggiu (TC)* [2000] ICTR ¶21; Elements of Crimes art 7(1)(h) (where accused 'seriously deprive[s]' the victim of one or more fundamental rights).

[229] *Krnojelac (AC)* [2003] ICTY ¶185.

[230] *Krnojelac (TC)* [2002] ICTY ¶432 ('without such a requirement, an accused could be convicted of persecution without anyone actually having been persecuted.') and ¶435 n 1306 (collecting cases).

[231] Compare *Naletilic (TC)* [2003] ICTY ¶636 n 1572 ('if a certain person is defined by the perpetrator as belonging to the targeted group, this definition becomes "discrimination in fact" for the victim as it may not be rebutted, even if such classification may be incorrect under objective criteria.') and *Kvocka (TC)* [2001] ICTY ¶195 ('if a person was targeted for abuse because she was suspected of belonging to the Muslim group, the discrimination element is met even if the suspicion proves inaccurate.') with *Krnojelac (TC)* [2002] ICTY ¶432 n 1292 (unsuccessful attempts to persecute theoretically constitute *attempted* persecution, but cannot be punished because no such offence exists within the ICTY jurisdiction) and *Krnojelac (AC)* [2003] ICTY ¶185 (disagreeing with trial chamber and suggesting that such cases of mistaken identity can constitute the persecution). As discussed below, the analysis of the trial chamber in *Krnojelac* is more analytically sound.

[232] The reasons for this were discussed in Chapter 3.

[233] Offences involving groups and their members typically involve *shared* agreement by perpetrators about the characteristics group members possess. In Nazi Germany, for example, membership in the group of 'Jews' was determined based on birth and the number of Jewish grandparents—these criteria represent the objective manifestation of the Nazis' subjective definition of 'Jews': Reich Citizenship Law: First Regulation (Germany 14 Nov 1935).

[234] Reich Citizenship Law: First Regulation (Germany 14 Nov 1935).

D is not liable for persecution for the injuries to V because he has not committed its *actus reus*—he has not discriminated in fact against a member of the group of communists.

Note that this is contrary to the view of the ICTY Appeals Chamber, which suggested that such cases of mistaken identity can constitute actual persecution.[235] In *Krnojelac*, the court opined in a similar example that 'a Serb mistaken for a Muslim may still be the victim of the crime of persecution. The Appeals Chamber considers that the act committed against him institutes discrimination in fact, *vis-à-vis* the other Serbs who were not subject to such acts, effected with the will to discriminate against a group on grounds of ethnicity.').

The difficulty with the tribunal's position is that it allows for a conviction for persecution without requiring parity between *actus reus* and *mens rea* in terms of the persecuted group. Even if the conduct was discriminatory in fact against the injured Serbs '*vis-à-vis* the other Serbs' not targeted, the fact remains that the offender never intended to discriminate against *Serbs*—he intended to discriminate against *Muslims*. The *actus reus* against one group cannot be combined with the *mens rea* against another to form persecution.

This is not to say that he has committed no crime. Among other things, he should be punished for an attempt. He had intent to discriminate and, had things been as he believed them to be, persecution would have been committed. To date, however, the punishment of international criminals for attempts has been more viable in theory than in practice. The ICTY and ICTR Statutes only recognize attempts for genocide,[236] such that 'attempted persecution' falls outside their jurisdiction. This weakness was corrected in the ICC Statute, which criminalizes attempts to complete *any* crime within its jurisdiction, including persecution.[237]

Mens rea of persecution

As noted previously, in addition to conscious awareness of the widespread or systematic attack on the civilian population (as required for all crimes against humanity),[238] persecution also requires discriminatory intent.[239] The offender must have the specific intent to discriminate on prohibited grounds. Discrimination must be a genuine aim of his conduct, though it need not be his sole criminal objective.[240] Unlawful discrimination must be the perpetrator's goal. It is not enough for him to know or even be virtually certain that discrimination will occur:[241] a mere awareness that a course of conduct will have a discriminatory effect is insufficient.[242]

235 *Krnojelac (AC)* [2003] ICTY ¶185.
236 ICTR Statute art 2(3)(d); ICTY Statute art 4(3)(d).
237 ICC Statute art 25(3)(f).
238 *Kordic & Cerkez (TC)* [2001] ICTY ¶212.
239 Lee, *The ICC* 95 (2001).
240 *Krnojelac (TC)* [2002] ICTY ¶435.
241 Compare MPC s 2.02(a) (purpose) with ibid s 2.02(b) (knowledge).
242 *Vasiljevic (TC)* [2002] ICTY ¶248.

As with any mental state, absent direct evidence, discriminatory intent can be inferred from the circumstances.[243] A discriminatory plan or policy against a particular group—while not an element of the crime—can serve as useful evidence that discriminatory intent existed.[244] The disparate treatment of members of one group versus another also can establish discriminatory intent against members of the disfavoured group.[245]

D. Comparative analysis

Genocide and crimes against humanity both emerged in response to Nazi atrocities during World War II. As noted previously, genocide initially was conceived as a type of crime against humanity.[246] It sometimes still is described in this way,[247] although obvious distinctions '[make] the relationship awkward'.[248] Nevertheless, '[g]enocide and crimes against humanity always overlapped, in that genocide was born of the persecution part of the already heinous category of crimes against humanity and was established as the most heinous of the heinous.'[249]

As noted previously, genocide is defined by its *dolus specialis vis à vis* the protected group, not results. This is counter-intuitive because the term conveys (in its normative sense) mass slaughters such as the Holocaust. Nevertheless, the destruction of a protected group is not required. Indeed, genocide can occur without a single member of the group dying or suffering any permanent injury.

Professor Cassese notes that genocide and crimes against humanity

> share at least three elements: (i) they encompass very serious offences that shock our sense of humanity in that they constitute attacks on the most fundamental aspects of human dignity; (ii) they do not constitute isolated events but are instead normally part of a larger context, either because they are large-scale and massive infringements of human dignity or because they are linked to a broader practice of misconduct; and (iii) although they need not be perpetrated by State officials or by officials of entities such as insurgents, they are usually carried out with the complicity, connivance or at least the toleration of the authorities.[250]

243 *Krnojelac (AC)* [2003] ICTY ¶184 (intent may be inferred provided that the facts of the case and 'circumstances surrounding the commission of the alleged acts substantiate the existence of such intent.').

244 *Krnojelac (TC)* [2002] ICTY ¶435.

245 *Krnojelac (AC)* [2003] ICTY ¶186 (differences in treatment and the fact that beatings were inflicted only upon the non-Serb detainees supported an inference of persecutory discrimination based on political or religious affiliation).

246 *Justice* [USMT 1947] 3 TWC 1; *RuSHA* [USMT 1948] 4 TWC 599.

247 *Jelisic (TC)* [1999] ICTY ¶68.

248 W Schabas, 'Problems of International Codification—Were the Atrocities in Cambodia and Kosovo Genocide?' (2001) 35 New England LR 287, 300–1.

249 Clark (n 65) 91–2 (discussing the development of war crimes, crimes against humanity and genocide and noting that '[s]ome of this expansion has been onto one another's turf.').

250 Cassese, *ICC* 339 (2002).

Assuming that the chapeau elements of crimes against humanity are established,[251] there often will be an overlap with genocide. The underlying acts constituting genocide (killing, maiming, etc) also qualify as 'murder' type crimes against humanity (extermination, torture, etc). Genocide in many cases also constitutes persecution, assuming that: (i) the acts constituting genocide per se discriminate in fact; and (ii) that the *mens rea* of genocide (to destroy the group) per se constitutes intent to discriminate against individual members of that group.[252]

Some diplomats and commentators suggest that it simply is unnecessary to revisit the question of political genocide because persecution is sufficient to protect political groups.[253] As shown below, this proposition is incorrect. Although genocide and crimes against humanity overlap *some* of the time, nevertheless they have different aims and differ in many respects. These distinctions will be demonstrated here in two key areas:

1. whether genocide and crimes against humanity are cumulative offences, such that a conviction for both crimes is permissible (and indeed necessary in order to fully describe the underlying criminal transaction at issue); and
2. whether the use of crimes against humanity as a proxy for a more precise concept of political genocide runs afoul of the fundamental principles of representative labelling of criminal offences.

Cumulative offences

The substantive definition of criminal offences is critical because

> [t]he criminal law plays a crucial role in defining behaviour and reconstructing it to fit the predetermined categories of existing offenses. It is the essential first step in determining which behaviour is subject to criminal justice and which [is] not. In defining what is and what is not crime, the law is far from merely responsive to offenses committed. It actively maps out the contours of criminal law.[254]

Any course of criminal conduct has the potential to implicate simultaneously the legal definition of more than one offence. When conduct falls within multiple definitions, a conviction for more than one crime may be required to fully describe the totality of the criminality at issue. In such cases, '[m]ultiple

[251] As discussed below, this assumption is critical. The chapeau elements are a key distinction between the offences.

[252] See *Vasiljevic (AC)* [2004] ICTY ¶140 ('the acts of the accused were *in fact* discriminatory, in that the men were killed only because they were Muslims'); ICC Statute art 7(1)(h) (serious deprivation under international law).

[253] *Cf* ICC Ad Hoc Committee Report (6 Sep 1995) UN Doc A/50/22 ¶61(declining to consider the issue during ICC negotiations); Schabas 171 (2009) (offering historical and legal support for the view that offences 'against groups not covered by Article II of the Genocide Convention are adequately addressed by other legal norms, in particular the prohibition of crimes against humanity.'); Benavides-Vanegas (n 2) 579, 612–13 (arguing that political groups are adequately protected already).

[254] Zedner 11 (2004).

convictions ... describe the full culpability of the accused and ... provide a complete picture of his criminal conduct'.[255] The legal principles on cumulation govern the question of whether the criminal transaction is sufficiently described by a single offence or whether multiple crimes must be recorded to fully delineate its scope.[256]

Cumulative convictions generally are permissible under both international[257] and domestic law.[258] The analysis, which presents a question of law,[259] determines whether an offender can be held liable for multiple crimes grounded in the same underlying conduct.[260] It is fundamental, however, that offenders cannot be sanctioned beyond the actual scope of their behaviour[261] or punished for multiple offences amounting to the same crime.[262]

There are three possibilities when a criminal transaction constitutes (or appears to constitute) more than one offence. The crimes will: (i) not overlap at all; (ii) overlap fully; or (iii) overlap partially. Taking these in order, in the first scenario the perpetrator commits multiple crimes simultaneously or as part of the same transaction but each offence has distinct elements.[263] An example would be a crime spree where D murders V, rapes V's wife and smashes V's television (a property offence). The offences share little more than temporal and physical proximity and convictions for all three are warranted.

This analysis applies equally to cases involving multiple victims. If D throws a bomb intended to kill V1, V2, V3 and V4, he is rightly convicted of four separate murders. Although his acts often are grouped together for trial and even sentencing, the transaction 'consists of a cluster of [distinct] offences'[264] that warrant separate convictions. In each of these cases, the temporal and physical proximity among the crimes does not alter their substantive criminality. D is equally guilty of multiple offences if the murder, rape and vandalism transpire weeks apart or

[255] *Krstic (AC)* [2004] ICTY ¶217. See also *Kordic & Cerkez (AC)* [2004] ICTY ¶1033 ('The cumulative convictions test serves twin aims: ensuring that the accused is convicted only for distinct offences, and at the same time, ensuring that the convictions entered fully reflect his criminality.').

[256] S Walther, 'Cumulation of Offences' in Cassese, *ICC* 475, 476 (2000).

[257] *Cf* Elements of Crimes pmbl ('A particular conduct may constitute one or more crimes.'). Although there is no international law per se on cumulation, international tribunals draw upon domestic jurisprudence as general principles of law and persuasive authority. *Kupreskic (TC)* [2000] ICTY ¶¶668–95; ICJ Statute art 38(1)(c),(d).

[258] *Cf Rezaq* (1998) 134 F3d 1121 (US Ct App (DC)) 1128–30 (conviction in Malta for murder and hostage taking did not bar US prosecution for air piracy); *Celebici (AC)* [2001] ICTY ¶¶406–9 (surveying domestic practice).

[259] *Kordic & Cerkez (AC)* [2004] ICTY ¶¶1032–3, 1040–1 (focusing on the legal elements of offences).

[260] It also gives rise to procedural issues, such as whether an indictment must charge cumulatively or in the alternative. Cumulative charging is the preferred practice in both international criminal tribunals, for example, The propriety of cumulative convictions arises only if an accused actually is convicted of both crimes. *Celebici (AC)* [2001] ICTY ¶400.

[261] *Krstic (AC)* [2004] ICTY ¶82 (Shahabuddeen J dissenting).

[262] *Kunarac (AC)* [2002] ICTY ¶170.

[263] This is 'real' concurrence (realkonkurrenz) under civil law: *Kupreskic (TC)* [2000] ICTY ¶661; Ambos and Wirth (n 102) 703.

[264] *Kupreskic (TC)* [2000] ICTY ¶678.

if he kills V1–V4 at separate times. These cases of 'real' concurrence are more a shorthand way to describe a series of connected acts than a delineation of the substantive legal distinctions between them.[265]

The second scenario, where the elements of one crime are subsumed fully within another, is known as 'false' concurrence[266] or 'merger'.[267] Robbery is a good example. Under many legal systems, robbery is 'theft' combined with a separate offence of 'intentionally causing serious bodily injury [battery]'.[268] Since robbery includes the elements of both theft and battery, the latter two are said to 'merge' into this larger offence.[269]

The offender must commit the acts constituting theft and battery in the same (or a closely-related) transaction. The temporal and spatial nexus is critical, and there can be no merger without meaningful correspondence in both respects. If, for example, D steals V's wallet and ten days later breaks V's nose, these separate crimes of theft and battery do not merge into robbery.

The general principle of *lex specialis* provides that more specific offences apply over less specific ones.[270] In our example, robbery is more specific because it provides a more comprehensive assessment of D's criminal conduct than can theft or battery independently. Nothing is lost through the merger. Robbery sufficiently describes the totality of his criminal conduct and ensures that he will account for all of it. Indeed, it would overstate his criminality to record that he committed theft, battery *and* robbery.

In the third scenario, a single act simultaneously breaches multiple legal prohibitions.[271] Although the offences derive from the same transaction, they warrant separate convictions because they have different elements and serve different underlying societal interests. A single forcible sexual penetration by a father of his daughter, for example, amounts to incest, rape, dereliction of parental duty and probably other offences. The single act simultaneously violates multiple legal prohibitions, each of which responds to a distinct social harm.

Distinguishing genocide and crimes against humanity

Several different methodologies for implementing the principles discussed above have been applied (or advocated in dissenting opinions or *dicta*) in the

265 We speak of a 'bank robbery' on the High Street, for example, as if it were one event. But this 'bank robbery' typically consists of a series of different offences, depending on the conduct during the transaction (eg, theft, assault, battery, robbery, possession of weapons, etc). On the international plane, there is the 'Rwandan Genocide' in 1994.

266 Walther (n 256) 478.

267 Ambos and Wirth (n 102) 701–2. It also is called 'apparent' concurrence. *Kupreskic (TC)* ¶662 (criminal conduct that 'appears' to violate multiple provisions, but actually violates only one).

268 MPC s 222(1).

269 In civil law, robbery 'consumes' theft and battery—hence the 'consumption' doctrine. Walther (n 256) 489–90. At common law, theft and battery are 'lesser included offences' because the proof of robbery also establish these crimes. *Kupreskic (TC)* [2000] ICTY ¶687.

270 *Kunarac (AC)* [2002] ICTY ¶170; Emerson and Ashworth 86 (2001).

271 *Kupreskic (TC)* [2000] ICTY ¶662; Ambos and Wirth (n 102) 702. This is known as 'ideal' concurrence (*idealkonkurrenz*) in civil law.

international criminal tribunals.[272] The ICTY Appeals Chamber settled on a uniform approach by adopting the 'materially distinct element' test, which mirrors the *Blockberger*[273] analysis used by federal courts in the United States:

> [M]ultiple criminal convictions entered under different statutory provisions but based on the same conduct are permissible only if each statutory provision involved has a *materially distinct element* not contained in the other. An element is materially distinct from another if it requires proof of a fact not required by the other. (Emphasis added.)[274]

The inquiry focuses upon the congruence of the elements themselves, not the facts used to establish the existence of those elements at trial.[275] In cases of 'real' concurrence, *Blockberger* allows multiple convictions because the offences have distinct elements (rape, murder, property damage, etc). It also allows cumulative convictions in cases of 'ideal' concurrence, where only *some* elements are shared and the offences overlap only partially. Cumulation is *not* allowed in cases of merger because there is no 'material' distinction: the elements of one offence exist fully within the other. But even if cumulative convictions are allowed, *Blockberger* does not sanction excessive punishment. Separate conduct establishing a distinct element is punished separately, but conduct common to both offences counts only once at sentencing.[276]

The inquiry into which distinctions are 'material' is largely fact dependant and is assessed on a case-by-case basis.[277] It aims to distinguish the 'gist' or 'gravamen' of offences aiming at different conduct and social ills.[278] Two offences whose elements differ technically but not 'materially' are treated as an instance of merger rather than one of 'ideal' concurrence.[279] *Blockberger* presumes an underlying course of conduct with temporal and spatial proximity. Offences too distinct in time or space do not cumulate because they are separate transactions. Again, this distinction is fact specific.[280]

[272] For additional detail, see Cassese, ICC 212–30 (2002).

[273] *Blockberger* (1932) 284 US 299 (US Sup Ct) 304. Civil law calls this the 'reciprocal specialty' test: *Kupreskic (TC)* [2000] ICTY ¶685.

[274] *Celebici (AC)* [2001] ICTY ¶412. The test also applies in the ICTR. *Musema (AC)* [2001] ICTR ¶369. It applies to intra-article convictions as well as different types of crimes. *Kunarac (AC)* [2002] ICTY ¶185.

[275] A variation that further distinguished the facts used to *prove* a particular element at trial generally has been discarded. *Cf Krstic (AC)* [2004] ICTY ¶90 (Shahabuddeen J dissenting) (distinguishing 'the legal elements of an offence and the evidence on which those elements are based') and *Crocker* (1981) 384 Mass 353 (Mass Sup Jud Ct) 359 (overruling prior doctrine).

[276] *Celebici (AC)* [2001] ICTY ¶769. See also *Krstic (AC)* [2004] ICTY ¶82 (Shahabuddeen J dissenting) (overlapping conduct should be 'taken into account in sentencing.').

[277] As explained below, the suggestion that chapeau elements per se are never 'material' should be rejected.

[278] *Krstic (AC)* [2004] ICTY ¶¶86–8 (Shahabuddeen J dissenting).

[279] *Cf Jones* (1981) 382 Mass 387 (Mass Sup Jud Ct) 394 (although vehicular homicide was not a lesser included offence of manslaughter, the crimes were sufficiently related to preclude conviction for both).

[280] Because it is not a bright line inquiry, the test can be criticized as subjective and inconsistent in application. Compare *Morin* (2001) 52 Mass App Ct 780 (Mass App Ct) 787–8 (touching V's breast, locking her in home, threatening to sodomize her and attempting to pull down her shorts

Genocide overlaps with crimes against humanity only when certain specified conditions exist as to *mens rea*, the victim at issue and the context in which the crimes are committed. The ICTY Appeals Chamber addressed some of these in *Krstic*[281] when it approved cumulative convictions for genocide and persecution.[282] The ICTY's analysis was incomplete, however, because there are potentially as many as five 'materially distinct elements' between the offences: (i) the *actus reus* of the chapeau; (ii) the *mens rea* of the chapeau; (iii) the victim classifications; and (in some jurisdictions) (iv) the so-called 'policy' element of the offences; and (v) the requirement that persecution be committed in conjunction with other international crimes.

Materially distinct elements

Required circumstances of the offences

The first distinction between genocide and persecution relates to the required circumstances of the offences—the *actus reus* of the chapeau. Like all crimes against humanity, persecution must be committed as part of a widespread or systematic attack on the civilian population. Genocide has no such contextual limitation.[283]

Although this distinction appears self-evident, the advent of the ICC has caused some confusion in this regard. In order to limit the treaty's application, genocide in the ICC is subject to a special restriction: that the offence transpired 'in the context of a manifest pattern of similar conduct directed against [the target group] or was conduct that itself could effect such destruction.'[284] This self-limiting constraint applies only in the ICC and is not binding outside that forum.[285] The clause limits only *which instances* of genocide fall within the ICC's jurisdiction. It has no impact on the substantive definition of the offence itself. Indeed, it could not: such treaty-based provisions can never alter the substance of *jus cogens* norms such as the prohibition of genocide.[286]

were 'so closely related in fact as to constitute in substance but a single crime') (internal quotations omitted) with *Wolinski* (2000) 431 Mass 228 (Mass Sup Jud Ct) 239 (even though they occurred just before offender threw victim out of a window, blows with flashlight were separate from armed robbery forming the basis of his felony murder conviction).

[281] *Krstic (AC)* [2004] ICTY ¶¶219–29. An ICTR Trial Chamber previously had allowed cumulative convictions for genocide and persecution without discussion or analysis: *Nahimana (TC)* [2003] ICTR ¶1090.

[282] This dovetailed with prior ICTR practice on genocide and other crimes against humanity, as well as that of prior domestic jurisprudence. *Musema (AC)* [2001] ICTR ¶¶358–70 (cumulative convictions for genocide and extermination); *Eichmann (AC)* [1961] 36 ILR 277 (Isr Sup Ct) ¶10 (affirming convictions for persecution and genocide).

[283] Genocide Convention art II.

[284] ICC Elements of Crimes art 6(a)(4)–(e)(4).

[285] ICC Statute art 9; Elements of Crimes (Item 1) (referring to art 22(1) of the ICC Statute). See also R Higgins, 'The Relationship Between the International Criminal Court and the International Court of Justice' in Von Hebel 163 (1999) (noting that elements are what two-thirds of the states-party to the ICC Statute manage to *agree upon*, which does not necessarily reflect international *lex lata*).

[286] VCLT art 53 ('a peremptory norm of general international law is a norm accepted and recognized by the international community of States as a whole as a norm from which no derogation

Nevertheless, the ICTY Trial Chamber in *Krstic* inexplicably adopted the ICC's jurisdictional limitation and used it to characterize genocide and persecution as cumulative offences. The court improperly conflated the 'manifest pattern' language with the widespread/systematic attack of crimes against humanity.[287] The Appeals Chamber reversed, finding the Elements of Crimes (and their added limitation of scale) 'inapposite' because they were not part of customary international law.[288]

This does not mean that considerations of scale are irrelevant. There is a pragmatic dimension to criminal law that is separate from whether a crime's substantive elements can be established. The fact that conduct satisfies the technical definition of genocide does not necessarily require prosecution at the international level. The locus of the trial, and the decision on whether even to charge genocide committed under limited circumstances, are best handled through prosecutorial and judicial discretion.[289]

Mental state relative to circumstances

The second distinction relates to the *mens rea* of the chapeau. All crimes against humanity (including persecution) require *knowledge* (or its equivalent) of the overarching widespread or systematic attack on the civilian population. This expands the *mens rea* of the underlying offence (intent to kill, to discriminate, etc) by adding a secondary fault element respecting circumstance.[290] In contrast, the *mens rea* of genocide focuses solely upon the intent to destroy the group. There is no required awareness of any larger context within which the crime is committed.[291]

There is some debate, however, over whether a distinction based upon chapeau elements alone can be sufficient. Some suggest that the chapeau should be seg-

is permitted and which can be modified only by a subsequent norm of general international law having the same character.'). Some criticize the Elements as a modification of the ICC Statute's definition of genocide without a legitimate amendment of the treaty. O Triffterer, 'Genocide, Its Particular Intent to Destroy in Whole or in part the Group as Such' (2001) 14 Leiden JIL 399, 407 (noting that arts 121 and 123 prohibit amendments to arts 5 and 6 during the first seven years of the ICC's operation).

287 *Krstic (TC)* [2001] ICTY ¶682.

288 *Krstic (AC)* [2004] ICTY ¶¶224, 229. The court also could have pointed out that the text of the Elements precludes their application outside the ICC. Elements of Crimes (General Introduction, Item 1) (referencing art 22(1) of the ICC Statute).

289 Good faith prosecutorial discretion does not violate the Convention's general obligation to prevent and punish genocide. States are obliged to punish the offence 'in accordance with their respective Constitutions.': Genocide Convention art V. This suggests that the prosecutorial discretion inherent in a given state's domestic law applies *mutatis mutandis* to the crime of genocide. Although common law and civil law systems draw the line in different places, there likely is a common baseline that informs such decision making in the international context. *Cf* ICJ Statute art 38(1)(c) (general principles of law common to domestic legal systems); ICC Statute art 17(1)(d) (case inadmissible when it 'is not of sufficient gravity to justify further action by the Court.').

290 *Kunarac (AC)* [2002] ICTY ¶102.

291 *Krstic (AC)* [2004] ICTY ¶223. Knowledge of such circumstances does support an evidentiary inference of genocidal intent, however. *Jelisic (TC)* [1999] ICTY ¶73.

regated from the underlying conduct elements for purposes of cumulation and should not count in the analysis.[292] Courts and commentators alike have drawn upon a key dissenting opinion in *Celebici*[293] to argue that chapeau elements should never qualify as 'materially distinct' under the *Blockberger* analysis.[294] This assessment is overly-simplistic and ultimately incorrect, however, because it fails to account for the nature of the crimes that actually were under discussion.

The *Celebici* dissenters discussed the chapeau of war crimes (international armed conflict, protected status of victims, etc) and noted that such 'abstract elements' had no bearing on the underlying offence itself.[295] They concurred in adopting *Blockberger*[296] but argued that only elements 'relating to the conduct and mental state of the accused [should] be taken into account'.[297] It vastly overstates the dissenting analysis, however, to suggest that chapeau elements are per se 'abstract' and hence never 'material'. The question turns more precisely on whether the chapeau elements bear upon personal culpability.

The *Celebici* dissenters discussed the example of rape as a war crime under Articles 2 and 3 of the ICTY Statute and rape as a crime against humanity under Article 5. The conduct elements were identical in both offences. But rape under Article 5 had a more specific *mens rea*. It required offenders to have additional knowledge of the context in which the offence was committed (widespread or systematic attack, etc). Since the underlying elements were identical except for an *additional* requirement under Article 5, convictions would not enter for both.[298] But this is a simple application of the merger rule, rather than a holding that the chapeau elements are irrelevant. Because rape under Article 5 included *all* elements of rape under Articles 2 and 3, plus one, rape as a crime against humanity was a more specific offence into which rape as a war crime would merge.

Subsequent developments in ICTY jurisprudence clarified the issue. In *Naletilic*, the ICTY Appeals Chamber held that the 'principle of individual guilt . . . demands sufficient awareness of factual circumstances establishing the armed conflict and its (international or internal) character'.[299] A required element for war crimes, not yet articulated at the time of the *Celebici* decision,[300] thus is

[292] *Finta* (1994) 1 SCR 701 (Can Sup Ct) ¶291 (LaForest J dissenting) ('The mental blameworthiness required for such crimes is already captured by the *mens rea* required for the underlying offence. The additional circumstances of the *actus reus* required in terms of the international system to justify extraterritorial jurisdiction do not require that the accused individually have knowledge of these matters.').

[293] *Celebici (AC)* [2001] ICTY ¶¶24–33 (Hunt and Bennouna JJ dissenting).

[294] *Cf Semanza (TC)* [2003] ICTR ¶12 (Dolenc J dissenting); HS Willis, 'Cumulative Convictions and the Double Jeopardy Rule: Pursuing Justice at the ICTY and the ICTR' (2003) 17 Emory ILR 341, 365.

[295] *Celebici (AC)* [2001] ICTY ¶¶26–7 (Hunt and Bennouna JJ dissenting).

[296] ibid ¶24. [297] ibid ¶33. [298] ibid.

[299] *Naletilic (AC)* [2006] ICTY ¶119.

[300] Prior to the ICTY's recent clarification, it appeared that the chapeau of war crimes in the international criminal tribunals required only proof of: (i) a nexus between the offender's acts and the existence of an armed conflict; and (ii) the victims' protected status under Geneva law, with

the offender's awareness of the factual circumstances of the armed conflict.[301] Rape as a war crime and rape as a crime against humanity thus should never cumulate because they punish different wrongs. In one, an offender knowingly takes advantage of a widespread or systematic attack on civilians. In the other, he knowingly takes advantage of an armed conflict. These chapeau elements thus relate directly to the offender's mental state and culpability, rendering them more than 'abstract elements'.

This analysis confirms that the chapeau are substantive elements of crimes against humanity, rather than 'abstract' jurisdictional provisions. Indeed, the overarching context in which the offender acts is both a critical aspect of his mental state and a fundamental characteristic of the offence. It is the existence of such heinous circumstances, together with the offender's use of them to his personal criminal advantage, that elevate 'ordinary' criminal offences to the level of crimes against humanity. Genocide, in contrast, requires no such awareness of larger contextual circumstances.

Additional bases of distinction

There are several additional grounds of distinction between genocide and crimes against humanity that do not apply in all cases but which provide further grounds for non-cumulation when they do. The third relates to the underlying victims of the crimes. Crimes against humanity apply only to a 'civilian population', whereas genocide applies equally to military personnel.[302]

A fourth distinction is the so-called 'policy' element of crimes against humanity. Although not required under customary international law,[303] many applications of crimes against humanity (such as the ICC's) require an attack 'pursuant to or in furtherance of a State or organizational policy to commit such attack'.[304] Although most genocides probably are so-organized in practice, 'policy' is not a constituent element of genocide.[305] Any requirement of legal proof of such a policy would be an additional material distinction between the crimes.

The fifth distinction—which applies specifically to persecution—is similar. In the ICC, persecution is not recognized as a stand-alone offence. It must be committed in conjunction with another crime specified in the ICC Statute—either a crime against humanity, a war crime, or genocide.[306] This mandatory nexus to

no *mens rea* element specified as to either of these circumstances: *Kordic & Cerkez (AC)* [2004] ICTY ¶1037.

[301] The ICC imposes similar requirements, although the accused need not form a conclusion about the legal character of these factual circumstances. Elements of Crimes art 8 intro ¶3; *Bemba (Confirmation of Charges-TC)* [2009] ICC ¶239.

[302] Genocide Convention arts I, II. Although crimes against humanity are linked in some cases to armed conflict, see ICTY Statute art 5, this has never been required for genocide: Genocide Convention art I.

[303] *Krstic (AC)* [2004] ICTY ¶225.

[304] ICC Statute art 7(2)(a). As noted previously, a similar requirement appears in French jurisprudence: *Barbie* (1985) 78 ILR 125 (Fr Ct Cass) 136–7 (policy of ideological hegemony).

[305] *Krstic (AC)* [2004] ICTY ¶225.

[306] ICC Statute art 7(1)(h); Lee, *The ICC* 95 (2001).

other international offences is not required under customary international law[307] or even many domestic formulations.[308] But in cases before the ICC, this additional element further distinguishes persecution from genocide, which need not be committed in conjunction with any other offence.

Further theories on cumulation

In addition to validating the *Blockberger* analysis, the ICTR in *Akayesu* suggested two alternative theories on cumulation. Under the first, independent of their substantive elements, offences may be cumulated when they uphold or protect divergent societal values or interests.[309] The second authorizes cumulative convictions in cases where 'it is necessary to record a conviction for both offences in order fully to describe what the accused did'.[310] Both of these 'tests' are problematic in application (hence their rejection in favour of *Blockberger*), but the result on cumulation between genocide and crimes against humanity would be identical even in jurisdictions that adopted them.

The alternate values/interests analysis would permit convictions for both persecution and genocide because the offences protect different underlying values. Broadly speaking, genocide protects enumerated groups from physical and biological destruction. Crimes against humanity protect individual members of the civilian population from serious, large-scale violence against the person (extermination, torture, etc) and unlawful discrimination on certain prohibited grounds.[311] That said, the legitimacy of this values/interests test as a stand-alone inquiry is questionable. It has not been applied to any factual situation in the international criminal tribunals.[312] The majority in *Celebici* noted the test but did not discuss it,[313] let alone dispute Judges Hunt's and Bennouna's assertion in dissent that it had no independent vitality.[314]

There is good reason for this. A free-standing 'values' test purportedly sufficient to justify *criminal conviction* necessarily requires an in-depth, detailed analysis of the rationale behind the offences at issue. Beyond the broadest level of generality, it is difficult to imagine that such an inquiry would involve the analysis of anything other than the substantive composition of the crimes themselves. The societal 'values' expressed by criminal offences presumably are reflected in legislative

307 *Tadic (Merits—TC)* [1997] ICTY ¶697. See also Duffy 42 (1998) (noting that the ICC eliminates 'the prosecution of persecution per se—a fundamental and long-established crime against humanity—from the Court's jurisdiction.').

308 *Cf Barbie* (1985) 78 ILR 125 (Fr Ct Cass) 143 ('it is not necessary to have a separate act of an inhumane nature to constitute persecution; the discrimination itself makes the act inhumane.').

309 *Akayesu (TC)* [1998] ICTR ¶468.

310 ibid.

311 ibid ¶470; Walther (n 256) ('genocide protects transindividual interests, whereas crimes against humanity protect individual interests....').

312 Judge Kahn referenced it as part of the fact-specific 'totality' analysis, as opposed to an independent test per se. *Kayishema (TC)* [1999] ICTR ¶¶32 (Kahn J dissenting). The totality analysis is discussed below.

313 *Celebici (AC)* [2001] ICTY ¶395.

314 ibid ¶17 (Hunt and Bennouna JJ dissenting). The Appeals Chamber also did not discuss it in *Kupreskic*, even though the Trial Chamber had (albeit in *dicta*). *Kupreskic (AC)* [2001] ICTY ¶¶386–96.

history, *travaux préparatoires*, prior case law, and the like. But because such materials inescapably intertwine with the legal terminology defining the offences, a separate 'values' test is unlikely to generate any new insights. The inquiry thus is circular and unhelpful.

A more troubling premise is that a separate inquiry into societal 'values' could justify cumulative convictions even where the substantive elements of offences forbid it. The problem is that societal 'values' dictating that the offences should *not* cumulate are reflected already in the *actus reus* and *mens rea* of the crimes themselves.[315] By seeking a separate justification for a different result, the test presumes an inherent conflict—that the societal values conveyed directly through the elements of the crimes themselves can be overridden by competing 'values' from some other source. This is fundamentally at odds with the well-established view that a society's 'most cherished values' are represented already in the substance of its criminal laws.[316] Given the high stakes, the questionable value added, and the inherent conflict, this separate inquiry has little to offer.

The third approach identified in *Akayesu* also has not been applied in the international tribunals. It is akin to the 'totality' approach, which obligates a court to 'address the criminal responsibility on each charge' proved. Under the totality approach, 'the verdict should be based upon the consideration of proven facts rather than the 'technicalities of pleading...."[317] Prejudice to the accused purportedly is addressed at the sentencing phase.[318]

Although its comprehensiveness and simplicity have some appeal, the benefits of this approach are outweighed by its substantial drawbacks. Convictions serve important expressive functions,[319] directing the stigmatizing condemnation of society toward the convicted offender. Judge Kahn rightly notes that, once labelled a genocidaire, the additional measure of guilt for committing crimes against humanity is negligible.[320] The implications of criminal convictions extend beyond mere stigma, however. Convictions carry serious collateral consequences for matters such as parole eligibility, classification under habitual offender laws,[321] and even credibility in future testimonial proceedings. These are serious matters that cannot be brushed aside lightly.[322]

[315] *Cf Albernaz* (1981) 450 US 333 (US Sup Ct) 343 (distinct conspiracy statutes aimed at the 'separate evils presented by drug trafficking' were permissible because "importation' and 'distribution' of marijuana impose diverse social harms.').

[316] Lawrence 169 (1999). See also *Celebici (AC)* [2001] ICTY ¶17 (Hunt and Bennouna JJ dissenting) (values are expressed in the substantive elements of the offences themselves and in the grouping of crimes into different types of offences).

[317] *Kayishema (TC)* [1999] ICTR ¶¶32 (Kahn J dissenting).

[318] ibid ¶34.

[319] The ICC, for example, must pronounce a separate sentence for each offence and a joint sentence specifying the total length of imprisonment or punishment. ICC Statute art 78(3). As a practical matter, this practice also creates a more detailed record to evaluate on appeal.

[320] *Kayishema (TC)* [1999] ICTR ¶35 (Kahn J dissenting).

[321] *Celebici (AC)* [2001] ICTY ¶23 (Hunt and Bennouna JJ dissenting).

[322] *Rutelidge* (1996) 517 US 292 (US Sup Ct) 301–2 (*de minimus* injury of a $50.00 fine provided sufficient grounds to vacate an impermissibly cumulative conviction, even for an offender serving multiple life sentences without the possibility of parole).

But even these important considerations are a secondary concern. As discussed in greater detail below, a criminal conviction is more than a proxy for a quantum of punishment. Convictions record historical facts of criminality. The totality approach risks overstating wrongdoing because it fails to account for the merger of offences. To return to a prior example, regardless of sentence, it would overstate D's culpability to record convictions for battery, theft and robbery arising out of the same transaction. It also is unnecessary. The historical facts of his criminal conduct are documented sufficiently through the more specific robbery conviction.

A more useful application of the totality approach is to record multiple convictions only when it is not apparent from the substance of the offence that the accused acted against different protected interests. With respect to genocide, such separate interests could be the protected groups themselves. The Nazis, for example, committed genocide against Jews, Gypsies, Slavs and other enumerated groups. A single conviction here for genocide would not adequately document the separate wrongs against each group. In this case, multiple convictions for genocide against the separate groups would be warranted.

Fair labelling

Regardless of which cumulation theory applies, it is clear that genocide and crimes against humanity are distinct offences. Convictions for both can be legitimately entered even for conduct arising out of a single criminal transaction (eg, a roadside massacre). Genocide and crimes against humanity thus are both available to describe the full scope of crimes committed against members of racial, national, religious and ethnic groups. But this is not the case for members of political groups because there is no analogous offence of political genocide.

Since only crimes against humanity are available, the question becomes whether (as some claim) these offences nevertheless are sufficient to respond to criminal violence intended to destroy a political group 'as such'. It should be clear that they are not. As detailed above, the two offences cover different legal ground. The absence of a parallel crime of political genocide demonstrates that less overall protection is afforded to political groups.

There is more to it, however. Using persecution as a proxy for a separate crime of political genocide also runs afoul of the principle of fair labelling. The fair labelling principle aims to ensure that the label describing criminal conduct accurately reflects both its wrongfulness and its severity. Broadly stated, it requires criminal offences to fairly represent both the injury[323] caused at issue and the wrongdoing at issue (what the offender did and what he meant to do).[324]

[323] Injury in criminal law includes potential harm and actual injury: B Mitchell, 'Multiple Wrongdoing and Offence Structure: A Plea for Consistency and Fair Labelling' (2001) 64 Modern LR 393, 393 n 2.

[324] G Williams, 'Convictions and Fair Labelling' (1983) 42 Cambridge LJ 85, 85–6. It also is called 'representative labelling'. AJ Ashworth, 'The elasticity of *mens rea*' in Tapper 49 (1981).

'Fair labelling' is not a precise science. Inevitably, decisions are needed on how 'representative' a label must be. 'Extreme fair labellers' seek 'detailed levels of specificity,'[325] while those on the other end of the spectrum advocate 'a small[er] number of very widely defined offences'.[326] There also are normative questions about whether the transgression of a given norm is best addressed through criminal law or should be handled in another way.[327] Although not an element of any offence, fair labelling nevertheless is a fundamental principle of criminal justice.[328] Its premise is that 'justice should not only be done, but should *manifestly and undoubtedly be seen to be done.*'[329] (Emphasis added.)

Labels tell the story of the accused's criminality.[330] The more specific the label, the more we know (from that label alone) about his conduct. This requires sensible line drawing between broad and narrow offences. A single offence of 'law breaking' covering everything from spitting on the sidewalk to homicide is equally unsatisfactory to an offence specifying 'non-consensual sexual intercourse by a male aged 35 years with a female child not his daughter aged 14 years, 6 months on a Tuesday afternoon....' The former conveys too little, and the latter too much.

A proper label reflects both the *essence* and the *totality* of the criminal conduct at issue. It is an amalgam of the interest invaded (bodily integrity, or property interests), the gravity of harm (taking human life, or destroying a shed), the mechanism of injury (stealing versus swindling, arson, or vandalism)[331] and the offender's mental state (deliberately causing injury, or profound carelessness). The latter is critical because offences are 'calibrated' to personal blameworthiness.[332]

Labelling relates to punishment but is not its sole determinant. If punishment must 'fit the crime,' murder obviously deserves greater sanction than spitting on the sidewalk. But this is more a question of hierarchy and comparative seriousness among offences, which are addressed below. Although the labels of offences often are paired with sentencing ranges, the link between them is more rhetorical than

325 Mitchell (n 323) 410. 326 Ashworth, *Elasticity* (n 324) 53.

327 Criminal prosecution is only one solution. On the international plane, 'self-help' and diplomatic sanctions, truth commissions, civil lawsuits and adjudicatory proceedings before the ICJ and human rights tribunals all have been used to address infringements that otherwise constitute criminal offences. 328 Williams (n 324) 49.

329 *Rex v Sussex Justices, Ex parte McCarthy* [1923] All ER 233 (Hewart J) [1924] 1 KB 256 (UK KB) 259.

330 Mitchell (n 323) 405 (labelling 'attempts to encapsulate in a very few words [the offender's] wrongful behaviour.').

331 Ashworth, *Elasticity* (n 324) 54–5 (discussing modes of offences and labelling).

332 Jacobs and Potter 79 (1998). See also Williams (n 324) 89 (offender must 'be punished according to his *mens rea* and not solely in accordance with the degree of injury he inflicted....'). Indeed, with inchoate crimes, there is no resulting injury at all—the criminal sanction is a function of his mental state and the *potential* for harm.

substantive.[333] Criminals are punished not based upon the label itself, but rather for the transgression of the societal and legal norms that the label *represents*.[334]

The principal function of labelling, then, is expression.[335] The label addresses both the offender and the larger community, stigmatizing the culpable conduct and conveying the 'nature of his transgression' to the public.[336] It expresses society's revulsion at the violation of important norms and values.[337]

As noted previously, these values are embodied in the very elements of the offences themselves. Rape, for example, could be addressed as a form of battery (non-consensual, offensive touching) with no special label to describe its unique features. But even if the penalty for 'battery' here was identical to that prescribed for 'rape,' something remains missing. That 'something' is legal and social recognition that the victim's unique sexual integrity was violated in a particularly repugnant way.[338] Society expresses the importance of sexual integrity by condemning and punishing violations of that right through a special offence that describes the unique wrongfulness of the infringement. The story told by 'rape' is more specific than that of 'battery' because it conveys that the perpetrator—now labelled a 'rapist'—violated additional (and more significant) legal norms by committing this offence.

Labelling also is important because a criminal conviction is an indelible historical record of what the offender did. The conviction ensures that the criminal conduct is not forgotten[339] and that its 'precise nature' can be ascertained later from the label itself.[340] The expression of values is inescapable. Even silence (*not* labelling certain conduct 'criminal') makes a statement. 'It is impossible for the

[333] Sentencing in international criminal law is a highly individualized practice that depends far more heavily on the specific aggravating and mitigating circumstances of an individual accused than on generalized practice for certain types of crimes. *Tadic (Sentencing-AC)* [2000] ICTY ¶¶21–2, 55–6. Although comparative analysis sometimes is helpful, it must be confined to its proper role: RD Sloane, 'The Evolving "Common Law" of Sentencing of the International Criminal Tribunal for Rwanda' (2007) 5 JICJ 718 (noting contribution of comparative analysis 'to the development of a fair, uniform and coherent penal jurisprudence.').

[334] It is an incomplete proxy at best. Punishment increases and decreases independent of the offence itself, depending on whether mitigating (remorse, cooperation with investigatory authorities, guilty plea, youth, infirmity, etc) or aggravating (abusing position of authority, nefarious motive, especially vulnerable victims, etc) factors are present. *Babic (Sentencing—TC)* [2004] ICTY ¶47. See also *Kajelijeli (AC)* [2005] ICTR ¶¶320–4 (reducing sentence from life imprisonment to 45 years for violations of accused's rights during pre-trial detention).

[335] J Steele, 'A Seal Pressed in the hot wax of Vengeance: A Girardian Understanding of Expressive Punishment' (2001) 16 J Law & Religion 35, 40 (describing the expressive theory of punishment).

[336] Simester and Sullivan 45 (2003).

[337] Lawrence 163 (1999) ('Criminal punishment carries with it social disapproval, resentment, and indignation . . . [and] inherently stigmatizes the offender.').

[338] *Cf* Simester and Sullivan 44 (2003) (discussing the undesirability of a general label conflating pickpockets with rapists).

[339] 'Who can but agree—forgetting makes a mockery of the dead.' A Cassese, 'Reflections on International Criminal Justice' (1998) 61 Modern LR 1, 3.

[340] Ashworth, Elasticity (n 324) 56. See also *Deronjic (Sentencing—TC)* [2004] ICTY ¶133 (international tribunals must 'search for and record, as far as possible, the truth of what happened . . . .' in addition to bringing justice to the victims and survivors).

punishment choices made by the society *not* to express societal values. There is no neutral position, no middle ground. The only question is the content of that expression and the resulting statement of those values.'[341]

Wrongfulness and culpability

The large scale context in which crimes against humanity are committed, coupled with either serious personal violence or extreme discrimination, elevates crimes against humanity to the status of offences under international law. Genocide, which is premised upon violence and deprives victims of the most fundamental right of all—the right to physical and biological *existence* as a group—is perhaps the ultimate form of personal violence and discrimination. In this sense, genocide is persecution and other crimes against humanity writ large:

> [T]he *mens rea* requirement for persecution is higher than for ordinary crimes against humanity, although lower than for genocide.... [P]ersecution as a crime against humanity is an offence belonging to the same *genus* as genocide. Both persecution and genocide are crimes perpetrated against persons that belong to a particular group and who are targeted because of such belonging. In both categories what matters is the intent to discriminate: to attack persons on account of their ethnic, racial, or religious characteristics (as well as, in the case of persecution, on account of their political affiliation). While in the case of persecution the discriminatory intent can take multifarious inhumane forms and manifest itself in a plurality of actions including murder, in the case of genocide that intent must be accompanied by the intention to destroy, in whole or in part, the group to which the victims of the genocide belong. Thus, it can be said that, *from the viewpoint of* mens rea, *genocide is an extreme and most inhuman form of persecution.* To put it differently, when persecution escalates to the extreme form of wilful and deliberate acts designed to destroy a group or part of a group, it can be held that such persecution amounts to genocide. (Emphasis added.)[342]

Once the chapeau elements are established, acts committed with intent to destroy a protected group undoubtedly also qualify as extermination, torture, persecution and other crimes against humanity against the group's individual members.[343] But the converse is not true because the *mens rea* of genocide is narrower. The genocidaire intends to *destroy*, whereas the persecutor intends to *discriminate*, the exterminator intends to engage in mass killing, the torturer intends to cause serious bodily or mental harm, etc. Genocide thus is a more specific (and nefarious) offence. Labelling a genocide 'crimes against humanity' tells us only that the offender aimed to kill, maim, discriminate, etc. It does not convey his more specific (and more blameworthy) intent to destroy the group 'as such.'

The *actus reus* of genocide also is more specific. It requires serious criminal violence against the person that actually could physically or biologically destroy

341 Lawrence 168 (1999). 342 *Kupreskic (TC)* [2000] ICTY ¶636.
343 ibid; *Eichmann (TC)* [1961] 36 ILR 5 (Isr Dist Ct) ¶201.

the group (killing, maiming, kidnapping, sterilization etc).[344] Crimes against humanity include such conduct but also many other acts that are substantially less serious. These need not even involve offences against the person or otherwise criminal acts.[345] The scope of persecutory conduct is potentially unlimited, whereas genocide is restricted to a detailed listing of violent acts.[346] The label of crimes against humanity thus fails to convey the more severe conduct inherent in genocide—a select group of serious crimes against the person of members of the protected group.

The victims: individuals versus groups

Apart from understating the seriousness of the offender's conduct and his mental state, labelling acts of political genocide 'persecution' also misidentifies the real victim of the crime. Persecution (like all crimes against humanity) is an offence against individuals. This is precisely the opposite of genocide, which is quintessentially an offence against groups.

Popular conceptions of crimes against humanity have created some confusion over the nature of the offence. This is because 'humanity' in this context has two potential meanings: (i) a common quality or standard of behaviour; or (ii) the human race as a whole.[347] The first view holds that crimes against humanity respond to the transgression of a legal standard common to civilized peoples.[348] In this sense, the offence describes the offender's conduct, rather than the identity of the victim. The second view posits humanity itself as a victim. The ICTR and the ICTY, for example, have addressed individual culpability but have further declared that:

> [C]rimes against humanity... *transcend the individual* because when the individual is assaulted, humanity comes under attack and is negated. It is therefore the concept of humanity as a victim which essentially characterizes crimes against humanity. (Emphasis added.)[349]
>
> Because of their heinousness and magnitude [crimes against humanity] constitute egregious attacks on human dignity, on the very notion of humaneness. They consequently affect, or should affect, each and every member of mankind, whatever his or her nationality, ethnic group and location.[350]

The first conception, that crimes against humanity transgress baseline human dignity common to all nations, is preferable. The notion of 'humanity' as a victim

[344] Genocide Convention art II(a)–(e).

[345] The *discrimination itself* makes it criminal in cases of persecution. *Barbie* (1985) 78 ILR 125 (Fr Ct Cass) 143.

[346] ICC Statute art 7(1)(k) ('other inhumane acts of similar character and gravity'). Persecution also extends to property interests and social and economic affairs. *Brdjanin (TC)* [2004] ICTY ¶¶1029–49 (denial of employment, freedom of movement, legal process, and medical care); *Blaskic (TC)* [2000] ICTY ¶234 (unlawful detention).

[347] Schwelb (n 3) 195.

[348] ibid; *Erdemovic (AC)* [1997] ICTY ¶26 (Li J dissenting).

[349] *Kambanda (TC)* [1998] ICTR ¶15 (internal quotations and citations omitted).

[350] *Erdemovic (AC)* [1997] ICTY ¶21 (McDonald and Vorah JJ).

is more rhetorical flourish than legal substance.[351] As horrible as atrocities in the former Yugoslavia and Rwanda were, it is doubtful that people in London or New York (equal members of 'humanity') are legitimately viewed as 'victims' of those tragedies. Exactly the opposite is true. It is demeaning to suggest that a woman who lost her husband and sons in Srebrenica and was herself raped somehow is on equal footing with a person in London or New York who read about such atrocities in the newspaper.

Crimes against humanity thus cannot be properly understood as attacks on collectives *qua* collectives. Rather, they are crimes against individuals under large scale or systematic circumstances.[352] Unlike genocide, offenders need not have any conception of a particular 'group' as their victim. Indeed, crimes against humanity can be committed specifically to *prevent* groups from forming in the first place:

> [C]rimes against humanity do not necessarily involve offences against or persecutions of groups.... [I]t is not necessary that the wronged person belong to an organized or well-defined group. In fact, it was the aim of such measures as, for instance, the hanging of a person for a trifling remark about the war, to *prevent* the formation of groups of dissenters against the continuation of the aggressive war.[353]

Genocide and crimes against humanity thus protect divergent underlying interests. Genocide defends the group's physical and biological existence 'as such' by making it a special offence to seek the group's physical and biological destruction. The victim is the group itself; any protection of the individuals comprising it is incidental. Crimes against humanity are exactly the opposite. They cover unlawful deprivations of fundamental rights on account of *individual* characteristics (race, religion, etc).[354] Protection of the larger groups is incidental:

> [W]hereas genocide is a crime directed at groups viewed as collective entities, with a moral dignity of their own, crimes against humanity are assaults on civilian populations viewed not as unified metaphysical entities but simply as collections of individuals whose own human interests and dignity are at risk and whose vulnerability arises from their presence in the target population.[355]

351 A Danner, 'Constructing a Hierarchy of Crimes in International Criminal Law Sentencing' (2001) 87 Virginia LR 415, 476 ('it is hyperbolic to assert...that the defendant's act has affected humanity as a whole.').

352 Ambos and Wirth (n 102) 704 ('crimes against humanity [protect] the individual from violations of his most important rights in situations where those rights are facing extreme danger, i.e. in cases of widespread or systematic attacks against civilians.').

353 Brand (n 150) 83 n 3 (emphasis in original).

354 The majority in *Kayishema* thus was incorrect when it held that 'the social interest protected [by both offences] is the prohibition of the killing of the protected class of persons.' *Kayishema (TC)* [1999] ICTR ¶635. The dissent correctly noted that the societal interests differed. ibid ¶32 (Kahn J dissenting). The opportunity for the Appeals Chamber to correct the majority's error vanished when the prosecutor's appeal was dismissed for late filing and 'lack of diligence and untimeliness, unaccompanied by any showing of good cause or a request for permission to file out of time'. *Kayishema (AC)* [2001] ICTY ¶42.

355 D Luban, 'A Theory of Crimes Against Humanity' 29 Yale JIL 85, 97.

A conviction for crimes against humanity alone thus cannot convey the reality of political genocide that a human group itself—independent of its individual members—was victimized by very serious criminal conduct aimed at its physical or biological destruction.

The absence of an international crime

Apart from the labelling issues discussed above, there are many circumstances where crimes against humanity are not even available as a chargeable offence (eg, where the chapeau cannot be established). As a practical matter, it is unlikely that genocide actually would transpire without some sort of widespread or systematic attack. Nevertheless, the offence was defined as it was at least in part to enable future genocides to be stopped early on, thereby achieving the Convention's twin goal of 'prevention'. The drafters deliberately chose an inchoate rather than a results-based offence, presumably because by the time genocidal intent manifested into the prohibited consequence (the group's partial or total destruction), intervention inevitably would arrive too late.[356] Genocide can be stopped and punished as soon as it starts; as an inchoate offence, it need not spiral into actual harm.

The disparity becomes even more significant in light of recent jurisprudence delineating the scope of the duty of states to *prevent* genocide under the Convention. The ICJ has made clear that the obligation has a legal[357]—as opposed to political or aspirational—character. States have an affirmative duty to prevent the crime when it is 'clear that there [is] a serious risk of genocide'.[358] The duty is triggered 'at the instant the State learns of, or should normally have learned of, the existence of a serious risk that genocide will be committed.'[359] No such obligation exists when the emergent genocide targets a political group. Members of political collectives must suffer the actual injury of the widespread or systematic attack contemplated by the chapeau (as well as discrimination 'in fact' in cases of persecution) before an international offence is deemed to have occurred.

The civilian versus military status of the underlying victims further impacts the charges that can be brought. An effective genocidal technique is the selective targeting of a group's military forces.[360] Consequently, the Genocide Convention allows no exception based upon military status. Atrocities against the military personnel of national, racial, ethnic and religious groups thus can constitute

[356] Efforts during the ICC negotiations to add results requirements to the genocide provisions of the ICC Statute were resoundingly rejected: 'Proposal Submitted by the United States of America: Draft Elements of Crimes' (4 Feb 1999) UN Doc PCNICC/1999/DP4 5–6; Lee, *The ICC* 52–3 (2001).

[357] Genocide Convention art I ('The Contracting Parties confirm that genocide...is a crime under international law which they undertake to prevent and to punish.').

[358] *Application of Genocide Convention—Merits* [2007] ICJ 1 ¶438. [359] ibid ¶431.

[360] *Krstic (AC)* [2004] ICTY ¶¶12, 19–21 (slaughter of 7,500 military and military-aged Muslim men in Srebrenica).

genocide against the group itself,[361] even though they would not qualify as crimes against humanity. Not so for political groups. Unless the underlying offences constitute war crimes (which have their own unique contextual requirements of armed conflict),[362] atrocities against military personnel of political groups are left unanswered entirely by international law.

The relative seriousness of crimes

The expressive function of criminal law goes beyond ensuring congruity between fair labelling and the totality of the offender's criminality. It also organizes individual crimes into a hierarchy that describes their seriousness relative to one another. This hierarchy aims, in part, to ensure that punishment is meted out fairly and sensibly (eg, that one cannot receive a life sentence for both murder and spitting on the sidewalk).[363]

It is plain that a redundancy exists within international criminal law, such that acts constituting murder under domestic law (to use one example) can be ascribed a number of labels under international law. The international label is a function of both the context in which the crime is committed and a more blameworthy mental state. In the known context of armed conflict, murder is a war crime. Committed during a widespread or systematic attack against a civilian population with knowledge of the attack, it is a crime against humanity. If the murder is committed with further intent to discriminate, it also is persecution.

Genocide is widely regarded as the most serious offence known to domestic and international law.[364] It is categorically different from other international offences because it is neither context-dependent nor results-based. Genocide is an international crime based solely upon the special intent required and the ultra-serious injury it aims to prevent.[365] Regardless of the broader context, the murder of a group member with intent to destroy a protected group is genocide, even if the group itself remains physically and biologically intact.

[361] Military force by itself does not establish genocidal intent, however. *Legality of Force—Provisional Measures* [1999] ICJ ¶35 ('the threat or use of [military] force against a State cannot in itself constitute an act of genocide within the meaning of... the Convention.').

[362] As noted previously, Geneva law protects military members of the group in the context of international armed conflict. If the armed conflict is not international in character, more limited protection exists under 'common' Article III to those treaties. Geneva Conventions I-IV art 3.

[363] Ashworth, *Sentencing* 72, 96–103 (2000) (describing scheme and parameters of this ordinal proportionality). Relativity has practical dimensions as well (eg, allocating limited police and judicial resources to responding to more serious crime).

[364] *Krstic (AC)* [2004] ICTY ¶36 (genocide is singled out for special condemnation and approbation); *Jelisic (AC)* [2001] ICTY ¶13 (Wald J dissenting in part) ('Indisputably, genocide is at the apex of [the] hierarchy [of international crimes]'); *Krstic (TC)* [2001] ICTY ¶700 (genocide is the 'most serious crime' within the tribunal's jurisdiction); *Akayesu (TC)* [1998] ICTR ¶16 (genocide is the 'crime of crimes').

[365] *Krstic (AC)* [2004] ICTY ¶134 ('Genocide is one of the worst crimes known to humankind, and its gravity is reflected in the stringent requirement of specific intent.').

As discussed above, genocide differs from crimes against humanity in terms of the conduct at issue, the requisite *mens rea*, the injury caused, and the victims of the crime. Its special label is a function of the distinct (and heightened) injury caused and society's increased revulsion at the act. Consequently, the label 'exterminator' or 'torturer' or 'persecutor' carries less moral censure than does 'genocidaire.'[366] Extermination simply is not genocide. Neither is persecution. Neither is torture, nor enslavement, nor any other crime under international law.

Incongruity in the relative seriousness of crimes is not an issue for racial, national, ethnic, and religious groups because, where otherwise appropriate, convictions can be recorded for crimes against humanity and genocide together. The availability of both labels enables a court to render a more precise judgment describing the totality of the criminal conduct. This validates an important legal distinction between serious violence against individuals on a massive scale and acts intended to destroy the larger groups to which those individuals belong. A given offender can be condemned for crimes against humanity, genocide, or both, with the accompanying consequences in both sentencing and social condemnation by the international community.[367]

Not so for political groups. At best, genocide against political collectives is sanctioned derivatively through the separate, less serious offence of crimes against humanity. At worst, international law fails to address it at all. The absence of a separate crime of political genocide has real-world consequences that should not lightly be put aside. Crimes against humanity and genocide have very different aims, availability, substance, and meaning. They simply cannot substitute for one another.

Taken together, the current state of international law reflects a value judgment by the international community about the relative worth of racial, national, religious and ethnic groups versus political groups. There is no overt recognition in international law that political groups deserve protection 'as such'. The existing legal structure thus makes the profound statement that identical acts committed with identical intent against members of political groups never merit the same degree of censure as such conduct against members of national, racial, ethnic and religious groups.

366 *Kayishema (TC)* [1999] ICTR ¶33 (Kahn J dissenting) ('the *full assessment* of charges and the *pronouncement* of guilty verdicts are important in order to reflect the totality of the accused's culpable conduct.'); Williams (n 324) 85 ('It may be said to be unfair to the prosecution or to the public if the conviction understates the offender's fault.').

367 Much is written on sentencing, which serves a 'heavily symbolic function'. Ashworth, *Sentencing* 344 (2001). That topic is beyond the scope of this writing. But it is worth noting here that although genocide is a more serious offence *in general*, there may be cases warranting less punishment for genocide than for a 'lesser' offence, depending on the factual circumstances. *Krstic (TC)* [2001] ICTY ¶700 ('Genocide embodies a horrendous concept, indeed, but a close look at the myriad of situations that can come within its boundaries cautions against prescribing a monolithic punishment for one and all genocides or similarly for one and all crimes against humanity or war crimes. A murder, whether qualified as a crime against humanity, a war crime or an act of genocide, may be a graver offence than imposing serious bodily or mental harm upon an individual.').

If this value judgment was the desired result of informed, reasoned decision making, so be it. But the discrepancy appears grounded largely in historical conditions and an invalid assumption that equivalent alternate protection exists. Political groups have extraordinarily high value to the international community, and yet the scope of available legal protection fails to correspond to the degree of worth. The inescapable conclusion is that a lacuna exists within international criminal law. It ought to be revisited.

The suggestion that the problem is less serious because some offenders might nevertheless be punished through the concept of crimes against humanity (rather than as genocidaires) misses the real point. After all, the Genocide Convention itself is largely symbolic. Articles II(a)–(e) prohibit murder, maiming, involuntary sterilization, kidnapping, etc—all of which are redundant of domestic offences. But such domestic crimes (and even less serious international offences) cannot possibly convey the true criminality operating in cases of genocide.

The labels ascribed to criminal offences are of prime importance. The Holocaust, for example, could accurately be labelled a case of 'murder'. But 'murder'—even 'mass murder'—is a woefully inadequate descriptor that fails to convey the true reality of Nazi atrocities and what the Third Reich was really trying to accomplish.[368] The international community recognized the need for new legal terminology, both to grapple with the sheer enormity of Nazi race policy and to convey a more complete and proportionate sense of the criminal wrongdoing at issue. International law thus labels murder and other crimes 'genocide' when they are committed with the intent to destroy protected groups.

The lack of a crime of political genocide leads to unusual, and even nonsensical, applications of international criminal law. During the 1994 Rwandan atrocities, for example, Hutu were massacred alongside Tutsis. Tutsis were targeted for destruction because of their ethnicity, while so-called 'moderate' Hutu were targeted for destruction because of their political beliefs (eg, opposing genocide against Tutsis). But even when faced with mass killings perpetrated at the same time, in the same place, by the same offenders, and as part of one overall scheme to create a Tutsi-free Rwanda, we label the dead Tutsi on the floor of the church a victim of genocide and call the dead Hutu lying next to him (at most) a victim of a crime against humanity or war crime.

The labels tell us something more about Tutsi versus Hutu victims, however. The individual Tutsi also represents a larger offence made manifest—genocide against the Rwandan Tutsi group as a whole. No such inference exists for the Hutu. At most, we can say he was killed for his individual political beliefs. The destruction of the larger political group to which he belonged, which was itself the object of destruction by the perpetrators, remains unrecognized and

[368] See *Göring* [1948] 19 IMT Proceedings 531 (final statement of French Prosecutor M. Auguste Champeteir De Ribes) ('This is a crime so monstrous, so undreamt of in history... that the term 'genocide' has had to be coined to define it....'). Winston Churchill previously called it 'a crime without a name'. R Lemkin, 'Genocide' (1946) 15 Am Scholar 227.

unanswered in international law. The absence of a specific crime of political genocide thus leaves us with an insufficient label to describe what really happened in Rwanda. In the same way that the labels of 'murder' and 'extermination' and 'persecution' fail to capture the essential quality of genocide, these terms cannot capture the essential characteristics of political genocide either. There is good reason, then, to revisit the wisdom of the decision, made sixty years ago, to exclude political groups from the protections of the Genocide Convention.

7

The Case for a Crime of Political Genocide

A. Political groups and international criminal law

The reprehensible underlying violence involved in political genocide is identical to that of genocide against enumerated groups. Likewise for the offender's mental state. 'Killing groups of people for political reasons has become the primary form of genocide (and mass killing) in our time. There is no reason to believe that the types of psychological and cultural influences differ in political and other group murders.'[1]

The force of law transforms social aspiration into binding obligation. Law simultaneously articulates and nourishes social values,[2] reflecting them in legal precepts that regulate human behaviour. It goes without saying that political genocide involves a severe infringement of fundamental human rights and the laws that protect them. The question is whether this violation is severe enough to require criminal prohibition, as opposed to other legal mechanisms for sanctioning offenders and compensating victims.

The conduct at issue rests at a complex intersection of human rights law and international criminal law. These inter-related doctrines ascended simultaneously after World War II and can be difficult to fully segregate analytically. Both created exceptions to the principle of absolute state sovereignty over citizens that applies absent some form of supervening international obligation.[3] The underlying principle—that domestic law cannot justify the breach of international obligations—is long-standing.[4] The innovation at Nuremberg was the application of this concept to *individuals*, together with the imposition of criminal sanctions for breaches. The two systems uphold shared international values through complementary mechanisms: 'where human rights law is the shield, [international criminal law] is the sword. The former is declarative or prescriptive, the latter is proscriptive.'[5]

[1] Staub 8 (1989).
[2] DM Amann, 'Group Mentality, Expressivism, and Genocide' (2002) 2 ICLR 93, 95.
[3] Bassiouni, *Introduction* 58 (2003). [4] VCLT art 26.
[5] Bassiouni, *Introduction* 134–5 (2003).

Any violation—large or small—of legal precepts can be called 'unlawful' or 'wrongful'.[6] But unlawfulness or wrongfulness alone cannot justify criminal punishment. The criminal law is more selective. Criminal sanctions attach only to infringements of values that have a certain intrinsic character (violations of life, bodily integrity, etc)[7] or to breaches of rules so centrally important that they merit similar treatment, irrespective of their intrinsic nature (laws providing for public order, distribution of social benefits, etc).[8]

The idea that international law has a criminal dimension is hardly new. In an oft-quoted comment, Grotius noted in the mid-17th century that:

> [K]ings, and those who possess rights equal to those kings, have the right of demanding punishments not only on account of injuries committed against themselves or their subjects, but also on account of injuries which do not directly affect them but [which] excessively violate the law of nature or of nations in regard to any persons whatsoever.[9]

Before analysing the question of political genocide, it is helpful to clarify more precisely what 'international criminal law' means in this context. The terminology is hardly self-evident. At least six potential meanings have been identified:

1. The application of domestic criminal law beyond a state's territory (eg, states punishing offences committed by nationals abroad);
2. Internationally mandated domestic criminal law (where international law requires states to make certain conduct a domestic offence);
3. Internationally authorized domestic criminal law (where the international community authorizes states to punish 'international' conduct such as piracy on the high seas as a function of domestic criminal law);
4. A baseline of domestic criminal law common to all civilized states (such as punishing certain infringements on life, liberty, or property);
5. International cooperation in the enforcement of domestic criminal law (extradition, rendition and the like); and
6. International criminal law in the 'material sense'—meaning the separate criminal justice system that exists and operates parallel to domestic criminal law and which involves the application of unique substantive and procedural legal rules.[10]

Categories 1–4 essentially are provisions of domestic law, albeit domestic law influenced substantially by rights and obligations derived from the international

[6] Fletcher 77 (1998).

[7] This is conduct *mala in se*—wrongful and harmful in and of itself. ibid 77–8.

[8] This is *malum prohibatum*—conduct that is prohibited but not intrinsically injurious. ibid 77. As a general matter, offences redressing injuries to life or personal interests are regarded as more serious than offences covering economic, cultural and social interests. Bassiouni, *Introduction* 127 (2003).

[9] Grotius 504 (1645).

[10] G Schwarzenberger, 'The Problem of an International Criminal Law' (1950) 3 Current Legal Probs 263, 264–73.

plane. Category 5 regulates interactions between states, but its primary purpose is facilitating the application of domestic criminal law.

International criminal law in the sense of Category 6 is the real emphasis of this writing, and political genocide will be considered here in that context. Category 6 is quintessentially international in character—a separate system with legal rules 'of a prohibitive character... strengthened by punitive sanctions of their own.'[11] Put another way:

> An 'international crime' is a grave offence against international law which the international community of States recognizes as a crime and for the committing of which the responsible individuals can be punished under international law even if the domestic law of a particular State does not declare it to be punishable.[12]

Particularly with respect to the 'core' crimes reflected in the ICC Statute, international criminal law concerns itself almost exclusively with violations that are *mala in se*.[13] The 'intrinsic nature' of international crimes is that they constitute 'serious attacks on fundamental values'.[14] But there are no set rules on the criteria for international crimes, the precise labels used to categorize them, or the distinctions between categories.[15] What is clear is that not all human rights violations—even serious violations—should be treated as international crimes.[16]

B. Characteristics of international crimes

The characteristics of international crimes were studied by leading experts in the International Law Commission, whose work on international crimes reflects vigorous international debate on the topic. The ILC's 1976 Draft Articles on State Responsibility addressed state responsibility for international crimes, distinguishing them from lesser infractions known as international delicts. Article 19 defined an international crime as:

> (2) An internationally wrongful act which results from the breach by a State of an international obligation so essential for the protection of fundamental interests of the

[11] ibid 273.

[12] Hannikainen 285 (1988). See also RD Sloane, 'The Expressive Capacity of International Punishment: The Limits of the National Law Analogy and the Potential of International Criminal Law' (2007) 43 Stanford JIL 39, 40–2 (noting three key differences between international and domestic criminal law—the communities served by criminal regulation; the collective character of the offences; and the international system's contravention of what were accepted social norms at the national level, as for example in Nazi Germany).

[13] Bassiouni, *Introduction* 121, 127 (2003) (placing 'core' international crimes at the top of a hierarchy of seriousness).

[14] Cassese, ICL 172 (2003).

[15] Bassiouni, *Introduction* 114 (2003).

[16] Study on Implementing Apartheid Convention (1981) UN Doc E/CN4/1426 ¶26 (discussing this issue in the context of apartheid).

international community that its breach is recognized as a crime by that community as a whole constitutes an international crime.

(3) Subject to paragraph 2, and on the basis of the rules of international law in force, an international crime may result, inter alia, from:
   (a) a serious breach of an international obligation of essential importance for the maintenance of international peace and security, such as that prohibiting aggression; .... [or]
   (c) a serious breach on a widespread scale of an international obligation of essential importance for safeguarding the human being, such as those prohibiting slavery, genocide and apartheid ....[17]

Article 19 was problematic from the start. An obvious difficulty was its circularity—that a breach constituted a crime when it generally was recognized as a crime.[18] It also failed the test of specificity, using modifiers such as 'serious breach', 'essential importance', etc without distinguishing crimes from delicts. Apart from the definitional problems, Article 19 was vague on implementation, indicating only that crimes 'may result' from such conduct.[19] More fundamentally, it was conceptually difficult for states to 'commit' a crime. Notions of 'criminal' regimes and 'rogue' states are more rhetorical flourish than substantive determinations. States are legal abstractions that cannot be imprisoned or punished through traditional criminal sanctions (beyond criminal restitution).[20]

The ILC's scheme for *all* wrongful acts created obligations both to desist and to make reparation—defined as restitution (re-establishing the status quo ante), compensation (monetary payments or other forms of value transfer) and satisfaction (additional symbolic remedies for moral or non-material injuries).[21] Wrongs constituting 'criminal' infractions were subject to additional consequences: (i) that 'all other states' were deemed injured (and thus had standing to claim reparations and institute countermeasures); (ii) that pragmatic limitations on reparations no longer applied; and (iii) that other states became obligated not to recognize the offending conduct as legitimate.[22]

State *punishment* certainly raises the spectre of group punishment of the nation's citizenry. Group punishment has been rejected as impermissible under international law. The IMT Charter, for example, allowed organizations to be

[17] Draft Articles on State Responsibility (1996) UN Doc A/51/10 art 19.

[18] Circularity is not unknown to international law. *Cf* VCLT art 53 ('a peremptory norm of general international law is a norm accepted and recognized by the international community of States as a whole as' peremptory in character). Circularity even appears in criminal law, although the legality principles can make it more problematic in that context. *Cf Adomako* [1995] 1 AC 171 (UK HL) (criminal conviction for involuntary manslaughter can be premised on gross negligence if the conduct in question is egregious enough to constitute a crime).

[19] Draft Articles on State Responsibility (1996) UN Doc A/51/10 art 19(3).

[20] Bassiouni, *Introduction* 61 (2003).

[21] Draft Articles on State Responsibility (1996) UN Doc A/51/10 arts 28, 34–36. See also ILC Report (23 Apr–1 Jun and 2 Jul–10 Aug 2001) UN Doc A/56/10 213–14, 235–68 (commentaries on same).

[22] Draft Articles on State Responsibility (1996) UN Doc A/51/10 arts 40(3), 52–53.

declared criminal and allowed individuals to be punished for membership.[23] But the IMT refused to punish membership alone, instead requiring personal knowledge or active facilitation of the organization's criminal aims.[24] Penalizing a state's citizens—many of whom are innocent of the state's 'crimes' and are perhaps even victims themselves—'raises fundamental questions of justice and fairness'.[25]

Article 19 also posed complications (if not outright conflicts) in connection with the Security Council's authority to restore international peace and security under Chapter VII.[26] There also were due process concerns. Just as individuals deserved procedural guarantees, it was 'no less unjust to visit on the community of the State the harsh consequences of condemnation and punishment without due process of law'.[27]

These concerns (and others) made Article 19 the 'single most controversial element in the draft articles on State responsibility'.[28] Positions varied widely, and no satisfactory consensus emerged.[29] As recommended by the Special Rapporteur,[30] Article 19 was deleted in the revised text.[31] But this does not mean that Article 19 has no analytic value. It was seen more favourably 'as an exercise not of codification but of development'.[32] Although hardly dispositive, it provides useful guidance on the *types* of conduct that qualifies as criminal on the international plane.

This is particularly true because similar characteristics are reflected in other work by the ILC on *individual* criminal responsibility. Beginning in 1954,[33] the ILC worked to develop a Draft Code of Offences Against the Peace and Security of Mankind. Some iterations were more controversial than others, leading to concerns about the unwarranted expansion of existing law, vagueness in the definition of offences, and the alteration of previously accepted definitions of crimes.[34]

23 IMT Charter arts 9–11.

24 *Göring* [IMT 1946] 1 IMT Proceedings 171, 262, 268, 273.

25 Bassiouni, *Introduction* 63 (2003).

26 *Cf Lockerbie* [1992] ICJ 3 ¶¶40–2 (legal assessment of sanctions by the ICJ was inappropriate where the Security Council authorized them).

27 First Report on State Responsibility (24 Apr 1998) UN Doc A/CN4/490/Add3 ¶¶80–1.

28 ibid ¶43. For detailed analysis of state positions during the drafting process, see M Spinedi, 'International Crimes of State: The Legislative History' in Weiler 45–79 (1989).

29 Government Commentary on State Responsibility (25 Mar 1998) UN Doc A/CN4/488 50–66. The US, France, Germany, UK, Austria, Ireland, and Switzerland opposed Article 19: ibid. The Czech Republic, Mongolia, Uzbekistan, Denmark, Mexico, Argentina, and Italy favoured the concept, albeit with qualifications to the existing text. ibid and ibid A/CN4/488/Add1–2 (Argentina and Italy). See also First Report on State Responsibility (24 Apr 1998) UN Doc A/CN4/490/Add3 ¶¶52–60 (summarizing positions).

30 First Report on State Responsibility (24 Apr 1998) UN Doc A/CN4/490/Add3 ¶101.

31 Report of the International Law Commission on the Work of its Fifty-Third Session (23 Apr–1 Jun and 2 Jul–10 Aug 2001) UN Doc A/56/10 ¶46. Debate continued in another form over the distinction between 'serious' and 'ordinary' breaches of international law. The Draft Articles were revised yet again to mirror the more familiar framework of VCLT art 53, which distinguishes peremptory norms (*jus cogens*) from other rules. ibid ¶¶45–9.

32 First Report on State Responsibility (24 Apr 1998) UN Doc A/CN4/490/Add3 ¶60.

33 [1954] Draft Code.

34 MN Leich, 'International Criminal Jurisdiction: ILC Draft Code of Crimes' (1993) 87 AJIL 607.

An expansive articulation of twelve offences in the 1991 Draft Code was reduced in 1996 to the three 'core' crimes now covered by the ICC Statute,[35] together with a fourth offence protecting UN personnel.[36] Substantive alterations of the definition of genocide in prior drafts[37] also were revised to mirror the Convention.

The Draft Code reflects substantial consensus on crimes that per se threaten international peace and security. Although not itself state practice,[38] the ILC's work is highly authoritative[39] and has been drawn upon as evidence of customary international law.[40] The Draft Code and Article 19 thus complement one another—the former addressing individual responsibility and the latter that of states.[41] But their underlying premise is the same. Both ground international criminal responsibility in threats to international peace and security and in conduct that shocks the collective international conscience.[42]

These criteria accord with authoritative academic commentary as well. Professor Bassiouni, for example, agrees that threats to international peace and security and acts that shock the world's conscience are the pre-eminent characteristics of international offences.[43] Others suggest that international crimes arise when the conduct involves fundamentally important human rights that are violated at a significant level of magnitude.[44] Even economic rationales support the primacy of these considerations as the principal justifications for international criminal regulation.[45]

[35] The ILC contemplated that the Draft Code might be implemented by incorporation into the ICC. 'Draft Code Commentary' (1996) UN Doc A/51/10 ¶¶47–8.

[36] ibid.

[37] [1954] Draft Code art II ¶10 (adding 'including' at the end of the first paragraph of art II of the Convention, thus rendering the prohibited acts in art II(a)–(e) illustrative rather than restrictive).

[38] *Hadzihasanovic (Interlocutory Appeal—AC)* [2003] ICTY ¶26 (Sep Op Hunt J).

[39] *Furundzija (TC)* [1998] ICTY ¶227 (this work of 'outstanding experts in international law... may (i) constitute evidence of customary law, or (ii) shed light on customary rules which are of uncertain contents or are in the process of formation, or, at the very least, (iii) be indicative of the legal views of eminently qualified publicists representing the major legal systems of the world.').

[40] *Jelisic (TC)* [1999] ICTY ¶61.

[41] Draft Code (1996) art 4 (code does not address state responsibility) and Draft Articles on State Responsibility (1996) UN Doc A/51/10 art 58 (Articles do not address individual responsibility).

[42] Draft Code (1996) art 7 cmt 1; Draft Articles on State Responsibility (1996) UN Doc A/51/10 art 19(3)(a) and (c).

[43] Bassiouni, *Introduction* 114–15, 173 (2003). Bassiouni's other suggested criteria—the involvement of multiple states, injury to internationally-protected persons or interests, and practical necessity—apply more to transnational offences and are not relevant here. ibid 115.

[44] Morris and Scharf, *The ICTR* 138–9 (1998). See also T Meron, 'International Criminalization of Internal Atrocities' (1995) 89 AJIL 554, 562 ('The extent to which the prohibition is addressed to individuals, whether the prohibition is unequivocal in character, the gravity of the act, and the interests of the international community are all relevant factors in determining the criminality of various acts.').

[45] EA Posner and AO Sykes, 'An Economic Analysis of State and Individual Responsibility Under International Law' (2007) 9 Am LER 100, 123–7 (international crimes arise when states agree that certain conduct is undesirable, that there are difficulties in enforcing prohibitions on that conduct solely at the domestic level, and that the benefit of increased probability of enforcement

Threats to international peace and security

The UN Security Council plays a unique role relative to threats to international peace and security. Its role under the UN Charter is to identify and respond to such threats.[46] The Security Council's assessments are 'essentially political judgments',[47] which makes their application as legal standards somewhat awkward. Nevertheless, the Security Council has determined that violations of 'core' criminal norms threaten international peace and security and that criminal prosecution is a proper restorative measure. This led to the creation of the ICTY and ICTR in the early 1990s.[48] In less egregious cases, the Security Council has resolved (under Chapter VII and otherwise) that certain human rights violations were criminal acts carrying individual responsibility. Examples of such offences included attacks on non-combatants, relief workers and medical personnel in Somalia.[49]

The Security Council's mandate certainly requires it to engage with and apply international law, and its resolutions can reflect the content of a particular legal rule.[50] The Security Council appears to adopt the view that large-scale attacks on fundamental human rights *ipso facto* threaten international peace and security. Nevertheless, Security Council resolutions are not usually seen as sources of international law.[51] They are *sui generis* to particular circumstances, and their application beyond those situations is unclear. The consequence of an *incorrect* determination on a legal issue by the Security Council is an open question, as is the related issue of whether Security Council resolutions are amenable to judicial review.[52]

In the *Lockerbie* case, Libya requested provisional measures barring the UK from imposing economic, air, and other sanctions.[53] The ICJ declined to adjudicate the legal merits of a Security Council resolution[54] authorizing the sanctions.[55] But it also denied Libya's request, holding the entry of provisional

outside of the domestic setting (in either international tribunals or other states) outweighs the costs of potential bias, unfairness, etc to each state's citizens).

[46] UN Charter art 39. [47] Bassiouni, *Introduction* 173 n 205 (2003).

[48] I Morris and Scharf, *The ICTY* 37–48 (1995); I Morris and Scharf, *The ICTR* 75–109 (1998).

[49] UNSC Res 794 (3 Dec 1992) UN Doc S/RES/794 and SC Res 814 (26 Mar 1993) UN Doc S/RES/814. [50] ibid.

[51] Higgins 28 (1994) (resolutions 'have an ad hoc effect and may create binding obligations, but they are not [legal] sources of general applicability.').

[52] Some tribunals have claimed such power, at least insofar as *jus cogens* rights are concerned. *Cf Kadi* [2005] ECJ ¶226 ('The Court is empowered to check, indirectly, the lawfulness of the resolutions of the Security Council in question with regard to jus cogens, understood as a body of higher rules of public international law binding on all subjects of international law, including the bodies of the United Nations, and from which no derogation is possible.'). For detailed discussion, see S Chesterman, 'The UN Security Council and the Rule of Law' (2008) *Final Report and Recommendations from the Austrian Initiative 2004–08* ¶¶25–30, 37.

[53] *Lockerbie* [1992] ICJ 3 ¶9. [54] UNSC Res 748 (31 Mar 1992) UN Doc S/RES/748.

[55] *Lockerbie* [1992] ICJ 3 ¶40.

measures inappropriate in light of the Security Council's action.[56] 'The fact that the ICJ has been able to apply resolutions of the Council without remarking upon the incompleteness of Article 38 strongly suggests that binding Council resolutions, both of a general and of a particular character, are still properly regarded as coming within the scope of traditional sources of international law.'[57]

The deeper intersection between international law and the Security Council's decision-making authority is unclear. The ICJ has come close to the line without forcing the issue. Judge Lauterpacht, for example, suggested that the Security Council's arms embargo on the former Yugoslavia might be invalid as actively contributing to Serbia's violation of *jus cogens* prohibitions on genocide. But he declined to decide the question, suggesting instead that the Security Council 'give due weight' to the issue in future proceedings.[58]

Although the Security Council can go quite far in its orders, its powers are not unlimited. If the Security Council orders the violation of a *jus cogens* norm, for example, the order is neither valid nor enforceable. The UN system is premised on a treaty—the UN Charter—which, like all treaties, cannot supersede *jus cogens* norms. Decisions violating *jus cogens* would be *ultra vires* the UN Charter and thus beyond the power of the Security Council created by that Charter.[59]

There is no need to ascertain here the outer limits of the Security Council's authority. It is enough that the Council clearly has the power to respond to violations of fundamental human rights through the mechanism of international criminal law. Political genocide fits within the existing paradigm of a threat to international peace and security because it almost always involves serious violence against human beings perpetrated on a similar scale to that of genocide.[60]

Numerous historical examples prove the point. In the four decades following World War II, the destruction of opposition groups on political grounds outnumbered destruction on xenophobic or hegemonical grounds by four to one.[61] Before that, some 5–6 million were killed in the Soviet Union during enforced

[56] ibid ¶¶40–2.

[57] S Talmon, 'The Security Council as World Legislature' (2005) 99 AJIL 175, 179.

[58] *Application of Genocide Convention—Prov Measures II* [1993] ICJ 325 ¶104 (Lauterpacht J).

[59] This assumes that the Security Council's power to enter orders itself is not a 'subsequent norm of general international law having the same character'. VCLT art 53. This is unlikely. Authority for the Security Council to violate *jus cogens* norms is not supported by state practice or *opinio juris*.

[60] That massive scale is not necessarily *required* is beside the point. Political genocide committed on a smaller scale that satisfies the elements of the offence would be handled in the same way as genocide against enumerated groups, either at the domestic level or otherwise. *Cf* ICC Elements of Crimes art 6(a)(4)-(e)(4) (premising ICC jurisdiction on 'conduct took place in the context of a manifest pattern of similar conduct directed against that group or was conduct that could itself effect such destruction.').

[61] B Harff and TR Gurr, 'Toward Empirical Theory of Genocides and Politicides: Identification and Measurement of Cases Since 1945' (1988) 32 ILQ 359, 368 (identifying six hegemonical and xenophobic genocides, compared with 36 repressive, retributive, revolutionary, and hegemonical politicides, with two mixed cases).

famine in Ukraine.[62] Millions more died in massive political repressions in the occupied Balkans[63] and Poland,[64] both before and after World War II.

More recent political genocides have transpired in the Far East and in Africa. Communists were targeted in Indonesia in the mid-1960s during a power struggle with military forces. Between 200,000 and 1 million were massacred—identified by party membership lists and denunciation by neighbours in smaller villages.[65] Likewise, during its 'most radical restructuring of the society,' the Khmer Rouge liquidated 2 million from 1975 to 1979—25 per cent of the Cambodian population.[66] Additional political massacres occurred in Uganda under Idi Amin (100,000–500,000 dead and 170,000 displaced) and in Equatorial Guinea under Macias (12.5 per cent of the population—50,000 people—killed and another 100,000 displaced). Further examples include 7,000–10,000 dead and 'disappeared' in Argentina's 'Dirty War' and 20,000 political murders in Guatemala.[67]

Violence on this scale—even when directed internally—unquestionably threatens international peace and security. Political genocide tears societies apart, creating cross-border crises in the form of food and resource shortages, refugees fleeing violence en masse, perpetrators fleeing justice and continuing to victimize political opponents abroad, and subsequent retaliatory measures taken by victims. Inter-state violence and armed conflict often follow. Atrocities by the Khmer Rouge, for example, ended only when Vietnam invaded the country and deposed Pol Pot. Likewise in Bangladesh, where India intervened amidst the violence in secessionist East Pakistan.

Political genocide almost always involves massive loss of life and widespread destruction of the social order. As noted above, this destruction ripples into neighbouring states and invites (or provides a convenient excuse for) armed conflict. Such matters pose significant risks to the international order and justify the proscription of political genocide at the international level.

Shocking the international conscience

The more egregious conduct is, the more likely it qualifies as an international crime.[68] The notion of 'shocking' the international conscience is more of an

[62] RCO Rezie, 'The Ukrainian Constitution: Interpretation of the Citizens Rights Provisions' (1999) Case Western JIL 169, 176 n 32.

[63] L Malksoo, 'Soviet Genocide? Communist Mass Deportations in the Baltic States and International Law' (2001) 14 Leiden JIL 757, 758, 763–6.

[64] SW Becker, 'Maintaining Secret Government Dossiers on the First Amendment Activities of American Citizens: the Law Enforcement Exception to the Privacy Act' (2000) 50 DePaul LR 675, 740 n 438.

[65] Kuper, *Prevention* 129–30 (1985).

[66] ibid 130–2. Atrocities in Cambodia were particularly vicious, leading one UN investigator to label them 'the most serious that had occurred anywhere in the world since Nazism'. ibid 135.

[67] ibid 132–43.

[68] *Flores v Southern Peru Copper Corp* (2003) 406 F3d 65 (US Ct App (2d Cir)) 85.

abstract description than substantive qualification. As a general matter, whether conduct qualifies is a function of the offences at issue and the scale upon which they are carried out. But it is not necessary here to concretely define the concept or to fully delineate all conduct that qualifies. Political genocide involves the most serious of human rights violations, typically committed on a massive scale. Whatever the outer limits of the doctrine, political genocide meets the criteria of egregiousness and scale and certainly qualifies.

Historically, political genocide has involved large-scale infringements on human rights. As noted previously, politically-based atrocities in Cambodia dwarf the carnage in Rwanda, both in temporal duration (four years versus four months) and the sheer loss of life (over 2 million, versus 800,000). The same is true for Soviet purges under Stalin, which exceeded even Nazi zeal in scope and duration. Indeed, many more have died as a result of political genocides than genocide against groups protected by the Convention.[69]

The nature of the rights at stake also favours treating political genocide as an international crime. As detailed in Chapter 4, the critical importance of political collectives is clear at both the national and international levels. The physical and biological destruction of such groups simultaneously infringes fundamental rights to life and bodily integrity and highly important rights of political identity and participation.

The criminal character of political genocide is beyond dispute. 'Amongst all human rights, the primacy of the right to life is unanimously agreed to be pre-eminent and essential: it is the *sine qua non*, for all other human rights... depend for their potential existence on the preservation of human life.'[70] Unjustified infringements on political rights also can be treated as criminal offences—either as unlawful deprivations of rights in and of themselves[71] or as discriminatory 'bias' or 'hate' crimes when linked to other violent acts.[72]

A direct criminal prohibition on political genocide is the natural consequence of recognizing and protecting the human rights implicated by the offence. It is illogical for international law to protect the political rights of individuals to organize in groups in the first place (rights to assemble, to form political parties, to communicate ideas to one another, etc) but not to treat the physical and biological destruction of the political groups arising out of that collective political activity as a criminal offence. Collective political rights are meaningful only if individuals are not subject to physical or biological destruction for exercising (or having the right to exercise or being perceived to exercise) political beliefs in concert with others. On the whole, political genocide is a penultimate form of guilt by association—egregious violence that 'shocks the conscience' of the

[69] Harff and Gurr 368 (politicides outnumbering genocides by more than four to one).

[70] 'Study (Second) on Genocide' (2 Jul 1985) UN Doc E/CN4/Sub2/1985/6 ¶17.

[71] Civil Rights Act (1968) 18 USC ss 241 (conspiracy to violate civil rights), 242 (deprivation of rights under colour of state law) and 245 (intimidation, interference or injury of federally-protected activities).

[72] Jenness and Grattet 79–86 (2001) (interference with civil rights).

international community. This meets the second generally-recognized criterion supporting proscription as an international crime.

C. The goals of international criminal justice

Entire libraries exist on the aims of criminal justice systems and the theoretical and philosophical justifications for criminal punishment.[73] The limited review here, which barely scratches the surface, seeks only to determine whether treating political genocide as a criminal offence is consistent with the major theories justifying criminalization.

Criminal proscription generally stems from the 'harm principle'—the minimization of injury to others (or the risk of such injury).[74] The principles of deterrence and retribution respond to this harm from opposite ends. Deterrence is the prospective answer. Provided that laws are enforced consistently, criminal prohibition provides 'a standing disincentive to crime and reinforces those social conventions and other inhibitions which are already in place'.[75] Retribution, in contrast, responds after the fact. It posits that 'offenders deserve punishment for their offences, and it is therefore right (and not just expedient) to provide that serious harms culpably caused should lead to punishment'.[76]

The ICTY has identified three general aims of criminal prosecution at the international level: (i) to do 'justice'; (ii) to deter future crimes; and (iii) to contribute to the restoration and maintenance of peace.[77] The first two correspond to the primary theoretical justifications for criminal punishment noted above—retribution and deterrence. The third is a characteristically different factor that is specific to *international* criminal justice.

Deterrence and retribution

Any application of deterrent and retributive principles must be tailored to the international context. This means, for example, that the concept of deterrence almost certainly is limited to 'general' deterrence. 'Specific' deterrence—inhibiting individual perpetrators from re-offending—has much less utility here. International offences (eg, the Rwandan genocide) tend to be *sui generis* events that are not susceptible to repetition in the same way as domestic offences (eg, serial bank robbery).

Deterrence is premised upon rational choice about conduct and consequences.[78] But in practice such choices are driven largely by surrounding social

[73] For details on the theoretical bases of criminal punishment, see Lacey, *Punishment* 1–17 (1994).

[74] The extent of injury required, and the tension between comprehensive criminalization and maximizing personal freedom, is much debated. Ashworth, *Principles* 32–42 (2003).

[75] ibid 16. [76] ibid 17. [77] *Tadic (Protective Measures—TC)* [1995] ICTY ¶18.

[78] F Hassan, 'The Theoretical Basis of Punishment in International Criminal Law' (1983) 15 Case Western JIL 38, 48–9.

circumstances. Social norms and morality can take tragic detours into criminality, such that 'ordinary' citizens transform into violent offenders committing extraordinarily brutal offences against former neighbours and friends. One need look no further than the historical example of Nazism to realize that personal violence that is anathema in ordinary circumstances can become socially desirable when times change.

International offences thus seek to deter criminal conduct in social contexts that tolerate, or even encourage, such behaviour by threatening prosecution in a *different* social context—either a successive domestic regime, another state enforcing international law, or an international forum.[79] There has been some suggestion, for example, that the death rates in Darfur dropped significantly following the ICC's issuance of an arrest warrant for Sudanese President Omar al-Bashir.[80] Even international oversight through the investigatory process is thought to have deterrent effect. Unless confidentiality obligations dictate otherwise, the ICC Prosecutor makes public information about its monitoring activities in order to help prevent criminal activity.[81]

The other principal justification for criminal justice—retribution—also fits less neatly at the international level. Few, if any, modern legal systems support a pure form of *lex talionis* (a tooth for a tooth, an eye for an eye). But domestic punishment typically is more proportionate to the injury caused by a crime. The retributive power of international justice often pales in comparison. Adolf Eichmann, for example, was hanged for committing genocide and similar offences.[82] As a key architect of the Nazi Final Solution, Eichmann was directly (albeit not solely) responsible for *millions* of deaths. The 'ultimate price' that he paid seems pitifully cheap relative to the incalculable damage he caused. The disparity can only broaden in light of the growing international trend away from the death penalty, especially for crimes involving massive deprivations of life.[83]

Such complications noted, it seems clear that proscribing political genocide would further both of these important goals of criminal justice. Political genocide is worth deterring on a forward-looking basis and is sufficiently blameworthy to punish after the fact. It is important not to overstate its contribution to these ends, however. The underlying criminal conduct involved (murder, torture, etc) already is subject to the harshest penalties under international and domestic

[79] ibid 56 ('the need for ensuring the sanctity of the most fundamental values of the international community also demands that potential violators be forewarned from committing breaches of the international order.').

[80] A de Waal and GH Stanton, 'Should President Omar al-Bashir of Sudan be Charged and Arrested by the International Criminal Court? An Exchange of Views' (2009) 4 Gen Stud & Prevent 329, 349.

[81] ICC 2008/09 UN Report (17 Sep 09) UN Doc A/64/356 ¶45 (current investigations in Afghanistan, Columbia, Code d'Ivorie, Georgia, Kenya, and Palestine). For more details on deterrence and the ICC, see JF Alexander, 'The International Criminal Court and the Prevention of Atrocities: Predicting the Court's Impact' (2009) 54 Vill LR 1.

[82] *Eichmann (AC)* [1961] 36 ILR 277 (Isr Sup Ct).

[83] ICC Statute art 77(1)(b), ICTR Statute art 23(1) and ICTY Statute art 24(1) (maximum penalty of life imprisonment).

law.[84] Except insofar as perpetrators of international crimes operate with a legalistic sense of impunity (eg, understanding the finer jurisdictional distinctions between persecution on political grounds and political genocide), the aims of deterrence and retribution appear largely accomplished already in connection with other international crimes. In this sense, the *incremental* deterrent and retributive value added by a separate crime of political genocide is marginal.

A crime of political genocide would contribute most strongly to the third factor identified by the ICTY—the expressive and restorative functions of international criminal justice. The greater value in recognizing political genocide is increased precision in labelling—identifying conduct for what it truly is and empowering the international community to take steps—both jurisdictionally and normatively—to condemn it. As discussed below, this is a critical factor in international criminal justice, whose emblematic dimensions have been paramount from the beginning.

Expression and restoration

Despite the massive scale of Nazi criminality at all levels of society, the major Nuremberg trials involved the prosecution of only 22 'major' Nazi war criminals before the IMT and 185 others under CC10.[85] These proceedings were neither comprehensive (13 trials of just over 200 defendants over four years) nor efficient.[86] Nevertheless, they delineated a new standard for criminal justice and individual criminal responsibility at the international level. The enduring symbolic value of Nuremberg as a clear record of the international community joining together to condemn almost unfathomable wrongdoing with a single voice is undeniable.[87]

The same holds true today. The ICTY has completed only 86 cases since its inception in 1993, with proceedings ongoing against an additional 37 defendants.[88] The ICTR has completed 45 cases at the trial level, 27 cases at the appellate

[84] The overlap between political genocide and other crimes was detailed in Chapter 6.

[85] Marrus 258–61 (1997) (IMT proceedings); Taylor 69, 118–19 (1949) (CC10 proceedings). There certainly were a number of other military trials of lower-level war criminals, although they were far less publicized. For a general description, see K Brand, 'Commentary' (1949) 15 LRTWC 1.

[86] At one point, the tribunals employed over 1,800 personnel. NJ Kritz, 'Coming to terms with Atrocities: A Review of Accountability Mechanisms for Mass Violations of Human Rights' (1996) 59 LCP 127, 133.

[87] *Cf* DE Arzt, 'Nuremberg, Denazification and Democracy: The Hate Speech Problem at the International Military Tribunal' (1995) 12 NYLS JHR 689, 705–6 ('If at the time it may have seemed a wasteful expenditure of funds—pouring the resources of four allied nations into a massive sixteen month endeavour, the result of which could have been attained with a mere two dozen bullets to the back of captured Nazi heads—the multi-volume historical record compiled at Nuremberg is of inestimable value today, in the face of persistent Holocaust denial and revisionism.').

[88] Sixteenth Annual Report of the International Tribunal for the Former Yugoslavia (31 Jul 2009) UN Doc A/64/205-S/2009/394 3–4. Two indictees remain at large. ibid.

level, and has 18 cases in process.[89] Despite limited 'progress', the international community continues to commit enormous political and financial resources—some $550 million for 2010 alone—to the ICTY ($302 million) and ICTR ($244 million).[90] Over $100 million recently was sought for 'mixed' domestic-international tribunals in Cambodia ($29 million),[91] Sierra Leone ($40 million),[92] and Lebanon ($35–45 million).[93] And the international community continues to preserve and expand international criminal justice through the permanent ICC, whose 2010 working budget was €102 million.[94]

Clearly there is tremendous symbolic value—far outweighing the usual adjudicative metrics and economic factors[95]—in the existence of a rules-based system that applies international criminal norms to a select group of perpetrators in a highly visible, transparent fashion. Professor Cassese has identified four distinct benefits that flow from international criminal justice.[96] First, international prosecution establishes individual responsibility so that entire societies (eg, all Germans, all Hutus, etc) are not assigned guilt collectively. Justice Jackson made a similar point at Nuremberg: '[c]rimes against international law are committed by men, not by abstract entities, and only by punishing individuals who commit such crimes can the provisions of international law be enforced.'[97] As noted previously, the problems of collective guilt through citizenship helped prompt the ILC to discontinue prior efforts to delineate criminal responsibility for states. International prosecution avoids this dilemma by fixing responsibility more precisely upon guilty individuals.

Second, international prosecution dissipates calls for revenge by channelling violence and retribution from private hands into legal processes. Criminal

[89] Fourteenth Annual Report of the International Tribunal for Rwanda (31 Jul 2009) UN Doc A/64/206-S/2009/396 3–5. Thirteen indictees remain at large. ibid.

[90] UN Press Release, 'Budget Committee Takes Up Proposed 2010–2011 Financing for International Criminal Tribunals for Rwanda, Former Yugoslavia' (10 Dec 2009) UN Doc GA/AB/3936. A major early critique was that the trial and investigatory processes for the ICTY and ICTR were substantially under-funded compared to the Nuremberg efforts. Kritz (n 86) 133 n 5.

[91] Extraordinary Chambers in the Courts of Cambodia for the Prosecution of Crimes Committed During the Period of Democratic Kampuchea: (Approved) Revised Budget Estimates from 2005 to 2009 (Jul 2008) 8–12.

[92] Sixth Annual Report of the President of the Special Court for Sierra Leone: June 2008 to May 2009 (21 Jul 09) 33–5, 66–7.

[93] Report of the Secretary-General Submitted Pursuant to Security Council Resolution 1757 (2007) of 30 May 2007 (4 Sep 2007) UN Doc S/2007/525 ¶22.

[94] Proposed Programme Budget for 2010 of the International Criminal Court (17 Jul 09) UN Doc ICC-ASP/8/10 (Advance Version) ¶¶1–3.

[95] *Cf* RA Mulligan, 'Enhancing the Delivery of Quality Justice: Report of the Court Metrics Project' Commonwealth of Massachusetts Administrative Office of the Trial Court (Mar 2007) (measuring clearance rate (outgoing cases as a percentage of incoming cases), time to disposition (percentage of cases resolved within established time frames), age of pending cases (active cases beyond established disposition dates), and trial date certainty (number of times cases were scheduled for trial).

[96] A Cassese, 'Reflections on International Criminal Justice' (1998) 61 Modern LR 1, 5–6.

[97] *Göring* [IMT 1946] 1 IMT Proceedings 171, 223.

punishment vindicates the victims' interests and restores a 'moral order disturbed by the crime'.[98] The absence of this restorative function—the appearance of impunity—is costly for the international community as a whole. When Turkish massacres went unpunished after World War I, for example, militant Armenians exacted violent retribution and assassinated Turkish officials throughout Europe in the early 1920s.[99]

Third, international prosecution creates an opportunity for reconciliation and societal renewal. This certainly includes the restoration of international peace and security.[100] But it extends beyond international stability into the broader healing of societies ripped apart by mass atrocities:

> One of the most important opportunities for promoting the transformation of the culture is the new government's response to past abuses... This response has the potential to inculcate the values of the new government in the society at large because it has a far greater hold on the public's attention than most other aspects of the transition.[101]

Fourth, international prosecution creates a reliable historical record of what happened. This was a primary aim of the Nuremberg proceedings.[102] It goes without saying that such trials must be fair and impartial exercises that demonstrate respect for human rights. 'Show' trials like that of deposed Romanian President Nicolae Ceausescu certainly create a record, but even truthful wrongs documented therein are overshadowed by the fundamental flaws of a pre-ordained result and unfairness. International criminal trials are a step removed from the offences themselves and are more likely to be conducted with the full panoply of due process guarantees. These factors help to ensure that the historic record is created accurately and fairly.

This does not mean that criminal prosecution is the only method of documenting international crimes. Other considerations may warrant the separation of documentation from criminal adjudication. The truth and reconciliation process in South Africa is a good example.[103] But such matters are the exception to a general policy against impunity. Criminal prosecution 'helps to bridge periods of diminished law. Trials offer a way to express both public condemnation of past violence and the legitimation of the rule of law necessary to the consolidation of future democracy.'[104]

The proscription of political genocide as a separate crime would facilitate all four of these goals. The separate offence allows greater precision in adjudication, thereby ensuring that the guilty are not sanctioned merely for 'lesser' criminal offences (or worse—not at all). On a wider scale, the violence-dissipating,

98 Fletcher 80 (1998).
99 Willis 163 (1982).
100 UN Charter arts 39–42.
101 E Daly, 'Transformative Justice: Charting a path to Reconciliation' (2002) 12 ILP 73, 74–5.
102 *Göring* [IMT 1946] 1 IMT Proceedings 171, 247 ('persecution of the Jews at the hands of the Nazi Government has been proved in the greatest detail before the Tribunal. It is a record of consistent and systematic inhumanity on the greatest scale.').
103 Promotion of National Unity and Reconciliation Act 1995.
104 Daly (n 101) 109.

restorative, and documentary aims of international criminal justice are all facilitated by the separate offence. Political genocide condemns more precisely the conduct at issue and documents more clearly the reality of what in almost all cases will be a massive violation of fundamental rights.

Just as the term 'genocide' was needed to convey the reality of the Holocaust and similar events, 'political genocide' is needed to convey the reality of Stalin's purges, the madness of the Khmer Rouge, and the underlying truth of atrocities against moderate Hutu in Rwanda. It is only when the end result of international prosecution corresponds meaningfully with the reality of criminal conduct that international 'justice' is truly done.

D. Responding to political genocide

Before a separate criminal proscription on political genocide is warranted, it is useful to evaluate whether existing international mechanisms can effectively deal with the problem. These include potential remedies through adjudication in the ICJ and human rights tribunals such as the ECHR, IACHR and the like.

ICJ proceedings

The 'classic statement' on diplomatic protection[105] for injuries to a state's citizens provides that:

> [i]t is an elementary principle of international law that a State is entitled to protect its subjects, when injured by acts contrary to international law committed by another State... By taking up the case of one of its subjects and by resorting to diplomatic action or international judicial proceedings on his behalf, a State is in reality asserting its own rights—its right to ensure, in the person of its subjects, respect for the rules of international law.[106]

The ICJ provides a forum for aggrieved states to pursue compensation on behalf of their nationals, provided that both states consent to its jurisdiction. The ICJ does not assess individual criminal responsibility or prosecute violations of international law. Its ability to respond to otherwise criminal acts is limited to adjudicating the breach of international law and ordering compensatory measures and injunctive relief.

Several conclusions are obvious from the very nature of the forum. First (apart from the court's advisory jurisdiction), the ICJ adjudicates disputes between *states*. This means that it has no jurisdiction over non-state actors who commit

[105] SM Schwebel, 'The treatment of human rights and of aliens in the International Court of Justice' in Lowe and Fitzmaurice 327, 328 (1996).

[106] *Mavrommatis Palestine Concessions* [1925] PCIJ Ser A No 2 (26 Mar) 12.

political genocide. Second, the ICJ is a consent-based system, which is incompatible with criminal activity. States that commit political genocide are highly unlikely to consent to the ICJ's jurisdiction, either on a compulsory or an ad hoc basis. Third, ICJ proceedings require a claim to be brought by a complaining state, which is unlikely unless the state's own interests or nationals are directly affected. Criminal conduct perpetrated by a state against its own citizens thus is highly unlikely to be brought before the ICJ.[107]

The ICJ also faces significant practical obstacles that further restrict its utility in adjudicating criminal infractions. The ICJ has no enforcement authority and relies principally upon voluntary compliance by states. Failing that, the UN Security Council (a decidedly political body) must take separate action to implement ICJ rulings.[108] This is a significant issue that places tremendous limitations on the utility of the ICJ in this context.

The divide between what is legally-binding versus pragmatically-effective became clear following the disintegration of the former Yugoslavia in the early 1990s. Faced with credible evidence of genocide against Bosnian Muslims, the ICJ ordered Serbia to immediately 'take *all measures* within its power to prevent commission of the crime of genocide' (emphasis added).[109] It also ordered Serbia not to aggravate the dispute and to prevent paramilitary and irregular units within its control from committing genocide.[110] By all accounts, the ICJ's order was ignored. Faced with a patent refusal to comply, the ICJ entered a nearly identical order five months later.[111] This too went unrecognized.

Both orders created legal obligations for Serbia to prevent genocide.[112] Neither had the desired effect. The massacres at Srebrenica took place some two years after the provisional measures were entered. There is no doubt that these massacres were genocide and fell within the ICJ's order. They were confirmed as such by the ICTY Appeals Chamber[113] and the ICJ itself, which *inter alia* held Serbia in breach of its international obligations for failing to comply with the court's provisional orders 14 years before.[114]

Even final international judgments that order specific remedies can lead to less than successful results. This is particularly true for states with a constitutionally divided system where federal and regional governments operate with different

[107] The prohibition on genocide extends *erga omnes*, which technically provides standing for states to institute ICJ proceedings even in respect of genocide by a state against its own citizens. This is not true for political genocide, however, which is not recognized under customary international law.

[108] This structure is problematic when a litigant is a permanent member of the Security Council that can veto enforcement measures against it. The US withdrawal from the *Nicaragua* case is a good example.

[109] *Application of Genocide Convention—Prov Measures I* [1993] ICJ 3 ¶52.

[110] ibid.

[111] *Application of Genocide Convention—Prov Measures II* [1993] ICJ 325 ¶61.

[112] ibid (Lauterpacht J) ¶¶7–13.

[113] *Krstic (AC)* [2004] ICTY ¶¶2–38.

[114] *Application of Genocide Convention—Merits* [2007] ICJ 1 ¶¶451–6. The court found other breaches for Serbia's failure to prevent genocide in Srebrenica when it could have done so and for failing to punish genocide after the fact through cooperation with the ICTY. ibid ¶¶428–38 (obligation to prevent), ¶¶439–50 (obligation to punish).

spheres of influence. The US federal government, for example, was denied authority to block state officials in Texas from executing a Mexican national for a violation of Texan law (murder). Despite the ICJ's order to stop the execution and the president's efforts to comply with it, the US Supreme Court held that constitutional provisions required the president to have express authorization from Congress before he could order Texas to halt the execution.[115]

This of course does not mean that the ICJ's order or the international obligation are invalid. Domestic law is never a defence to the breach of an international obligation, and the US will face repercussions on the international plane.[116] It demonstrates, however, the pragmatic divide between validity and effectiveness, even when states undertake to implement their international obligations in good faith.

Adjudication in the ICJ thus lacks critical measures needed to respond to political genocide. It cannot punish perpetrators and has no practical ability to stop criminal conduct from occurring. The glacial pace of dispute resolution in the ICJ (14 years in the case of genocide in the former Yugoslavia) further indicates that the forum is ill-suited to respond to international crimes. None of this is a failing of the ICJ. It was never designed to play such a role. Nevertheless, it is clear that ICJ proceedings alone are insufficient to address the problem of political genocide.

Human rights adjudication

A UN Special Rapporteur studying genocide in 1978 suggested that political groups were 'effectively' protected under other international instruments such as the UDHR and ICCPR.[117] This is questionable. The UDHR is a non-binding general assembly resolution. And the ICCPR is a human rights treaty, not a *criminal* convention. Even assuming that these instruments reflect binding obligations of customary international law, neither is supported by compulsory adjudication to enforce the obligation.

Human rights treaties (and their concomitant adjudicatory mechanisms) depend upon voluntary and good faith participation by states party to the instruments themselves. Human rights tribunals thus suffer from the same drawback as adjudication in the ICJ. The states most likely to commit or tolerate political genocide are least likely to consent to jurisdiction. And although individuals have standing to assert claims, the responding parties are *states*, which likewise precludes a human rights tribunal from bringing non-state actors directly to account.

In any event, the mechanisms of enforcement and available remedies are vastly different. Criminal responsibility is far more significant than a 'mere' human

[115] *Medellin v Texas* [2008] 129 S Ct 360 (US Sup Ct).

[116] *Avena–Further Proceedings* [2009] ICJ 1 (holding that the United States breached its obligations to respect provisional orders entered by the ICJ and reaffirming US obligations but declining to require the US to provide Mexico with guarantees of non-repetition).

[117] 'Study on Genocide' (4 Jul 1978) UN Doc E/CN4/Sub2/416 ¶87.

rights violation.[118] Without detracting from the importance of human rights tribunals, it is important to recognize their limitations. Adjudicated violations (including those amounting to political genocide) create at most an obligation to desist from the offending practice and to pay compensation. The enforcement paradigm itself is insufficient: cases involving the eradication of a political group's physical and biological existence would be adjudicated with the same mechanisms utilized to assess the validity of a poll tax.

Operating alone, the existing rubric of human rights law is incapable of accounting for the crucial differences between rights violations and the smaller subset of severe violations constituting international crimes. Human rights adjudication thus is not a workable substitute for the separate criminal proscription of political genocide.

The need for criminal prosecution

Neither the ICJ nor the various human rights adjudicatory bodies were designed to adjudicate criminal violations or to enforce criminal legal norms. As such, they are incapable of delivering a truly effective response to political genocide (or other international crimes, for that matter). In cases of gross infringements of internationally-guaranteed human rights, the only way to genuinely uphold the rights at issue is through criminal investigation and prosecution.[119]

These duties are separate from obligations of compensation and restoration.[120] The failure to prosecute breaches a separate *international* obligation, even where international law requires states to criminalize certain matters as domestic offences. Domestic amnesties involving gross criminal conduct, for example, have been invalidated as inconsistent with supervening international duties to uphold non-derogable human rights.[121]

[118] *Kunarac (TC)* [2001] ICTY ¶170 (discussing divergent roles of states and individuals in international humanitarian law and human rights law).

[119] *Kondewa (Amnesty—AC)* [2004] SC-SL ¶41 ('When the right to life is violated, certainly on the scale of genocide or massacre, only prosecution could be 'effective' [as a remedy for human rights violations]'); *Velásquez Rodríguez* (IACHR 1988) ¶176 ('If... the violation goes unpunished... the State has failed to comply with its duty to ensure the free and full exercise of those rights to the persons within its jurisdiction. The same is true when the State allows private persons or groups to act freely and with impunity to the detriment of the rights recognized by the Convention.').

[120] ibid ¶166 ('States must prevent, investigate and punish any violation of the rights recognized by the Convention and... attempt to restore the right violated and provide compensation....') and ¶¶174–5 (the 'State has a legal duty to take reasonable steps to prevent human rights violations and to use the means at its disposal to carry out a serious investigation of violations committed within its jurisdiction, to identify those responsible, to impose the appropriate punishment and to ensure the victim adequate compensation.... This duty to prevent includes all those means of a legal, political, administrative and cultural nature that... ensure that any violations are considered and treated as illegal acts, which, as such, may lead to the punishment of those responsible and the obligation to indemnify the victims for damages....).

[121] *Barrios Altos* (IACHR 2001) ¶41 (holding amnesty 'impermissible' for government officials implicated in mass killing of 15 students because such provisions 'prevent the investigation and

A narrow distinction must be drawn for temporary *immunity* provided to high-level government officials while they remain in office. In the *Arrest Warrant* case,[122] the ICJ invalidated a Belgian arrest warrant for Congo's Minister of Foreign Affairs in a case involving alleged war crimes and crimes against humanity. But the court was careful to distinguish *procedural* immunity 'for a certain period' from *substantive impunity* absolving the offender. Immunity does not extend to offences before or after the official held office or to purely private conduct committed at any time. Immunity also can be waived by the responding state or invalidated by other measures (such as treaty obligations under the ICC Statute or Chapter VII enforcement measures of the Security Council).[123]

As a general matter, gross human rights violations require criminal prosecution and punishment. The UN Commission on Human Rights recently affirmed Principles and Guidelines on the compulsory prosecution of criminal violations of human rights.[124] States are *obligated* to investigate violations, to prosecute alleged offenders and to punish the guilty.[125] These Principles and Guidelines reflect broader duties under customary international law. They were expressly cast as reiterating *existing* international obligations—not creating new ones.[126] More importantly, they were adopted unanimously 40–0,[127] with 13 abstentions.[128] Four permanent members of the UN Security Council voted in favour—only the US abstained. This significant consensus on mandatory criminal prosecution for egregious human rights violations provides further support for responding to political genocide through criminal law.[129]

Nothing here would eliminate the panoply of self-help measures available to states in responding to acts of genocide abroad.[130] It also would allow civil litigation for monetary damages to proceed against individual offenders, states and international organizations responsible for genocide (which, with some

punishment of those responsible for serious human rights violations such as torture, extrajudicial, summary or arbitrary execution and forced disappearance, all of them prohibited because they violate non-derogable rights recognized by international human rights law.').

[122] *Arrest Warrant* [2002] ICJ 121 ¶¶58–78. [123] ibid ¶¶60–1.

[124] UNCHR Res 2005/35 (19 Apr 2005) UN Doc E/CN4/2005/L10/Add11 (Annex).

[125] ibid ¶4. [126] ibid pmbl.

[127] Argentina, Armenia, Bhutan, Brazil, Burkina Faso, Canada, China, Congo, Costa Rica, Cuba, Dominican Republic, Ecuador, Finland, France, Gabon, Guatemala, Guinea, Honduras, Hungary, Indonesia, Ireland, Italy, Japan, Kenya, Malaysia, Mexico, Netherlands, Nigeria, Pakistan, Paraguay, Peru, Republic of Korea, Romania, Russian Federation, South Africa, Sri Lanka, Swaziland, Ukraine, UK, and Zimbabwe. ibid ¶68.

[128] Australia, Egypt, Eritrea, Ethiopia, Germany, India, Mauritania, Nepal, Qatar, Saudi Arabia, Sudan, Togo, and US. ibid.

[129] This is not to suggest that the duty to investigate, prosecute and punish all derive from precisely the same source. Seiberg-Fohr, for example, conceptualizes the duty to investigate as a necessary corollary of providing victims with an effective remedy but prosecution and punishment as a procedural obligation stemming from a general human rights obligation to prevent further violations and re-establish trust in the rule of law. Seiberg-Fohr 222–5 (2009).

[130] J Fowler and Z Heckscher, 'Introductory Note to the Sudan Accountability and Investment Act of 2007 and the Signing Statement of President George W. Bush to the Act' (2008) 47 ILM 127 (divestment law aimed at responding to genocide by government of Sudan).

exceptions,[131] have proved largely unsuccessful to date).[132] But criminal prosecution must also be a viable option.

More importantly, criminal prosecution must be a viable option at the international level. It is not enough that the gross infringements involved in political genocide simply to be pursued as criminal violations under domestic law. As discussed below, political genocide must be proscribed as an *international* crime in order to genuinely uphold the rights at issue.

State failures

The more politically and economically viable a state is, the more likely it is to protect human rights successfully.[133] Conversely, in states subject to disorder and internal conflicts, 'normal constitutional and other legal checks and balances are singularly ineffective'.[134] Although this certainly warrants strengthening domestic legal, political, and economic structures, it also weighs in favour of handling large scale atrocities such as political genocide as *international* crimes.

The international character of criminal activity is most evident when the conduct is perpetrated by (or committed with the tacit acquiescence of) a state, although this is not required per se:

> While State action or policy may be decisive in causing an abuse to threaten international peace and security, and the abuse of power and authority by State agents may make conduct rise to a level that is deemed to shock the conscience of humanity, this will not always necessarily be the case. For example, war crimes are frequently committed with no policy element, and genocide could conceivably occur without such a policy, even if such an occurrence is rare.... Particularly in light of the growing prominence of non-State actors, State action or policy should be seen as relevant, but should not always be read into the crimes themselves or their underlying rationales....[135]

This makes sense. If Al Qaeda operatives had detonated a nuclear weapon in Manhattan on September 11, 2001 instead of committing an aerial attack, such a crime (no doubt intended to cause death and injury to millions) could legitimately be prosecuted as genocide regardless of a lack of state involvement.[136]

[131] *Kadic v Karadzic* (1995) 70 F3d 232 (US Ct App (2d Cir)) (tort case against Serb leaders in former Yugoslavia for genocide and other offences).

[132] *Mothers of Srebrenica* [2008] 295247/HA ZA 07–2973 (Hague Dist Ct Neth) (dismissing case on immunity grounds).

[133] C Beyani, 'The Legal Premises for the International Protection of Human Rights' in Goodwin-Gill and Talmon 22 (1999).

[134] T Meron and A Rosas, 'A Declaration of Minimum Humanitarian Standards' (1991) 85 AJIL 375, 376.

[135] Broomhall 51 (2003).

[136] This is a point of departure from Professor Bassiouni's view that a '*jus cogens* crime [like genocide] is essentially characterized, explicitly or implicitly, by state policy or conduct, irrespective of whether it is manifested by commission or omission'. Bassiouni, *Introduction* 173 (2003). Note that the responsibility of a state for sheltering terrorist organizations is a separate question.

Although state failures are not *necessary* conditions for international criminal regulation,[137] they provide additional support for it when they are present. In a great many cases, political genocide is the product of misapplied state sovereignty—a state policy supporting the practice or tacitly sanctioning it.[138] In this sense political genocide is an *abuse* of state power. But it also can be prompted by the *absence* of state power—a breakdown in government control over territory and citizens during civil insurrection or the like. In either context, political genocide cannot be handled effectively as a domestic offence.

Despite an implementation structure contemplating prosecution at the domestic level, the spectre of domestic failure has been present in relation to genocide from the very beginning.[139] Official immunity was abrogated in the Convention because genocide is not a legitimate exercise of sovereignty.[140] It has never been considered to be a lawful exercise of governmental power, and genocide is never a 'political' offence for extradition purposes.[141]

So too in cases of political genocide. It is not a legitimate exercise of state power to commit genocide against political groups. The provisions abrogating immunity and the political offence exception were established in the draft Convention *before* political groups were deleted. There was no suggestion that genocide against political groups should be evaluated under a different standard. Indeed, a substantial motivation for deleting the reference to political groups in the first place was the fear that government officials could be prosecuted internationally for violently eliminating their political opposition.

The substantial likelihood of state failure in most cases of political genocide weighs in favour of international proscription. Domestic mechanisms needed to protect the fundamental human rights at issue are most likely to fail when they are needed most. International prosecution is the only way to ensure that the underlying rights of political existence will have a genuine opportunity to be upheld.

Discretion and judgment in application

Political genocide should be proscribed as a distinct international crime. But this does not mean that every instance must be *prosecuted* internationally. There may be cases where the technical elements of the international crime are satisfied

137 Broomhall 50–1 (2003) (role of state action or policy in international crimes).

138 *Cf* Text to nn 61–67. Bassiouni notes an inverse relationship between penal characteristics appearing in international law and state action or sponsorship. The more state conduct is implicated, the less willing states are to characterize certain behaviour as criminal. Bassiouni, *Introduction* 164 (2003).

139 Genocide Convention art VI. Presumably, domestic prosecution would take place in another state or in a successor regime.

140 ibid art IV.

141 ibid art VII; *Decision on the Extradition of RM Cavallo* (10 Jun 2003) No 140/2002 (2003) 42 ILM 884 (Mex Sup Ct) (extraditing former Argentine navy captain to Spain on charges of genocide and crimes against humanity and holding that the offences were not political in nature nor subject to the political offence exception to extradition).

but which are better handled in another way. Just as with genocide under the Convention, judgment and discretion are required in the application of the substantive proscription.[142]

Prosecutorial judgment and discretion exist already in other aspects of international criminal law. In the ICC, for example, the court can deem a case inadmissible where it is not of 'sufficient gravity to justify further action by the court'.[143] Whether 'prosecution is not in the interests of justice' depends upon many factors, 'including the gravity of the crime, the interests of the victims and the age and infirmity of the alleged perpetrator, and his or her role in the alleged crime'.[144] This is a key line of demarcation for when matters should be handled domestically instead of internationally.

But legal rules must be drafted to cover the generalities, not the exceptions. There is good reason to recognize political genocide as a separate crime subject to international prosecution. Whatever challenges this poses, it must be remembered that consequences also follow from *not* acting. On balance, the international community is better served handling exceptions on a case-by-case basis than to remain paralysed. No sound justification exists to continue to actively sanction this costly lacuna in international criminal law.

[142] Professor Bassiouni, for example, suggests that international prosecution should be limited to high level actors—'leaders, policy makers and senior executors'—leaving other offenders to be prosecuted domestically: Bassiouni, *Introduction* 706 (2003).

[143] ICC Statute art 17(a)(d).

[144] ICC art 53(2)(c). Prosecutorial discretion is subject to review in the Pre-Trial Chamber. ICC Statute art 53(3).

8

The Way Forward: Rethinking the Crime of Crimes

A. The protection of political groups

There are good reasons to treat genocide against political groups as a separate international crime. The concept is supported by strong theoretical and public policy grounds, and the need is great. Prohibiting political genocide directly furthers the underlying goals of international criminal justice, particularly given the inability of other aspects of international criminal law to sufficiently address the problem.

'Political genocide' here is defined as conduct against a political group that would constitute genocide if committed against a racial, national, ethnic or religious group. It is any of the acts listed in Article II(a)-(e) in the Genocide Convention committed with intent to destroy, in whole or in part, a political group 'as such'. The prohibition would incorporate *mutatis mutandis* all other law on genocide, including the related offences prohibited under Article III of the Convention. The only difference is the application of the concept to attacks on political groups instead of racial, religious, national, and ethnic groups.

Action will be required if the solution advocated here is to be meaningful, and the dialogue must begin someplace. One logical starting point is the International Law Commission, which could continue its past work in codifying and progressively developing international criminal law by studying the issue further. Another avenue would be the ICC, which is structured to allow for amendments to the ICC Statute over time.[1]

The Convention itself contemplated future revision, and any contracting party can make a request to alter the Convention by writing to the UN Secretary General.[2] As noted previously, however, any efforts to directly amend the Genocide Convention itself would be likely to prove unworkable in practice. States generally are reluctant to alter the terms of such widely ratified and

[1] ICC Statute arts 121–123.

[2] Genocide Convention art XVI (request by state party to the Convention for revision of the treaty 'may be made at any time . . . .').

universally accepted instruments.[3] The nearly universal acceptance of the definition of genocide in Article II as part of customary international law creates additional barriers. Apart from potential confusion about the degree of interplay between genocide as a matter of treaty and customary law, states may well have additional concerns about potentially enshrining a revised definition into a customary regime whose scope they can control far less than their treaty obligations.

A better approach would be to follow the progressive example utilized with the Geneva Conventions and to create an Optional Protocol to the Genocide Convention, which states could ratify if they wish. As noted previously, a number of states already cover political genocide under domestic law, which suggests a natural initial constituency for the optional protocol and body of support for an amended ICC Statute.

A draft proposal on the offence appears as follows:

Political Genocide—Defined

For the purpose of this Statute, 'political genocide' means any of the following acts committed with intent to destroy, in whole or in part, a political group, as such:

(a) Killing members of the political group;
(b) Causing serious bodily or mental harm to members of the political group;
(c) Deliberately inflicting on the political group conditions of life calculated to bring about its physical destruction in whole or in part;
(d) Imposing measures intended to prevent births within the political group;
(e) Forcibly transferring children of the political group to another political group.

Political Genocide—Prohibited

The following acts shall be punishable:

(a) Political genocide;
(b) Conspiracy to commit political genocide;
(c) Direct and public incitement to commit political genocide;
(d) Attempt to commit political genocide;
(e) Complicity in political genocide.[4]

The simple definition set forth above by no means suggests that the actual *creation* and *implementation* of a crime of political genocide under international law also is a simple matter. History demonstrates many obstacles to translating

[3] Quigley 83 (2006) ('The historical record with human rights treaties shows no instance of subsequent revision. Treaties once adopted remain as they are.').

[4] In the case of either an optional protocol to the Convention or an amendment to the ICC Statute, additional conforming amendments to the instruments to accommodate political genocide would be required. *Cf* Genocide Convention arts I, IV–IX; ICC Statute arts 5, 25, 33; Elements of Crimes art 6.

theory into reality, often grounded squarely in the absence of political will to create and implement broader protections. Although certain practicalities must be accounted for, they render the substantive justifications no less potent:

> No one now objects to [international protection of] the category 'human rights' on the ground that the level of actual protection of those rights in many countries remains problematic, that the machinery for their protection in most cases remains embryonic, or that there are still important areas of uncertainty about the content and application of those rights. These things may be true, but they are taken either as reasons for improving the articulation and enforcement of international human rights standards, or at least as inevitable concomitants, in a diverse, disorganized, and disorderly international community, of recognizing human rights at all.[5]

B. Pragmatic considerations

The theoretical complexities involved in creating a separate international offence to protect political groups were addressed in the foregoing chapters. But it also is important to address some of the key *pragmatic* arguments that have been raised against a separate prohibition on genocide for political groups. The strongest of these—that a separate crime is unnecessary because of the availability of other international offences—was addressed at length in Chapter 6. As noted there, this argument fails because the crimes have very different aims, availability, substance, and meaning. They simply cannot substitute for one another.

Most other 'pragmatic' arguments appear to fall within one of four broad categories. They include claims that proscribing political genocide will:

(1) Impede ongoing progress and acceptance of the crime of genocide in the international community;
(2) Create an asymmetrical prohibition on the crime—where some provisions on genocide cover political groups and others do not, leading to a state of confusion in international law;
(3) Impermissibly interfere with law enforcement and military efforts against terrorist organizations, rebel forces, and the like; and
(4) Unnecessarily dilute the meaning of the 'crime of crimes', to the detriment of groups now protected by the Convention.

These claims are discussed *seriatim*.

Ongoing progress on the Genocide Convention and the ICC Statute

During the drafting of the Convention, some states argued against including political groups on the grounds that their presence would preclude widespread

[5] Crawford 162 (1988).

acceptance and ratification of the treaty.[6] The point was renewed thirty years later by a UN Special Rapporteur, who suggested that ongoing exclusion was warranted because states would decline participation in new international instruments providing a broader definition of genocide.[7] It arose again early in the drafting process for the ICC Statute, where various constituencies expressed concern that altering the definition of genocide could limit participation in the ICC treaty.[8]

Whatever the validity of such arguments in 1948 or even 1978, they have considerably less force today. The Convention is widely-ratified, with 141 states party.[9] Another 36 states not party to the Convention either participate in or have at least signed the ICC treaty,[10] which mirrors the Convention's substantive prohibition on genocide[11] and itself has 110 parties.[12] Entirely separate from the broad participation in both treaties, the prohibition on genocide also is part of customary international law and binds *all* states as a matter of *jus cogens*.[13] At this point, it is farcical to suggest that subsequent evolution to accommodate the concept of political genocide would in any way limit the application of the Convention itself or the many other international instruments implementing its provisions.

International criminal law is an inherently evolutionary system. As one author put it, to the extent they are predicated 'on the protection of fundamental rights and the promotion of common values, which are subject to evolution . . . ', international crimes likewise 'may be expected to develop over time'.[14] Tempered by the inherent limitations of the principles of legality,[15] ongoing evolution is fully consistent with the evolution of the doctrine since Nuremberg. The Nuremberg

[6] Official Records (6th Comm 1948) (SR65) 21 (Venez) ('States would not accept such limitations to their right to suppress internal disturbances.'); ibid (SR69) 58 (Sweden) (claiming that the value of the Convention was linked to the number of ratifications and that a less controversial definition facilitated that goal); Final Report of the Commission of Experts Established Pursuant to Security Council Resolution 935 (9 Dec 1994) UN Doc S/1994/1405 ¶157 (drafters' concerns that including political groups 'would create an obstacle to the Convention's ratification').

[7] 'Study on Genocide' (4 Jul 1978) UN Doc E/CN4/Sub2/416 ¶87. Another Special Rapporteur reached the opposite conclusion seven years later. 'Study (Second) on Genocide' (2 Jul 1985) UN Doc E/CN4/Sub2/1985/6 ¶30.

[8] Amnesty International *The International Criminal Court: Making the Right Choices—Part 1* AI-Index IOR 40/001/1997 (1 Jan 1997) 21–2 ('The definition of the crime of genocide in that treaty could at some point be expanded to cover political and social groups, as originally envisaged by the General Assembly, and other aspects of that treaty could be improved. Nevertheless, it is likely that any attempt to change the definition for the purposes of the statute at this date could lead to weakening the definition and prolonged debate which would risk delaying the establishment of the international criminal court indefinitely. Moreover, some of the limits in the scope of the application of the Genocide Convention are addressed in the definition of crimes against humanity.').

[9] Appendix A, Table IV.

[10] Appendix A, Table III.

[11] ICC Statute art 6.

[12] Multilateral Treaties Deposited with the Secretary-General: ICC Statute (11 Jan 2010).

[13] *Application of Genocide Convention—Prov Measures II* [1993] ICJ 325, 440 (Lauterpacht J) ('the prohibition on genocide has long been regarded as one of the few undoubted examples of *jus cogens*').

[14] Broomhall 49 (2003) (discussing crimes against humanity).

[15] Other constraints that may exist under domestic law, such as a temporal limitation after which criminal prosecution is prohibited, do not prevent the application of international criminal law

proceedings themselves reflect an evolution of international criminal law between the two world wars. Early 20th century ambivalence over the viability of certain international crimes and the prosecution of government officials[16] clearly had dissipated prior to the start of World War II.[17]

Numerous other examples prove the point. Evolution is clear, for example, with crimes against humanity. The narrow 'chapeau' of Nuremberg,[18] which required a nexus to international armed conflict, later was discarded in favour of the context of a widespread or systematic attack on a civilian population.[19] The underlying conduct constituting such crimes also expanded over the years, from vague criminal breaches of the 'laws of humanity' after World War I[20] to detailed proscriptions articulated at Nuremberg[21] and under CC10.[22] The ICC Statute reflects further evolution in its expansion of the offences proscribed as crimes against humanity, as well as additional categories of prohibited discrimination in the crime of persecution.[23]

Other examples of conduct prohibited under international law now constituting an international crime include the prohibitions on enforced disappearances[24] (now a crime against humanity)[25] and the exploitation of children as child soldiers[26] (now a war crime).[27] Likewise for the modes of commission of international crimes. As recently as the early 1990s, for example, attempts were

because 'core' international crimes are not subject to domestic statutes of limitation. Convention on Non-Applicability of Statutory Limitations (26 Nov 1968) UN Doc A/7218 art 1.

16 Commission on the Responsibility of the Authors of the War and on the Enforcement of Penalties, Report Presented to the Preliminary Peace Conference (29 Mar 1919) (1920) 14 AJIL 95, 128–44 (US and Japanese objections).

17 London Agreement 280 (establishing IMT at Nuremberg); IMT Charter art 6 (offences under international law); *Göring* [IMT 1946] 1 IMT Proceedings 171, 218 (IMT Charter codified pre-existing law governing Nazi conduct during World War II).

18 IMT Charter art 6(c) (offences 'in execution of or in connection with any crime within the jurisdiction of the Tribunal, whether or not in violation of the domestic law of the country where perpetrated').

19 ICC Statute art 7(1).

20 Commission on Responsibility (n 16) 122 (proposed international tribunal to apply 'the principles of the law of nations as they result from the usages established among civilized peoples... the laws of humanity and... the dictates of public conscience.').

21 IMT Charter art 6(c) (murder, extermination, enslavement, deportation, and other inhumane acts committed against any civilian population, before or during the war, or persecutions on political, racial or religious grounds....).

22 CC10 art II(1)(c) (adding specific references to imprisonment, torture and rape, rendering the list of offences illustrative rather than exhaustive, and deleting the textual nexus to the war crimes and crimes against peace).

23 ICC Statute art 7.

24 'Declaration on the Protection of All Persons from Enforced Disappearances' (18 Dec 1992) UN Doc A/47/49 arts 1–4; Inter-American Convention on Forced Disappearance of Persons (9 Jun 1994) arts 1–2.

25 ICC Statute art 7(1)(i) and (2)(i).

26 Geneva Protocol I art 77(2) (contracting states must 'take all feasible measures in order that children who have not attained the age of fifteen years do not take a direct part in hostilities and... refrain from recruiting them into their armed forces'); CRC art 38 (minimum age for military service).

27 ICC Statute art 8(2)(b)(xxvi) and (e)(vii). Law further develops in parallel on the domestic plane. *Cf* Child Soldiers Accountability Act (2008) 18 USC s 2442 (US law providing criminal liability for the use of children in armed conflict).

recognized only for the crime of genocide[28] in the ICTY and ICTR Statutes.[29] The ICC Statute is more progressive and includes attempts to commit any ICC offence that are prevented by reasons independent of the accused's wishes.[30] Evolutionary forces extend even to broad principles of international justice, such as the requirements of the legality principles themselves.[31]

Broad recognition of the need for international criminal law to evolve over time is built into the structure of the ICC itself. Amendment is governed by Article 121 of the ICC Statute. Article 121(5) applies to the definitions of crimes in Articles 5–8 and provides that amendments to such offences will only enter into force for states that affirmatively 'opt in'. Otherwise, 'the Court shall not exercise its jurisdiction regarding a crime covered by the amendment when committed by that State Party's nationals or on its territory'.[32]

This is in contrast to other amendments to the ICC Statute, which are governed by Article 121(4). Article 121(4) amendments are binding upon *all* states party to the ICC Statute as soon as the amendment is ratified by a 7/8 majority.[33] Participation remains voluntary, however. If a state party within the 1/8 minority finds the modification unacceptable, it is entitled to withdraw fully from the ICC Statute within one year of the amendment entering force.[34]

There is little danger of states withdrawing from the ICC as a consequence of political genocide being included, however. The creation of such an offence in the ICC clearly would operate as a modification of Article 6 on genocide, which would bring it within the provisions of Article 121(5). The crime of political genocide simply would not apply with respect to any state that refused to affirmatively support it.

Criminalizing political genocide through an optional protocol to the Genocide Convention or an amendment to the ICC Statute would in no way detract from participation in those instruments or enforcement of the existing prohibition on genocide. The available evidence is to the contrary. Twenty states[35] already prohibit political genocide under domestic law, which hardly seems to have impeded the operation of the Convention, the ICC Statute, or any other application of the prohibition on genocide. The speculative risk that some states might withdraw from the Genocide Convention or the ICC Statute to protest the decision of other states to recognize political genocide is far outweighed by the ongoing costs of continuing to exclude the crime from international criminal law.

The fact that international criminal law is *meant* to evolve does not mean that evolution is an easy process, however. Far from it. The IMT Charter for Nuremberg, for example, was the subject of arduous negotiation between the

[28] Genocide Convention art III(d)(attempts).

[29] ICTR Statute art 2(3)(d); ICTY Statute art 4(3)(d).

[30] ICC Statute art 25(3)(f).

[31] Broomhall 35–6 (2003) (noting divergence between codification of legality principles in ICC Statute and their content and application under general international law).

[32] ICC Statute art 121(5).

[33] ibid art 121(4).

[34] ibid art 121(6).

[35] Appendix A, Table I.

former Allies at the outset of the Cold War.[36] So was the Genocide Convention.[37] More recently, the states party to the ICC Statute continue to wrangle over the crime of aggression, despite a decade's worth of work on the subject.[38]

Inherent difficulties do not excuse the failure to act, however. Nor do they necessarily suggest that years of gruelling negotiations lie ahead. The complexities of achieving consensus on aggression do not signal a similar fate for political genocide or imply that the process is doomed to failure. The issues at stake in applying genocide to political groups—while controversial—are both narrower and clearer. As defined and advocated herein, political genocide is the further application of an existing crime to a different group (much akin to the expansion of crimes against humanity in the ICC Statute). There is a tremendous body of existing jurisprudence on genocide from international criminal tribunals and other courts as well as domestic legislation from 20 states.[39]

Aggression, in contrast, is a far more murky concept that has not been applied since Nuremberg. Consensus is much harder to reach in part because of its unique typology as a 'leadership' crime addressed to government officials,[40] which complicates the traditional bases of criminal liability.[41] Additional questions exist over whether *threats* of military action can constitute 'attempts' to commit the crime of aggression.[42] Other complicating factors include the scope of the right to self-defence, the role of the UN Security Council, and the crime's intersection with humanitarian intervention.

Asymmetry in application

A related claim is that recognition of a separate offence of political genocide will create uncertainty and lead to the asymmetric application of international law. Some states would recognize political genocide for purposes of the ICC, but not for the Convention. Others may ascribe to the optional protocol but not an amended ICC Statute. Others may join the optional protocol but either not participate in the ICC at all or refuse to participate in the ICC's prohibition on political genocide. Other states may refuse outright, thus limiting the concept solely to national, racial, ethnic, and religious groups.

36 R Overy (2003), 'The Nuremberg Trials: International law in the Making' in Sands 1 (2003); Bassiouni, *CAH* 19–40 (1999) (definition of crimes against humanity); IMT Charter art 6(a)–(c).

37 This was detailed in Chapter 5.

38 ICC Statute arts 5(1)(d), 5(2) (ICC will have jurisdiction over the crime of aggression after the states party to the ICC Statute define the offence).

39 Appendix A, Table I.

40 ICC Report on Aggression (5 Sep 2006) UN Doc ICC-ASP/5/SWGCA/INF1 ¶¶84–93; T Meron, 'International Criminalization of Internal Atrocities' (1995) 89 AJIL 554, 562 ('That an obligation is addressed to governments is not dispositive of the penal responsibility of individuals, if individuals clearly must carry out that obligation').

41 ICC Report on Aggression (n 40) ¶92 (debating liability for individual who 'plans, prepares, initiates or executes' aggression as these terms 'would not adequately represent the activities of a leader, who in particular did not personally execute the use of armed force, but rather directed or led that execution.').

42 ibid ¶¶36–50.

There is little doubt that things could become confusing. Terminology here is critical, hence the separate labels: 'political genocide' for attacks on political groups; 'genocide' for attacks on national, racial, ethnic, and religious groups. The separate label makes clear which offence is being applied and provides ample notice to potential offenders under the principles of legality.

More fundamentally, however, international criminal law is inherently an asymmetric system. The development and application proceed at varying paces depending on the specific context. Geneva law on non-international armed conflict, for example, operates with different underlying thresholds depending on whether or not a state has adopted Additional Protocol II.[43] And as discussed in Chapter 6, the definition of crimes against humanity varies considerably in many domestic and international settings.

Another good example is torture. Torture is prohibited under customary international law[44] and in a variety of international instruments. It is a crime in and of itself[45] but also can constitute genocide, war crimes and crimes against humanity.[46] Further disparity exists in the numerous definitions of 'torture' appearing in various international instruments.[47] Multiple definitions of the concept of genocide thus are entirely permissible under international law, provided that certain minimum requirements are complied with.[48]

[43] Compare Geneva Conventions I–IV art III (applying to 'armed conflict not of an international character occurring in the territory of one of the High Contracting Parties') with Geneva Protocol II art 1(1) (protocol that 'develops and supplements' Common Article III applies 'to all armed conflicts which are not covered by Article 1 of [Geneva Protocol I] . . . and which take place in the territory of a High Contracting Party between its armed forces and dissident armed forces or other organized armed groups which, under responsible command, exercise such control over a part of its territory as to enable them to carry out sustained and concerted military operations and to implement this Protocol.'). A (less-controversial) third optional protocol creates an additional distinct emblem for the ICRC to obviate religious and political concerns raised by the red cross and red crescent emblems: Geneva Protocol III arts 1–2.

[44] *Furundzija (TC)* [1998] ICTY ¶153 (criminal prohibition against torture is mandatory under customary international law as a *jus cogens* obligation).

[45] CAT arts 1, 4–5.

[46] *Brdjanin (TC)* [2004] ICTY ¶690 (genocide); *Furundzija (TC)* [1998] ICTY ¶162 (war crimes and crimes against humanity).

[47] Compare CAT art 1(1) ('any act by which *severe* pain or suffering, whether physical or mental, is intentionally inflicted on a person for such purposes as obtaining from him or a third person information or a confession, punishing him for an act he or a third person has committed or is suspected of having committed, or intimidating or coercing him or a third person, or for any reason based on discrimination of any kind, when such pain or suffering is inflicted by or at the instigation of or with the consent or acquiescence of a *public official or other person acting in an official capacity*') with Inter-American Convention to Prevent and Punish Torture (9 Dec 1985) OAS Doc OEA/Ser P, AG/Doc 2023/85 Rev 1 art 2 ('any act intentionally performed whereby physical or mental pain or suffering is inflicted on a person for purposes of *criminal investigation*, as a means of intimidation, as personal punishment, *as a preventive measure*, as a penalty, or *for any other purpose*. Torture shall also be understood to be *the use of methods upon a person intended to obliterate the personality of the victim or to diminish his physical or mental capacities, even if they do not cause physical pain or mental anguish*') with ICC Statute art 7(2)(e) ('the intentional infliction of severe pain or suffering, whether physical or mental, upon a person *in the custody or under the control of the accused*') (emphasis added).

[48] CAT art 1(2) ('This article is without prejudice to any international instrument or national legislation which does or may contain provisions of wider application').

Asymmetry appears in the jurisdictional application of international criminal law as well as its substance. The ICC, for example, is overtly asymmetrical in its jurisdiction over war crimes; it allowed states party the option of a seven-year 'transitional' exception for this offence.[49] The UN Security Council also can require the ICC to desist from the investigation and prosecution of international crimes within its mandate.[50] Domestic agreements also can entitle a state to refuse certain forms of cooperation with the court.[51]

This is true even for the prohibition on genocide. The ICC's Elements of Crimes clearly narrow the circumstances in which the court will take jurisdiction over cases involving genocide.[52] Although this is not a substantive change to the definition per se, as a practical matter, it demonstrates that the offence may be applied differently in the ICC than in the international criminal tribunals, the ICJ, or domestic courts.

The high level of comfort with asymmetry even for international crimes reflects the international community's recognition of a high degree of context dependency. Different understandings of international crimes will apply depending upon the context, location, and circumstances. Provided that sufficient notice is provided to perpetrators about which rules apply, and when, variability in application in no way violates the principles of legality.

Asymmetry in application thus poses no more of an obstacle to recognizing political genocide than it does already with respect to other international crimes. In practice things would be *more* clear. The prohibition on political genocide would have a distinct label ('political genocide'). This makes the contours of the offence far clearer in application than is the case with other crimes (torture, war crimes, crimes against humanity, etc) that apply identical terminology to multiple definitions and jurisdictional settings throughout international and domestic law.

Law enforcement and military activity

It has been a long-standing worry that the protection of political groups from genocide could impact a state's ability to deal with threats and oppose subversive elements.[53] This is a legitimate concern. The power of the label is significant, and there is no shortage of willingness to distort the definition to facilitate a particular agenda.[54] It would hardly advance the international community's interests to provide terrorist organizations and similar groups with a legal weapon that could impede a state's ability to respond to threats.

[49] ICC Statute art 124. [50] ibid art 16. [51] ibid art 98.

[52] ICC Elements of Crimes art 6(a)(4)–(e)(4) (requiring that the offence transpired 'in the context of a manifest pattern of similar conduct directed against [the target group] or was conduct that itself could effect such destruction.').

[53] 'Study (Second) on Genocide' (2 Jul 1985) UN Doc E/CN4/Sub2/1985/6 ¶35.

[54] *Cf* text to nn 73–74, below.

But this concern does not survive scrutiny as a basis for denying protection to political groups. There is a marked distinction between legitimate state opposition to subversive elements and political genocide. Even when motivated by political ends, terrorist organizations like Al Qaeda simply are not 'political' groups for purposes of genocide, any more than terrorists constitute a 'political social group' entitled to protection under international refugee law.[55] The destruction of Al Qaeda is premised upon its criminal, not 'political', characteristics. Law enforcement is not hampered by religious, national, ethnic or racial influences in certain crimes and would not be disrupted by political characteristics, either.[56]

The distinction between genocide and war precedes the Convention itself. Genocide

> refers to the actual destruction of a human group and not to restrictions, ill-treatment, or oppression of that group.... The destruction of the human group is the actual aim in view. In the case of foreign or civil war, one side may inflict extremely heavy losses on the other but its purpose is to impose its will on the other side and not to destroy it.[57]

The Convention distinguishes armed conflict from genocide by treating genocide as a crime in both peace and war.[58] If war equated to genocide, the crime hardly could be committed 'in time of war'—acts of war alone would establish the offence. Military force thus is distinct from genocide.[59] Similar considerations apply *mutatis mutandis* to law enforcement.

ICJ jurisprudence recognizes the distinction. In Serbia's case against NATO, the ICJ held that 'the threat or use of [military] force against a State cannot in itself constitute an act of genocide within the meaning of... the Convention.'[60] This reaffirmed prior jurisprudence applying the principle even to the massive destructive power of nuclear weapons.[61]

The distinction is further supported in state practice. As discussed previously, the US ratified the Convention with extensive reservations, declarations and understandings. One understanding provided that 'acts in the course of armed conflicts committed without the specific intent required by Article II are

[55] *Ward v Canada* [1993] 2 SCR 689 (Can Sup Ct) ¶79 (LaForest J) (noting jurisprudence determining that terrorists simply are ineligible for inclusion within the definition of 'particular social group' but deciding issue on alternate grounds of 'explicit exclusionary provisions' elsewhere in Canada's refugee law).

[56] *Cf* 'Threats to international peace and security caused by terrorist acts' UNSC Res 1566 (8 Oct 2004) UN Doc S/Res/1566 ¶5 (terrorist acts 'are under no circumstances justified by consideration of a political, philosophical, ideological, racial, ethnic, religious or other similar nature....').

[57] Relations Between the Convention on Genocide on the one hand and the Formulation of the Nurnberg Principles and the Preparation of a Draft Code of Offences Against Peace and Security on the Other—Note by the Secretariat (2 Apr 1948) UN Doc E/AC25/3 6.

[58] Genocide Convention art I.

[59] 'Study on Genocide' (4 Jul 1978) UN Doc E/CN4/Sub2/416 ¶384.

[60] *Legality of Force—Provisional Measures* [1999] ICJ ¶35.

[61] *Nuclear Weapons* [1996] ICJ 227, 240.

not sufficient to constitute genocide as defined by this Convention'.[62] Although states objected to other US reservations and understandings, none objected to this one.[63]

This is not to suggest that military activities cannot *become* genocidal if taken too far. Drawing the distinction early on, the drafters reported that

> War is not normally directed at the destruction of the enemy: such destruction is only the means used by a belligerent to impose his will on the opponent. When that result has been achieved, peace is concluded. However harsh the conditions imposed on the defeated party may be, it retains the right to existence.... War may, however, be accompanied by the crime of genocide. This happens when one of the belligerents aims at exterminating the population of enemy territory and systematically destroys what are not genuine military objectives. Examples of this are the execution of prisoners of war, the massacre of the populations of occupied territory and their gradual extermination. These are clearly cases of genocide.[64]

Absent a transition from lawful belligerency to unlawful genocide, states are no more impeded by the coverage of political groups than they are by the protection of groups covered already in the Convention.

Religious groups, in particular, prove the point. Many terrorist groups and other criminal organizations are 'strongly influenced by religious extremism and fanaticism'.[65] The shared international response to such criminal organizations has been to eliminate them. International efforts against Al Qaeda have included the killing, incapacitation and incarceration of its members. On the domestic front, Japan proceeded in similar fashion against Aum Shinri Kyo—the religious cult that released deadly saren nerve gas in the subways of Tokyo in 1995.[66] Spain has long fought against ETA and other 'national' Basque separatist groups. But these are not cases of genocide against national or religious groups 'as such'. Criminal organizations, even when motivated by national, religious, or political ends, have no right to exist 'as such', and are not protected by international law. States are entitled to take appropriate measures to render such groups harmless and to punish crimes by their members.

Military and law enforcement efforts are, however, properly subject to the limits of necessity and proportionality.[67] Once the law enforcement or military objective is satisfied, the justification for killing, etc the group's members declines. A state is not entitled to send members of a captured Al Qaeda terrorist cell to an extra-judicial firing squad, even if its soldiers would have been entitled to kill them during a military operation aimed at destroying the cell. When

[62] Multilateral Treaties Deposited with the Secretary-General: Genocide Convention (11 Jan 2010).

[63] ibid.

[64] Comments on the Draft Convention (26 Jun 1947) UN Doc E/447 23.

[65] Lerner 76 (2003).

[66] S Harzenski, 'Terrorism, A History: Stage One' (2003) 12 JTLP 137, 144.

[67] T Meron and A Rosas, 'A Declaration of Minimum Humanitarian Standards' (1991) 85 AJIL 375, 378–9.

legitimate military and law enforcement objectives can be achieved through less severe means, the failure to adopt such measures marks a departure toward the impermissible boundaries of international criminal law and genocide.

These balancing considerations apply *mutatis mutandis* to criminal organizations that might assert some claim to protected status as political groups. The legitimate objectives of law enforcement and military activity provide no grounds for refusing to proscribe political genocide as a separate international offence.

Diluting the concept

The stigma of genocide is avoided at all costs by individuals and states. Despite pleading guilty to 31 counts of war crimes and crimes against humanity, for example, 'Serbian Adolf' Goran Jelisic went to trial in the ICTY on a single count of genocide.[68] States resist the label with equal vehemence. A non-binding resolution in the US House of Representatives, for example, labelled massacres of Armenians in the early 20th century 'genocide.' The resolution was withdrawn at President Clinton's request following Turkish threats to retaliate by reopening ties with Iraq and withdrawing strategic military support and defence contracts.[69] Turkey even temporarily recalled its ambassador when a more recent proposal cleared a committee in the US House of Representatives.[70] Turkey declared a similar French resolution 'an offence against the Turkish people'.[71]

Some suggest that proscribing political genocide risks negative collateral consequences. 'Diluting the definition, either by formal amendment of its terms or by extravagant interpretation of the existing text, risks trivializing the horror of the real crime when it is committed.'[72] Dilution is a genuine concern. The power of the label creates a magnetism that invites propaganda, normative expansion, and application to concepts far beyond its original meaning.[73] Genocide has been applied, for example, to:

> 'race mixing' (integration of blacks and non-blacks); drug distribution; methadone programs; and the practice of birth control and abortions among Third World people; sterilization and 'Mississippi appendectomies' (tubal ligations and hysterectomies); medical treatment of Catholics; and the closing of synagogues in the Soviet Union.[74]

[68] *Jelisic (AC)* [2001] ICTY ¶¶2, 24–58.

[69] Murphy 265, 274–5 (2002).

[70] 'Affirmation of the US Record on the Armenian Genocide Resolution' 110th US Congress (10 Oct 2007) HR Res 106; MJ Kelly, '"Genocide"—The Power of a Label' (2008) 40 Case Western JIL 147, 150–3.

[71] DM Amann, 'Group Mentality, Expressivism, and Genocide' (2002) 2 ICLR 93, 126 n 149.

[72] Schabas 133 (2009). See also DM Amann, 'Group Mentality, Expressivism, and Genocide' (2002) 2 ICLR 93, 95 (noting tension between ensuring that 'deserving groups' are protected and disturbing 'the singular status of the proscription against genocide.').

[73] Professor Akhavan calls this 'moral scavenging': Akhavan 310 (2001).

[74] JN Porter, 'Introduction' in Porter 2, 9–10 (1982).

However serious these matters may be, it seems wrong to speak of them in the same breath as massacres of millions during the Holocaust. They do not involve genocide at all, and yet the power of the term creates clear incentives to draw upon it for purposes of empowering an agenda that has little to do with international criminal justice.[75]

But this does not mean that the concept of genocide is untouchable. Rather, any departure from the traditional definition must be justified by rigorous legal analysis and other stringent measures of 'quality control'.[76] The definition of political genocide offered herein departs from Article II only in terms of the group protected. It retains the core concept of genocide as serious personal violence committed with specific intent to destroy the group 'as such'. The *actus reus* and *mens rea* are identical—the only difference is the group against whom the conduct is directed.

It may be true that the drafters of the Convention intended to cover only a restrictive, and in some sense, holistic concept of 'national minorities'[77] within which political groups simply did not fit. But even if this proposition is correct, it does not necessarily follow that the Convention cannot or should not be altered. What the drafters intended for the Convention six decades ago is no longer the relevant question. The real issue is whether the status quo of excluding political groups continues to make sense today. It does not. The exclusion of political groups has proved to be an utterly impractical distinction over the past 60 years, and there is no justifiable reason to continue to hold reasonable progress on this crime hostage out of a misguided sense of fidelity to the past.

Does it honestly work an injustice to Jews or Armenians to equate what happened to them with Soviet atrocities against non-Communists in Poland or the barbarity of the Khmer Rouge? As the paradigmatic 20th century genocide, the Holocaust probably is fairly characterized as a unique historical event. But its singularity derives from the massive scale involved, the devilish creativity of the Nazis in perverting technology to their own twisted ends, and because it was tragically successful—all but eliminating the last vestiges of Jews from certain parts of Europe.[78] The human evil at issue in the Holocaust—reduced to a legal

[75] Fein, *Human Wrongs* 126 (2007) ('To some, genocide is a discredited charge, because the term is so often used as rhetoric and hyperbole in political attacks....').

[76] C Beyani, 'The Legal Premises for the International Protection of Human Rights' in Goodwin-Gill and Talmon 21 (1999).

[77] Schabas 132 (2009); *Krstic (TC)* [2001] ICTY ¶556 (Convention 'was designed more to describe a single phenomenon, roughly corresponding to what was recognized, before the second world war, as "national minorities," rather than to refer to several distinct prototypes of human groups.').

[78] Some maintain that the Holocaust was unique for other reasons that separate it from all other cases of genocide. ST Katz, 'The Uniqueness of the Holocaust: The Historical Dimension' in Rosenbaum 19, 37 (1996) (arguing that only the Holocaust was directed toward the absolute annihilation of the victim populace).

proscription through the Genocide Convention—is unique only in degree, not in substance or wrongfulness.

As noted previously, the most coherent understanding of the groups enumerated in the Convention derives from the underlying rights of group shared members to engage in various forms of collective physical and biological existence. The defining rights underlying political groups are closer than any other category. When those political rights are infringed in the manner contemplated by genocide, they are close enough.

There is good reason to separately label and punish that infringement. It does not detract from the uniqueness and wrongfulness of genocide to suggest that a political group also can be the victim of nearly (but not exactly) identical conduct that is condemned through a separate label. The real injustice is to maintain the status quo—to leave international law mute: incapable of labelling, condemning and punishing the extraordinary criminality inherent in political genocide for what it really is.

Concluding Thoughts

The Genocide Convention recognizes that certain aspects of collective identity are so fundamental that no one should have to sacrifice them in order to avoid physical or biological destruction. There are many good reasons to bring political groups within this concept through a separate international crime. All too many examples attest that the problem remains very real. Genocidal attacks upon collective political identities necessarily entail serious violence committed with the most blameworthy of mental states. Such infringements qualify for proscription at the international level because they threaten international peace and security and because their egregiousness shocks the world's collective conscience.

Regrettably, a prohibition on political genocide falls short as a matter of *lex lata*. There simply is insufficient state practice and *opinio juris* to legitimately recognize the crime under customary international law. However strong the underlying justifications, the formalities of law-making on the international plane cannot be dispensed with. At heart, international law is a consent-based system that creates legal rules through mutual agreement (whether overt or tacit) among states. A strong moral claim, cogent analytical grounds and exigent needs justify the recognition of a new international crime no more than wishful thinking or speculation. Recognizing new international crimes simply because it is a good idea to do so violates other equally important fundamental rights—the legality principles and the prohibition on *ex post facto* offences.

This is no reason to put the question aside, however. The concept of political genocide clearly poses difficulties for states and the international community as a whole. It has been studiously avoided whenever possible. But there always will be some divide between what states *should* do and what they are *willing* to do. The pragmatic complexities of creating and implementing a crime of political genocide in no way lessen the need or invalidate the many justifications for engaging directly with the problem.

Proposed international crimes—whether recognized as a matter of customary international law or created through treaties—are properly subject to rigorous measures of 'quality control'. But when these tests are passed, international law should be flexible enough to respond to modern requirements. Political genocide merits a genuine response, and there are a number of good reasons to actively rethink outmoded conceptions in the Genocide Convention. The need is great. Just as the label 'murder' was insufficient to reflect the essential criminality of the Nazi Holocaust, our current legal terminology cannot convey the true magnitude or nature of political genocide.

This is not to suggest that a new international crime would be a panacea for human barbarity. Far from it. International criminal law is a limited system that cannot (and should not be expected to) solve all of the world's ills. The ever-present struggle to muster political will continues to demonstrate the wide gulf between condemning atrocities and actually doing something about them.[1] And even where political will exists, experience suggests that even well-functioning international criminal tribunals can—at best—hope to prosecute a handful of perpetrators of mass atrocities.

As of early 2010, the ICC prosecutor was actively pursuing criminal cases in four states: Uganda, the Democratic Republic of the Congo, the Central African Republic, and Sudan.[2] The office also was formally investigating and monitoring situations in six other jurisdictions[3] and had begun trying cases against three defendants.[4] But the massive suffering and loss of life that continues despite the ICC's efforts demonstrates—painfully—the inherent limitations of international criminal justice.

The most public face of mass atrocity today is the ongoing crisis in Darfur, which reflects all of the ambivalence that the international community has felt about genocide since it first recognized the crime in response to Nazi horrors during World War II. Estimates of the death toll in Sudan range from 200,000 to 450,000,[5] with even greater numbers displaced and at serious risk of starvation, disease, and future violence. The suffering continues despite nearly a decade of political machination and diplomatic manoeuvring among the UN Security Council and other UN organs, the ICC and its prosecutor, the Sudanese government, powerful western states, neighbouring states and regional blocs lining up in support or opposition, and numerous non-governmental organizations and other international constituencies.[6]

It is clear that the violence in Darfur constitutes a number of serious international crimes. But there is significant debate about whether that criminal activity amounts to genocide, and if so, who is responsible for it. An investigation by the US government determined that at least some of the offences constituted genocide and that both the Sudanese government and state-sponsored militias were

[1] Gourevitch 170 (1999) ('The West's post-Holocaust pledge that genocide would never again be tolerated proved to be hollow, and for all the fine sentiments inspired by the memory of Auschwitz, the problem remains that denouncing evil is a far cry from doing good.').

[2] ICC 2008/09 UN Report (17 Sep 09) UN Doc A/64/356 ¶6.

[3] ibid ¶45 (Afghanistan, Columbia, Code d'Ivorie, Georgia, Kenya, and Palestine).

[4] *Katanga & Ngudjolo (Confirmation of Charges—TC)* [2008] ICC 1; *Lubanga (Confirmation of Charges—TC)* [2007] ICC 1.

[5] A de Waal and GH Stanton, 'Should President Omar al-Bashir of Sudan be Charged and Arrested by the International Criminal Court? An Exchange of Views' (2009) 4 Gen Stud & Prevent 329, 344 (citing differing estimates); J Hagan and A Palloni, 'Death in Darfur' (2006) Science 1578, 1579 (analysing social science data and determining that death toll was much higher than previously estimated).

[6] *Cf* V Peskin, 'The International Criminal Court, the Security Council, and the Politics of Impunity in Darfur' (2009) 4 Gen Stud & Prevent 304.

responsible.[7] A subsequent UN investigation found that while war crimes and crimes against humanity had been committed, there was insufficient evidence to conclude that genocide was being perpetrated by the Sudanese government.[8] The committee acknowledged, however, that individual perpetrators (including government officials) might have acted with genocidal intent.[9]

Following a referral of the matter to the ICC by the UN Security Council,[10] the ICC prosecutor concluded that there was sufficient prima facie evidence to seek an arrest warrant on genocide charges (among others) for Sudan's sitting president, Omar Al Bashir.[11] Not surprisingly, the Sudanese government vehemently denied the allegations, decrying the ICC as a 'stooge' operating at the behest of the state's enemies.[12] A divided Pre-trial Chamber subsequently ruled against the genocide charges but did issue a warrant for President Al Bashir on charges of war crimes and crimes against humanity.[13] Following the prosecutor's appeal,[14] the ICC Appeals Chamber held that the pretrial chamber had applied an incorrect standard of proof and remanded with instructions to reconsider issuing an arrest warrant on the genocide allegations.[15]

Apart from the legal questions, the wider political and diplomatic implications of the term 'genocide' are significant as well. States have an affirmative duty to prevent genocide 'at the instant the State learns of, or should normally have learned of, the existence of a serious risk that genocide will be committed'.[16] Apart from this, however, the mere use of the 'G-word' substantially ups the rhetorical ante in international diplomacy, sometimes irretrievably. As one commentator noted, '[h]aving labelled a group or a government as "genocidal," it is difficult to make

[7] J Fowler, 'A New Chapter of Irony: The Legal Definition of Genocide and the Implications of Powell's Determination' in Totten and Markusen 127, 130–2 (2006).

[8] ibid 132–4; SC Darfur Report (25 Jan 2005) ¶520. For a critique of the report as analytically flawed and the product of an unduly hurried and underfunded investigation, see S Totten, 'The UN International Commission of Inquiry on Darfur: New and Disturbing Findings' (2009) 4 Gen Stud & Prevent 354. It is worth pointing out that other investigations suffered from similar limitations. Security Council Expert Report (Addendum) (27 May 1994) UN Doc A/1994/674/Add2 (Vol I) ¶7 (investigatory commission for the former Yugoslavia noting limited funding and staffing, as well as time pressure).

[9] ibid. This apparently led to a sealed list of 51 individuals being provided to the ICC prosecutor for further investigation. Fein, *Human Wrongs* 150 (2007).

[10] UNSC Res 1593 (31 Mar 2005) UN Doc S/Res/1593.

[11] *Al Bashir—Request for Arrest Warrant* [2008] ICC 1, 3 ('after negotiations and armed action both failed to end in Darfur a rebellion whose members belonged mostly to the three target groups, Al Bashir decided and set out to destroy in part the Fur, Masalit and Zaghawa groups, on account of their ethnicity. His motives were largely political. His pretext was a "counterinsurgency". His intent was genocide.').

[12] M Simons, L Polgreen and J Gettleman, 'Arrest is Sought of Sudan Leader in Genocide Case' (15 Jul 08) NY Times A1.

[13] *Al Bashir (Arrest Warrant—TC)* [2009] ICC 1 ¶¶147–223 (evidence of genocide insufficient for warrant); ibid (Usacka J dissenting) ¶105 (evidence of genocide was sufficient to justify arrest).

[14] *Al Bashir (Leave to Appeal—TC)* [2009] ICC 1, 5–6.

[15] *Al Bashir (Arrest Warrant—AC)* [2010] ICC ¶¶29–42. As this book goes to press, the matter is still pending before the ICC Pre-trial Chamber.

[16] *Application of Genocide Convention—Merits* [2007] ICJ 1 ¶431.

the case that a political compromise needs to be found with them'.[17] The inability to achieve diplomatic resolution leaves the international community with far fewer—and far less palatable—options to respond (eg, sanctions, prosecution, and military intervention).[18]

This, then, is the wider context in which the prohibition on political genocide advocated here would operate. The myriad political and diplomatic realities connected to genocide would apply *mutatis* to political genocide as well—perhaps with even greater intensity. But the inherent difficulties do not justify inaction. The law—even criminal law—always has been an imperfect mechanism for labelling and condemning the unimaginable horror of genocide:

> The scene that unfolded before us... is one steeped in blood and tears, in which the story of the Holocaust and of European Jewry is revealed. No human pen, no human tongue can ever succeed in describing the barest outline of the suffering of the millions who were killed—slaughtered and burned in extermination camps and gas chambers by the murderous tools invented and perfected by the 'fertile' brain and the perverse fantasy of the Nazi scum.[19]

Still, a step in the right direction is better than nothing. Lethargy carries its own serious consequences. The failure to act is a *choice*, purchased here at the expense of human life. The reality of doing nothing is scarcely a decade past. Consider the opening narrative. Two men lay dead on the floor of Mubuga Church in Rwanda in 1994. One is Hutu, the other Tutsi. They were massacred at the same time, in the same way, by the same people and for the same perverse reason—to create a Tutsi-free Rwanda. But international law forces apart the irrefutable commonality of their suffering and deaths through legal terminology. Reality is divided through words of inclusion and exclusion: one is a victim of genocide, and the other is a victim of some lesser offence. And the attack on the larger political group—and all of the cherished rights and values that it represents—goes unrecognized, and unanswered.

At the end of the day, the absence of political genocide as a stand-alone crime reflects a lacuna in international law. It leaves us mute: unable to condemn directly the physical and biological destruction of the right to collective political identity. International law can do better. Political genocide should be proscribed as a separate international crime. The failure to condemn political genocide for what it truly is—openly, directly and publicly—should be put right.

[17] A de Waal, 'Reflections on the Difficulties of Defining Darfur's Crisis as Genocide' (2007) Harv HRJ 25, 31.

[18] ibid.

[19] *Eichmann (AC)* [1961] 36 ILR 277 (Isr Sup Ct) 322.

Bibliography

Books

Note on abbreviations

To provide less cumbersome internal citations, books are referenced by author, page and year—eg Drost 100 (1959). For authors of multiple works, the italicized abbreviation preceding the description below further identifies the volume—eg Ashworth, *Principles* 100 (1999).

Works cited

Payam Akhavan *Reducing Genocide to Law* (Harvard Law School Cambridge 2001)

Amnesty International *The International Criminal Court: Making the Right Choices—Part 1* (Report) (1 Jan 2007) AI-Index IOR 40/001/1997

George J Andreopoulos (ed) *Genocide: Conceptual and Historical Dimensions* (Univ Penn Press Philadelphia 1994)

Ivo Andrić *The Bridge on the Drina* (LF Edwards trans Harvill Press 1995) (1945)

Aristotle *Nicomachean Ethics* (JAK Thompson trans Penguin Books 2004)

Alejandro Artucio *The Trial of Macias in Equatorial Guinea* (Int'l Comm Jurists Geneva 1979)

Ashworth, Principles, Andrew Ashworth *Principles of Criminal Law* (3rd edn Oxford Univ Press Oxford 1999)

Ashworth, Principles 4th edn, Andrew Ashworth *Principles of Criminal Law* (4th edn Oxford Univ Press Oxford 2003)

Ashworth, Sentencing, Andrew Ashworth *Sentencing and Criminal Justice* (3rd edn Cambridge Univ Press Cambridge 2000)

Bassiouni, CAH, M Cherif Bassiouni *Crimes Against Humanity in International Criminal Law* (2nd edn Kluwer Boston 1999)

Bassiouni, Conventions, M Cherif Bassiouni *International Criminal Law Conventions and Their Penal Provisions* (Transnational NY 1997)

Bassiouni, Draft Code and Statute, M Cherif Bassiouni *A Draft International Criminal Code and Draft Statute for an International Criminal Court* (Kluwer Boston 1987)

Bassiouni, Introduction, M Cherif Bassiouni *Introduction to International Criminal Law* (Transnational NY 2003)

Bassiouni and Manikas, M Cherif Bassiouni and P Manikas *The Law of the International Criminal Tribunal for the Former Yugoslavia* (Transnational NY 1996)

Rudolf Bernhardt *Encyclopaedia of Public International Law* (North Holland NY 1993)

Machteld Boot *Genocide, Crimes Against Humanity, War Crimes* (Intersentia nv 2002)

Ove Bring *International Criminal Law in Historical Perspective* (Juridiska Fakulteten Stockholm 2001)

Brody and Ratner, Reed Brody and Michael Ratner (eds) *The Pinochet Papers: The Case of Augusto Pinochet in Spain and Britain* (Kluwer London 2000)

Bruce Broomhall *International Justice and the International Criminal Court* (Oxford Univ Press Oxford 2003)

Ian Brownlie *Principles of Public International Law* (5th edn Oxford Univ Press Oxford 1998)

Michael Byers *Custom, Power and the Power of Rules—International Relations and Customary International Law* (Cambridge Univ Press Cambridge 1999)

Cassese, ICC, Antonio Cassese, Paola Gaeta, and John RWD Jones (eds) *The Rome Statute of the International Criminal Court: A Commentary* (Oxford Univ Press Oxford 2002)

Cassese, ICL, Antonio Cassese *International Criminal Law* (Oxford Univ Press Oxford 2003)

Israel W Charny (ed) *Genocide: A Critical Bibliographic Review* (Facts on File Publishers NY 1988)

Simon Chesterman 'The UN Security Council and the Rule of Law' *Final Report and Recommendations from the Austrian Initiative 2004–08* (Fed Ministry for Eur and Int'l Affairs 2008)

Comparative Encyclopaedia, Rene David (ed) *The International Encyclopaedia of Comparative Law* (Oceana NY 1973)

James Crawford (ed) *The Rights of Peoples* (Clarendon Press Oxford 1988)

Erica IA Daes *Protection of minorities under the International Bill of Human Rights and the Genocide Convention* (Katsikalis Netherlands 1973)

Meir Dan-Cohen *Rights, Persons and Organizations* (Univ California Press Berkeley 1986)

De Nike, Howard J De Nike, John Quigley and Kenneth J Robinson *Genocide in Cambodia—Documents from the Trial of Pol Pot and Ieng Sary* (Univ Penn Press Philadelphia 2000)

Dekker and Post, Ige F Dekker and Harry HG Post (eds) *On the Foundations and Sources of International Law* (TMC Asser Press Hague 2003)

Pieter N Drost *The Crime of State: Vol II—Genocide* (AW Sythoff Leyden 1959)

Helen Duffy *Justice in the Balance: Recommendations for an Independent and Effective International Criminal Court* (Hum Rts Watch NY 1998)

Emerson and Ashworth, Ben Emerson and Andrew Ashworth *Human Rights and Criminal Justice* (Sweet & Maxwell London 2001)

Helen Fein *Genocide: A Sociological Perspective* (Sage London 1993)

Fein, Human Wrongs, Helen Fein *Human Rights and Wrongs: Slavery, Terror and Genocide* (Paradigm Boulder 2007)

George P Fletcher *Basic Concepts of Criminal Law* (Oxford Univ Press Oxford 1998)

Sheldon Glueck *The Nuremberg Trial and Aggressive War* (AA Knopf NY 1946)

Goodwin-Gill and Talmon, GS Goodwin-Gill and Stefan Talmon (eds) *The Reality of International Law: Essays in Honour of Ian Brownlie* (Clarendon Press Oxford 1999)

Philip Gourevitch *We wish to inform you that tomorrow we will be killed with our families* (Picador NY 1999)

John H Griffin *Black Like Me* (Signet NY 1962)

Hugo Grotius *Vol 2 De Jure Belli ac Pacis—Libri Tres* (Francis W Kelsey trans Oxford Univ Press Oxford 1925) (1645)

Lauri Hannikainen *Peremptory Norms (Jus Cogens) in International Law* (Finnish Lawyers Helsinki 1988)

Barbara Harff *Genocide and Human Rights: International Legal and Political Issues* (Univ Denver Press Denver 1984)

Harris and Joseph, David Harris and Sarah Joseph (eds) *The International Covenant on Civil and Political Rights and United Kingdom Law* (Clarendon Press Oxford 1995)

Jean-Marie Henckaerts and Louise Doswald-Beck *Customary International Humanitarian Law Volume I: Rules* and *Volume II: Practice* (Cambridge Univ Press Cambridge 2005)

Rosalyn Higgins *Problems and Process: International Law and How We Use It* (Clarendon Press Oxford 1994)

Raul Hilberg *The Destruction of the European Jews: Vol I* (3rd edn Yale Univ Press New Haven 2003)

Tim Hillier *Sourcebook on Public International Law* (Cavendish London 1998)

David Hirsch *Law Against Genocide: Cosmopolitan Rivals* (Glasshouse Press London 2003)

Samuel N Hoenig *The Essence of Talmudic Law and Thought* (Jason Aronson Northvale 1993)

Oliver Wendell Holmes *The Common Law* (Dover NY 1991) (1881)

Jeremy Horder (ed) *Oxford Essays in Jurisprudence* (Clarendon Press Oxford 2000)

Jacobs and Potter, James B Jacobs and Kimberly Potter *Hate Crimes—Criminal Law and Identity Politics* (Oxford Univ Press Oxford 1998)

Raoul M Jennar *The Cambodian Constitutions 1953–1993* (White Lotus Co Bangkok 1995)

Jenness and Grattet, Valerie Jenness and Ryken Grattet *Making a Hate Crime* (Russell Sage NY 2001)

Klip and Suiter, Andre Klip and Goran Suiter (eds) *Annotated Leading Cases of the International Criminal Tribunals* (Intersentia Antwerp 2001)

Martti Koskenniemi (ed) *Sources of International Law* (Ashgate Aldershot 2000)

Kuper, Genocide—Political Use, Leo Kuper *Genocide: Its Political Use in the Twentieth Century* (Yale Univ Press New Haven 1981)

Kuper, Prevention, Leo Kuper *The Prevention of Genocide* (Yale Univ Press New Haven 1985)

Nicola Lacey *State Punishment: Political Principles and Community Values* (Routledge London 1994)

Frederick M Lawrence *Punishing Hate* (Harvard Univ Press Cambridge 1999)

Lawrence J LeBlanc *The United States and the Genocide Convention* (Duke Univ Press Durham 1991)

Lee, The ICC, Roy S Lee *The International Criminal Court: Elements of Crimes and Rules of Procedure and Evidence* (Transnational NY 2001)

Lee, Making of the ICC, Roy S Lee (ed) *The International Criminal Court: The Making of the Rome Statute* (Kluwer Boston 1999)

Raphael Lemkin *Axis Rule in Occupied Europe* (Carnegie Washington 1944)

Natan Lerner *Group Rights and Discrimination in International Law* (2nd edn Martinus Nijhoff London 2003)

Lowe and Fitzmaurice, A Vaughan Lowe and Malgosia Fitzmaurice (eds) *Fifty Years of the International Court of Justice* (Cambridge Univ Press Cambridge 1996)

Farhad Malekian *The Concept of Islamic International Criminal Law: A Comparative Study* (Martinus Nijhoff London 1994)

Michael Marrus *The Nuremberg War Crimes Trials: A Documentary History* (Bedford Books Boston 1997)

McDonald and Goldman, Gabrielle McDonald and Olivia Swaak-Goldman (eds) *Substantive and Procedural Aspects of International Criminal Law: the Experience of International and National Courts* (Kluwer Boston 2000)

Meron, Humanitarian Norms, Theodor Meron *Human Rights and Humanitarian Norms as Customary Law* (Clarendon Press Oxford 1989)

Meron, Law Making, Theodor Meron *Human Rights Law Making in the United Nations* (Clarendon Press Oxford 1986)

Guenael Mettraux *International Crimes and the Ad Hoc Tribunals* (Oxford Univ Press Oxford 2005)

Robert Michels *Political Parties* (Eden and Cedar Paul trans Peter Smith Boston 1978) (1915)

Morris and Scharf, The ICTR, Virginia Morris and Michael Scharf *The International Criminal Tribunal for Rwanda Vols I–II* (Transnational NY 1998)

Morris and Scharf, The ICTY, Virginia Morris and Michael Scharf *An Insider's Guide to the International Criminal Tribunal for the Former Yugoslavia Vols I-II* (Transnational NY 1995)

MPC, Model Penal Code (Proposed Official Draft) (American Law Institute Philadelphia 1962)

Sean P Murphy *US Practice in International Law (1999–2001)* (Cambridge Univ Press Cambridge 2002)

Oxford English Dictionary, JA Simpson and ESC Weiner (eds) *The Oxford English Dictionary* (Clarendon Press Oxford 1989)

Paust, Jordan Paust et al (eds) *International Criminal Law: Cases and Materials* (2nd edn Carolina Academic Press 2000)

Jordan Paust et al *International Criminal Law Documents Supplement* (3rd edn Carolina Academic Press Durham 2006)

Edgar Allen Poe *The Tell Tale Heart* (1895)

Mauro Polti and Giuseppe Nesi *The Rome Statute of the International Criminal Court: A Challenge to Impunity* (Aldershot Hants 2001)

Jack N Porter (ed) *Genocide and Human Rights: A Global Anthology* (Wash DC Press of America Washington DC 1982)

John B Quigly *The Genocide Convention: An International Law Analysis* (Ashgate Hampshire 2006)

Ratner and Abrams, Jason Ratner and Steven Abrams *The Criminalization of Atrocities in International Law* (Oxford Univ Press Oxford 1997)

Restatement (Second) of Contracts (West St Paul 1981)

Restatement (Third) of Foreign Relations, Restatement (Third) of Foreign Relations Law of the United States (West St Paul 1987)

Roberts and Guelff, Adam Roberts and Richard Guelff (eds) *Documents on the Laws of War* (2nd edn Oxford Univ Press Oxford 1989)

Nehemiah Robinson *The Genocide Convention—A Commentary* (World Jewish Congress NY 1960)

Alan S Rosenbaum (ed) *Is The Holocaust Unique? Perspectives on Comparative Genocide* (2nd edn Westview Press Boulder 2001)

Philippe Sands (ed) *From Nuremberg to the Hague* (Cambridge Univ Press Cambridge 2003)

William Schabas *Genocide in International Law* (2nd edn Cambridge Univ Press Cambridge 2009)

Anja Seibert-Fohr *Prosecuting Serious Human Rights Violations* (Oxford Univ Press Oxford 2009)

Sewall and Kaysen, Sarah Sewall and Carl Kaysen (eds) *The United States and the International Criminal Court* (Rowman & Littlefield Lanham 2000)

William Shakespeare *The Second Part of King Henry the Sixth* (1591)

Simester and Sullivan, AP Simester and GR Sullivan *Criminal Law Theory and Doctrine* (2nd edn Hart Oxford 2003)

Bruno Simma *International Human Rights and General International Law: A Comparative Analysis*—The Protection of Human Rights in Europe Vol IV/2 153 (Collected Courses—Academy of European Law 1993)

Ian Sinclair *The Vienna Convention on the Law of Treaties* (2nd edn Manchester Univ Press Manchester 1984)

Peter Smith (ed) *Criminal Law: Essays in Honour of JC Smith* (Butterworths London 1987)

Kazimierz Smoleń *State Museum in Oświęcim, Auschwitz Birkenau Guide-Book* (Stephen Lee trans 1999)

Aviam Soifer *Law and the Company We Keep* (Harvard Univ Press Cambridge 1995)

Ervin Staub *The Roots of Evil—The Origins of Genocide and Other Group Violence* (Cambridge Univ Press Cambridge 1989)

Scott Straus *The Order of Genocide: Race Power, and War in Rwanda* (Cornell Univ Press Ithaca 2006)

Lyal S Sunga *The Emerging System of International Criminal Law* (Kluwer Boston 1997)

CHF Tapper (ed) *Crime, Proof and Punishment: Essays in Memory of Sir Rupert Cross* (Butterworths London 1981)

Telford Taylor *Anatomy of Nuremberg the Trials: A Personal Memoir* (Knopf NY 1992)

Telford Taylor *Final Report to the Secretary of the Army on the Nuernberg War Crimes Trials Under Control Council Law No 10* (WS Hein Buffalo 1997) (1949)

Totten and Markusen, Samuel Totten and Eric Markusen *Genocide in Darfur: Investigating the Atrocities in Sudan* (Routledge NY 2006)

UNCHR Refugee Handbook, Office of the United Nations High Commissioner for Refugees—Handbook on Procedures and Criteria for Determining Refugee Status under the 1951 Convention and the 1967 Protocol relating to the Status of Refugees UN Doc HCR/IP/4/Eng/REV1 (1979) (Re-edited edn Geneva 1992)

Mark E Villiger *Customary International Law and Treaties* (2nd edn Kluwer Boston 1997)

Von Hebel, Herman von Hebel, Johan Lammers and Jolien Schukking (eds) *Reflections on the International Criminal Court* (TMC Asser Press Hague 1999)

Weiler, Joseph Weiler, Anthony Cassese, and Marina Spinedi (eds) *International Crimes of State* (De Gruyter Berlin 1989)
James F Willis *Prologue to Nuremberg* (Greenwood Press Westport 1982)
Lucia Zedner *Criminal Justice* (Oxford Univ Press Oxford 2004)

Articles and Periodical Literature

Note on abbreviations

The initial references to scholarly articles and periodical literature within each chapter are accompanied by a full OSCOLA citation. Subsequent references within that chapter are cross-referenced by author to the footnote containing the initial appearance.

Each chapter is self-contained. There are no cross-references to footnotes in preceding or later chapters.

Journal abbreviations

AJCL	American Journal of Comparative Law
AJIL	American Journal of International Law
Am LER	American Law and Economics Review
Am Scholar	American Scholar
Am Univ LR	American University Law Review
Arizona JICL	Arizona Journal of International & Comparative Law
Asian YBIL	Asian Yearbook of International Law
ASILPROC	American Society of International Law Proceedings
BC TWLJ	Boston College Third World Law Journal
BCLR	Boston College Law Review
BU ILJ	Boston University International Law Journal
BYBIL	British Yearbook of International Law
Cal LR	California Law Review
Can YBIL	Canadian Yearbook of International Law
Case Western JIL	Case Western Reserve Journal of International Law
Cardozo LR	Cardozo Law Review
Columbia LR	Columbia Law Review
Criminal LF	Criminal Law Forum
DePaul LR	DePaul Law Review
Duke LR	Duke Law Review
EJIL	European Journal of International Law
Fletcher Forum	Fletcher Forum of World Affairs
Fordham ILJ	Fordham International Law Journal
Fordham LR	Fordham Law Review
Florida JIL	Florida Journal of International Law
Gen Stud & Prevent	Genocide Studies and Prevention
Hastings ICLR	Hastings International & Comparative Law Review
Harvard ILJ	Harvard International Law Journal
Harv HRJ	Harvard Human Rights Journal
Houston JIL	Houston Journal of International Law
ICLR	International Criminal Law Review
ILP	International Legal Perspectives
ILQ	International Studies Quarterly

ILSA JICL	International Law Students Association Journal of International & Comparative Law
ILSA Quarterly	International Law Students Association Quarterly
Indiana ICLR	Indiana International & Comparative Law Review
J Gen Res	Journal of Genocide Research
J Law & Religion	Journal of Law & Religion
JICJ	Journal of International Criminal Justice
JTLP	Journal of Transnational Law and Policy
LCP	Law & Contemporary Problems
Leiden JIL	Leiden Journal of International Law
Legal Stud	Legal Studies
Loy LA LR	Loyola of Los Angeles Law Review
LQR	Law Quarterly Review
Michigan JIL	Michigan State Journal of International Law
Mo LR	Missouri Law Review
Modern LR	Modern Law Review
Nat'l Black LJ	National Black Law Journal
New England LR	New England Law Review
NYLS JHR	New York Law School Journal of Human Rights
Oxford JICJ	Oxford Journal of International Criminal Justice
So Cal LR	Southern California Law Review
Stanford JIL	Stanford Journal of International Law
Texas ILJ	Texas International Law Journal
UN Bull	United Nations Bulletin
Vill LR	Villanova Law Review
W&M LR	William & Mary Law Review
Wis ILJ	Wisconsin International Law Journal
YB-IHL	Yearbook of International Humanitarian Law
YB-IHRL	Yearbook of International Human Rights Law
YB-ILC	Yearbook of The International Law Commission
YB-UN	Yearbook of the United Nations
Yale JIL	Yale Journal of International Law
Yale HRDLJ	Yale Human Rights and Development Law Journal
Yale LJ	Yale Law Journal

Works cited

J Abrams, 'Universal Jurisdiction: Myths, Realities and Prospects: The Atrocities in Cambodia and Kosovo: Observations on the Codification of Genocide' (2001) 35 New England LR 303

H Afchar, 'The Muslim Concept of Law' in 2 Rene David (ed) *The International Encyclopaedia of Comparative Law* 84 (Oceana NY 1973)

M Akehurst, 'Custom as a Source of International Law' (1976) 47 BYBIL 1

LG Albrecht, BL Apt, EM Condon, GJ Garland, AD Giampolo, M Hansel, RS Kerr, V Mascarenhas, and LJ Shields, 'International Human Rights' (2007) 41 Int'l Lawyer 643

JF Alexander, 'The International Criminal Court and the Prevention of Atrocities: Predicting the Court's Impact' (2009) 54 Vill LR 1

DM Amann, 'Group Mentality, Expressivism, and Genocide' (2002) 2 ICLR 93

DM Amann, 'Under Destruction' (2000) 3 Green Bag 369

K Ambos and S Wirth, 'Commentary' in 2 Andre Klip and Goran Suiter (eds) *Annotated Leading Cases of the International Criminal Tribunals* 701 (Intersentia Antwerp 2001)

DE Arzt, 'Nuremberg, Denazification and Democracy: The Hate Speech Problem at the International Military Tribunal' (1995) 12 NYLS JHR 689

AJ Ashworth, 'Defining Criminal Offences Without Harm' in Peter Smith (ed) *Criminal Law: Essays in Honour of JC Smith* 8 (Butterworths London 1987)

AJ Ashworth, 'The elasticity of mens rea' in CHF Tapper (ed) *Crime, Proof and Punishment: Essays in Memory of Sir Rupert Cross* 45 (Butterworths London 1981)

AJ Ashworth and E Steiner, 'Criminal Omissions and public duties; the French experience' (1990) 10 Legal Stud 153

KD Askin, 'Crimes Within the Jurisdiction of the International Criminal Court' (1999) 10 Criminal LF 33

MC Bassiouni, 'The Commission of Experts Established Pursuant to Security Council Resolution 780: Investigating Violations of International Humanitarian Law in the Former Yugoslavia' (1994) 5 Criminal LF 279

E Beckenhauer, 'Redefining Race: Can Genetic Testing Provide Biological Proof of Indian Ethnicity?' (2003) 56 Stan LR 161

SW Becker, 'Maintaining Secret Government Dossiers on the First Amendment Activities of American Citizens: the Law Enforcement Exception to the Privacy Act' (2000) 50 DePaul LR 675

JB Bellinger and WJ Haynes, 'A U.S. Government Response to the International Committee of the Red Cross's Customary International Humanitarian Law Study' (2007) 89 Int'l Rev of the Red Cross 443

FS Benavides-Vanegas, 'The Elimination of Political Groups under International Law and the Constitution of Political Claims' (2003) 15 Florida JIL 575

C Beyani, 'The Legal Premises for the International Protection of Human Rights' in GS Goodwin-Gill and Stefan Talmon (eds) *The Reality of International Law: Essays in Honour of Ian Brownlie* (Clarendon Press Oxford 1999) 21

A Botha, 'Genocide perpetrators to die' News24 (12 Oct 2004), available at <http://www.news24.com/News24/Africa/News/0,,2–11-1447_1608472,00.html> (visited 11 Jan 2010)

K Brand, 'Commentary' (1949) 15 LRTWC 1

I Brownlie, 'The Rights of Peoples in Modern International Law' in James Crawford (ed) *The Rights of Peoples* (Clarendon Press Oxford 1988) 1

B Bryant, 'The United States and the 1948 Genocide Convention' (1975) 16 Harvard ILJ 686

A Cassese, 'Reflections on International Criminal Justice' (1998) 61 Modern LR 1

F Chalk and K Jonassohn, 'The History and Sociology of Genocidal Killings' in Israel W Charny (ed) *Genocide: A Critical Bibliographic Review* (Facts on File Publishers NY 1988)

S Chesterman, *The UN Security Council and the Rule of Law—The Role of the Security Council in Strengthening a Rules-based International System* (2008) Final Report and Recommendations from the Austrian Initiative, 2004–2008 (Federal Ministry for European and International Affairs)

C Cisse, 'The End of a Culture of Impunity in Rwanda?' (1998) 1 YB-IHL 161
A Clapham, 'Issues of complexity, complicity, and complementarity: from the Nuremberg trials to the dawn of the new International Criminal Court' in Philippe Sands (ed) *From Nuremberg to the Hague* 31 (Cambridge Univ Press Cambridge 2003)
R Clark, 'Crimes Against Humanity and the Rome Statute of the International Criminal Court' in Mauro Polti and Giuseppe Nesi *The Rome Statute of the International Criminal Court: a Challenge to Impunity* (Aldershot Hants 2001) 77
I Cotler, 'Case Comment: Regina v Finta' (1996) 90 AJIL 460
VN Dadrian, 'The Armenian Genocide and the Legal and Political Issues in the Failure to Prevent or Punish the Crime' (1998) 29 UWLA LR 43
VN Dadrian, 'Genocide as a Problem of National and International Law: The World War I Armenian Case and its Contemporary Legal Ramifications' (1989) 14 Yale JIL 221
VN Dadrian, 'The Turkish Military Tribunal's Prosecution of the Authors of the Armenian Genocide: Four Major Court-Martial Series' (1997) 11 Holocaust and Genocide Studies 28
E Daly, 'Transformative Justice: Charting a path to Reconciliation' (2002) 12 ILP 73
A Danner, 'Constructing a Hierarchy of Crimes in International Criminal Law Sentencing' (2001) 87 Virginia LR 415
G Dawson and R Boynton, 'Reconciling Complicity in Genocide and Aiding and Abetting Genocide in the Jurisprudence of the United Nations Ad Hoc Tribunals' (2008) 21 Harv HRJ 241
JDM Derrett and TK Krishnamurthy, 'The Hindu Conception of Law' in 2 Rene David (ed) *The International Encyclopaedia of Comparative Law* (Oceana NY 1973) 107
A de Waal, 'Reflections on the Difficulties of Defining Darfur's Crisis as Genocide' (2007) Harv HRJ 25
A de Waal and GH Stanton, 'Should President Omar al-Bashir of Sudan be Charged and Arrested by the International Criminal Court? An Exchange of Views' (2009) 4 Gen Stud & Prevent 329
MA Drumbl, 'Law and Atrocity: Settling Accounts in Rwanda' (2005) 31 Ohio NU LR 41
H Fein, 'Genocide, Terror, Life Integrity and War Crimes: The Case for Discrimination' in George J Andreopoulos (ed) *Genocide: Conceptual and Historical Dimensions* 95 (Univ Pennsylvania Press Philadelphia 1994)
AT Feindel, 'Reconciling Sexual Orientation: Creating A Definition of Genocide That Includes Sexual Orientation' (2005) 13 Michigan JIL 197
CE Feuss and JD Sosna, 'Courts are Warming to Claims of "Unconscious Bias" as a Result, Employers Face Bigger Class Actions and Costlier Litigation' (2007) 30 Nat'l LJ S2
SK Fisher, 'Occupation of the Womb: Forced Impregnation as Genocide' (1996) 46 Duke LJ 91
GG Fitzmaurice, 'Some Problems Regarding the Formal Sources of International Law' [1958] Symbolae Verzijil 153, reprinted in Martti Koskenniemi (ed) *Sources of International Law* (Ashgate Aldershot 2000) 57
GP Fletcher, 'The Storrs Lectures: Liberals and Romantics at War: the Problem of Collective Guilt' (2002) 111 Yale LJ 1499
AR Ford, 'A Race Apart: Genocide and the Protection of Disabled Persons Under International Law' (2009) Review of Disability Studies 15

J Fowler, 'A New Chapter of Irony: The Legal Definition of Genocide and the Implications of Powell's Determination' in Samuel Totten and Eric Markusen, *Genocide in Darfur: Investigating the Atrocities in Sudan* (Routledge NY 2006)] 127 (2006)

J Fowler and Z Heckscher, 'Introductory Note to the Sudan Accountability and Investment Act of 2007 and the Signing Statement of President George W. Bush to the Act' (2008) 47 ILM 127

RR Garet, 'Communality and Existence: The Rights of Groups' (1983) 56 So Cal LR 1001

AE Giardino, 'Using Extraterritorial Jurisdiction to Prosecute Violations of the Law of War: Looking Beyond the War Crimes Act' (2007) 48 BCLR 699

AM Gilbert and ED Marchand, 'Splitting the Atom or Splitting Hairs—The Hate Crimes Prevention Act of 1999' (1999) 30 Saint Mary's LJ 931

J Goodman, 'Divine Judgment: Judicial Review of Religious Legal Systems in India and Israel' (2009) Hastings ICLR 477

J Gordon, 'When Intent Makes all the Difference in the World: Economic Sanctions on Iraq and the Accusation of Genocide' (2002) 5 Yale HRDLJ 57

AKA Greenawalt, 'Re-Thinking Genocidal Intent: The Case for a Knowledge-Based Interpretation' (1999) 99 Columbia LR 2259

AS Greene, 'The Pledge of Allegiance Problem' (1995) 64 Fordham LR 451

J Hagan and A Palloni, 'Death in Darfur' (2006) Science 1578

B Harff and TR Gurr, 'Toward Empirical Theory of Genocides and Politicides: Identification and Measurement of Cases Since 1945' (1988) 32 ILQ 359

S Harzenski, 'Terrorism, A History: Stage One' (2003) 12 JTLP 137

F Hassan, 'The Theoretical Basis of Punishment in International Criminal Law' (1983) 15 Case Western JIL 38

JM Henckaerts, 'Customary International Humanitarian Law: a Response to US Comments' (2007) 89 Int'l Rev of the Red Cross 473

R Higgins, 'The Relationship Between the International Criminal Court and the International Court of Justice' in Herman von Hebel, Johan Lammers and Jolien Schukking (eds) *Reflections on the International Criminal Court* (TMC Asser Press 1999) 163

R Hirschl, 'The Theocratic Challenge to Constitution Drafting in Post-Conflict States' (2008) 49 W&M LR 1179

J Horder, 'On the Irrelevance of Motive in Criminal Law' in Jeremy Horder (ed) *Oxford Essays in Jurisprudence* (Clarendon Press Oxford 2000) 173

R Jahan, 'The Bengalis of East Pakistan' in JN Porter (ed) *Genocide and Human Rights: A Global Anthology* (Wash DC Press of America Washington DC 1982) 256

RY Jennings, 'What is International Law and How Do We Tell It When We See It?' (1981) 37 Schweitzerisches Jahrbuch fur Internationales Recht 59, reprinted in Martti Koskenniemi (ed) *Sources of International Law* (Ashgate Aldershot 2000) 27

S Joseph, 'Rights of Political Participation' in David Harris and Sarah Joseph (eds) *The International Covenant on Civil and Political Rights and United Kingdom Law* (Clarendon Press Oxford 1995) 535

ST Katz, 'The Uniqueness of the Holocaust: The Historical Dimension' in Alan S Rosenbaum (ed) *Is The Holocaust Unique? Perspectives on Comparative Genocide* (2nd edn Westview Press Boulder 2001) 19

KMF Keith, 'The Mens Rea of Superior Responsibility as Developed by ICTY Jurisprudence' (2001) 14 Leiden JIL 617

MJ Kelly, '"Genocide"—The Power of a Label' (2008) 40 Case Western JIL 147
O Kimminich, (1984) 'History of the Law of Nations Since World War II' in R Bernhardt (ed) *Encyclopaedia of Public International Law* (North Holland NY 1993) 849
O Kranzbuhler, 'Nuremberg Eighteen Years Afterwards' (1964) 14 DePaul LR 333
NJ Kritz, 'Coming to terms with Atrocities: A Review of Accountability Mechanisms for Mass Violations of Human Rights' (1996) 59 LCP 127
FM Lawrence, 'The Case for a Federal Bias Crime Law' (1999) 16 Nat'l Black LJ 144
LJ LeBlanc, 'The United Nations Genocide Convention and Political Groups: Should the United States Propose an Amendment?' (1988) 13 Yale ILJ 268
MN Leich, 'Contemporary Practice of the United States Relating to International Law' (1986) 80 AJIL 612
MN Leich, 'International Criminal Jurisdiction: ILC Draft Code of Crimes' (1993) 87 AJIL 607
Lemkin, Genocide, R Lemkin, 'Genocide' (1946) 15 Am Scholar 227
Lemkin, Genocide as a Crime, R Lemkin, 'Genocide as a Crime under International Law' (1947) 41 AJIL 145
Lemkin, Genocide Under International Law, R Lemkin, 'Genocide as a Crime Under International Law' (15 Jan 1948) UN Bulletin 70
Lord Lester of Herne Hill and S Joseph, 'Obligations of Non-Discrimination' in David Harris and Sarah Joseph (eds) *The International Covenant on Civil and Political Rights and United Kingdom Law* (Clarendon Press Oxford 1995) 563
HS Levie, 'Indo-Pakistani Agreement' (1974) 68 AJIL 95
HS Levie, 'Legal Aspects of the Continued Detention of the Pakistani Prisoners of War by India' (1973) 67 AJIL 512
M Lippman, 'The Convention on the Prevention and Punishment of the Crime of Genocide: Fifty Years Later' (1998) 15 Arizona JICL 414
M Lippman, 'The Drafting of the 1948 Convention on the Prevention and Punishment of the Crime of Genocide' (1985) 3 BU ILJ 1
M Lippman, 'The Evolution and Scope of Command Responsibility' (2000) 13 Leiden JIL 139
M Lippman, 'Genocide: The Crime of the Century—The Jurisprudence of Death at the Dawn of the new Millennium' (2001) 23 Houston JIL 467
M Lippman, 'The Other Nuremberg: American Prosecutions of Nazi War Criminals in Occupied Germany' (1992) 3 Indiana ICLR 1
DG Littman, 'Universal Human Rights & Human Rights in Islam' (1999) 45 Midstream 2
D Luban, 'A Theory of Crimes Against Humanity' (2004) 29 Yale JIL 85
D Luban, 'Calling Genocide by its Rightful Name: Lemkin's Word, Darfur, and the UN Report' (2006) 7 Chicago JIL 303
L Malksoo, 'Soviet Genocide? Communist Mass Deportations in the Baltic States and International Law' (2001) 14 Leiden JIL 757
MJ Matheson, 'Current Development: The Fifty-Eighth Session of the International Law Commission' (2007) 101 AJIL 424
MJ Matheson, 'The Fifty-Eighth Session of the International Law Commission' (2007) 101 AJIL 407
B Mawhinney, 'Canadian Practice in International Law' (1993) Can YBIL 343
JV Mayfield, 'The prosecution of War Crimes and Respect for Human Rights: Ethiopia's Balancing Act' (1995) 9 Emory ILR 553

WA McKean, 'The Meaning of Discrimination in International and Municipal Law' (1970) 44 BYBIL 177

M Mendelson, 'The International Court of Justice and the Sources' in AV Lowe and M Fitzmaurice (eds) *Fifty Years of the International Court of Justice* (Cambridge Univ Press Cambridge 1996) 70

T Meron, 'The Geneva Conventions as Customary Law' (1987) 81 AJIL 348

T Meron and A Rosas, 'A Declaration of Minimum Humanitarian Standards' (1991) 85 AJIL 375

ER Milhizer, 'Group Status and Criminal Defences: Logical Relationship or Marriage of Convenience?' (2006) 71 Mo LR 547

B Mitchell, 'Multiple Wrongdoing and Offence Structure: A plea for Consistency and Fair Labelling' (2001) 64 Modern LR 393

J Mukimbiri, 'The Seven Stages of the Rwandan Genocide' (2005) 3 Oxford JICJ 823

RA Mulligan, 'Enhancing the Delivery of Quality Justice: Report of the Court Metrics Project' Commonwealth of Massachusetts Administrative Office of the Trial Court (Mar 2007)

S Murphy, 'Department of State Legal Analysis of 1994 Genocide in Rwanda' (2002) 96 AJIL 258

WP Nagan and VF Rodin, 'Racism, Genocide, and Mass Murder: Toward a Legal Theory About Group Deprivation' (2004) 17 Nat'l Black LJ 33

A Neier, 'Peaceful Transitions to Constitutional Democracy' (1998) 19 Cardozo LR 1953

D Nersessian, 'The Contours of Genocidal Intent: Troubling Jurisprudence from the International Criminal Tribunals' (2002) 37 Texas ILJ 231 (2002)

D Nersessian, 'Whoops—I Committed Genocide! The Anomaly of Constructive Liability for Serious International Crimes' (2006) 30 Fletcher Forum 81

A Nitoiu, 'Accountability for State-Sponsored Human Rights Abuses in Eastern Europe and the Soviet Union' (1992) 12 BC Third World LJ 241

J Oraa, 'The Protection of Human Rights in Emergency Situations under Customary International Law' in GS Goodwin-Gill and Stefan Talmon (eds) *The Reality of International Law: Essays in Honour of Ian Brownlie* (Clarendon Press Oxford 1999) 413

MJ Osiel, 'Obeying Orders: Atrocity, Military Discipline and the Law of War' (1998) 86 Cal LR 944

R Overy, 'The Nuremberg Trials: International law in the Making' in Philippe Sands (ed) *From Nuremberg to the Hague* (Cambridge Univ Press Cambridge 2003) 1

J Paust, 'Aggression Against Authority: The Crime of Oppression, Politicide and Other Crimes Against Human Rights' (1986) 18 Case Western JIL 283

PB Perlman, 'The Genocide Convention' (1950) 30 Nebraska LR 1

V Peskin, 'The International Criminal Court, the Security Council, and the Politics of Impunity in Darfur' (2009) 4 Gen Stud & Prevent 304

JN Porter, 'Introduction' in JN Porter (ed) *Genocide and Human Rights: A Global Anthology* (Washington DC Press of America Washington DC 1982) 2

EA Posner and AO Sykes, 'An Economic Analysis of State and Individual Responsibility Under International Law' (2007) 9 Am LER 129

HHG Post, 'The Role of State Practice in the Formation of Customary International Humanitarian Law' in IF Dekker and HHG Post (eds) *On the Foundations and Sources of International Law* (TMC Asser Press Hague 2003) 129

S Powles, 'Joint Criminal Enterprise—Criminal Liability by Prosecutorial Ingenuity and Judicial Creativity?' (2004) 2 Oxford JICJ 606

'Race in a Genetic World' (2008) 110 Harvard Magazine 62

SR Ratner, 'The Genocide Convention After Fifty Years: Contemporary Strategies for Combating a Crime Against Humanity' (1998) 92 ASILPROC 1

SR Ratner, 'The Schizophrenias of International Criminal Law' (1998) 33 Texas ILJ 237

AE Ray, 'The Shame of It: Gender-Based Terrorism in the Former Yugoslavia and the Failure of International Human Rights Law to Comprehend the Injuries' (1997) 46 Am Univ LR 793

WM Reisman, 'Why Regime Change is (Almost Always) a Bad Idea' (2004) 98 AJIL 516

RCO Rezie, 'The Ukrainian Constitution: Interpretation of the Citizens Rights Provisions' (1999) Case Western JIL 169

T Sapru, 'Into the Heart of Darkness: The Case Against the Foray of the Security Council Into the Rwandan Crisis' (1997) 32 Texas ILJ 329

G Sawer, 'The Western Concept of Law' in 2 Rene David (ed) *The International Encyclopaedia of Comparative Law* (Oceana NY 1973) 14

WA Schabas, 'Groups Protected by the Genocide Convention: Conflicting Interpretations from the International Criminal Tribunal for Rwanda' (2000) 6 ILSA JICL 375

WA Schabas, 'National Courts Finally Begin to Prosecute Genocide—the 'Crime of Crimes'' (2003) 1 Oxford JICJ 39.

WA Schabas, 'Problems of International Codification—Were the Atrocities in Cambodia and Kosovo Genocide?' (2001) 35 New England LR 287

MP Scharf, 'Justice versus Peace' in Sarah Sewall and Carl Kaysen (eds) *The United States and the International Criminal Court* (Rowman & Littlefield Lanham 2000) 184

A Schlogel, 'Genocide' in 2 R Bernhardt (ed) *Encyclopaedia of Public International Law* (North Holland NY 1981) 541

G Schwarzenberger, 'The Problem of an International Criminal Law' (1950) 3 Current Legal Probs 263

SM Schwebel, 'The Effect of Resolutions of the UN General Assembly on Customary International Law' (1979) 73 ASILPROC 301

E Schwelb, 'Crimes Against Humanity' (1946) 23 BYBIL 178

B Simma and AL Paulus, 'Responsibility of Individuals for Human Rights Abuses in Internal Conflicts: A Positivist View' (1999) 93 AJIL 302

TW Simon, 'Defining Genocide' (1996) Wis ILJ 243

M Simons, L Polgreen and J Gettleman, 'Arrest is Sought of Sudan Leader in Genocide Case' (15 Jul 08) NY Times A1

RD Sloane, 'The Evolving "Common Law" of Sentencing of the International Criminal Tribunal for Rwanda' (2007) 5 Oxford JICJ 718

RD Sloane, 'The Expressive Capacity of International Punishment: The Limits of the National Law Analogy and the Potential of International Criminal Law' (2007) 43 Stanford JIL 39

M Spinedi, 'International Crimes of State: The Legislative History' in Joseph Weiler, Anthony Cassese and Marina Spinedi (eds) *International Crimes of State* (De Gruyter Berlin 1989) 45

GH Stanton, 'Blue Scarves and Yellow Stars: Classification and Symbolization in the Cambodian Genocide' (1987), The Faulds Lecture, Warren Wilson College,

Swannanoa, North Carolina, March 1987, available at <http://www.genocidewatch.org> (visited 12 Jan 2010)

GH Stanton, 'The Eight Stages of Genocide' (1998) Genocide Watch, available at <http://www.genocidewatch.org/images/8StagesBriefingpaper.pdf> (visited 11 Jan 2010)

J Steele, 'A Seal Pressed in the hot wax of Vengeance: A Girardian Understanding of Expressive Punishment' (2001) 16 J Law and Religion 35

S Straus, 'Contested meanings and conflicting imperatives: a conceptual analysis of genocide' (2001) 3 J Gen Res 349

O Swaak-Goldman, 'Persecution' in Gabrielle McDonald and Olivia Swaak-Goldman (eds) *Substantive and Procedural Aspects of International Criminal Law: the Experience of International and National Courts, Vol I—Commentary* (Kluwer Boston 2000) 249

I Szabo, 'The Socialist Conception of law' in 2 Rene David (ed) *The International Encyclopaedia of Comparative Law* (Oceana NY 1973) 49

S Talmon, 'The Security Council as World Legislature' (2005) 99 AJIL 175

S Taylor, 'Nepal's deposed king leaves palace for last time' USA Today (11 Jun 2008)

FK Tiba, 'The Mengistu Genocide Trial in Ethiopia' (2007) 5 Oxford JICJ 513

S Totten, 'The UN International Commission of Inquiry on Darfur: New and Disturbing Findings' (2009) 4 Gen Stud & Prevent 354

O Triffterer, 'Genocide, Its Particular Intent to Destroy in Whole or in part the Group as Such' (2001) 14 Leiden JIL 399

J Turley, 'Transformative Justice and the Ethos of Nuremberg' (2000) 33 Loy LA LR 655

JD Van der Vyver, 'Prosecution and Punishment of the Crime of Genocide' (1999) 23 Fordham ILJ 286

B Van Schaak, 'The Crime of Political Genocide: Repairing the Genocide Convention's Blind Spot' (1997) 106 Yale LJ 2259

G Verdirame, 'The Genocide Definition in the Jurisprudence of the Ad Hoc Tribunals' (2000) 49 ICLQ 578

P Verwimp, 'Death and survival during the 1994 genocide in Rwanda' (2004) 58 Population Studies 233

J Walberg, 'The Conflict of Muslim and Secular Law in Nigeria' (2004) 12 ILSA Quarterly 4

S Walther, 'Cumulation of Offences' in Antonio Cassese, Paola Gaeta and John RWD Jones (eds) *The Rome Statute of the International Criminal Court: A Commentary* (Oxford University Press Oxford 2002) 475

L Sadat Wexler, 'Prosecutions for Crimes Against Humanity in French Municipal Law: International Implications' (1998) 91 ASILPROC 270

G Williams, 'Convictions and Fair Labelling' (1983) 42 Cambridge LJ 85

HS Willis, 'Cumulative Convictions and the Double Jeopardy Rule: Pursuing Justice at the ICTY and the ICTR' (2003) 17 Emory ILR 341

International Materials

Note on abbreviations

United Nations documents and other international materials are referenced by the italicized abbreviation accompanying the full document citation below, together with the document's date and UN document number. Subsequent references to the same document within that chapter are cross-referenced to the footnote containing the initial appearance.

Each chapter is self-contained. There are no cross-references to footnotes in preceding or later chapters.

International Agreements and Conventions

ACHR, Inter-American Convention on Human Rights (22 Nov 1969) 1144 UNTS 123 OAS Official Records Ser K/XVI/1.1 (Doc 65) Rev1 and Corr1

AfCHR, African [Banjul] Charter on Human and Peoples' Rights (27 Jun 1981) OAU Doc CAB/LEG/67/3 Rev5

Apartheid Convention, International Convention on the Suppression and Punishment of the Crime of 'Apartheid' (30 Nov 1973) UN Doc A/9030

Convention Against Torture, Convention against Torture and Other Cruel, Inhuman or Degrading Treatment or Punishment (10 Dec 1984) 1465 UNTS 85

Convention for the Protection of Individuals with Respect to Automatic Processing of Personal Data (28 Jan 1981) Eur TS No 108

Convention on Non-Applicability of Statutory Limitations (26 Nov 1968) UN Doc A/7218

CRC, Convention on the Rights of the Child (20 Nov 1989) 1577 UNTS 3

ECHR, European Convention for the Protection of Human Rights and Fundamental Freedoms (4 Nov 1950) 218 UNTS 262

Geneva Convention I, Geneva Convention for the Amelioration of the Condition of the Wounded and Sick in Armed Forces in the Field (12 Aug 1949) 75 UNTS 31

Geneva Convention II, Geneva Convention II for the Amelioration of the Condition of Wounded, Sick and Shipwrecked Members of Armed Forces at Sea (12 Aug 1949) 75 UNTS 85

Geneva Convention III, Geneva Convention Relative to the Treatment of Prisoners of War (12 Aug 1949) 75 UNTS 135

Geneva Convention IV, Geneva Convention Relative to the Protection of Civilian Persons in Time of War (12 Aug 1949) 75 UNTS 287

Geneva Protocol I, Protocol I Additional to the Geneva Conventions of 12 August 1949, and Relating to the Protection of Victims of International Armed Conflicts (12 Dec 1977) 1125 UNTS 3

Geneva Protocol III, Protocol Additional to the Geneva Convention of 12 August 1949 and relating to the Adoption of an Additional Distinctive Emblem (8 Dec 2005)

Genocide Convention, 'Convention on the Prevention and Punishment of the Crime of Genocide' UNGA Res 260 (III) (9 Dec 1948) 78 UNTS 277

Genocide Convention—Spanish Text, 'Convención Para la Prevención y la Sanción del Delito de Genocidio' UNGA Res 260 (III) (9 Dec 1948) 78 UNTS 296

[1899] Hague Convention II, Convention with Respect to the Laws and Customs of War on Land (Hague II) (29 Jul 1899)

ICCPR, International Covenant on Civil and Political Rights, 999 UNTS 171, UNGA Res 2200A (XXI) (16 Dec 1966) UN Doc A/6316

ICESCR, International Covenant on Economic, Social and Cultural Rights, 993 UNTS 3, UNGA Res 2200A (XXI) (16 Dec 1966) UN Doc A/6316

ICJ Statute, Statute of the International Court of Justice (26 Jun 1945) 59 Stat 1055

Inter-American Convention on Forced Disappearance, Inter-American Convention on Forced Disappearance of Persons (9 Jun 1994) OAS Treaty Series No 68, 33 ILM 1429

'Inter-American Convention to Prevent and Punish Torture' (9 Dec 1985) OAS Doc OEA/Ser P, AG/Doc 2023/85 Rev 1

Moscow Declaration, Declaration of Four Nations on General Security (US-UK-USSR-PRC) (30 Oct 1943) 9 US Dep't of State Bull 307

Refugee Convention, Convention Relating to the Status of Refugees (28 Jul 1951) 189 UNTS 150

UN Charter, Charter of the United Nations (26 Jun 1945) 59 Stat 1031 (1945)

VCLT, Vienna Convention on the Law of Treaties (23 May 1969) 1155 UNTS 331

UN General Assembly

Draft Resolution relating to the crime of genocide proposed by the delegations of Cuba, India and Panama (2 Nov 1946) UN Doc A/BUR50

Multilateral Treaties Deposited with the Secretary-General: United Nations Treaty Collection—Charter of the United Nations [UN Charter] (11 Jan 2010) available at <http://www.treaties.un.org/Pages/ViewDetails.aspx?src=IND&mtdsg_no=I-1&chapter=1&lang=en> (visited 11 Jan 2010)

Multilateral Treaties Deposited with the Secretary-General: United Nations Treaty Collection—International Covenant on Civil and Political Rights [ICCPR] (11 Jan 2010) available at http://www.treaties.un.org/Pages/ViewDetails.aspx?src=TREATY&mtdsg_no=IV-4&chapter=4&lang=en> (visited 11 Jan 2010)

Multilateral Treaties Deposited with the Secretary-General: United Nations Treaty Collection—Convention on the Prevention and Punishment of the Crime of Genocide [Genocide Convention] (11 Jan 2010) available at http://www.treaties.un.org/Pages/ViewDetails.aspx?src=TREATY&mtdsg_no=IV-1&chapter=4&lang=en> (visited 11 Jan 2010)

Multilateral Treaties Deposited with the Secretary-General: United Nations Treaty Collection—Rome Statute of the International Criminal Court [ICC Statute] (11 Jan 2010) available at <http://www.treaties.un.org/Pages/ViewDetails.aspx?src=IND&mtdsg_no=XVIII-10&chapter=18&lang=en> (visited 11 Jan 2010)

Official Records of the Second Part of the First Session of the General Assembly—Plenary Meetings (Verbatim Record 23 Oct–16 Dec 1946)

Union of Soviet Socialist Republics: Amendments to the draft convention on the prevention and punishment of genocide proposed by the Sixth Committee (5 Dec 1948) UN Doc A/760

UN General Assembly Resolutions

Declaration on Enforced Disappearance, UNGA Res 47/133 'Declaration on the Protection of All Persons from Enforced Disappearances' (18 Dec 1992) UN Doc A/47/49

'Declaration on the Protection of All Persons from Enforced Disappearances' (18 Dec 1992) UN Doc A/47/49

Declaration on Religious Belief, UNGA Res 36/55 'Declaration on the Elimination of All Forms of Intolerance and of Discrimination Based on Religion or Belief' (25 Nov 1981) UN Doc A/36/684

Friendly Relations Declaration, UNGA Res 2625 (XXV) 'Declaration on Principles of International Law Concerning Friendly Relations and Cooperation among States' (24 Oct 1970) UN Doc A/8082

UDHR, 'Universal Declaration of Human Rights' UNGA Res 217-A (III) (10 Dec 1948) UN Doc A/810

UNGA Res 60/232 'Final report of the Ad Hoc Committee on a Comprehensive and Integral International Convention on the Protection and Promotion of the Rights and Dignity of Persons with Disabilities on its eighth session' (6 Dec 2006) UN Doc A/61/611

UNGA Res 47/121 'The Situation in Bosnia and Herzegovina' (7 Apr 1993) UN Doc A/ Res/47/121/Rev1

UNGA Res 95 (I) 'Affirmation of the Principles of International Law Recognized by the Charter of the Nurnberg Tribunal' (11 Dec 1946) UN Doc A/64/Add1

UNGA Res 96 (I) 'The Crime of Genocide' (11 Dec 1946) UN Doc A/BUR/50

UNGA Res 180 (II) 'Draft Convention on the Crime of Genocide' (21 Nov 1947) UN Doc A/519

UNGA Res 260-A (III) 'Prevention and Punishment of the Crime of Genocide' (9 Dec 1948) UN Doc A/810

UNGA Res 1803 (XVII) 'Permanent Sovereignty over Natural Resources' (14 Dec 1962)

UNGA Res 2131 (XX) 'Declaration on the Inadmissibility of Intervention in the Domestic Affairs of States and the Protection of Their Independence and Sovereignty' (21 Dec 1965) UN Doc A/6014

UNGA Res 3447 (XXX) 'Declaration on the Rights of Disabled Persons' (9 Dec 1975) UN Doc A/10034

UN Security Council Resolutions

UNSC Res 748 'Libyan Arab Jamahiriya' (31 Mar 1992) UN Doc S/RES/748

UNSC Res 794 'Somalia' (3 Dec 1992) UN Doc S/RES/794

UNSC Res 814 'Somalia' (26 Mar 1993) UN Doc S/RES/814

UNSC Res 1566 'Threats to international peace and security caused by terrorist acts' (8 Oct 2004) UN Doc S/RES/1566

UNSC Res 1593 'Reports of the Secretary-General on the Sudan' (31 Mar 2005) UN Doc S/RES/1593

UNSC Res 1888 'Women and peace and security' (30 Sept 2009) UN Doc S/RES/ 1888

Resolutions on International Criminal Tribunals

UNSC Res 827 'Tribunal (Former Yugoslavia)' (25 May 1993) UN Doc S/RES/827

UNSC Res 955 'Tribunal (Rwanda)' (8 Nov 1994) UN Doc S/RES/955

UNSC Res 1315 'Tribunal (Sierra Leone)' (14 Aug 2000) UN Doc S/RES/1315

UN Commission on Human Rights

UNCHR Res 1997/33 'International Guidelines on HIV/AIDS and Human Rights' (11 Apr 1997) UN Doc E/CN4/1997/150

UNCHR Res 2005/35 'Basic Principles and Guidelines on the Right to a Remedy and Reparation for Victims of Gross Violations of International Human Rights Law and Serious Violations of International Humanitarian Law' (19 Apr 2005)

UN Committee on the Elimination of Racial Discrimination

CERD General Recommendation No 8 (22 Aug 1990) UN Doc A/45/18

UN Educational, Scientific and Cultural Organization

United Nations Educational, Scientific and Cultural Organization 'International Meeting of Experts on Further Study of the Concept of the Rights of Peoples' (22 Feb 1990) UN Doc SHS-89/CONF602/7

Sixth (Legal) Committee

Official Records (6th Comm 1946), (1946) Official Records of the First Part of the First Session of the General Assembly—Sixth Committee: Legal Questions

Official Records (6th Comm 1948), (1948) Official Records of the Third Session of the General Assembly—Sixth Committee: Legal Questions

Sixth Committee Materials (By Date)

'Draft report and resolution adopted by Sub-Committee 3 relating to the crime of genocide' (6 Dec 1946) UN Doc A/C6/120

'France: Draft convention on genocide' (1 Oct 1948) UN Doc A/C6/211

'USA: Amendments to the draft convention on genocide (E/794)' (4 Oct 1948) UN Doc A/C6/214

'USSR: Amendments to the draft convention on genocide (E/794)' (4 Oct 1948) UN Doc A/C6/215/Rev1

'Draft Resolutions and draft convention on genocide proposed by the Drafting Committee' (23 Nov 1948) UN Doc A/C6/289

Sixth Committee Report, 'Genocide: Draft Convention and Report of the Economic and Social Council—Report of the Sixth Committee' (3 Dec 1948) UN Doc A/760

'Memorandum Submitted by the Kingdom of Saudi Arabia to International Organizations on Human Rights and their Implementation within its Territory' (15 Jun 1970) UN Doc 10/6/10/J6/1350

'Cairo Declaration on Human Rights in Islam' (5 Aug 1990) UN Doc A/CONF157/PC/62/Add18

'Final Report of the Commission of Experts Established Pursuant to Security Council Resolution 935' (9 Dec 1994) UN Doc S/1994/1405

'Report of the Independent Inquiry into the Actions of the United Nations During the 1994 Genocide in Rwanda' (16 Dec 1999) UN Doc S/1999/1257

Economic and Social Council

Official Records (Ec/Soc 6th Sess 1948), Economic and Social Council: Official Records, 3rd Year, 6th Session (2 Feb–11 Mar 1948)
Official Records (Ec/Soc 7th Sess 1948), Economic and Social Council Official Records, 3rd Year, 7th Session (19 Jul–28 Aug 1948)
Summary Records (Ad Hoc Comm 1948), Ad Hoc Committee on Genocide: Summary Records (5 Apr–10 May 1948) UN Docs E/AC25/SR1-SR 28

Economic and Social Council Resolutions

Ec/Soc Res 47(IV) 'Crime of Genocide' (28 Mar 1947) UN Doc E/325
Ec/Soc Res 77(V) 'Genocide' (6 Aug 1947)
Ec/Soc Res 117(VI) 'Genocide' (3 Mar 1948) UN Doc E/734

Economic and Social Council Materials (By Date)

Opinion of the Committee on the Progressive Development of International Law and Its Codification (17 Jun 1947) UN Doc E/447
Genocide Convention—Secretariat Draft, Draft [First] Convention on the Prevention and Punishment of the Crime of Genocide Prepared by the Secretariat (26 Jun 1947) UN Doc E/447 p5
Comments on the Draft Convention (26 Jun 1947) UN Doc E/447
Comments on the Draft Convention—Consultative Council of Jewish Organizations (24 Jul 1947) UN Doc E/C2/49
Comments on the Draft Convention—World Jewish Congress (8 Aug 1947) UN Doc E/C2/52
Comments on the Draft Convention—Commission of Churches on International Affairs (31 Oct 1947) UN Doc E/C2/63
Comments on the Draft Convention—World Federation of United Nations Organizations (12 Nov 1947) UN Doc E/C2/64
Prevention and Punishment of Genocide: Historical Summary (2 Nov 1946—20 Jan 1948) (26 Jan 1948) UN Doc E/621
Prevention and Punishment of Genocide—Comments by Governments on the Draft Convention Prepared by the Secretariat—Communications from Non-Governmental Organizations (30 Jan 1948) UN Doc E/623
Terms of reference given to the Council by General Assembly Resolution 180(II)—Note by the Secretary General (3 Feb 1948) UN Doc E/622
Report of the Social Committee (23 Feb 1948) UN Doc E/690
Relations Between the Convention on Genocide on the one hand and the Formulation of the Nurnberg Principles and the Preparation of a Draft Code of Offences Against Peace and Security on the Other—Note by the Secretariat (2 Apr 1948) UN Doc E/AC25/3

Basic Principles of a Convention on Genocide Submitted by the Delegation of the Union of Soviet Socialist Republics' (7 Apr 1948) UN Doc E/AC25/7
Draft articles for the Inclusion in the Convention on Genocide Proposed by the Delegation of China (16 Apr 1948) UN Doc E/AC25/9
Prevention and Punishment of Genocide—Comments by Governments on the Draft Convention Prepared by the Secretariat (19 Apr 1948) UN Doc E/623/Add2
Prevention and Punishment of Genocide—Comments by Governments on the Draft Convention Prepared by the Secretariat (19 Apr 1948) UN Doc E/623/Add3
Prevention and Punishment of Genocide—Comments by Governments on the Draft Convention Prepared by the Secretariat (19 Apr 1948) UN Doc E/623/Add4
Ad Hoc Committee Report on Genocide, Report to the Economic and Social Council on the Meetings of the Committee held at Lake Success, New York, from 5 April to 10 May 1948 (26 May 1948) UN Doc E/794
Genocide Convention—Ad Hoc Draft, Draft [Second] Convention on the Prevention and Punishment of the Crime of Genocide Prepared by the *Ad Hoc* Committee (26 May 1948) UN Doc E/794 p18
Study on Genocide, Study of the Question of the Prevention and Punishment of the Crime of Genocide (4 Jul 1978) UN Doc E/CN4/Sub2/416
Study (Second) on Genocide, Revised and Updated Report on the Question of the Prevention and Punishment of the Crime of Genocide (2 Jul 1985) UN Doc E/CN4/Sub2/1985/6

International Law Commission

Nationality and statelessness

'Draft Articles on Nationality of Stateless Persons in Relation to the Succession of States' in Report of the International Law Commission on the work of its 51st Session (3 May—23 Jul 1999) UN Doc A/54/10

Draft Code of Offences

[1954] Draft Code, Draft Code of Offences Against the Peace and Security of Mankind (1954) UN Doc A/CN4/SERA/1954d
[1996] Draft Code, Draft Code of Crimes Against the Peace and Security of Mankind: Titles and Texts of Articles on the Draft Code of Crimes Against the Peace and Security of Mankind (1996) UN Doc A/51/10
Fourth Report on the Draft Code of Offences Against the Peace and Security of Mankind (1986) UN Doc A/CN4/398

State responsibility

First Report on State Responsibility, International Law Commission 'First Report on State Responsibility' (24 Apr 1998) UN Doc A/CN4/490/Add3
Government Commentary on State Responsibility, International Law Commission 'State Responsibility—Comments and observations received from Governments' (25 Mar 1998) UN Doc A/CN4/488

International Law Commission 'The Obligation to Extradite or Prosecute (*aut dedere aut judicare*)' (2007) UN Doc A/CN4/579
International Law Commission 'Responsibility of States for Internationally Wrongful Acts: Comments and information received from governments' (2007) UN Doc A/62/63
International Law Commission 'Responsibility of States for Internationally Wrongful Acts: Compilation of decisions of international courts, tribunals, and other bodies' (2007) UN Doc A/62/62
International Law Commission 'Responsibility of States for Internationally Wrongful Acts: Compilation of decisions of international courts, tribunals, and other bodies' (2007) UN Doc A/62/62/Add1
International Law Commission 'Second Report on the Obligation to Extradite or Prosecute (*aut dedere aut judicare*)' (2007) UN Doc A/CN4/585
Report of the International Law Commission on the Work of its Fifty-Third Session (23 Apr–1 Jun & 2 Jul–10 Aug 2001) UN Doc A/56/10
Report of the International Law Commission on the Work of its Forty-Eighth Session (6 May–26 Jul 1996) UN Doc A/51/10
Third Report on the Expulsion of Aliens, International Law Commission 'Third report on the expulsion of aliens' (19 Apr 2007) UN Doc A/CN4/581

International Criminal Tribunals

Post-World War II tribunals

Berlin Protocol, Protocol Rectifying Discrepancy in Text of Charter (6 Oct 1945) in (1947) 1 IMT Proceedings 17
CC10, Control Council Law No 10 'Punishment of Persons Guilty of War Crimes Against Peace and Against Humanity' (20 Dec 1945) reprinted in (1946) 3 Official Gazette of the Control Council for Germany 50
IMT Charter, Charter of the International Military Tribunal (8 Aug 1945) in (1947) 1 IMT Proceedings 10
IMTFE Charter, Charter of the International Military Tribunal for the Far East (19 Jan 1946) (amended 26 Apr 1946) US Dep't of State Pub No 2675 in Treaties & Int'l Acts Series No 1589
London Agreement, Agreement by the Government of the United Kingdom of Great Britain and Northern Ireland, the Government of the United States of America, the Provisional Government of the French Republic and the Government of the Soviet Socialist Republics for the Prosecution and Punishment of the Major War Criminals of the European Axis (8 Aug 1945) in (1947) 1 IMT Proceedings 8
Military Government Ordinance No 7 (18 Oct 1946), as modified by Military Government Ordinance No 11 (17 Feb 1947) in Telford Taylor *Final Report to the Secretary of the Army on the Nuernberg War Crimes Trials Under Control Council Law No 10* 286–93 (1949) (WS Hein Buffalo 1997)
Motion Adopted by all Defence Counsel (19 Nov 1945) in (1947) 1 IMT Proceedings 168
Nuremberg Principles, Principles of International Law Recognized by the Charter of the Nürnberg Tribunal and in the Judgment of the Tribunal, adopted by the UN International Law Commission (2 Aug 1950) 2 YB-ILC 374

Royal Warrant 0160/2498 (14 Jun 1945) in Telford Taylor *Final Report to the Secretary of the Army on the Nuernberg War Crimes Trials Under Control Council Law No 10* 254–57 (1949) (WS Hein Buffalo 1997)

International Criminal Court

Draft Statute for an International Criminal Court (1952) UN Doc A/2136 (Annex)
Draft Statute for an International Criminal Court (1954) in 'Report of the 1953 Committee on International Criminal Jurisdiction' (1954) UN Doc A/2645
Elements of Crimes, Report of the Preparatory Commission for the International Criminal Court—Finalized Draft Text of the Elements of Crimes (6 Jul 2000) UN Doc PCNICC/2000/INF/3/Add2
ICC 2008/09 UN Report, Report of the International Criminal Court to the United Nations for 2008/09 (17 Sep 09) UN Doc A/64/356
ICC Ad Hoc Committee Report, Report of the Ad Hoc Committee on the Establishment of an International Criminal Court (6 Sep 1995) UN Doc A/50/22
ICC Preparatory Committee Report, Report of the Preparatory Committee on the Establishment of an International Criminal Court (13 Sep 1996) UN Doc A/51/22
ICC Report on Aggression, International Criminal Court—Assembly of States Parties, Report of the Informal Inter-Sessional Meeting of the Special Working Group on the Crime of Aggression, Special Working Group on the Crime of Aggression, 5th Sess, The Hague (23 Nov–1 Dec 2006) UN Doc ICC-ASP/5/SWGCA/INF1 (5 Sep 2006)
ICC Statute, Statute of the International Criminal Court (17 Jul 1998) UN Doc A/CONF183/9
Proposal Submitted by the United States of America: Draft Elements of Crimes (4 Feb 1999) UN Doc PCNICC/1999/DP4
Proposed Programme Budget for 2010 of the International Criminal Court (17 Jul 09) UN Doc ICC-ASP/8/10 (Advance Version)

International Criminal Tribunal for the Former Yugoslavia

Final Report to the Prosecutor by the Committee Established to Review the NATO Bombing Campaign Against the Federal Republic of Yugoslavia (13 Jun 2000) 39 ILM 1257
ICTY Statute, Statute of the International Tribunal for the Prosecution of Persons Responsible for Serious Violations of International Humanitarian Law in the Territory of the Former Yugoslavia Since 1991 (25 May 1993) UN Doc S/25704
Secretary General ICTY Report, Report of the Secretary General Pursuant to Paragraph 2 of Security Council Resolution 808 (3 May 1993) UN Doc S/25704
Security Council Expert Report, Final Report of the Commission of Experts Established Pursuant to Security Council Resolution 780 (27 May 1994) UN Doc A/1994/674
Security Council Expert Report (Addendum), Annexes to the Final Report of the Commission of Experts Established Pursuant to Security Council Resolution 780 (27 May 1994) UN Doc A/1994/674/Add2 (Vol I) Annexes I-V
Sixteenth Annual Report of the International Tribunal for the Former Yugoslavia (31 July 2009) UN Doc A/64/205–S/2009/394

International Criminal Tribunal for Rwanda

Fourteenth Annual Report of the International Tribunal for Rwanda (31 Jul 2009) UN Doc A/64/206–S/2009/396

ICTR Statute, Statute of the International Tribunal for the Prosecution of Persons Responsible for Genocide and Other Serious Violations of International Humanitarian Law Committed in the Territory of Rwanda and Rwandan Citizens Responsible for Genocide and Other Such Violations Committed in the Territory of Neighbouring States, Between 1 January 1994 and 31 December 1994 (8 Nov 1994) UN Doc S/RES/955 (Annex)

IPEP Report, Organization of African Unity—International Panel of Eminent Personalities: Report on the 1994 Genocide in Rwanda and Surrounding Events (7 Jul 2000) 40 ILM 141

Special Court for Sierra Leone

Sierra Leone Statute, Agreement between the United Nations and the Government of Sierra Leone on the Establishment of the Special Court for Sierra Leone (Annex) (16 Jan 2002)

Sixth Annual Report of the President of the Special Court for Sierra Leone: June 2008 to May 2009 (21 Jul 09)

Special Tribunal for Lebanon

Report of the Secretary-General Submitted Pursuant to Security Council Resolution 1757 (2007) of 30 May 2007 (4 Sep 2007) UN Doc S/2007/525

Extraordinary Chambers in the Courts of Cambodia

Report of Experts on Cambodia, Report of the Group of Experts for Cambodia established pursuant to General Assembly Resolution 52/135 (16 Mar 1999) UN Doc A/53/850

Extraordinary Chambers in the Courts of Cambodia for the Prosecution of Crimes Committed During the Period of Democratic Kampuchea (Approved) Revised Budget Estimates from 2005 to 2009 (Jul 2008)

International Criminal Law Materials (By Date)

Study on Implementing Apartheid Convention, Implementation of the International Convention on the Suppression and Punishment of the crime of Apartheid—Study on Ways and Means of Insuring the Implementation of International Instruments such as the International Convention on the Suppression and Punishment of the Crime of Apartheid, Including the International Jurisdiction Envisaged by the Convention (1981) UN Doc E/CN4/1426

'Documenting Atrocities in Darfur' Bureau of Democracy, Human Rights, and Labour and the Bureau of Intelligence and Research (9 Sep 2004) US State Dep't Pub No 11182

SC Darfur Report, Report of the International Commission of Inquiry on Darfur to the United Nations Secretary General, Pursuant to Security Council Resolution 1564 of 18 September 2004 (25 Jan 2005)

Human Rights Materials

Amnesty International 'Human rights trials and delayed justice' (29 Jul 1996) AI Index AFR 25/011/1996

Amnesty International 'International Criminal Court: The failure of states to enact effective implementing legislation' (1 Sep 2004) AI Index IOR 40/019/2004

Bahamonde v Equatorial Guinea, UN Human Rights Committee Communication No 468/1991 (10 Nov 1993) UN Doc CCPR/C/49/D/468/1991

CCPR General Comment No 5 'Derogation of Rights' (31 Jul 1981)

CCPR General Comment No 10 'Freedom of Opinion' (29 Jun 1983)

CCPR General Comment No 18 'Non-discrimination' (10 Nov 1989)

CCPR General Comment No 24 'Reservations Upon Ratification or Accession' (4 Nov 1994)

CCPR General Comment No 29 'States of Emergency' (31 Aug 2001)

Expert Report on Protecting Human Rights, Report of the Independent Expert on the Protection of Human Rights and Fundamental Freedoms While Countering Terrorism (7 Feb 2005) UN Doc E/CN4/2005/103

Prevention of Discrimination and Protection of Indigenous Peoples and Minorities: 'Working paper by Mr Rajendra Kalidas Wimala Gooneskere on the topic of discrimination based on work and descent, submitted pursuant to Sub-Commission Resolution 2000/4' (14 Jun 2001) UN Doc E/CN4/Sub2/2001/16

Yogyakarta Principles, Yogyakarta Principles on the Application of International Human Rights Law in relation to Sexual Orientation and Gender Identity (Mar 2007)

Miscellaneous Materials

'Chart showing markings for categories of prisoners—Dachau, Germany ca 1942' available at <http://www.ushmm.org/research/library/faq/details.php?topic=02> (visited 11 Jan 2010)

United Kingdom Home Secretary: Response of Her Majesty's Government Regarding the Spanish Extradition Request (9 Dec 1998)

UN Press Release *'Risk of Genocide Remains Frighteningly Real', Secretary-General Tells Human Rights Commission as He Launches New Plan to Prevent Genocide* (7 Apr 2004) UN Doc SG/SM/9197

UN Press Release *Budget Committee Takes Up Proposed 2010–2011 Financing for International Criminal Tribunals for Rwanda, Former Yugoslavia* (10 Dec 2009) UN Doc GA/AB/3936

Domestic Legislation

General Legislation

Cambodia

Constitution of Democratic Kampuchea (5 Jan 1976), reproduced in RM Jennar *The Cambodian Constitutions (1953–1993)* 81 (White Lotus Co Bangkok 1995)

France

Code Penal (France) 1997–98 (Dixième ed 1997)

Law No 64–1326 (26 Dec 1964) Journal Officiel de la République Française (29 Dec 1964)

Germany

Reich Citizenship Law: First Regulation (Germany) (14 Nov 1935)

Poland

Polish Decree on Punishment, Decree of 31 Aug 1944 Concerning the Punishment of Fascist-Hitlerite Criminals Guilty of Murder and Ill-Treatment of the Civilian Population and of Prisoners of War, and the Punishment of Traitors to the Polish Nation, as amended 16 Feb 1945 and 10 Dec 1946, reproduced in (1948) 7 LRTWC 82–91 (Annex)

United Kingdom

Extradition Act 2003

United States

Alien Tort Claims Act 1789 28 USC s 1350

Civil Rights Act 1968 18 USC ss 241–42, 245

Voting Rights Act 1965 42 USC s 1973

Domestic Legislation on Genocide

Albania

Criminal Code of the Republic of Albania, Law No 7895 (27 Jan 1995) 'Crimes Against Humanity' art 73

Argentina

Draft Code of Crimes within the Competence of the International Criminal Court pt 2 tit 1 art 13 [Genocide]

Armenia

Criminal Code of the Republic of Armenia s 13 c 33 'Crimes against peace and human security' art 393 [Genocide]

Australia

International Criminal Court (Consequential Amendments) Act (No 42) 2002 ss 268.3—268.37

Austria

Penal code (Austria) par 25 'Genocide' s 321

Azerbaijan

Criminal Code (Azerbaijan) s 7 pt 16 'Crimes against peace and security of humanity' art 103 [Genocide]

Bangladesh

Bangladesh International Crimes (Tribunals) Act (20 Jul 1973) art 3

Belarus

Belarus Criminal Code s 6 c 17 'Crimes against peace, the safety of humanity and war crimes' art 127 [Genocide]

Belgium

Law relating to the repression of the serious violations of humanitarian international law (10 Feb 1999) art 3(1)

Bolivia

Penal Code (Bolivia) Law No 1768 Title 1 Ch 4 art 138

Bosnia-Herzegovina

Criminal Code of Bosnia and Herzegovina 'Official Gazette' of Bosnia and Herzegovina No. 3/03 (22 Nov 2003) 'Genocide' art 171

Brazil

Draft [ICC] legislation presented to the Minister of Justice of Brazil (Oct 2002) c 2 arts 18–21 [Genocide]

Burkina Faso

Penal Code (Burkina Faso) c 2 art 313 [Genocide]

Cambodia

Decree Law No 1 (15 Jul 1979)

Cambodian Genocide Law, Law on the Establishment of the Extraordinary Chambers in the Courts of Cambodia for the Prosecution of Crimes Committed During the Period of Democratic Kampuchea with Inclusion of Amendments as Promulgated on 27 Oct 2004 (10 Aug 2001) No NS/RKM/0801/12

Loi sur la création des chambres extraordinaires, avec inclusion d'amendements, promulguée le 27 octobre 2004 (NS/RKM/1004/006) [French Text—Law on the Establishment of the Extraordinary Chambers in the Courts of Cambodia for the Prosecution of Crimes Committed During the Period of Democratic Kampuchea]

Canada

Crimes Against Humanity and War Crimes Act Offences Within Canada SC 2000 c 24 s 4

Crimes Against Humanity and War Crimes Act Offences Within Outside SC 2000 c 24 s 6

China

Translation of the Convention for the Prevention and Punishment of the Crime of Genocide into simplified (jaintizi) Chinese, Published in the 'People's Republic of China State Gazette' upon ratification and accession in April 1983

Columbia

Penal Code of Columbia (2000 LAW 599) (Jul 24) art 101 [Genocide]

Congo (Democratic Republic)

Law No 8—98 (31 Oct 1998) c 1 art 1 [Genocide]

Costa Rica

Penal Code of Costa Rica (14 Apr 1998) art 127

Côte d'Ivoire

Penal Code (Côte d'Ivoire) c 1 s 1 title 1 art 137

Croatia

Croatian Penal Code c 13 'Criminal Acts against Values Protected by International Law' art 156

Cuba

Law No 62 Penal Code (Cuba), as modified by Law No 87 bk 1 c 3 s 6 art 116(1)

Czech Republic

Criminal Code (Czech Republic) c 20 s 259 [Genocide] CERD/C/289/Add1 ¶29

Denmark

Act No 132 of 29 of April 1955 Concerning the Punishment of Genocide

Ecuador

Penal Code (Ecuador): Law on Crimes Against Humanity art 19

El Salvador

Penal Code of the Republic of El Salvador (Decree No 1030) title 19 art 361 [Genocide]

Estonia

Estonian Penal Code (9 Nov 1994) s 61
Estonian Criminal Code (2001) art 611(1)

Ethiopia

Penal Code of the Empire of Ethiopia of 1957 art 281 (Negarit Gazeta, Extraordinary Issue No 1 of 1957)

Fiji

Penal Code (Fiji) 1945 pt 2 div I 'Offences against Public Order' c 8 s 69 [Genocide]

Finland

The Penal Code of Finland No 39/1889 c 11 s 6, as affirmed in the Act on the Implementation of the Legislative Provisions of the Rome Statute of the International Criminal Court and on the Application of the Statute (28 Dec 2000) No 1285/2000

France

Code Penal (France) art 211–1 as affirmed by Law No 2002–268 of 26 Feb 2002 on co-operation with the International Criminal Court

Georgia

Georgian Criminal Code s 14 c 47 'Crimes against peace and security of the mankind and international humanitarian law' art 407 [Genocide]

Germany

Jorgic (AC) [1999], Prosecutor v Jorgic, Judgment (20 Apr 1999) 2 BvR 1290/99, 3 StR 215/98F (Fed Const Ct Germany)

Völkerstrafgesetzbuch [VStGB] [Code of Crimes Against International Law] BGBl 2002 I at 2254 (30 Jun) art 1 pt 2 c 1 s 6(1)

Ghana

Ghana: Criminal Code (Amendment) Act 1993 s 1 [Genocide]

Guatemala

Penal Code (Guatemala) art 376

Hungary

Criminal Code 1978 (Hungary) c 11 'Crimes Against Humanity' title 1 s 155 [Genocide]

Iraq

The Statute of the Iraqi Special Tribunal (10 Dec 2003) art 11

Ireland

International Criminal Court Bill 2003 (No. 36 of 2003) pt 2 s 6(1)

Israel

Crime of Genocide (Prevention and Punishment) Law No 5710–1950 art 1 (29 Mar 1950)

Nazi and Nazi Collaborators (Punishment) Law No 5710 (29 Mar 1950)

Italy

Law No 962 of 9 Oct 1967 on the Prevention and Punishment of the Crime of Genocide

Kyrgyzstan

Criminal Code (Kyrgyzstan) s 12 c 34 'Crimes against Peace and Security of Mankind' art 373 [Genocide]

Liechtenstein

Penal code (StGB) (Liechtenstein) (24 Jun 1987) c 25 s 321

Lithuania

Criminal Code of the Republic of Lithuania art 71

Luxembourg

Law of 8 August 1985 on the Repression of Genocide

Mali

Penal Code (2001) bk 3 tit 1 c 2 art 30 [Genocide]

Malta

International Criminal Court Act (13 Dec 2003) sch 1 art 6

Mexico

Federal Penal Code 1931 bk 2 title 3 c 2 art 149-bis [Genocide]

Moldova

Criminal Code of the Republic of Moldova c 1 'Crimes against Peace, Security of humanity and War crimes' art 135 [Genocide]

Netherlands

International Crimes Act (9 Jun 2003) pt 2 s 3(1)

New Zealand

New Zealand: International Crimes and International Criminal Court Act 2000 (No 26 2000, Amendment No 67 2002) pt 2 s 9(2)

Nicaragua

Penal Code (Nicaragua) bk 2 title 14 art 549 [Genocide]

Panama

Penal Code (Panama) title 9 c 3 art 311 'Crimes against the international community'

Paraguay

Penal Code (Paraguay) bk 2 title 9 art 308 art 319 [Genocide]

Peru

Law No. 26926 (19 Feb 1998) title14 c 1 [Genocide] art 319

Poland Penal Code, Law of 6 June 1997 c 16 'Offences Against Peace, Humanity and War Crimes' art 118 [Genocide]

Portugal

Penal Code of 1982 (Portugal) art 189

Penal Code (Portugal) tit 3 c 2 art 239 [Crimes against peace and humanity—Genocide

Law No 31/2004 (22 Jul 2004) Republic Daily I Ser A art 218

Romania

Romanian Socialist Republic Penal Code (1976 Special Part) title 9 art 356

Russian Federation

Criminal Code s 12 c 34 'Crimes against the peace and security of mankind' art 357 [Genocide]

Rwanda

Organic Law No 8/96 of 30 August 1996 on the Organization of Prosecutions for Offences Constituting the Crime of Genocide or Crimes Against Humanity Committed since 1 October 1990, Official Gazette of the Republic of Rwanda, Year 35 No 17 (1 Sep 1996) arts 1(a) and 2

Scotland

International Criminal Court (Scotland) Act 2001 (2001 asp 13) sch 1

Slovenia

Penal Code 1994 (Slovenia) c 35 art 373

South Africa

Law No 27 of 2002: Implementation of the Rome Statute of the International Criminal Court Act 2002 (12 Jul 2002) sch 1 pt 1 [Genocide]

Spain

Penal Code (Spain) Law No 10/1995 (23 Nov), as modified by Law No 15/2003 (25 Nov) art 607

Sweden

Swedish Penal Code: Law 169 (20 Mar 1963) 'Act relating to the punishment of genocide' s 1

Switzerland

Penal Code (Switzerland) bk 2 c 12(a) 'Offences against the interests of the international community' art 264 [Genocide]

Tajikistan

Penal Code (Tajikistan) s1 c1 art 398 'Genocide'

Trinidad and Tobago

Genocide Act 1977 s 2

Uganda

International Criminal Court Bill (19 Apr 2004) art 7(2) and sch 1 art 6

United Kingdom

International Criminal Court Act 2001 c 17 ss 50–52, 58–59 sch 8 ¶1 art 6

United States

Affirmation of the US Record on the Armenian Genocide Resolution (10 Oct 2007) HR Res 106

Genocide Accountability Act of 2007 (21 Dec 2007) Pub Law No 110–151 s 2

Child Soldiers Accountability Act (2008) 18 USC s 2442

Genocide Convention Implementation (Proxmire) Act (1988) 18 USC ss 1091–1093

Uruguay

Implementation of the Rome Statute of the International Criminal Court 2003 (17 Jan 2003) Art II.2.B

Venezuela

Legislative Proposal on the Implementation of the Rome Statute of the International Criminal Court (25 Jul 2002) art 5(1)(a) and n 26

Cases

Abbreviations

ECJ European Court of Justice
ICC International Criminal Court

ICJ	International Court of Justice
ICTR	Ad hoc International Criminal Tribunal for Rwanda
ICTY	Ad hoc International Criminal Tribunal for the Former Yugoslavia
ILR	International Law Reports
IMT	International Military Tribunal—Trial of the Major War Criminals Before the International Military Tribunal, 14 Nov 1945–1 Oct 1946 (William S Hein & Co1995) (1946)
IMTFE	International Military Tribunal for the Far East
LRTWC	Law Reports of Trials of War Criminals Compiled by the United Nations War Crimes Commission (WS Hein & Co Buffalo 1997) (UN War Crimes Comm 1947–1949)
SC-SL	Special Court for Sierra Leone
TWC	Trials of War Criminals Before the Nuernberg Military Tribunals Under Control Council Law No 10 (US Gov't Printing Office Washington DC 1949–53)
USMT	United States Military Tribunal

European Court of Justice

Yassin Abdullah Kadi v Council of the European Union and Commission of the European Communities (2005) Case No T-315/01 (Eur Ct Justice)

International Criminal Court

Al Bashir (Arrest Warrant—AC), Prosecutor v Omar Hassan Ahmad Al Bashir, Judgment on the appeal of the Prosecutor against the 'Decision on the Prosecution's Application for a Warrant of Arrest against Omar Hassan Ahmad Al Bashir' (3 Feb 2010) Case No ICC-02/05-01/09-OA

Al Bashir (Arrest Warrant—TC), Prosecutor v Omar Hassan Ahmad Al Bashir, Decision on the Prosecution's Application for a Warrant of Arrest against Omar Hassan Ahmad Al Bashir (4 Mar 2009) Case No ICC-02/05–01/09

Al Bashir (Leave to Appeal—TC), Prosecutor v Omar Hassan Ahmad Al Bashir, Decision on the Prosecutor's Application for Leave to Appeal the 'Decision on the Prosecution's Application for a Warrant of Arrest Against Omar Hassan Ahmad Al Bashir' (24 Jun 2009) Case No ICC-02/05–01/09

Al Bashir—Request for Arrest Warrant, Prosecutor v Omar Hassan Ahmad Al Bashir, Prosecutor's Application for Warrant of Arrest under Article 58 Against Omar Hassan Ahmad Al Bashir (14 Jul 2008) Case No ICC-02/05–01/09

Bemba (Confirmation of Charges—TC), Prosecutor v Jean-Pierre Bemba Gombo, Decision Pursuant to Article 61(7)(a) and (b) of the Rome Statute on the Charges of the Prosecutor Against Jean-Pierre Bemba Gombo (15 Jun 09) Case No ICC-01/05–01/08

Lubanga (Confirmation of Charges—TC), Prosecutor v Thomas Lubanga Dyilo, Decision on the Confirmation of Charges (29 Jan 07) Case No ICC-01/04–01/06

Katanga & Ngudjolo (Confirmation of Charges—TC), Prosecutor v Germain Katanga and Mathieu Ngudjolo Chui, Decision on the Confirmation of Charges (30 Sept 08) Case No ICC-01/04–01/07

International Court of Justice

Application of Genocide Convention—Counter Claims, Application of the Convention on the Prevention and Punishment of the Crime of Genocide (B&H v Yugo (Serb & Mont)) [1997] ICJ 243 (17 Dec) (Counter-Claims)

Application of Genocide Convention—Judgment, Application of the Convention on the Prevention and Punishment of the Crime of Genocide (B&H v Yugo (Serb & Mont)) [2007] ICJ 1 (26 Feb) (Merits)

Application of Genocide Convention—Jurisdiction, Application of the Convention on the Prevention and Punishment of the Crime of Genocide (B&H v Yugo (Serb & Mont)) [1996] ICJ 595 (11 Jul) (Jurisdiction)

Application of Genocide Convention—Merits, Application of the Convention on the Prevention and Punishment of the Crime of Genocide (B&H v Yugo (Serb & Mont)) [2007] ICJ 1 (26 Feb) (Merits)

Application of Genocide Convention—Prov Measures I, Application of the Convention on the Prevention and Punishment of the Crime of Genocide (B&H v Yugo (Serb & Mont)) [1993] ICJ 3 (8 Apr) (Prov measures)

Application of Genocide Convention—Prov Measures II, Application of the Convention on the Prevention and Punishment of the Crime of Genocide (B&H v Yugo (Serb & Mont)) [1993] ICJ 325 (13 Sept) (Prov measures)

Arrest Warrant, Arrest Warrant of 11 April 2000 (Congo v Belg) [2002] ICJ 121 (14 Feb) (Merits)

Asylum, Asylum Case (Colum v Peru) [1950] ICJ 266 (20 Nov) (Merits)

Avena—Further Proceedings, Request for Interpretation of the Judgment of 31 March 2004 in the Case Concerning Avena and Other Mexican Nationals (Mex v US) [2009] ICJ 1 (19 Jan) (Merits)

Barcelona Traction, Barcelona Traction (Belg v Sp) [1970] ICJ 3 (5 Feb) (Second Phase)

Corfu Channel, Corfu Channel Case (UK v Alb) [1949] ICJ 4 (9 Apr) (Merits)

Fisheries Jurisdiction, Fisheries Jurisdiction Case (UK v Ice) [1974] ICJ 3 (25 Jul) (Merits)

Legality of Force—Provisional Measures, Legality of the Use of Force (Yugo v Belg, Can, Fr, Ger, Italy, Neth, Port, Sp, UK and USA) [1999] ICJ 1 (2 Jun) (Prov Measures)

Lockerbie, Case Concerning Questions of Interpretation and Application of the 1971 Montreal Convention Arising from the Aerial Incident at Lockerbie (Lib v UK) [1992] ICJ 3 (14 Apr) (Prov Measures)

Namibia, Legal Consequences for States of the Continued Presence of South Africa in Namibia notwithstanding Security Council Resolution 276 [1971] ICJ 16 (Advisory Opinion)

Nicaragua, Military and Paramilitary Activities in and Against Nicaragua (Nic v US) [1986] ICJ 14 (27 Jun) (Merits)

North Sea Continental Shelf (Ger v Den and Neth) [1969] ICJ 3 (20 Feb) (Merits)

Nottebohm (Licht v Guat) [1955] ICJ 4 (6 Apr) (Second Phase)

Nuclear Weapons, Legality of the Threat or Use of Nuclear Weapons [1996] ICJ 227 (8 Jul) (Advisory Opinion)

Pakistani POWs, Trial of Pakistani Prisoners of War (Pak v Ind) [1973] ICJ 1 (13 Jul) (Prov Measures)

Reparations, Reparation for Injuries Suffered in the Service of the United Nations [1949] ICJ 174 (11 Apr) (Advisory Opinion)

Reservations, Reservations to the Convention on the Prevention and Punishment of Genocide [1951] ICJ 15 (28 May) (Advisory Opinion)
SW Africa, South West Africa Cases (Eth and Lib v SA) [1966] ICJ 1 (18 Jul) (2nd Phase—Judgment)
Voting Procedure, Voting Procedure on Questions Relating to Reports and Petitions Concerning the Territory of South-West Africa [1955] ICJ 67 (7 Jun) (Advisory Opinion)
Western Sahara [1975] ICJ 12 (16 Oct) (Advisory Opinion)

Permanent Court of International Justice

Lotus, Case of the SS 'Lotus' (Fr v Turk) [1927] PCIJ Ser A No 10 (7 Sep) 3
Mavrommatis Palestine Concessions (Greece v Gr Brit) [1924] PCIJ Ser A No 2 (30 Aug) 5
Minorities in Upper Silesia, Rights of Minorities in Upper Silesia (Minority Schools) (Ger v Pol) [1928] PCIJ Ser A No 15 (26 Apr) 5

International Criminal Tribunal for the Former Yugoslavia

Babic (Sentencing—TC), Prosecutor v Babic, Sentencing Judgment (29 Jun 2004) Case No ICTY-03–72-S
Banovic (TC), Prosecutor v Banovic, Judgment (28 Oct 2003) Case No ICTY-02–65/1-S
Blagojevic (TC), Prosecutor v Blagojevic and Jokic, Judgment (17 Jan 2005) Case No ICTY-02–60-T
Blaskic (TC), Prosecutor v Blaskic, Judgment (3 Mar 2000) Case No ICTY-95–14-T
Brdjanin (TC), Prosecutor v Brdjanin, Judgment (1 Sep 2004) Case No ICTY-99–36-T
Celebici (AC), Prosecutor v Delalic, Appeal Judgment (20 Feb 2001) Case No ICTY-96–21-A
Celebici (TC), Prosecutor v Delalic, Judgment (16 Nov 1998) Case No ICTY-96–21-T
Deronjic (Sentencing—TC), Prosecutor v Deronjic, Sentencing Judgment (30 Mar 2004) Case No ICTY-02–61-S
Erdemovic (AC), Prosecutor v Erdemovic, Appeal Judgment (7 Oct 1997) Case No ICTY-96–22-A
Furundzija (TC), Prosecutor v Furundzija, Judgment (10 Dec 1998) Case No ICTY-95–17/1-T
Galic (TC), Prosecutor v Galic, Judgment (5 Dec 2003) Case No ICTY-98–29-T
Hadzihasanovic (Interlocutory Appeal—AC), Prosecutor v Hadzihasanovic, Decision on Interlocutory Appeal Challenging Jurisdiction in Relation to Command Responsibility (16 Jul 2003) Case No ICTY-01–47-AR72
Jelisic (AC), Prosecutor v Jelisic, Appeal Judgment (5 Jul 2001) Case No ICTY-95–10
Jelisic (TC), Prosecutor v Jelisic, Judgment (14 Dec 1999) Case No ICTY-95–10-T
Karadzic and Mladic—Rule 61, Prosecutor v Karadzic and Mladic, Confirmation of Indictment Pursuant to Rule 61 (11 Jul 1996) Case Nos ICTY-95–5-T and ICTY-95–18-T
Kordic & Cerkez (AC), Prosecutor v Kordic & Cerkez, Appeal Judgment (17 Dec 2004) Case No ICTY-95–14/2-A
Kordic & Cerkez (TC), Prosecutor v Kordic & Cerkez, Judgment (21 Feb 2001) Case No ICTY-95–14/2-T

Krnojelac (AC), Prosecutor v Krnojelac, Appeal Judgment (17 Sept 2003) Case No ICTY-97–25-A
Krnojelac (TC), Prosecutor v Krnojelac, Judgment (15 Mar 2002) Case No ICTY-97–25-T
Krstic (AC), Prosecutor v Krstic, Appeal Judgment (19 Apr 2004) Case No ICTY-98–33-A
Krstic (TC), Prosecutor v Krstic, Judgment (2 Aug 2001) Case No ICTY-98–33-T
Kunarac (AC), Prosecutor v Kunarac, Appeal Judgment (12 Jun 2002) Case Nos ICTY-96–23-A and 96–23-23/1-A
Kunarac (TC), Prosecutor v Kunarac, Judgment (22 Feb 2001) Case Nos ICTY-96–23-T and 96–23-23/1-T
Kupreskic (AC), Prosecutor v Kupreskic, Appeal Judgment (23 Oct 2001) Case No ICTY-95–16-A
Kupreskic (TC), Prosecutor v Kupreskic, Judgment (14 Jan 2000) Case No ICTY-95–16-T
Kvocka (AC), Prosecutor v Kvocka, Appeal Judgment (28 Feb 2005) Case No ICTY-98–30-30/1-A
Kvocka (TC), Prosecutor v Kvocka, Judgment (2 Nov 2001) Case No ICTY-98–30-30/1-T
Milosevic (Motion to Acquit—TC), Prosecutor v Milosevic, Decision on Motion for Judgment of Acquittal (16 Jun 2004) Case No ICTY-02–54-T
Naletilic (AC), Prosecutor v Naletilic, Judgment (5 Mar 2006) Case No ICTY-98–34-T
Naletilic (TC), Prosecutor v Naletilic, Judgment (31 Mar 2003) Case No ICTY-98–34-T
Obrenovic (TC), Prosecutor v Obrenovic, Sentencing Judgment (10 Dec 2003) Case No ICTY-02–60/2-S
Sikirica (TC), Prosecutor v Sikirica, Judgment on Defence Motions to Acquit (3 Sep 2001) Case No ICTY-95–8
Simic (TC), Prosecutor v Simic, Judgment (17 Oct 2003) Case No ICTY-95–9-T
Stakic (AC), Prosecutor v Stakic, Judgment (22 Mar 2006) Case No ICTY-97–24-A
Stakic (TC), Prosecutor v Stakic, Judgment (31 Jul 2003) Case No ICTY-97–24-T
Tadic (Indictment—TC), Prosecutor v Tadic, Decision on Defence Motion on the Form of the Indictment (14 Nov 1995) Case No ICTY-94–1-T
Tadic (Jurisdiction—AC), Prosecutor v Tadic, Decision on Defence Motion for Interlocutory Appeal on Jurisdiction (5 Oct 1995) Case No ICTY-94–1-A
Tadic (Merits—AC), Prosecutor v Tadic, Appeal Judgment (15 Jul 1999) Case No ICTY-94–1-A
Tadic (Merits—TC), Prosecutor v Tadic, Judgment (7 May 1997) Case No ICTY-94–1-T
Tadic (Protective Measures—TC), Prosecutor v Tadic, Decision on the Prosecutor's Motion Requesting Protective Measures for Victims and Witnesses (10 Aug 1995) Case No ICTY-94–1-T
Tadic (Sentencing—AC), Prosecutor v Tadic, Judgment in Sentencing Appeals (26 Jan 2000) Case No ICTY-94–1-A
Vasiljevic (AC), Prosecutor v Vasiljevic, Appeal Judgment (25 Feb 2004) Case No ICTY-98–32-A
Vasiljevic (TC), Prosecutor v Vasiljevic, Judgment (29 Nov 2002) Case No ICTY-98–32-T

International Criminal Tribunal for Rwanda

Akayesu (AC), Prosecutor v Akayesu, Appeal Judgment (1 Jun 2001) Case No ICTR-96–4-A

Akayesu (TC), Prosecutor v Akayesu, Judgment (2 Sep 1998) Case No ICTR-96–4-T

Bagilishema (AC), Prosecutor v Bagilishema, Appeal Judgment (3 Jul 2002) Case No ICTR-95–1A-A

Bagilishema (TC), Prosecutor v Bagilishema, Judgment (7 Jun 2001) Case No ICTR-95–1A-T

Kajelijeli (AC), Prosecutor v Kajelijeli, Appeal Judgment (23 May 2005) Case No ICTR-98–44A-A

Kajelijeli (TC), Prosecutor v Kajelijeli, Judgment and Sentence (1 Dec 2003) Case No ICTR-98–44A-T

Kambanda (TC), Prosecutor v Kambanda, Judgment and Sentence (4 Sep 1998) Case No ICTR-97–23-S

Kamuhanda (AC), Prosecutor v Kamuhanda, Judgment (19 Sep 2005) Case No ICTR-9 5–54A-A

Kamuhanda (TC), Prosecutor v Kamuhanda, Judgment (22 Jan 2004) Case No ICTR-9 5–54A-T

Kayishema (AC), Prosecutor v Kayishema and Ruzindana, Appeal Judgment (1 Jun 2001) Case No ICTR-95–1-A

Kayishema (TC), Prosecutor v Kayishema and Ruzindana, Judgment (21 May 1999) Case No ICTR-95–1-T

Musema (AC), Prosecutor v Musema, Appeal Judgment (16 Nov 2001) Case No ICTR-96–13-A

Musema (TC), Prosecutor v Musema, Judgment (27 Jan 2000) Case No ICTR-96–13-T

Nahimana (TC), Prosecutor v Nahimana, Barayagwiza and Ngeze, Judgment and Sentence (3 Dec 2003) Case No ICTR-99–52-T

Ndindabahizi (TC), Prosecutor v Ndindabahizi, Judgment and Sentence (15 Jul 2004) Case No ICTR-2001–71-I

Ntakirutimana (AC), Prosecutor v Elizaphan and Gérard Ntakirutimana, Appeal Judgment (13 Dec 2004) Cases Nos ICTR-96–10-A and ICTR-96–17-A

Ruggiu (TC), Prosecutor v Ruggiu, Judgment and Sentence (1 Jun 2000) Case No ICTR-97–32-I

Rutaganda (TC), Prosecutor v Rutaganda, Judgment (6 Dec 1999) Case No ICTR-96–3-T

Semanza (TC), Prosecutor v Semanza, Judgment and Sentence (15 May 2003) Case No ICTR-97–20-T

Special Court for Sierra Leone

Kondewa (Amnesty—AC), Prosecutor v Kondewa, Appeals Chamber Decision on lack of Jurisdiction/Abuse of Process: Amnesty Provided by the Lome Accord (25 May 2004) Case No SCSL-2004–14AR72(E)

Norman (Judicial Independence—AC), Prosecutor v Norman, Appeals Chamber Decision on Preliminary Motion Based on lack of Jurisdiction (Judicial Independence) (13 Mar 2004) Case No SCSL-2004–14-AR72(E)

International Military Tribunal at Nuremberg

IMT Indictment, Prosecutor v Hermann Göring—Indictment (1945) 1 IMT Proceedings 27 (International Military Tribunal at Nuremberg)

IMT Proceedings, Prosecutor v Hermann Göring—Legal Proceedings (14 Nov 1945—1 Oct 1946) Vols 1–22 Trial of the Major War Criminals Before the International Military Tribunal, 14 Nov 1945—1 Oct 1946 (William S Hein & Co 1995) (International Military Tribunal at Nuremberg)

Göring [IMT 1946], Prosecutor v Hermann Göring—Judgment and Sentence (1 Oct 1946) 1 IMT Proceedings 171 (International Military Tribunal at Nuremberg)

International Military Tribunal for the Far East (Tokyo)

Araki [IMTFE 1946], United States v Araki—Judgment and Sentence (4–12 Nov 1948) 101–03 IMTFE Proceedings 48413—48858 (International Military Tribunal at Tokyo)

IMTFE Proceedings, Prosecutor v Araki—Legal Proceedings (29 Apr 1946—12 Nov 1948) Vols 1–124 RJ Pritchard (ed) *The Tokyo War Crimes Trial—Records of the International Military Tribunal for the Far East* (Edwin Meller Press Wales 1998) (International Military Tribunal at Tokyo)

US military trials under Control Council Law No 10

Concentration Camp [USMT 1947], Prosecutor v Pohl (1947) 5 TWC 195 (US Military Tribunal at Nuremberg—Case No 4)

Einsatzgruppen [USMT 1948], Prosecutor v Ohlendorf (1948) 4 TWC 1 (US Military Tribunal at Nuremberg—Case No 9)

Flick [USMT 1947], Prosecutor v Flick (1947) 6 TWC 3 (US Military Tribunal at Nuremberg—Case No 5)

High Command [USMT 1948], Prosecutor v von Leeb (1948) 10–11 TWC 3 (US Military Tribunal at Nuremberg—Case No 12)

Hostages [USMT 1948], Prosecutor v List (1948) 11 TWC 759 (US Military Tribunal at Nuremberg—Case No 7)

IG Farben [USMT 1948], Prosecutor v Krauch (1948) 7 TWC 1 (US Military Tribunal at Nuremberg—Case No 6)

Justice [USMT 1947], Prosecutor v Alstötter (1947) 3 TWC 1 (US Military Tribunal at Nuremberg—Case No 3)

Krupp [USMT 1948], Prosecutor v Krupp (1948) 9 TWC 1 (US Military Tribunal at Nuremberg—Case No 10)

Medical [USMT 1947], Prosecutor v Brandt (1947) 1 TWC 1 (US Military Tribunal at Nuremberg—Case No 1)

Milch [USMT 1947], Prosecutor v Milch (1947) 2 TWC 773 (US Military Tribunal at Nuremberg—Case No 2)

Ministries [USMT 1949], Prosecutor v von Weizsaecker (1949) 12 TWC 3 (US Military Tribunal at Nuremberg—Case No 11)

RuSHA [USMT 1948], Prosecutor v Greifelt (1948) 4 TWC 599 (US Military Tribunal at Nuremberg—Case No 8)

Iran-US Claims Tribunal

Islamic Rep of Iran v United States of America Case No A/18 (6 Apr 1984) Decision No DEC 32-A18-FT (Iran/United States Claim Tribunal)

Italy-US Claims Tribunal

Flegenheimer Claim (Ital v US) (20 Sep 1958) 25 ILR 91 (Italy/US Conciliation Commission)

European Court of Human Rights

Ireland v United Kingdom (1 Oct 1972) ECHR Case No A/5310/71
Soering v United Kingdom (7 Jul 1989) ECHR Ser A No 161

Inter-American Court of Human Rights

Barrios Altos (IACHR 2001), *Barrios Altos Case (Chumbipuma Aguirre v Peru)* (14 Mar 2001) Judgment [2001] IACHR 5
Diaz (IACHR 1997), *Diaz v Columbia* (No 11.227) Report No 5/97 (Admissibility) OEA/SerL/V/II95 Doc 7 rev (1997)
Velásquez Rodríguez (IACHR 1988), *Velásquez Rodríguez Case* (29 Jul 1988) Judgment [1988] IACHR 1

United Nations Human Rights Committee

Bahamonde v Equatorial Guinea (UNHRC 1993), *Oló Bahamonde v Equatorial Guinea* (468/1991) (10 Nov 1993) UN Doc CCPR/C/49/D/468/1991
Lovelace v Canada (UNHRC 1981), *Lovelace v Canada* (R 6/24) (30 Jul 1981) UN Doc A/36/40 p166

Australia

Kruger v Australia (1997) 126 ALR 126 (High Ct Austr)
Nulyarimma v Thompson (1999) 165 ALR 621 (High Ct Austr)

Cambodia

Verdict of the Phnom Penh Revolutionary Tribunal, (Aug 1979) *Verdict of the People's Revolutionary Tribunal Held in Phnom Penh for the Trial of the Genocide Crime of*

Pol Pot—Ieng Sary Clique (on file with author) (courtesy of Cambodian Genocide Project—Yale University)

Canada

Regina v Finta [1994] 1 SCR 701 (Can Sup Ct)
Ward v Canada [1993] 2 SCR 689 (Can Sup Ct)

Estonia

Paulov Judgment, Prosecutor v Paulov, Cassation Judgment (21 Mar 2000) Case No 3–1-1–31-00, Official Gazette Riigi Teataja—RT pt III (Sup Ct Estonia), excerpted in Oxford Reports on International Law ILDC 198 (EE 2000)

Ethiopia

Mengistu Judgment, Special Prosecutor v Col Mengistu Haile Mariam and 173 Others, Final Judgment (Merits) (11 Jan 2007) Criminal File No 1/87 [Unreported Decision] (Fed High Ct Ethiopia), excerpted in Oxford Reports on International Law ILDC 555 (ET 1995)

France

Fédération Nationale des Déportés et Internés Résistants et Patriotes and Others v Barbie (20 Dec 1985) 78 ILR 125 (Court de Cassation (Criminal Chamber))
Prosecutor v Munyeshyaka (6 Jan 1998) No X 96–82.491 Pf Nr Y 96–82-491 (Court de Cassation (Criminal Chamber)), excerpted in (1999) 1 YB-IHRL 598
Prosecutor v Touvier (13 Apr 1992) 100 ILR 338 (Court de Cassation (Criminal Chamber))

Germany

Jorgic (AC) [Ger Fed Const Ct 1999], Prosecutor v Jorgic (20 Apr 1999) 2 BvR 1290/99, 3 StR 215/98F (Germany—Fed Const Ct)
Jorgic (TC) [Ger Dist Ct 1997], Prosecutor v Jorgic (26 Sept 1997) 2 StE 8/96, IV-26/96 (Germany—Dist Ct Dusseldorf)

Israel

Eichmann (AC) [Isr Sup Ct 1961], Attorney General of Israel v Eichmann (1961) 36 ILR 277 (Isr Sup Ct)
Eichmann (TC) [Isr Dist Ct 1961], Attorney General of Israel v Eichmann (1961) 36 ILR 5 (Isr Dist Ct)
Enigster [Isr Dist Ct 1952], Attorney-General of Israel v Enigster (1952) 18 ILR 541 (Isr Dist Ct)
Israel v John (Ivan) Demjanjuk (29 Jul 1993) Crim App No 347/88 (Isr Sup Ct)

Japan

X v Japan (5 Oct 1994) in (1996) 6 Asian YBIL 221 (Japan—Fukui Dist Ct)

Mexico

Decision on the Extradition of RM Cavallo (10 Jun 2003) No 140/2002 in (2003) 42 ILM 884 (Sup Ct Mexico)

Netherlands

Mothers of Srebrenica, Mothers of Srebrenica v The State of the Netherlands, Rechtbank's-Gravenhage (10 Jun 2008) Case No 295247/HA-ZA-07–2973 (Hague Dist Ct Netherlands)

Philippines

Wright v CA (15 Aug 1994) GR No 113213 (Philippines) 235 SCRA 341 in (1995) 5 Asian YBIL 265

Poland

Goeth [Pol Sup Nat'l Trib 1947], Poland v Haupsturmfuhrer Amon Goeth (1948) 7 LRTWC 1 (Supreme National Tribunal—Poland)

Greiser [Pol Sup Nat'l Trib 1946], Poland v Gauleiter Artur Greiser, Poland v Haupsturmfuhrer Amon Goeth (1949) 13 LRTWC 70 (Supreme National Tribunal—Poland)

Hoess [Pol Sup Nat'l Trib 1947], Poland v Obersturmbannfuhrer Rudolf Hoess (1948) 7 LRTWC 11 (Supreme National Tribunal—Poland)

Spain

Pinochet: Spanish Jurisdiction [Audencia Nacional 1998], Order Affirming Spain's Jurisdiction to Take Cognizance of the Crimes of Genocide and Terrorism Committed During the Chilean Dictatorship (5 Nov 1998) Appeal No 173/98 Crim Inv No 1/98 (*Audiencia Nacional* Crim Ch 1st sec) (en banc) reprinted in R Brody and M Ratner (eds) *The Pinochet Papers—The Case of Augusto Pinochet in Spain and Britain* 95 (Kluwer London 2000) (unofficial translation—original available in original language at <http://www.derechos.org/nizkor/arg/espana/audi.html>) (visited 11 Jan 2010)

Scilingo [2005], *Prosecutor v Adolfo Scilingo, Sentence for Crimes Against Humanity in the Case of Adolfo Scilingo* (19 Apr 05) (Sup Ct Spain) (unofficial translation by author)

United Kingdom

Adomako [1995] 1 AC 171 (HL)

Attorney General's Reference (No 3 of 1994) [1998] AC 245 (HL)
Blaue [1975] 3 All ER 446 (CA)
Clarkson [1971] 3 All ER 344 (CMAC)
Cunningham [1957] 2 QB 396 (CA)
Ex Parte Pinochet (Pinochet III) [1999] 2 WLR 827 (HL)
Hipperson [1996] CLY 1445 (QB)
Powell and Daniels [1998] 1 Cr App R 261 (HL)
Rex v Sussex Justices, Ex parte McCarthy [1923] All ER 233, [1924] 1 KB 256 (UK-KB)
Satnam and Kewal (1983) 78 Cr App R 149 (CA)
Siracusa (1990) 90 Cr App R 340 (CA)
Woollin [1999] 1 AC 82 (HL)

United States

Albernaz v United States (1981) 450 US 333 (US Sup Ct)
Amanfi v Ashcroft (2003) 328 F3d 719 (US Ct App (3rd Cir))
Beanal v Freeport-McMoran (1999) 197 F3d 161 (US Ct App (5th Cir))
Blockberger v United States (1932) 284 US 299 (US Sup Ct)
Brounstein v American Cat Fanciers Assn (1993) 839 FSupp 1100 (US Dist Ct (NJ))
Buck v Bell (1927) 274 US 200 (US Sup Ct)
Commonwealth v Crocker (1981) 384 Mass 353 (Mass Sup Jud Ct)
Commonwealth v Jones (1981) 382 Mass 387 (Mass Sup Jud Ct)
Commonwealth v Morin (2001) 52 Mass App Ct 780 (Mass App Ct)
Commonwealth v Wolinski (2000) 431 Mass 228 (Mass Sup Jud Ct)
Demjanjuk v Petrovsky (1985) 776 F2d 571 (US Ct App (6th Cir))
Democratic Party v Jones (2000) 530 US 567 (US Sup Ct)
Employment Division v Smith (1990) 494 US 872 (US Sup Ct)
Ferrall v Ferrall (1910) 69 SE 60 (Sup Ct NC)
Filartiga v Pena-Irala (1980) 630 F2d 876 (US Ct App (2d Cir))
Flores v Southern Peru Copper Corp (2003) 406 F3d 65 (US Ct App (2d Cir))
Hadamar [USMT 1945], United States v Klein (8–15 Oct 1945) 1 LRTWC 46 (US Military Tribunal)
Hudgins v Wright (1806) 11 Va (1 Hen & M) 134 (Sup Ct App VA)
Kadic v Kardizic (1995) 70 F3d 232 (US Ct App (2d Cir))
Medellin v Texas (2008) 129 SCt 360 (US Sup Ct)
NAACP v Alabama ex rel Patterson (1958) 357 US 449 (US Sup Ct)
Quinn v Robinson (1986) 783 F2d 776 (US Ct App (9th Cir))
Respublica v De Longchamps (1784) 1 US 111, 1 Dall 111 (Pa Sup Ct)
Reynolds v United States (1878) 98 US 145 (US Sup Ct)
Roper v Simmons (2005) 125 S Ct 1183 (US Sup Ct)
Rutelidge v United States (1996) 517 US 292 (US Sup Ct)
St Francis College v Al-Khazraji (1987) 481 US 604 (US Sup Ct)
Siderman de Blake v Republic of Argentina (1992) 965 F2d 699 (US Ct App (9th Cir))
Toyoda [USMT 1949] *United States v Toyoda* (26 Oct 1946–6 Sept 1949) (US Mil Tribunal—General Headquarters, Supreme Commander for the Allied Forces) (excerpted pages from trial transcript and judgment on file with author) (pp 1–32 and pp 4999–5021) (courtesy of RJ Pritchard)

United States v Noriega (1990) 746 FSupp 1506 (US Dist Ct (SD Fla))
United States v Rezaq (1998) 134 F3d 1121 (US Ct App (DC Cir))
United States v Smith (1820) 18 US (5 Wheat) 153 (US Sup Ct)
Vialpando v State (1982) 640 P2d 77 (Sup Ct Wyo)
Vieth v Jubelirer (2004) 541 US 267 (US Sup Ct)
In re Yamashita (1946) 327 US 1 (US Sup Ct)

Appendix A
Data Tables—State Practice on Genocide

Table I 84-State Survey
Groups Covered by Domestic Legislation Implementing Either the Genocide Convention or the ICC Statute

State	Relevant Law	Political Groups?	Social Groups?	'Other' Groups?
Albania	Criminal Code Law No 7895 (27 Jan 1995) art 73	No	No	No
Antigua & Barbuda	Genocide Act, Laws vol 4 c 191	No	No	No
Argentina	Draft Code of Crimes Within the Competence of the [ICC] pt 2 tit 1 art 13	No	No	No
Armenia	Criminal Code s 13 c 33 art 393	No	No	No
Australia	[ICC] Act (No 42) 2002 ss 268.3 - 268.37	No	No	No
Austria	Penal Code c 25 s 321	No	No	No
Azerbaijan	Criminal Code s 7 pt 16 art 103	No	No	No
Bangladesh	International Crimes (Tribunals) Act (19 Jul 1973) art 3	Yes	No	No
Barbados	Genocide Act 1980, Laws of Barbados vol 6 tit 9 c 133A	No	No	No
Belarus	Criminal Code s 6 c 17 art 127	Implicit	Implicit	Yes[1]
Belgium	Law on the Repression of Serious Violations of Humanitarian International Law (10 Feb 1999) art 3	No	No	No
Bolivia	Penal Code Law No 1768 tit 1 c 4 art 138	No	No	No
Bosnia-Herzegovina	Criminal Code: 'Official Gazette' of Bosnia and Herzegovina No 3/03 (22 Nov 2003) art 171	No	No	No
Brazil	Draft implementing Legislation Presented to the Minister of Justice (Oct 2002) c 2 art 18	No	No	No
Bulgaria	Criminal Code c 14 s 3	No	No	No
Burkina Faso	Penal Code c 2 art 313	Implicit	Implicit	Yes[2]
Cambodia	Decree Law No 1 (15 Jul 1979)[3] Cambodian Genocide Law (10 Aug 2001) No NS/RKM/1004/006	Yes	Yes	No[4]

(*continued*)

[1] Including 'groups formed on the basis of another criterion chosen arbitrarily'.

[2] Including 'a group established from any other arbitrary criterion'.

[3] 'Planned destruction of innocent people; Evacuation of people from towns and villages; Concentrating people and forcing them to do hard labour in physically and morally exhausting conditions; Abolition of religion and destruction of economic and cultural structures and familial and social relations'.

[4] Cambodia initially proposed enlarging the groups protected to include: 'wealth, level of education, sociological environment (urban/rural), allegiance to a political system or regime (old people/ new people), social class or social category (merchant, civil servant etc)'. The additional categories were rejected out of concern for the principles of legality. Schabas 145–6 (2000).

Table I 84-State Survey
Groups Covered by Domestic Legislation Implementing Either the Genocide Convention or the ICC Statute (*continued*)

State	Relevant Law	Political Groups?	Social Groups?	'Other' Groups?
Canada	Crimes Against Humanity and War Crimes Act Offences Within Canada SC 2000 c 24 s 4 Crimes Against Humanity and War Crimes Act Offences Outside Canada SC 2000 c 24 s 6	Implicit	Implicit	Yes[5]
China	Translation of Genocide Convention 'People's Republic of China State Gazette' upon ratification in April 1983	No	No	No
Columbia	Crimes Against Life and Personal Integrity, Penal Law No 599 (24 Jul 2000) bk 2 tit 1 arts 101–02	Yes	No	No
Congo (DR)	Law No 8–98 (31 Oct 1998) c 1 art 1	Implicit	Implicit	Yes[6]
Costa Rica	Penal Code (14 Apr 1998) art 127	Yes	Yes	Yes[7]
Côte d'Ivoire	Penal Code c 1 s 1 tit 1 art 137	Yes	No	No
Croatia	Penal Code c 13 art 156	No	No	No
Cuba	Penal Code Law No 62, as modified by Law No 87 bk 1 c 3 s 6 art 116	No	No	No
Czech Republic	Criminal Code c 20 s 259	No	No	No
Denmark	Act No 132 (29 Apr 1955) s 1	No	No	No
Ecuador	Law on Crimes Against Humanity art 19	Yes	Implicit	Yes[8]
El Salvador	Penal Code (Decree No 1030) tit 19 art 361	No	No	No
Estonia	Penal Code 1994 (9 Nov) s 61 and Penal Code 2001 s 61	Implicit	Yes	Yes[9]
Ethiopia	Penal Code 1957 art 281	Yes	No	No
Fiji	Penal Code 1945 pt 2 div 1 c 8 s 69	No	No	No
Finland	Penal Code No 39/1889 c 11	Implicit	Implicit	Yes[10]
France	Code Penal art 211–1, affirmed by Law No 2002–268 (26 Feb 2002) on Co-operation with the [ICC]	Implicit	Implicit	Yes[11]
Georgia	Criminal Code s 14 c 47 art 407	No	No	No
Germany	VStGB [Code of Crimes Against International Law] BGBl 2002 I at 2254 (30 Jun) art 1 pt 2 c 1 s 6(1)	No	No	No

(*continued*)

5 Including 'any identifiable group'.
6 Including 'a group determined starting from any other arbitrary criterion'.
7 Including 'gender, age, sexual preference, social position, economic situation or civil status'.
8 Including 'gender, sexual orientation, age, health or conscience'.
9 Including 'groups offering resistance to the occupation regime'.
10 Including 'another comparable group'.
11 Including 'a group determined by any other arbitrary criterion'.

Table I 84-State Survey
Groups Covered by Domestic Legislation Implementing Either the Genocide Convention or the ICC Statute (*continued*)

State	Relevant Law	Political Groups?	Social Groups?	'Other' Groups?
Ghana	Criminal Code (Amendment) Act 1993 s 1	No	No	No
Guatemala	Penal Code art 376	No	No	No
Hungary	Criminal Code 1978 c 11 tit 1 s 155	No	No	No
Indonesia[12]	Law No 26 (2000) c 3 art 8	No	No	No
Iraq	Statute of the Iraqi Special Tribunal (10 Dec 2003) art 11	No	No	No
Ireland	[ICC] Bill 2003 (No 36) pt 2 s 6	No	No	No
Israel	Crime of Genocide (Prevention and Punishment) Law No 5710–1950	No	No	No
Italy	Law No 962 (9 Oct 1967) art 1	No	No	No
Jamaica	Offences against the Person Act (Amendment 1968) Laws vol 8 s 33	No	No	No
Kiribati[13]	Penal Code s 8 art 62	No	No	No
Kyrgyzstan	Criminal Code s 12 c 34 art 373	No	No	No
Latvia	Criminal Code (17 Jun 1998) c 8 s 71	Implicit	Yes	Yes[14]
Liechtenstein	Penal Code StGB (24 Jun 1987) c 25 s 321	No	No	No
Lithuania	Criminal Code art 71	Yes	Yes	No
Luxembourg	Law on the Repression of Genocide (8 Aug 1985) art 1	No	No	No
Mali	Penal Code (2001) bk 3 tit 1 c 2 art 30	No	No	No
Malta[15]	[ICC] Act (13 Dec 2003) sch 1 art 6	No	No	No
Mexico	Penal Code 1931 bk 2 tit 3 c 2 art 149-bis (as amended)	No	No	No
Moldova	Criminal Code c 1 art 135	No	No	No
Netherlands	International Crimes Act (9 Jun 2003) pt 2 s 3	No	No	No
New Zealand	International Crimes and [ICC] Act 2000 No 26 and Amendment No 67 (2002) pt 2 s 9	No	No	No
Nicaragua	Penal Code bk 2 tit 14 art 549	No	No	No
Panama	Penal Code: Crimes Against the International Community tit 9 c 3 art 311	Yes	No	No
Paraguay	Penal Code bk 2 tit 9 art 308 art 319	No	No	No
Peru	Law No 26926 (19 Feb 1998) tit 14 c 1 art 319	No	No	No
Poland	Penal Code: Law of 6 Jun 1997 c 16 art 118	Yes[16]	No	No

(*continued*)

[12] Indonesia is party to neither the Genocide Convention nor the ICC Statute.
[13] Kiribati is party to neither the Genocide Convention nor the ICC Statute.
[14] Including 'ethnic origin, race, social class or a defined collective belief or faith'.
[15] Malta is party to neither the Genocide Convention nor the ICC Statute.
[16] Including 'political group or a group of persons with a definite philosophical conviction'.

Table I 84-State Survey
Groups Covered by Domestic Legislation Implementing Either the Genocide Convention or the ICC Statute (*continued*)

State	Relevant Law	Political Groups?	Social Groups?	'Other' Groups?
Portugal	Penal Code 1982 art 189, as modified by Penal Code tit 3 c 2 art 239 and Law No 31/2004 (22 Jul 2004) art 218	No	No[17]	No
Romania	Romanian Socialist Republic Penal Code (1976 Special Part) tit 9 art 356	Implicit	Implicit	Yes[18]
Russian Federation	Criminal Code s 12 c 34 art 357	No	No	No
Rwanda	Organic Law 8/96 (1 Sep 1996) arts 1(a) and 2	No	No	No
Scotland[19]	[ICC] Act 2001 (2001 asp 13) sch 1	No	No	No
Seychelles	Genocide Act 1969 sch 1 art 6	No	No	No
Slovenia	Penal Code 1994 c 35 art 373	Yes	Yes	No
Solomon Islands[20]	Penal Code: Law No 46A of 1978 pt 7 art 52	No	No	No
South Africa	Law No 27 of 2002: Implementation of the [ICC Statute] Act 2002 (12 Jul) sch 1 pt 1	No	No	No
Spain	Penal Code: Law No 10/1995 (23 Nov) and Law No 15/2003 (25 Nov) art 607	No	No	No
Sweden	Penal Code: Law No 169 (20 Mar 1963) s 1	No	No	No
Switzerland	Penal Code bk 2 c 12(a) art 264	No	No	No
Tajikistan[21]	Penal Code s 1 c 1 art 398	No	No	No
Tonga	Genocide Act 1969 Law No 8 c 19 s 2	No	No	No
Trinidad and Tobago	Genocide Act 1977 s 3	No	No	No
Tuvalu[22]	Penal Code c 8 pt 8 art 62	No	No	No
Uganda	[ICC] Bill (19 Apr 2004) art 7 sch 1	No	No	No
Ukraine	Criminal Code (1 Sep 2001) c 20 art 442	No	No	No
United Kingdom	[ICC] Act 2001 c 17 sch 8 pt 1art 6	No	No	No
United States	Genocide Implementation Act of 1987 18 USC s 1091, as amended by Law No 110–141 (21 Dec 07) s 2	No	No	No
Uruguay	Implementation of the [ICC] Statute 2003 (17 Jan 2003) art 2	No	No	No
Venezuela	Proposed Legislation on Implementation of the [ICC] Statute (25 Jul 2002) art 5	No	No	No

17 Portugal's original law, which included social groups, was revised to conform to the four categories in the Genocide Convention in Decree Law no 48/95 (15 March 1995). Schabas 146 (2000).
18 Including 'a collectivity or a national, ethnic, racial, or religious group'.
19 Scotland is part of the UK but has its own domestic legislation implementing the ICC Statute.
20 Solomon Islands is party to neither the Genocide Convention nor the ICC Statute.
21 Tajikistan is not party to the Genocide Convention but has ratified the ICC Statute.
22 Tuvalu is party to neither the Genocide Convention nor the ICC Statute.

Table II 20 States Covering Political Groups in Domestic Provisions on Genocide

State	Relevant Law	Political Groups?	Social Groups?	'Other' Groups?
Bangladesh	International Crimes (Tribunals) Act (19 Jul 1973) art 3	Yes	No	No
Belarus	Criminal Code s 6 c 17 art 127	Implicit	Implicit	Yes[23]
Burkina Faso	Penal Code c 2 art 313	Implicit	Implicit	Yes[24]
Cambodia	Decree Law No 1 (15 Jul 1979)[25] Cambodian Genocide Law (10 Aug 2001) No NS/RKM/1004/006	Yes	Yes	No[26]
Canada	Crimes Against Humanity and War Crimes Act Offences Within Canada SC 2000 c 24 s 4 Crimes Against Humanity and War Crimes Act Offences Outside Canada SC 2000 c 24 s 6	Implicit	Implicit	Yes[27]
Columbia	Crimes Against Life and Personal Integrity, Penal Law No 599 (24 Jul 2000) bk 2 tit 1 arts 101–02	Yes	No	No
Congo (DR)	Law No 8–98 (31 Oct 1998) c 1 art 1	Implicit	Implicit	Yes[28]
Costa Rica	Penal Code (14 Apr 1998) art 127	Yes	Yes	Yes[29]
Côte d'Ivoire	Penal Code c 1 s 1 tit 1 art 137	Yes	No	No
Ecuador	Law on Crimes Against Humanity art 19	Yes	Implicit	Yes[30]
Estonia	Penal Code 1994 (9 Nov) s 61 and Penal Code 2001 s 61	Implicit	Yes	Yes[31]
Ethiopia	Penal Code 1957 art 281	Yes	No	No
Finland	Penal Code No 39/1889 c 11	Implicit	Implicit	Yes[32]
France	Code Penal art 211–1, affirmed by Law No 2002–268 (26 Feb 2002) on Co-operation with the [ICC]	Implicit	Implicit	Yes[33]

(*Continued*)

[23] Including 'groups formed on the basis of another criterion chosen arbitrarily'.

[24] Including 'a group established from any other arbitrary criterion'.

[25] 'Planned destruction of innocent people; Evacuation of people from towns and villages; Concentrating people and forcing them to do hard labour in physically and morally exhausting conditions; Abolition of religion and destruction of economic and cultural structures and familial and social relations'.

[26] Cambodia initially proposed enlarging the groups protected to include: 'wealth, level of education, sociological environment (urban/rural), allegiance to a political system or regime (old people/new people), social class or social category (merchant, civil servant etc)'. The additional categories were rejected out of concern for the principles of legality. Schabas 145–6 (2000).

[27] Including 'any identifiable group'.

[28] Including 'a group determined starting from any other arbitrary criterion'.

[29] Including 'gender, age, sexual preference, social position, economic situation or civil status'.

[30] Including 'gender, sexual orientation, age, health or conscience'.

[31] Including 'groups offering resistance to the occupation regime'.

[32] Including 'another comparable group'.

Table II 20 States Covering Political Groups in Domestic Provisions on Genocide (*Continued*)

State	Relevant Law	Political Groups?	Social Groups?	'Other' Groups?
Latvia	Criminal Code (17 Jun 1998) c 8 s 71	Implicit	Yes	Yes[34]
Lithuania	Criminal Code art 71	Yes	Yes	No
Panama	Penal Code: Crimes Against the International Community tit 9 c 3 art 311	Yes	No	No
Poland	Penal Code: Law of 6 Jun 1997 c 16 art 118	Yes[35]	No	No
Romania	Romanian Socialist Republic Penal Code (1976 Special Part) tit 9 art 356	Implicit	Implicit	Yes[36]
Slovenia	Penal Code 1994 c 35 art 373	Yes	Yes	No

Table III 51 States not Party to the Genocide Convention

State	Date of UN Membership	Party to ICC Statute?
Angola	1 Dec 1976	**S**[37]
Benin	20 Sep 1960	**R**
Bhutan	21 Sep 1971	**N**
Botswana	17 Oct 1966	**R**
Brunei Darussalam	21 Sep 1984	**N**
Cameroon	20 Sep 1960	**S**
Cape Verde	16 Sep 1975	**S**
Central African Republic	20 Sep 1960	**R**
Chad	20 Sep 1960	**R**
Congo	20 Sep 1960	**R**
Djibouti	20 Sep 1977	**R**
Dominica	18 Dec 1978	**R**
Dominican Republic[38]	24 Oct 1945	**R**
Equatorial Guinea	12 Nov 1968	**N**
Eritrea	28 May 1993	**S**

(*Continued*)

33 Including 'a group determined by any other arbitrary criterion'.

34 Including 'ethnic origin, race, social class or a defined collective belief or faith'.

35 Including 'political group or a group of persons with a definite philosophical conviction'.

36 Including 'a collectivity or a national, ethnic, racial, or religious group'.

37 N = Not Party; S = Signatory; R = Ratified/Acceded. As of January 2010, there are 192 member states in the United Nations: Multilateral Treaties Deposited with the Secretary-General: United Nations Treaty Collection—Charter of the United Nations (13 Jan 2010) available at <http://www.treaties.un.org/Pages/ViewDetails.aspx?src=IND&mtdsg_no=I-1&chapter=1&lang=en> (visited 13 Jan 2010).

38 The Dominican Republic is a signatory to the Genocide Convention (13 Dec 1948), but has not ratified the treaty.

Table III 51 States not Party to the Genocide Convention (*Continued*)

State	Date of UN Membership	Party to ICC Statute?
Grenada	17 Sep 1974	**N**
Guinea-Bissau	17 Sep 1974	**S**
Guyana	20 Sep 1966	**R**
Indonesia	28 Sep 1950	**N**
Japan	18 Dec 1956	**R**
Kenya	16 Dec 1963	**R**
Kiribati	14 Sep 1999	**N**
Madagascar	20 Sep 1960	**R**
Malawi	1 Dec 1964	**R**
Malta	1 Dec 1964	**R**
Marshall Islands	17 Sep 1991	**R**
Mauritania	27 Oct 1961	**N**
Mauritius	24 Apr 1968	**R**
Micronesia	17 Sep 1991	**N**
Nauru	14 Sep 1999	**R**
Niger	20 Sep 1960	**R**
Oman	7 Oct 1971	**S**
Palau	15 Dec 1994	**N**
Qatar	21 Sep 1971	**N**
Saint Lucia	18 Sep 1979	**S**
Samoa	15 Dec 1976	**R**
San Marino	2 Mar 1992	**R**
Sao Tome and Principe	16 Sep 1975	**S**
Sierra Leone	27 Sep 1961	**R**
Solomon Islands	19 Sep 1978	**S**
Somalia	20 Sep 1960	**N**
St. Kitts and Nevis	23 Sep 1983	**R**
Suriname	4 Dec 1975	**R**
Swaziland	24 Sep 1968	**N**
Tajikistan	2 Mar 1992	**R**
Thailand	16 Dec 1946	**S**
Timor-Leste	27 Sep 2002	**R**
Turkmenistan	2 Mar 1992	**N**
Tuvalu	5 Sep 2000	**N**
Vanuatu	15 Sep 1981	**N**
Zambia	1 Dec 1962	**R**

[ICC] Ratifying States: 26
[ICC] Signatory States: 10
[ICC] Non-Party States: 15

Source on Genocide Convention:

Multilateral Treaties Deposited with the Secretary-General: United Nations Treaty Collection—Genocide Convention (13 Jan 2010) available at <http://www.treaties.un.org/Pages/ViewDetails.aspx?src=TREATY&mtdsg_no=IV-1&chapter=4&lang=en> (visited 13 Jan 2010).

Source on ICC:

Multilateral Treaties Deposited with the Secretary-General: United Nations Treaty Collection—Rome Statute of the International Criminal Court (13 Jan 2010) available at <http://www.treaties.un.org/Pages/ViewDetails.aspx?src=IND&mtdsg_no=XVIII-10&chapter=18&lang=en> (visited 13 Jan 2010).

Table IV 141 States Party to the Genocide Convention

State	Signature	Ratified / Acceded
Afghanistan		22 Mar 1956
Albania		12 May 1955
Algeria		31 Oct 1963
Andorra		22 Sep 2006
Antigua and Barbuda		25 Oct 1988
Argentina		5 Jun 1956
Armenia		23 Jun 1993
Australia	11 Dec 1948	8 Jul 1949
Austria		19 Mar 1958
Azerbaijan		16 Aug 1996
Bahamas		5 Aug 1975
Bahrain		27 Mar 1990
Bangladesh		5 Oct 1998
Barbados		14 Jan 1980
Belarus	16 Dec 1949	11 Aug 1954
Belgium	12 Dec 1949	5 Sep 1951
Belize		10 Mar 1998
Bolivia	11 Dec 1948	14 Jun 2005
Bosnia and Herzegovina		29 Dec 1992
Brazil	11 Dec 1948	15 Apr 1952
Bulgaria		21 Jul 1950
Burkina Faso		14 Sep 1965
Burundi		6 Jan 1997
Cambodia		14 Oct 1950
Canada	28 Nov 1949	3 Sep 1952
Chile	11 Dec 1948	3 Jun 1953
China	20 Jul 1949	18 Apr 1983
Colombia	12 Aug 1949	27 Oct 1959
Comoros		27 Sep 2004
Congo (Democratic Republic of)		31 May 1962
Costa Rica		14 Oct 1950
Côte d'Ivoire		18 Dec 1995
Croatia		12 Oct 1992
Cuba	28 Dec 1949	4 Mar 1953
Cyprus		29 Mar 1982
Czech Republic		22 Feb 1993
Denmark	28 Sep 1949	15 Jun 1951
Ecuador	11 Dec 1948	21 Dec 1949
Egypt	12 Dec 1948	8 Feb 1952
El Salvador	27 Apr 1949	28 Sep 1950
Estonia		21 Oct 1991
Ethiopia	11 Dec 1948	1 Jul 1949
Fiji		11 Jan 1973
Finland		18 Dec 1959
France	11 Dec 1948	14 Oct 1950
Gabon		21 Jan 1983

(*Continued*)

Table IV 141 States Party to the Genocide Convention (*Continued*)

State	Signature	Ratified / Acceded
Gambia		29 Dec 1978
Georgia		11 Oct 1993
Germany		24 Nov 1954
Ghana		24 Dec 1958
Greece	29 Dec 1949	8 Dec 1954
Guatemala	22 Jun 1949	13 Jan 1950
Guinea		7 Sep 2000
Haiti	11 Dec 1948	14 Oct 1950
Honduras	22 Apr 1949	5 Mar 1952
Hungary		7 Jan 1952
Iceland	14 May 1949	29 Aug 1949
India	29 Nov 1949	27 Aug 1959
Iran (Islamic Republic of)	8 Dec 1949	14 Aug 1956
Iraq		20 Jan 1959
Ireland		22 Jun 1976
Israel	17 Aug 1949	9 Mar 1950
Italy		4 Jun 1952
Jamaica		23 Sep 1968
Jordan		3 Apr 1950
Kazakhstan		26 Aug 1998
Korea (Democratic People's Republic of [North])		31 Jan 1989
Korea (Republic of [South])		14 Oct 1950
Kuwait		7 Mar 1995
Kyrgyzstan		5 Sep 1997
Laos People's Democratic Republic		8 Dec 1950
Latvia		14 Apr 1992
Lebanon	30 Dec 1949	17 Dec 1953
Lesotho		29 Nov 1974
Liberia	11 Dec 1948	9 Jun 1950
Libyan Arab Jamahiriya		16 May 1989
Liechtenstein		24 Mar 1994
Lithuania		1 Feb 1996
Luxembourg		7 Oct 1981
Macedonia (Former Yugoslav Republic of)		18 Jan 1994
Malaysia		20 Dec 1994
Maldives		24 Apr 1984
Mali		16 Jul 1974
Mexico	14 Dec 1948	22 Jul 1952
Moldova (Republic of)		26 Jan 1993
Monaco		30 Mar 1950
Mongolia		5 Jan 1967
Montenegro	19 July 2006	23 Oct 2006
Morocco		24 Jan 1958

(*Continued*)

Table IV 141 States Party to the Genocide Convention

State	Signature	Ratified / Acceded
Mozambique		18 Apr 1983
Myanmar	30 Dec 1949	14 Mar 1956
Namibia		28 Nov 1994
Nepal		17 Jan 1969
Netherlands		20 Jun 1966
New Zealand	25 Nov 1949	28 Dec 1978
Nicaragua		29 Jan 1952
Nigeria		27 Jul 2009
Norway	11 Dec 1948	22 Jul 1949
Pakistan	11 Dec 1948	12 Oct 1957
Panama	11 Dec 1948	11 Jan 1950
Papua New Guinea		27 Jan 1982
Paraguay	11 Dec 1948	3 Oct 2001
Peru	11 Dec 1948	24 Feb 1960
Philippines	11 Dec 1948	7 Jul 1950
Poland		14 Nov 1950
Portugal		9 Feb 1999
Romania		2 Nov 1950
Russian Federation	16 Dec 1949	3 May 1954
Rwanda		16 Apr 1975
Saint Vincent and the Grenadines		9 Nov 1981
Saudi Arabia		13 Jul 1950
Senegal		4 Aug 1983
Serbia		12 Mar 2001
Seychelles		5 May 1992
Singapore		18 Aug 1995
Slovakia		28 May 1993
Slovenia		6 Jul 1992
South Africa		10 Dec 1998
Spain		13 Sep 1968
Sri Lanka		12 Oct 1950
Sudan		13 Oct 2003
Sweden	30 Dec 1949	27 May 1952
Switzerland		7 Sep 2000
Syrian Arab Republic		25 Jun 1955
Tanzania (United Republic of)		5 Apr 1984
Togo		24 May 1984
Tonga		16 Feb 1972
Trinidad and Tobago		13 Dec 2002
Tunisia		29 Nov 1956
Turkey		31 Jul 1950
Uganda		14 Nov 1995
Ukraine	16 Dec 1949	15 Nov 1954
United Arab Emirates		11 Nov 2005
United Kingdom		30 Jan 1970

(*Continued*)

Table IV 141 States Party to the Genocide Convention (*Continued*)

State	Signature	Ratified / Acceded
United States of America	11 Dec 1948	25 Nov 1988
Uruguay	11 Dec 1948	11 Jul 1967
Uzbekistan		9 Sep 1999
Venezuela		12 Jul 1960
Viet nam		9 Jun 1981
Yemen		9 Feb 1987
Zimbabwe		13 May 1991

Source: Multilateral Treaties Deposited with the Secretary-General: United Nations Treaty Collection—Genocide Convention (13 Jan 2010) available at <http://www.treaties.un.org/Pages/ViewDetails.aspx?src=TREATY&mtdsg_no=IV-1&chapter=4&lang=en> (visited 13 Jan 2010).

Table V 64 States Parties to the Genocide Convention (Domestic Legislation Unavailable)

State	Signature	Ratified / Acceded
Afghanistan		22 Mar 1956
Algeria		31 Oct 1963
Andorra		22 Sep 2006
Bahamas		5 Aug 1975
Bahrain		27 Mar 1990
Belize		10 Mar 1998
Burundi		6 Jan 1997
Chile	11 Dec 1948	3 Jun 1953
Comoros		27 Sep 2004
Cyprus		29 Mar 1982
Egypt	12 Dec 1948	8 Feb 1952
Gabon		21 Jan 1983
Gambia		29 Dec 1978
Greece	29 Dec 1949	8 Dec 1954
Guinea		7 Sep 2000
Haiti	11 Dec 1948	14 Oct 1950
Honduras	22 Apr 1949	5 Mar 1952
Iceland	14 May 1949	29 Aug 1949
India	29 Nov 1949	27 Aug 1959
Iran (Islamic Republic of)	8 Dec 1949	14 Aug 1956
Jordan		3 Apr 1950
Kazakhstan		26 Aug 1998
Korea (Democratic People's Republic of [North])		31 Jan 1989
Korea (Republic of [South])		14 Oct 1950
Kuwait		7 Mar 1995
Laos People's Democratic Republic		8 Dec 1950

(*Continued*)

Table V 64 States Parties to the Genocide Convention (Domestic Legislation Unavailable) (*Continued*)

State	Signature	Ratified / Acceded
Lebanon	30 Dec 1949	17 Dec 1953
Lesotho		29 Nov 1974
Liberia	11 Dec 1948	9 Jun 1950
Libyan Arab Jamahiriya		16 May 1989
Macedonia (Former Yugoslav Republic of)		18 Jan 1994
Malaysia		20 Dec 1994
Maldives		24 Apr 1984
Monaco		30 Mar 1950
Mongolia		5 Jan 1967
Montenegro	19 July 2006	23 Oct 2006
Morocco		24 Jan 1958
Mozambique		18 Apr 1983
Myanmar	30 Dec 1949	14 Mar 1956
Namibia		28 Nov 1994
Nepal		17 Jan 1969
Nigeria		29 Jul 2009
Norway	11 Dec 1948	22 Jul 1949
Pakistan	11 Dec 1948	12 Oct 1957
Papua New Guinea		27 Jan 1982
Philippines	11 Dec 1948	7 Jul 1950
Saint Vincent and the Grenadines		9 Nov 1981
Saudi Arabia		13 Jul 1950
Senegal		4 Aug 1983
Serbia		12 Mar 2001
Singapore		18 Aug 1995
Slovakia		28 May 1993
Sri Lanka		12 Oct 1950
Sudan		13 Oct 2003
Syrian Arab Republic		25 Jun 1955
Tanzania (United Republic of)		5 Apr 1984
Togo		24 May 1984
Tunisia		29 Nov 1956
Turkey		31 Jul 1950
United Arab Emirates		11 Nov 2005
Uzbekistan		9 Sep 1999
Viet nam		9 Jun 1981
Yemen		9 Feb 1987
Zimbabwe		13 May 1991

Source: Multilateral Treaties Deposited with the Secretary-General: United Nations Treaty Collection—Genocide Convention (13 Jan 2010) available at <http://www.treaties.un.org/Pages/ViewDetails.aspx?src=TREATY&mtdsg_no=IV-1&chapter=4&lang=en> (visited 13 Jan 2010).

Appendix B
Unofficial Translations of Domestic Laws on Genocide from 84 States

Table of Contents

NB. Except where noted to the contrary, all translations herein are unofficial versions created by the author.

Albania

Criminal Code of the Republic of Albania, Law No 7895 (27 Jan 1995) 'Crimes Against Humanity' art 73 [Genocide]

Whoever executes a premeditated plan aiming at the total or partial destruction of a national, ethnic, racial or religious group directed towards its members, and combined with the following acts, such as—

- intentionally killing a group's members,
- causing them serious physical and psychological harm,
- placement in difficult living conditions which cause physical destruction,
- applying birth preventing measures,
- the obligatory transfer of children from one group to another,

shall be punished with no less than 10 years of imprisonment, or with life imprisonment, or the death penalty.

Antigua & Barbuda

The Genocide Act, Laws of Antigua & Barbuda vol 4 c 191

II. In this Act 'the Genocide Convention' means the Convention on the Prevention and Punishment of the Crime of Genocide approved by the General Assembly of the United Nations on the 9th day of December 1948.

III. (1) A person shall commit an offence of genocide if he commits any act falling within the definition of 'genocide' as set out in Article II of the Genocide Convention contained in the Schedule to this Act.
   (2) A person guilty of an offence of genocide shall on conviction on indictment:
      (a) If the offence consists of the killing of any person, be sentenced to imprisonment for life; and
      (b) In any other case, be liable to imprisonment for 14 years.

IV. Proceedings for an offence of genocide shall not be instituted except by or with the consent of the Director of Public Prosecutions.

Schedule—Article II of the Geneva Convention

In the present Convention, genocide means any of the following acts committed with intent to destroy, in whole or in part, a national, ethnic, racial or religious group, as such—

(a) Killing members of the group;
(b) Causing serious bodily or mental harm to members of the group;
(c) Deliberately inflicting on the group conditions of life calculated to bring about its physical destruction in whole or in part;
(d) Imposing measures intended to prevent births within the group;
(e) Forcibly transferring children of the group to another group.

Argentina

Draft Code of Crimes within the Competence of the International Criminal Court pt 2 title 1 art 13 [Genocide]

Whoever, with the intention to destroy totally or partially a national, ethnic, racial or religious group as such, commits any of the following acts, will be punished with imprisonment of 5 to 25 years or lifetime imprisonment:

(a) Serious injury to the physical or mental integrity of the members of the group;
(b) Intentional submission of the group to conditions of existence meant to cause its total or partial physical destruction;
(c) Measures destined to prevent births in the group;
(d) Transfer by force of children of the group to another group.

The penalty will be lifetime imprisonment for killing members of the group.

Armenia

Criminal Code of the Republic of Armenia s 13 c 33 'Crimes Against Peace and Human Security' art 393 [Genocide]

Actions aimed at the complete or partial extermination of national, ethnic, racial or religious groups by means of killing the members of the group, inflicting severe damage to their health, forcibly preventing them from childbearing, forced transfer of children, violent re-settlement directed at the physical elimination of the members of this group, are punishable by imprisonment for the term of 13 to 15 years or with a life sentence.

Australia

International Criminal Court (Consequential Amendments) Act (No 42) 2002

268.3 Genocide by killing

(1) A person (the perpetrator) commits an offence if:

(a) the perpetrator causes the death of one or more persons; and
(b) the person or persons belong to a particular national, ethnical, racial or religious group; and
(c) the perpetrator intends to destroy, in whole or in part, that national, ethnical, racial or religious group, as such.

Penalty: Imprisonment for life.

268.4 Genocide by causing serious bodily or mental harm

(1) A person (the perpetrator) commits an offence if:
(a) the perpetrator causes serious bodily or mental harm to one or more persons; and
(b) the person or persons belong to a particular national, ethnical, racial or religious group; and
(c) the perpetrator intends to destroy, in whole or in part, that national, ethnical, racial or religious group, as such.

Penalty: Imprisonment for life.

(2) In subsection (1): causes serious bodily or mental harm includes, but is not restricted to, commits acts of torture, rape, sexual violence or inhuman or degrading treatment.

268.5 Genocide by deliberately inflicting conditions of life calculated to bring about physical destruction

(1) A person (the perpetrator) commits an offence if:
(a) the perpetrator inflicts certain conditions of life upon one or more persons; and
(b) the person or persons belong to a particular national, ethnical, racial or religious group; and
(c) the perpetrator intends to destroy, in whole or in part, that national, ethnical, racial or religious group, as such; and
(d) the conditions of life are intended to bring about the physical destruction of that group, in whole or in part.

Penalty: Imprisonment for life.

(2) In subsection (1): conditions of life includes, but is not restricted to, intentional deprivation of resources indispensable for survival, such as deprivation of food or medical services, or systematic expulsion from homes.

268.6 Genocide by imposing measures intended to prevent births

(1) A person (the perpetrator) commits an offence if:

(a) the perpetrator imposes certain measures upon one or more persons; and
(b) the person or persons belong to a particular national, ethnical, racial or religious group; and
(c) the perpetrator intends to destroy, in whole or in part, that national, ethnical, racial or religious group, as such; and
(d) the measures imposed are intended to prevent births within that group.

Penalty: Imprisonment for life.

268.7 Genocide by forcibly transferring children

(1) A person (the perpetrator) commits an offence if:
(a) the perpetrator forcibly transfers one or more persons; and
(b) the person or persons belong to a particular national, ethnical, racial or religious group; and
(c) the perpetrator intends to destroy, in whole or in part, that national, ethnical, racial or religious group, as such; and
(d) the transfer is from that group to another national, ethnical, racial or religious group; and
(e) the person or persons are under the age of 18 years; and
(f) the perpetrator knows that, or is reckless as to whether, the person or persons are under that age.

Penalty: Imprisonment for life.

(2) In subsection (1): forcibly transfers one or more persons includes transfers one or more persons:
(a) by threat of force or coercion (such as that caused by fear of violence, duress, detention, psychological oppression or abuse of power) against the person or persons or against another person; or
(b) by taking advantage of a coercive environment.

Austria

Penal code (Austria) c 25 s 321 'Genocide'

Whoever, with the intent to exterminate a group, on the basis of its affiliation with a church or a religious society, a race, an ethnicity, or a national group, as such, in whole or in part—

- kills members of the group, or
- causes them heavy physical (Penal Code s 84 abs 1) or mental damage, or
- deliberately imposes living conditions intended to cause the death of all members or a section of the group, or

– imposes measures intended to prevent births within the group, or
– transfers by force or by threat of force children of the group into another group,

shall be punished with life imprisonment.

Azerbaijan

Criminal Code (Azerbaijan) s 7 pt 16 'Crimes against Peace and Security of Humanity' art 103 [Genocide]

Killing members of any national, ethnical, racial or religious group, with intent to destroy it, in whole or in part, as a group, causing serious bodily or mental harm to members of the group, or deliberately inflicting on the group conditions of life calculated to bring about its physical destruction in whole or in part, or imposing measures intended to prevent births within the group, or forcibly transferring children of the group to another group, shall be punished by deprivation of liberty for a period of 10 to 15 years or by life imprisonment.

Bangladesh

Bangladesh International Crimes (Tribunals) Act (20 Jul 1973) art 3

(1) A Tribunal shall have the power to try and punish any person irrespective of this [sic] nationality who, being a member of any armed, defence or auxiliary forces commits or has committed, in the territory of Bangladesh, whether before or after the commencement of this Act, any of the following crimes:....

(2)(c): Genocide: meaning and including any of the following acts committed with intent to destroy, in whole or in part, a national, ethnic, racial, religious or political group, such as:

(a) Killing members of the group;
(b) Causing serious bodily or mental harm to members of the group;
(c) Deliberately inflicting on the group conditions of life calculated to bring about its physical destruction in whole or in part;
(d) Imposing measures intended to prevent births within the group;
(e) Forcibly transferring children of the group to another group.

Barbados

Laws of Barbados vol 6 tit 11 c 133A 'The Genocide Act'

(1) This Act may be cited as the *Genocide Act*.
(2) For the purposes of this Act, 'Convention' means the Convention on the Prevention and Punishment of the Crime of Genocide approved by the

General Assembly of the United Nations on the 9th of December 1948, the text of which is set out in the Schedule; 'Genocide' has the meaning assigned to it in Article II of the Convention.

(3) Articles II, III and IV of the Convention have the force of law in Barbados.

(4) Any person who commits any of the acts set out in Article III of the Convention is guilty of an offence and is liable on conviction on indictment,
  (a) In respect of the acts specified in paragraphs (a) and (e) of that Article, to imprisonment for life; and
  (b) In respect of the acts specified in paragraphs (b) to (d) of that Article, to imprisonment for a term of 14 years.

(5) No proceedings for an offence under this Act shall be instituted without the consent of the Director of Public Prosecutions.

Belarus

Criminal Code of Belarus s 6 c 17 'Crimes against Peace, the Safety of Humanity and War Crimes' art 127 [Genocide]

Intentional acts aimed at destroying, totally or partially, a racial, national, ethnic or religious group or groups established on the basis of another arbitrarily-chosen criterion, by the murder of members of the group, serious attacks on the physical integrity of members of the group, deliberately placing the group into conditions of existence meant to cause its total or partial physical destruction, the forced transfer of children of the group to another group, or measures aimed at blocking births within the group, are punishable by imprisonment from 10 to 25 years, by life imprisonment, or by the death penalty.

Belgium

Law on the Repression of Serious Violations of International Humanitarian Law (10 Feb 1999) art 3(1)

The Crime of Genocide, as defined below, constitutes a crime of international law and is punishable in accordance with the provisions of this law, whether in time of peace or of war. In accordance with the Convention for the Prevention and Punishment of the Crime of Genocide of December 9, 1948, and without prejudice to the penal provisions applicable to infringements through negligence, 'genocide' means one of the following acts done with the intention to destroy, in whole or part, a national, ethnic, racial or religious group as such:

(1) Murder of members of the group;
(2) A serious attack on the physical or mental integrity of members of the group;
(3) Intentionally placing the group in conditions of existence intended to cause its total or partial physical destruction;

(4) Measures aimed at blocking births within the group;
(5) Forced transfer of children of one group to another group.

Bolivia

Penal Code (Bolivia) Law No 1768 tit 1 c 4 art 138

Whoever, with the purpose of destroying totally or partially a national, ethnic or religious group, causes death or injury to the members of the group, or places them in conditions of cruel subsistence, or imposes upon them measures intended to impede their reproduction, or violently displaces children or adults to other groups, will be punished with military imprisonment for 10 to 20 years. Punishment shall include the direct or indirect authors or others directly guilty of massacres within the country.

Bosnia-Herzegovina

Criminal Code of Bosnia and Herzegovina: 'Official Gazette' of Bosnia and Herzegovina No. 3/03 (22 Nov 2003) 'Genocide' art 171

Whoever, with an aim to destroy, in whole or in part, a national, ethnical, racial or religious group, orders the perpetration of or perpetrates any of the following acts:

(a) Killing members of the group;
(b) Causing serious bodily or mental harm to members of the group;
(c) Deliberately inflicting on the group conditions of life calculated to bring about its physical destruction in whole or in part;
(d) Imposing measures intended to prevent births within the group;
(e) Forcibly transferring children of the group to another group,

shall be punished by imprisonment for a term not less than 10 years or lifetime imprisonment.

Brazil

Draft [ICC] Legislation Presented to the Minister of Justice of Brazil (Oct 2002) c 2

Article 18—Genocide

Whoever, with the intention of annihilating, in whole or in part, a national, racial or religious group, as such:

(a) Kills a member of the group;
Penalty—imprisonment for 12 to 30 years.

(b) Causes grievous bodily harm, or physical or mental harm, to a member of the group;
Penalty—imprisonment for 5 to 12 years.
(c) Intentionally, submits the group to living conditions capable of causing total or partial physical annihilation;
Penalty—imprisonment for 5 to 12 years.
(d) Takes steps designed to prevent births within the group;
Penalty—imprisonment for 5 to 12 years.
(e) Carries out the forced transfer of children of the group to another group—
Penalty—imprisonment for 5 to 12 years.

commits the offence of genocide.

Article 19—Formation of an Association to Commit Genocide
Where three or more people associate to commit the crimes referred to in the preceding article.

Penalty: One half of that set for the crime for which they formed the association to commit.

Article 20—Incitement to Commit Genocide
Inciting someone, directly and publicly, to commit genocide

Penalty: One half of the penalties for the crime incited.

(1) The penalty for the crime of incitement will be the same as the crime incited, if the latter actually takes place.
(2) The penalty will be increased by one third, where the incitement takes place through the press.

Article 21—Increase of the Penalty
The penalty is increased by one to two thirds, when:

(a) the crime is committed by a public authority or agent thereof;
(b) the crime is committed by means of an association of people;
(c) the victim is less than 14 years of age, more than 65 years of age, is pregnant, has special needs, or, for any reason, has any reduction in his or her ability to resist.

Bulgaria

Criminal Code of Bulgaria c 14 s 3 art 416

(1) Whoever, with the purpose of annihilating entirely or partially a definite national, ethnic, racial or religious group:
    (a) Causes death, severe bodily injury or permanent mental disorder to a person belonging to such a group;
    (b) Places the group in living conditions meant to cause its complete or partial physical extermination;

(c) Undertakes measures aimed at obstructing the childbirth in such a group;
(d) Forcibly transfers children from one group to another,

shall be punished for genocide by imprisonment of 10 to 20 years or by life imprisonment.

Burkina Faso

Penal Code (Burkina Faso) c 2 art 313 [Genocide]

Those who, in execution of a concerted plan aimed at the total or partial destruction of a national, ethnic, racial or religious group or of a group established from any other arbitrary criterion, commit one of the following acts against members of this group:

- attack on the life of group members;
- attack on the physical or psychic integrity of group members;
- placing group members in conditions of life likely to cause the total or partial destruction of the group;
- measures aimed at blocking reproduction of group members;
- forced transfers of children of the group,

are subject to punishment by the death penalty.

Cambodia

Law on the Establishment of the Extraordinary Chambers in the Courts of Cambodia for the Prosecution of Crimes Committed during the Period of Democratic Kampuchea (10 Aug 2001) with Amendments (27 Oct 2004) No NS/RKM/0801/12 art 4

The Extraordinary Chambers shall have the power to bring to trial all suspects who committed the crime of genocide as defined in the Convention on the Prevention and Punishment of the Crime of Genocide of 1948, and which were committed during the period from 17 April 1975 to 6 January 1979.

The acts of genocide, which have no statute of limitations, mean any acts committed with the intent to destroy, in whole or in part, a national, ethnical, racial or religious group such as:

- killing members of the group;
- causing serious bodily or mental harm to members of the group;
- deliberately inflicting on the group conditions of life calculated to bring about its physical destruction in whole or in part;

- imposing measures intended to prevent births within the group;
- forcibly transferring children from one group to another group.

The following acts shall be punishable under this Article:

- attempts to commit acts of genocide;
- conspiracy to commit acts of genocide;
- participation in acts of acts of genocide.

Canada

Crimes Against Humanity and War Crimes Act Offences Within Canada SC 2000 c 24 s 4

(1) Genocide, etc, committed in Canada
Every person is guilty of an indictable offence who commits

(a) genocide;
(b) a crime against humanity; or
(c) a war crime.

(1.1) Conspiracy, attempt, etc

Every person who conspires or attempts to commit, is an accessory after the fact in relation to, or counsels in relation to, an offence referred to in subsection (1) is guilty of an indictable offence.

(2) Punishment
Every person who commits an offence under subsection (1) or (1.1)

(a) shall be sentenced to imprisonment for life, if an intentional killing forms the basis of the offence; and
(b) is liable to imprisonment for life, in any other case.

(3) Definitions
The definitions in this subsection apply in this section....

'genocide' means an act or omission committed with intent to destroy, in whole or in part, an identifiable group of persons, as such, that, at the time and in the place of its commission, constitutes genocide according to customary international law or conventional international law or by virtue of its being criminal according to the general principles of law recognized by the community of nations, whether or not it constitutes a contravention of the law in force at the time and in the place of its commission.

(4) Interpretation—customary international law

For greater certainty, crimes described in Articles 6 and 7 and paragraph 2 of Article 8 of the Rome Statute are, as of July 17, 1998, crimes according to customary international law. This does not limit or prejudice in any way the application of existing or developing rules of international law.

Canada Federal Statutes Crimes Against Humanity and War Crimes Act Offences Outside Canada SC 2000, c 24 s 6

(1) Genocide, etc, committed outside Canada
Every person who, either before or after the coming into force of this section, commits outside Canada

(a) genocide,
(b) a crime against humanity, or
(c) a war crime,

is guilty of an indictable offence and may be prosecuted for that offence in accordance with section 8.

(1.1) Conspiracy, attempt, etc

Every person who conspires or attempts to commit, is an accessory after the fact in relation to, or counsels in relation to, an offence referred to in subsection (1) is guilty of an indictable offence.

(2) Punishment
Every person who commits an offence under subsection (1) or (1.1)

(a) shall be sentenced to imprisonment for life, if an intentional killing forms the basis of the offence; and
(b) is liable to imprisonment for life, in any other case.

(3) Definitions
The definitions in this subsection apply in this section....

'genocide' means an act or omission committed with intent to destroy, in whole or in part, an identifiable group of persons, as such, that at the time and in the place of its commission, constitutes genocide according to customary international law or conventional international law or by virtue of its being criminal according to the general principles of law recognized by the community of nations, whether or not it constitutes a contravention of the law in force at the time and in the place of its commission.

(4) Interpretation—customary international law

For greater certainty, crimes described in articles 6 and 7 and paragraph 2 of article 8 of the Rome Statute are, as of July 17, 1998, crimes according to customary international law, and may be crimes according to customary international law before that date. This does not limit or prejudice in any way the application of existing or developing rules of international law.

(5) Interpretation—crimes against humanity

For greater certainty, the offence of crime against humanity was part of customary international law or was criminal according to the general principles of law recognized by the community of nations before the coming into force of either of the following:

(a) the Agreement for the prosecution and punishment of the major war criminals of the European Axis, signed at London on August 8, 1945; and

(b) the Proclamation by the Supreme Commander for the Allied Powers, dated January 19, 1946.

Schedule—Article 6 [Genocide]—Provisions of Rome Statute

For the purpose of this Statute, 'genocide' means any of the following acts committed with intent to destroy, in whole or in part, a national, ethnical, racial or religious group, as such:

(a) killing members of the group;
(b) causing serious bodily or mental harm to members of the group;
(c) deliberately inflicting on the group conditions of life calculated to bring about its physical destruction in whole or in part;
(d) imposing measures intended to prevent births within the group;
(e) forcibly transferring children of the group to another group.

China

Translation of the Convention for the Prevention and Punishment of the Crime of Genocide into Simplified (Jaintizi) Chinese, Published in the 'People's Republic of China State Gazette' upon Ratification and Accession in April 1983

Article II
In the present Convention, genocide means any of the following acts committed with intent to destroy, in whole or in part, a national, ethnical, racial or religious group, as such:

(a) Killing members of the group;
(b) Causing serious bodily or mental harm to members of the group;
(c) Deliberately inflicting on the group conditions of life calculated to bring about its physical destruction in whole or in part;
(d) Imposing measures intended to prevent births within the group;
(e) Forcibly transferring children of the group to another group.

Columbia

Penal Code of Columbia (2000 Law No 599) (Jul 24) art 101 [Genocide]

Whoever, in order to destroy totally or partially a national, ethnic, racial, religious or legally constituted political group, or because of its property, causes the death of its members, will incur imprisonment of 30 to 40 years, a fine of 2,000 to 10,000 effective legal minimum monthly wages, and loss of public rights and functions for 15 to 20 years.

The penalty will be imprisonment of 10 to 25 years, a fine of 1,000 to 10,000 effective legal minimum monthly wages, and the loss of public rights and functions for 5 to 15 years when with the same intention any one of the following acts is committed:

(1) Serious injury to the physical or mental integrity of members of the group.
(2) Forced pregnancy.
(3) Submission of members of the group to conditions of total or partial existence meant to cause its physical destruction.
(4) Measures destined to prevent births in the group.
(5) Transfer by force of children of the group to another group.

US State Department Bureau of Democracy, Human Rights, and Labour: Country Reports on Human Rights Practices—Columbia (2001) (4 Mar 2002):

In response to the killings of thousands of members of the Patriotic Union (UP) leftist coalition ... a May 2000 law classified 'political genocide' as a crime; however, it provided that political genocide could be committed only against members of legally constituted (i.e., non-guerrilla) groups.

Congo (Democratic Republic)

Law No 8 - 98 (31 Oct 1998) c 1 art 1 [Genocide]

Genocide is perpetrating, or making others perpetrate pursuant to a concerted plan, the intentional destruction, in all or part, of a national, ethnic, racial, or religious group, or a group determined from any other arbitrary criterion, through one of the following acts:

(a) Murder of the members of the group;
(b) Serious harm to the physical or mental integrity of the members of the group;
(c) Intentionally placing the group in conditions of existence meant to cause its partial or total destruction;
(d) Measures aimed at blocking births within the group;
(e) Forced transfer of the group's children.

Costa Rica

Penal Code of Costa Rica (14 April 1998) art 127

Whoever participates in the total or partial destruction of a definite group of human beings for reasons of race, nationality, gender, age, political, religious or sexual preference, social position, economic situation or civil status, will be punished with 15 to 35 years imprisonment.

The following will be punished with the same penalty:

(1) Causing members of those groups serious bodily or mental damage;
(2) Placing those groups in conditions of life leading to the destruction of all or some of the individuals that comprise them;

(3) Taking measures intended to prevent pregnancies or births within those groups; or
(4) Transferring, by means of force or intimidation, people from one of those groups to different groups.

Côte d'Ivoire

Penal Code (Côte d'Ivoire) c 1 s 1 tit 1 art 137

This article describes and punishes all acts aimed at the total or partial elimination of a national, ethnic, confessional [religious] or political group. These acts include the following:

- murder, serious bodily injury or attacks on the physical or mental health of the members of the group, in whatever form;
- measures taken to prevent the procreation or the survival of the descendants of members of the group;
- forced displacement or dispersal of the group's children or placing the group in living conditions meant to cause its death or disappearance [destruction].

Alternate translation from 'International Convention on the Elimination of all Forms of Racial Discrimination—Reports Submitted by Parties Under Article 9 of the Convention: Côte d'Ivoire' (1 Oct 2002) UN Doc CERD/C/382/Add2 ¶18

Article 137. To be punished by the death penalty, whoever, in times of war as in times of peace, acts with the intention of totally or partially destroying completely a national, ethnic, denominational or political group, organizes, orders or commits:

- Murder, serious bodily injury or attacks on the physical or mental health of the members of the group, in whatever form;
- Measures taken to prevent the procreation or the survival of the descendants of members of the group;
- Forced displacement or dispersal of population groups or children or their placing in living conditions such that they must lead to their death or disappearance.

Croatia

Croatian Penal Code c 13 art 156 'Criminal Acts against Values Protected by International Law' [Genocide]

Whoever orders, with an aim to completely or partially destroy a national, ethnic, racial or religious group, that members of such group be killed or severely injured, or that their physical or psychological health be severely damaged, or that civilians be forcibly displaced, or that a group be placed into such conditions of life as would lead to its complete or partial extermination, or that measures be taken to prevent procreation among members of such group, or that children be forcibly moved to another group, or whoever with the same aim commits any of the above-mentioned acts, shall be punished with at least 10 years imprisonment or with lifetime imprisonment.

Cuba

Law No 62: Penal Code (Cuba), as modified by Law No 87 bk 1 c 3 s 6 art 116(1)

Whoever, with intent to destroy, totally or partially, a national, ethnic, racial or religious group as such:

(a) Puts the group into conditions of existence that constitute a threat of extermination of the group or some of its members;
(b) Takes measures to prevent or prevents births in the group;
(c) Executes the forcible transfer of the children from the group to another one;
(d) Kills members of the group, or seriously injures their physical or mental integrity,

shall incur the sanction of imprisonment for 10 to 20 years, or death.

Czech Republic

Criminal Code (Czech Republic) c 20 s 259 [Genocide], reproduced from 'International Convention on the Elimination of all Forms of Racial Discrimination—Second Report of States Parties Due in 1996: Czech Republic' (17 Jul 1997) UN Doc No CERD/C/289/Add 1 ¶29

(1) A person who, acting with the intent to destroy, in whole or in part, any national, ethnic, racial, or religious group,
   (a) Deliberately inflicts on persons belonging to any such group conditions of life calculated to bring about its physical destruction in whole or in part,
   (b) Imposes measures intended to prevent births within the group,
   (c) Forcibly transfers children of the group to another group, or
   (d) Causes a person belonging to the group grievous bodily harm or death,

   shall be punished by imprisonment for a term of 12 to 15 years or by an exceptional penalty.
(2) Complicity in the act defined in Paragraph 1 shall be punished in like manner.

Denmark

Act No 132 of 29 of April 1955 Concerning the Punishment of Genocide

(1) Whoever, with intent to destroy in whole or in part a national, ethnical, racial or religious group as such—
   (a) Kills members of the group,

(b) Causes serious bodily or mental harm to members of the group,
(c) Deliberately inflicts on the group conditions of life calculated to bring about its physical destruction in whole or in part,
(d) Imposes measures intended to prevent births within the group,
(e) Forcibly transfers children of the group to another group,

is punishable for genocide by imprisonment for life or for not less than 16 years.

(2) Attempt and complicity in the acts enumerated in section 1 shall be punished according to Chapter 4 of the Civil Criminal Code.

Ecuador

Penal Code (Ecuador): Law on Crimes Against Humanity art 19

Genocide is any one of the following acts, perpetrated in time of peace or war, with the intention to destroy totally or partially a group defined by its national, ethnic, racial, religious, or political condition, or by gender, sexual orientation, age, health or conscience as such:

(a) Killing a member or members of the group;
(b) Causing serious injury to the physical or mental integrity of a member or members of the group;
(c) Submission of one or more people or members of the group to conditions of existence that will cause the total or partial physical destruction of that group;
(d) Measures designed to prevent the births in the group; and
(e) Transfer by force of a child or children to another group.

El Salvador

Penal Code of the Republic of El Salvador (Decree No 1030) tit 19 art 361 [Genocide]

Whoever, in order to destroy partially or totally a definite human group, because of its nationality, race or religion—

- commits homicide, or
- causes bodily or psychic injury to members of the group, or
- places them into conditions that will make their subsistence difficult, or
- imposes measures on them destined to prevent reproduction, or
- forcibly displaces group members to other groups,

will be punished by imprisonment for 10 to 25 years.

The sanction is increased up to 30 years if the person directly responsible for any act of genocide is a government employee or member of the military.

Ordering or conspiracy to commit genocide will be punished by imprisonment for 6 to 12 years; and public incitement to commit genocide will be punished by imprisonment for 4 to 8 years.

Estonia

Estonian Penal Code (9 Nov 1994) s 61, reproduced from Lauri Malksoo 'Soviet Genocide? Communist Mass Deportations in the Baltic States and International Law' (2001) 14 Leiden JIL 757, 772

(1) For committing crimes against humanity, including genocide, as these crimes are defined in norms of international law, ie, for wilful acts which aimed to completely or partially destroy a national, ethnic, racial, religious group, a group offering resistance to the occupation regime or other social group, for killing a member of such group or inflicting upon him serious or very serious bodily or mental damage or for torturing him, for forced removal of children, for the deportation or expulsion of the indigenous population during an armed attack, occupation or annexation, or the denial of their economic, political and social human rights or the stripping of such rights – will be punished with the loss of freedom from eight until fifteen years or with the life sentence or with death penalty.

(2) The representative of the state authorities, with whose approval the crimes mentioned in this article's first paragraph were committed, shall be punished due to his involvement as an accessory in accordance with [Section] 17 [Paragraph] 6.

Estonian Criminal Code 2001 art 611(1)

For crimes against humanity, including genocide, as per the definition of these crimes in international law, that is for deliberate acts whose aim it is to fully or partially eradicate a group based on national, ethnic, racial or religious distinction, which is resisting an occupation regime, or any other social group; for the killing of a member of such a group or for causing him/her grave or very grave bodily injuries or mental dysfunction or for torturing him/her; for removal of his/her children by force; for deportation of the indigenous population or for banishment into exile once an armed invasion, occupation or annexation has occurred, and for depriving them of their economic, political and social human rights or for restriction of these rights—the penalty is deprivation of liberty for between 8 to 15 years or the death penalty.

Ethiopia

Penal Code of the Empire of Ethiopia of 1957 [Genocide; Crimes against Humanity] (Negarit Gazeta, Extraordinary Issue No 1 of 1957) art 281

Whosoever, with intent to destroy, in whole or in part, a national, ethnic, racial, religious or political group, organizes, orders or engages in, be it in time of war or in time of peace:

(a) Killings, bodily harm or serious injury to the physical or mental health of members of the group, in any way whatsoever; or
(b) Measures to prevent the propagation or continued survival of its members or their progeny; or
(c) The compulsory movement or dispersion of peoples or children, or placing them under living conditions calculated to result in their death or disappearance,

shall be punished with rigorous imprisonment from 5 years to life, or, in cases of exceptional gravity, with death.

Fiji

Penal Code (Fiji) 1945 pt 2 div 1 'Offences against Public Order' c 8 s 69 [Genocide]

(1) A person commits the offence of genocide if he commits any of the following acts with intent to destroy, in whole or in part, a national, ethnical, racial or religious group as such:
    (b) Killing members of the group;
    (c) Causing serious bodily or mental harm to members of the group;
    (d) Deliberately inflicting on the group conditions of life calculated to bring about its physical destruction in whole or in part;
    (e) Imposing measures intended to prevent births within the group;
    (f) Forcibly transferring children of the group to another group.
(2) A person guilty of an offence of genocide shall, on conviction:
    (a) If the offence consists of the killing of any person, be sentenced to death;
    (b) In any other case, be liable to imprisonment for a term not exceeding 14 years.
(3) Proceedings for an offence of genocide shall not be instituted except by or with the consent of the Director of Public Prosecutions.

Finland

The Penal Code of Finland No 39/1889 c 11 s 6, affirmed by the Act on the Implementation of the Legislative Provisions of the Rome Statute of the International Criminal Court and on the Application of the Statute (28 Dec 2000) No 1285/2000

Section 6—Genocide (578/1995)

(1) A person who for the purpose of entirely or partially destroying a race, a national, ethnic or religious group or another comparable group:
  (1) Kills members of the group;
  (2) Inflicts grievous bodily or mental damage or illness upon members of the group;
  (3) Takes forcible measures to prevent procreation among the group;
  (4) Forcibly moves children from one group to another; or
  (5) In another comparable manner essentially impairs the survival of the group,

  shall be sentenced for genocide to imprisonment for at least 4 years or for life.

(2) An attempt is punishable.

Section 7—Preparation for genocide (578/1995)
A person who for the purpose referred to in Section 6

(1) Conspires with another to commit genocide; or
(2) Makes a plan for genocide,

shall be sentenced for preparation of genocide to imprisonment for at least 4 months and at most 4 years.

France

Code Penal (France) art 211-1, affirmed by Law No 2002-268 (26 Feb 2002) on Co-operation with the International Criminal Court

Genocide occurs where, in the enforcement of a concerted plan aimed at the partial or total destruction of a national, ethnic, racial or religious group, or of a group determined by any other arbitrary criterion, one of the following actions is committed or caused to be committed against members of that group:

- wilful attack on life;
- serious attack on psychic or physical integrity;
- subjection to living conditions meant to entail the partial or total destruction of that group;
- measures aimed at preventing births;
- enforced transfer of children.

Genocide is punishable by criminal imprisonment for life.

Georgia

Georgian Criminal Code s 14 c 47 'Crimes against peace and security of the mankind and international humanitarian law' art 407 [Genocide]

Acts committed with intent to destroy, in whole or in part, a national, ethnic, racial or religious group by way of killings, causing serious harm to health, intentionally inflicting on the group aggravated conditions of life, forced prevention of births, or transferring children of the group to another group,

shall be punished by deprivation of liberty for a term of 8 to 20 years or by life imprisonment.

Germany

Völkerstrafgesetzbuch [VStGB] [Code of Crimes Against International Law] BGBl 2002 I at 2254 (30 Jun) art 1 pt 2 c 1 s 6(1)

(1) Whoever with the intent of destroying as such, in whole or in part, a national, racial, religious or ethnic group
  1. kills a member of the group,
  2. causes serious bodily or mental harm to a member of the group, especially of the kind referred to in section 226 of the Criminal Code,
  3. inflicts on the group conditions of life calculated to bring about their physical destruction in whole or in part,
  4. imposes measures intended to prevent births within the group,
  5. forcibly transfers a child of the group to another group

  shall be punished with imprisonment for life.

(2) In less serious cases referred to under subsection (1), numbers 2 to 5, the punishment shall be imprisonment for not less than five years.

Ghana

Ghana: Criminal Code (Amendment) Act 1993 s 1 [Genocide]

A person commits genocide where, with intent to destroy, in whole or in part, any national, ethnical, racial or religious group, he

(a) Kills members of the group;
(b) Causes serious bodily or mental harm to members of the group;
(c) Deliberately inflicts on the group conditions of life calculated to bring about its physical destruction in whole or in part;
(d) Imposes measures intended to prevent births within the group; or
(e) Forcibly transfers children of the group to another group.

Guatemala

Penal Code (Guatemala) art 376, reproduced from *Guatemala v Lucas Garcia (Criminal Complaint)* (Fiscal General Ministerio Publico) (3 May 2000) ¶70

A person commits genocide if (s)he, with the intention to destroy in whole or in part a national, ethnic or religious group, carries out any of the following acts:

(1) Killing of members of the group,
(2) Causing injury which seriously affects the physical or mental integrity of members of the group,
(3) Submission of the group or members thereof to conditions of existence which may produce its (or their) total or partial physical destruction,
(4) Forced displacement of children or adults from one group to another, and
(5) Measures designed to sterilize members of the group or in any other manner impede their reproduction.

A person responsible for genocide will be sentenced to between 30 and 50 years imprisonment.

Article 377 (Instigation to commit genocide):

Whoever publicly instigates the commission of genocide will be sentenced to the same period of imprisonment.

Hungary

Criminal Code 1978 (Hungary) c 11 'Crimes Against Humanity' tit 1 s 155 [Genocide]

(1) Anyone who—with the aim of the total or partial extermination of a national, ethnic, racial or religious group—
    (a) Kills members of the group,
    (b) Causes serious bodily or mental injury to members of the group because they belong to the group,
    (c) Places the group into conditions of life that threaten the group or members thereof with death,
    (d) Takes measures aimed at the impediment of births within the group,
    (e) Transfers children belonging to the group into another group,

    commits a felony and shall be punishable with imprisonment from 10 to 15 years or life imprisonment.
(2) The person who commits preparation for genocide, shall be punished for a felony with imprisonment from 2 to 8 years.

Indonesia

Republic of Indonesia Law No 26 (2000) c 3 art 8

Article 4
The Human Rights Court shall have jurisdiction over serious violations of human rights.

Article 5
The Human Rights Court also shall have jurisdiction over serious violations of human rights that were perpetrated outside the territorial limits of the Republic of Indonesia by Indonesian citizens.

Article 6
The Human Rights Court shall have no jurisdiction over serious violations of human rights committed by persons aged under 18 years at the time the offence was perpetrated.

Article 7
The Human Rights Court shall have jurisdiction over the following serious violations of human rights:

1. The crime of genocide;
2. Crimes against humanity.

Article 8
The crime of genocide in Article 7 means acts carried out with the intention to destroy all or part of a national, racial, ethnic or religious group by means of:

(a) Killing the group's members;
(b) Causing serious physical or mental suffering to the group's members;
(c) Imposing conditions of life on the group that will result in the physical destruction of all or some of the group's members;
(d) Forcibly imposing measures whose purpose is to prevent births within the group;
(e) Forcibly moving children from the group to another group.

Iraq

The Statute of the Iraqi Special Tribunal (10 Dec 2003) art 11

(a) For the purposes of this Statute and in accordance with the Convention on the Prevention and Punishment of the Crime of Genocide, dated December 9, 1948, as ratified by Iraq on January 20, 1959, 'genocide' means any of the following acts committed with intent to destroy, in whole or in part, a national, ethnical, racial or religious group, as such:
    1. Killing members of the group;
    2. Causing serious bodily or mental harm to members of the group;
    3. Deliberately inflicting on the group conditions of life calculated to bring about its physical destruction in whole or in part;
    4. Imposing measures intended to prevent births within the group; and
    5. Forcibly transferring children of the group to another group.

(b) The following acts shall be punishable:
1. Genocide;
2. Conspiracy to commit genocide;
3. Direct and public incitement to commit genocide;
4. Attempt to commit genocide; and
5. Complicity in genocide.

Ireland

International Criminal Court Bill 2003 (No 36) pt 2 s 6(1) [Domestic Jurisdiction in ICC Offences]

6(1) In this Part, unless the context otherwise requires... 'genocide' means any of the acts specified in Article 6 [of the ICC Statute].

Israel

Crime of Genocide (Prevention and Punishment) Law No 5710–1950 art 1(a) (29 Mar 1950), reproduced from 'International Convention on the Elimination of all Forms of Racial Discrimination—Second Report of States Parties Due in 1993: Israel' (9 Apr 1998) UN Doc CCPR/C/81/Add 13 ¶163:

In this Law, genocide means any of the following acts committed with intent to destroy, in whole or in part, a national, ethnic, racial or religious group (hereinafter referred to as the group) as such:

(1) Killing members of the group;
(2) Causing serious bodily harm to members of the group;
(3) Inflicting on the group conditions of life calculated to bring about its physical destruction, in whole or in part;
(4) Imposing measures intended to prevent births within the group;
(5) Forcibly transferring children of the group to another group.

Italy

Law No 962 of 9 Oct 1967 on the Prevention and Punishment of the Crime of Genocide

Article 1—Acts directed towards the commission of genocide

Anyone who, in order to destroy, in whole or in part, a national, ethnical, racial or religious group, as such, commits acts which are intended to cause serious personal harm to persons belonging to the group shall be punished by imprisonment for 10 to 18 years.

Anyone who, in order to destroy, in whole or in part, a national, ethnical, racial or religious group, as such, commits acts which are intended to cause death or very serious personal injury to persons belonging to the group shall be punished by imprisonment for 24 to 30 years.

The same penalty shall apply to those who, for the same purpose, inflict on persons belonging to the group conditions of life calculated to bring about the physical destruction, in whole or in part, of the said group.

Article 2—Deportation for the purpose of genocide

Anyone who, for the purpose indicated in the foregoing article, deports persons belonging to a national, ethnical, racial or religious group shall be punished with imprisonment for 15 to 24 years.

Article 3—Aggravating circumstances

If the death of one or more persons arises as a result of any of the facts envisaged in the foregoing articles the penalty of life imprisonment shall apply.

Article 4—Acts intended to commit genocide by restricting births

Anyone who imposes or implements measures intended to prevent or limit births within a national, ethnical, racial or religious group in order to destroy, in whole or in part, the group shall be punished with imprisonment for 12 to 20 years.

Article 5—Acts intended to commit genocide through the transfer of minors

Anyone who, for the purpose indicated in the foregoing articles, transfers minors under the age of 14 belonging to a national, ethnical, racial or religious group to a different group shall be punished with imprisonment for 12 to 21 years.

Article 6—Imposition of distinguishing marks or signs

Anyone who forces persons belonging to a national, ethnical, racial or religious group to bear distinguishing marks or signs indicating their membership in that group shall be punished, for that very fact, with imprisonment for 4 to 10 years.

If the act is committed to facilitate the destruction, in whole or in part, of the group imprisonment for 12 to 21 years shall apply.

Article 7—Agreement to commit genocide

When several persons agree to commit one of the crimes defined in articles 1 to 5 and in the second subsection of article 6 of this law, and the crime is not perpetrated, each of these persons shall be punishable, by sole virtue of the agreement, with imprisonment for 1 to 6 years.

Whenever several persons agree to commit the crime defined in the first subsection of article 6 of this law, and the crime is not perpetrated, each of them shall be punishable with imprisonment, by sole virtue of the agreement, for three months to one year.

The penalty shall be higher for the instigators.

Article 8—Public incitement and defence

Anyone who publicly incites another to commit one of the crimes defined in articles 1 to 5 shall be punished with imprisonment for 3 to 12 years, by sole virtue of the incitement.

The same penalty shall apply to anyone who publicly defends any of the crimes specified in the foregoing subsection.

Jamaica

Offences Against the Person Act (Amendment 1968), Laws of Jamaica vol 8 s 33

Whosoever shall advocate or promote genocide is guilty of an indictable offence, and shall be liable to be imprisoned for a term not exceeding ten years, with or without hard labour.

In this section 'genocide' means any of the following acts committed with the intent to destroy in whole or in part any national, ethnical, racial or religious group, as such:

- killing members of the group;
- causing serious bodily or mental harm to members of the group;
- deliberately inflicting on the group conditions of life calculated to bring about its physical destruction in whole or in part;
- imposing measures intended to prevent births within the group;
- forcibly transferring children of the group to another group.

Kiribati

Laws of the Gilbert Islands: Penal Code c 67 s 8 art 62

(1) A person commits the felony of genocide if he commits any of the following acts with intent to destroy, in whole or in part, a national, ethnical, racial or religious group, as such—
  (a) Killing members of the group;
  (b) Causing serious bodily or mental harm to members of the group;
  (c) Deliberately inflicting on the group conditions of life calculated to bring about its physical destruction in whole or in part;
  (d) Imposing measures intended to prevent births within the group;
  (e) Forcibly transferring children of the group to another group.

(2) A person guilty of the felony of genocide shall on conviction—
  (a) If the offence consists of the killing of any person, be sentenced to imprisonment for life;
  (b) In any other case, be liable to imprisonment without the option of a fine for 14 years (section 26 notwithstanding).
(3) Proceedings for an offence of genocide shall not be instituted except by or with the consent of the Attorney-General.

Kyrgyzstan

Criminal Code (Kyrgyzstan) s 12 c 34 'Crimes against Peace and Security of Mankind' art 373 [Genocide]

Acts aimed at the full or partial extermination of a national, ethnical, racial or religious group by murdering the members of such group, infliction of serious harm to their health, forced prevention of procreation, compulsory transfer of children, forced resettlement or the creation of other living conditions intended for the physical extermination of the members of such group, shall be punished by imprisonment for 12 to 20 years or by the death penalty.

Latvia

Criminal Code (17 Jun 1998) c 8 s 71

For a person who commits genocide, that is, commits intentional acts for purposes of destroying in whole or in part of any group of persons identifiable as such by nationality, ethnic origin, race, social class or a defined collective belief or faith, by killing members of the group, inflicting upon them physical injuries hazardous to life or health or causing them to become mentally ill, intentionally causing conditions of life for them as to result in their physical destruction in whole or in part, utilizing measures intended to prevent the birth of children in such group, or forcibly transferring children from one group of persons into another, the applicable sentence is life imprisonment or imprisonment for 3 to 20 years.

Liechtenstein

Penal code (StGB) (Liechtenstein) (24 Jun 1987) c 25 s 321

(1) Whoever with the intention of destroying totally or partly, by a group affiliated to a church or a church society, a people, a race, or a national group as such,
  – kills members of the group,
  – causes them physical (s 84 Abs 1) or mental injury,

– subjects the group to living conditions which are meant to cause the death of all or part of the members of the group,
– imposes measures upon the group to prevent births, or
– transfers by force or threat of force children of the group force into another group,

shall be punished with life imprisonment.

(2) Whoever with another in the common execution of an act in Article 1, orders or arranges such punishable actions, shall be punished with imprisonment for 1 to 10 years.

Lithuania

Criminal Code of the Republic of Lithuania art 71, reproduced from 'International Convention on the Elimination of all Forms of Racial Discrimination—Reports of States Parties Under Article 9 of the Convention: Lithuania' (13 Feb 2001) UN Doc CERD/C/369/Add 2 ¶57

Article 71 of the Criminal Code of the Republic of Lithuania provides for criminal liability for the crime of genocide:

Any of the acts which aim at physical destruction, in whole or in part, of people of a particular national, ethnic, religious, social or political group by torturing or injuring members of such a group, hampering their mental development; deliberately inflicting on the group conditions of life calculated to bring about its physical destruction in whole or in part; forcibly transferring their children over to other groups or imposing measures intended to prevent births within such groups, shall be punished by imprisonment for a term from 5 to 20 years.

Any act provided for in paragraph 1 of this article manifesting itself in the massacre of people, as well as the organization or ordering of any of the acts provided for in paragraphs 1 and 2 of the said article shall be punished by imprisonment for a term from 10 to 20 years or by life imprisonment.

Luxembourg

Law of 8 Aug 1985 on the Repression of Genocide

1. Whoever, with intention to destroy, totally or partially, a national, ethnic, racial or religious group as such, commits one of the following acts, is guilty of genocide:
   (a) Murders members of the group;
   (b) Causes serious injury to the physical or mental integrity of members of the group;
   (c) Intentionally places the group or members of the group in conditions of existence likely to cause their total or partial physical destruction;

(d) Imposes measures aimed at preventing births within the group;
(e) Forcibly transfers children of the group to another group.
The offender shall be condemned to life imprisonment.

2. Conspiracy to commit genocide is punished with hard labour from 10 to 15 years, if some preparatory act towards its execution is committed, and of imprisonment in the contrary case. Conspiracy exists as soon as the resolution to act was adopted between several people.
3. Without excepting the application of Articles 66 and 67 of the Penal Code, ordering, proposing or offering, even not followed or ineffective, to commit one of the infringements envisaged by Article 1, and the acceptance of similar proposals or offers, are punishable by imprisonment.
4. Those who, being informed of the execution of an infringement envisaged in Article 1 or of facts which begin the execution of it, and being able to prevent or stop its commission, failed to act within the limits of this possibility of action, shall be punished by imprisonment.

Mali

Penal Code (2001) bk 3 tit 1 c 2 art 30 [Genocide]

Genocide is one of the following acts committed with intent to destroy, totally or partly, a national, ethnic, racial or religious group, as such:

(a) Murder of members of the group;
(b) Serious injury to the physical or mental integrity of members of the group;
(c) Intentionally subjecting the group to conditions of existence likely to lead to its total or partial physical destruction;
(d) Imposing measures aimed at blocking births within the group;
(e) Forcibly transferring children of the group to another group.

Malta

International Criminal Court Act (13 Dec 2003) sch 1 art 6 [Genocide]

For the purpose of this Statute, 'genocide' means any of the following acts committed with intent to destroy, in whole or in part, a national, ethnical, racial or religious group, as such—

(a) Killing members of the group;
(b) Causing serious bodily or mental harm to members of the group;
(c) Deliberately inflicting on the group conditions of life calculated to bring about its physical destruction in whole or in part;
(d) Imposing measures intended to prevent births within the group;
(e) Forcibly transferring children of the group to another group.

Mexico

Federal Penal Code 1931 (as amended) bk 2 tit 3 c 2 art 149-bis [Genocide]

Whoever, in order to destroy, totally or partially, one or more groups of national, ethnic, racial or religious character, perpetrates by any means, offences against the life of group members, or imposes massive sterilization with the purpose of preventing the reproduction of the group, commits the crime of genocide.

Moldova

Criminal Code of the Republic of Moldova c 1 'Crimes against Peace, Security of humanity and War crimes' art 135 [Genocide]

Genocide is the commission of one of the following acts with the purpose to destroy, in whole or in part, a national, ethnic, racial or religious group:

(a) Killing members of the group;
(b) Causing serious harm to the physical or mental health of members of the group;
(c) Imposing measures intended to decrease the birth rate within the group;
(d) Illegal trafficking in children belonging to the group;
(e) Deliberate creation of conditions of life bringing about physical destruction of the group in whole or in part.

Genocide shall be punishable with imprisonment for 16 to 25 years or by life imprisonment.

Netherlands

International Crimes Act (9 Jun 2003) pt 2 s 3

Anyone who, with intent to destroy, wholly or partly, any national, ethnic or religious group or a group belonging to a particular race, as such:

(a) kills members of the group;
(b) causes serious bodily or mental harm to members of the group;
(c) deliberately inflicts upon the group conditions of life calculated to bring about the physical destruction of the group, in whole or in part;
(d) imposes measures intended to prevent births within the group; or
(e) forcibly transfers children of the group to another group,

is guilty of genocide and liable to life imprisonment or a term of imprisonment not exceeding 30 years or a sixth category fine.

New Zealand

New Zealand: International Crimes and International Criminal Court Act 2000 (No 26 2000, amendment No 67 2002) pt 2 s 9(2)

For the purposes of this section, 'genocide' is an act referred to in article 6 of the [ICC] Statute.

Nicaragua

Penal Code (Nicaragua) bk 2 tit 14 art 549 [Genocide]

Whoever commits or orders measures to destroy, partly or totally, an ethnic or religious group, as such, through attacks on the personal integrity of its members, mass deportations, forcible displacement of group children or adults to other groups, the imposition of conditions that make subsistence difficult, or imposes operations or practices intended to prevent the group's reproduction, commits the crime of genocide and will be punished with military imprisonment for 15 to 20 years.

Article 550

The organization of groups intended to commit the crime of genocide, and public incitation of the same, will be punished by military prison for 5 to 8 years.

Panama

Penal Code (Panama) tit 9 c 3 art 311 'Crimes against the International Community'

Whoever participates in the total or partial destruction of a definite group of human beings, because of the group's nationality, race, or religious or political belief, will be punished with 15 to 20 years imprisonment.

It is punishable to, with intent to partially or totally destroy a definite group of people according to the reasons set forth in the previous paragraph, engage in the following acts:

(a) Causing members of those groups bodily or psychic damage;
(b) Placing those groups in dangerous living conditions;
(c) Preventing births, and
(d) Transferring, by force or intimidation, children of one of those groups to other groups.

Paraguay

Penal Code (Paraguay) bk 2 tit 9 art 308 art 319 [Genocide]

Whoever, with intent to destroy, totally or partially, a community or national, ethnic, religious or social group:

(1) Kills or seriously injures members of the group;
(2) Subjects the community to cruel processes or conditions of existence that could destroy it totally or partially;
(3) Transfers, by force or intimidation, children or adults to other groups, or transfers other peoples from their habitual domicile;
(4) Prevents the exercise of their religion or customary practices;
(5) Imposes measures to prevent the births within the group; or
(6) Forcibly disperses the community,

will be punished with not less than 5 years' imprisonment.

Peru

Law No 26926 (19 Feb 1998) tit 14 c 1 art 319 [Genocide]

Whoever, with intention to destroy, totally or partially, a national, ethnic, social or religious group, commits any of the following acts:

(1) Killing members of the group;
(2) Causing serious injury to the physical or mental integrity of members of the group;
(3) Subjecting the group to conditions of existence intended to cause its total or partial physical destruction;
(4) Imposing measures to prevent births in the group;
(5) Forcibly transferring the group's children to another group;

shall be liable to a minimum period of imprisonment of 20 years.

Poland

Penal Code, Law of 6 Jun 1997 c 16 'Offences Against Peace, Humanity and War Crimes' art 118 [Genocide]

(1) Any person who, with the intent to destroy, in whole or in part, a national, ethnic, racial, political or religious group or a group of persons with a definite philosophical conviction, kills a member of the group or causes serious harm to the health of a member of the group, shall be punished with imprisonment for a time not less than 12 years, with imprisonment for 20 years, or with imprisonment for life.
(2) Any person who, with the intent specified in s 1, inflicts on persons belonging to such a group conditions of life calculated to bring about its biological destruction, or imposes measures intended to prevent births within the group, or forcibly transfers children of the group to another group, shall be

punished with imprisonment for a time not less than 5 years, or with imprisonment for 25 years.

(3) Any person who attempts to commit an offence specified in sections 1 or 2, shall be punished with imprisonment for a time not less than 3 years.

Portugal

Penal Code of 1982 (Portugal) art 189 [Genocide]

[Original law that included social groups was revised to conform to the Genocide Convention in Decree Law No 48/95 (15 Mar 1995). See Schabas 146 (2000)]

Penal Code (Portugal) tit 3 c 2 art 239 [Crimes Against Peace and Humanity—Genocide]

(1) Whoever, with intent to destroy, in whole or part, a national, ethnic, racial or religious group, as such, through:
   (a) Homicide of members of the group;
   (b) Serious offences against the physical integrity of members of the group;
   (c) Subjecting the group to cruel, degrading or inhuman conditions of existence or to conditions contemplated to cause its partial or total destruction;
   (d) Forcibly transferring the children of the group to another group; or
   (e) Impeding procreation or births within the group;

   will be punished with 12 to 25 years' imprisonment.
(2) Whoever, publicly and directly, incites genocide will be punished with 2 to 8 years imprisonment.
(3) Conspiracy to commit genocide is punishable with 1 to 5 years imprisonment.

Law No 31/2004 (22 July 2004) art 218 'Adapting Portuguese Criminal Legislation to the Statute of the International Criminal Court, Typifying the Behaviours that Constitute Crimes Against International Humanitarian Law'

[Same definition as in Penal Code tit 3 c 2 art 239 above]

Romania

Romanian Socialist Republic Penal Code (1976 Special Part) tit 9 art 356

The commission of any of the following acts for the purpose of completely or partially destroying a collectivity or a national, ethnic, racial, or religious group:

(a) Murder of the members of the collectivity or group;
(b) Severe injury to the physical or mental integrity of the members of the collectivity or group;

(c) Forcing the collectivity or group to submit to conditions of existence which cause physical harm;
(d) Taking measures to prevent births within a collectivity or group;
(e) Forced transfer of the minors belonging to a collectivity or group to another collectivity or group—

constitutes genocide and is punishable by death and total confiscation of property, or by 15 to 20 years' imprisonment, prohibition of the exercise of certain rights, and partial confiscation of property.

If the act is committed during wartime, the penalty is death and total confiscation of property.

An agreement for the purpose of committing the offence of genocide is punishable by 5 to 15 years' imprisonment, prohibition of the exercise of certain rights, and partial confiscation of property.

Russian Federation

Criminal Code s 12 c 34 'Crimes against the Peace and Security of Mankind' art 357 [Genocide]

Acts aimed at the full or partial extermination of a national, ethnical, racial or religious group by way of killing the members of such group, causing serious harm to their health, forced prevention of procreation, forced transfer of children, forced resettlement or the creation of other living conditions intended to physically exterminate the members of this group, shall be punished by imprisonment for 12 to 25 years, by the death penalty, or by life imprisonment.

Rwanda

Organic Law No 8/96 of 30th August 1996 on the Organization of Prosecutions for Offences Constituting the Crime of Genocide or Crimes Against Humanity Committed since 1 October 1990, Official Gazette of the Republic of Rwanda, Year 35 No 17 (1 Sep 1996), reproduced from *Virginia Morris and Michael Scharf, The International Criminal Tribunal for Rwanda* Vol II 369 (Transnational NY 1998)

Article 1
The purpose of this organic law is the organization of criminal proceedings against persons who are accused of having, since 1 October 1990, committed acts set out and sanctioned under the Penal Code and which constitute:

(a) either the crime of genocide or crimes against humanity as defined in the Convention on the Prevention and Punishment of the Crime of Genocide of 9 December 1948, in the Geneva Convention relative to the Protection of Civilian Persons in Time of War of 12 August 1949 and its additional protocols, as well as in the Convention on the Non-Applicability of Statutory Limitations to War Crimes and Crimes Against Humanity of 26 November 1968, the three of which were ratified by Rwanda; or

(b) offences set out in the Penal Code which the Public Prosecution Department alleges or the defendant admits were committed in connection with the events surrounding the genocide and crimes against humanity.

Article 2
Persons accused of offences set out in Article 1 of this organic law and committed during the period between 1 October 1990 and 31 December 1994 shall, on the basis of their acts of participation, be classified into one of the following categories:

Category 1:

(a) persons whose criminal acts or whose acts of criminal participation place them among the planners, organizers, instigators, supervisors and leaders of the crime of genocide or of a crime against humanity;
(b) persons who acted in positions of authority at the national, prefectural, communal, sector or cell level, or in a political party, the army, religious organizations, or in a militia and who perpetuated or fostered such crimes;
(c) notorious murderers who by virtue of the zeal or excessive malice with which they committed atrocities, distinguished themselves in their areas of residence or where they passed;
(d) persons who committed acts of sexual torture;

Category 2:

[P]ersons whose criminal acts or whose acts of criminal participation place them among perpetrators, conspirators or accomplices of intentional homicide or of serious assault against the person causing death;

Category 3:

[P]ersons whose criminal acts or whose acts of criminal participation make them guilty of other serious assaults against the person;

Category 4:

[P]ersons who committed offences against property;

Article 3
For the purposes of this organic law, an accomplice is a person who provided essential assistance in the commission of the offence or who, by any means, diverted criminal prosecution of persons referred to in Article 2 of this organic law or failed to give information about them.

The fact that any of the acts referred to in this organic law were committed by a subordinate does not relieve his superior of criminal responsibility if he knew or had reason to know that the subordinate was about to commit such acts or had done so and the superior failed to take the necessary and reasonable measures to punish or prevent such acts while these measures were available to him.

Scotland

International Criminal Court Act 2001 (2001 asp 13) sch 1

Article 6
For the purpose of this Statute, 'genocide' means any of the following acts committed with intent to destroy, in whole or in part, a national, ethnical, racial or religious group, as such—

(a) Killing members of the group;
(b) Causing serious bodily or mental harm to members of the group;
(c) Deliberately inflicting on the group conditions of life calculated to bring about its physical destruction in whole or in part;
(d) Imposing measures intended to prevent births within the group;
(e) Forcibly transferring children of the group to another group.

Seychelles

The Genocide Act of 1969 Order 1970 (No 146) sch 1

(1) A person commits an offence of genocide if he commits any act falling within the definition of 'genocide' in Article II of the Genocide Convention as set out in the Schedule to this Act.
(2) A person guilty of an offence of genocide shall on conviction in the Seychelles or the Turks and Caicos Islands and on conviction on indictment in Bermuda, the British Virgin Islands or the Falkland Islands and Dependencies—
    (a) if the offence consists of the killing of any person, be sentenced to imprisonment for life;
    (b) in any other case, be liable to imprisonment for a term not exceeding 14 years.
(3) Proceedings for an offence of genocide shall not be instituted in a territory specified in Schedule 2 to the Genocide Act, 1969 (Overseas Territories) Order 1970 except by or with the consent of—
    (a) in Bermuda, the British Virgin Islands or the Seychelles, the person for the time being performing the functions of Attorney-General of the territory concerned;
    (b) in the Falkland Islands and Dependencies, the officer for the time being administering the Government;

(c) in the Turks and Caicos Islands, the person for the time being performing the functions of Administrator.

Slovenia

Penal Code 1994 (Slovenia) c 35 art 373

(1) Whoever, with the intention of destroying, in whole or in part, a national, ethnic, racial or religious group, gives orders to kill members of the group or inflict severe injury upon them, to cause serious bodily or mental harm to members of the group, to forcibly displace the population, to inflict upon the group conditions of life calculated to bring about its physical destruction in whole or in part, to impose measures to prevent births within the group, or to forcibly transfer children of the group to another group, or whoever, with the same intention, commits any of the above acts, shall be sentenced to imprisonment for not less than 10 to 20 years.
(2) The same punishment shall be imposed on whoever commits any of the acts under the previous paragraph against a social or political group.

Solomon Islands

Law No 46A of 1978, Laws of the Solomon Islands c 26: Penal Code pt 7 art 52 s 5

(1) Any person who with intent to destroy, in whole or in part, a national, ethnical, racial or religious group as such, commits any of the following acts—
    (a) Killing members of the group;
    (b) Causing serious bodily or mental harm to members of the group;
    (c) Deliberately inflicting on the group conditions of life calculated to bring about its physical destruction in whole or in part;
    (d) Imposing measures intended to prevent births within the group;
    (e) Forcibly transferring children of the group to another group,

    is guilty of genocide and shall:
    (i) if the offence consists of the killing of any person, be sentenced to imprisonment for life;
    (ii) in any other case, be liable to imprisonment for 14 years and notwithstanding section 24(3) may not be sentenced to pay a fine instead of imprisonment.
(2) Proceedings for an offence of genocide shall not be instituted except by or with the consent of the Director of Public Prosecutions.

South Africa

Law No 27 of 2002: Implementation of the Rome Statute of the International Criminal Court Act 2002 (12 Jul 2002) sch 1 pt 1 [Genocide]

'Genocide' means any of the following conduct committed with intent to destroy, in whole or in part, a national, ethnical, racial or religious group, as such:

(a) Killing members of the group;
(b) Causing serious bodily harm or mental harm to members of the group;
(c) Deliberately inflicting on the group conditions of life calculated to bring about its physical destruction in whole or in part;
(d) Imposing measures intended to prevent births within the group; or
(e) Forcibly transferring children of the group to another group.

Spain

Penal Code (Spain) Law No 10/1995 (23 Nov), as modified by Law No 15/2003 (25 Nov) art 607

Whoever, with intent to destroy totally or partially a national, ethnic, racial or religious group, through one of the following acts, will be punished—

With 15 to 20 years' imprisonment, if they kill the group's members. If two or more aggravating circumstances occurred, the increased penalty will prevail.

With imprisonment for 15 to 20 years, if they sexually assaulted some of its members or produced injuries specified in article 149.

With imprisonment for 8 to 15 years, if they placed the group or any of its members in conditions of existence that endanger their life or seriously disturb their health, or which caused the injuries in Article 150.

With the same imprisonment, if they carried out forcible displacements of the group or its members, or if they adopted any measures to prevent their reproduction, or transferred by force individuals from the group to another.

With imprisonment of 4 to 8 years, if they produced any injury other than those specified in sections 2 and 3 of this section.

Sweden

Swedish Penal Code: Law No 169 (20 Mar 1963) 'Act relating to the Punishment of Genocide' s 1

(1) Any person that commits a crime which, by law, is punishable with 4 or more years' imprisonment, against a national, ethnic, racially defined or religious group with the intention to destroy the group, completely or partially, shall be punished for genocide to imprisonment for 4 to 10 years, or for life.
(2) Attempt, preparations or conspiracy to commit genocide, and also the failure to report such a crime, shall be sentenced under the provisions of Chapter 23 of the Criminal Code.

Switzerland

Penal Code (Switzerland) bk 2 c 12(a) 'Offences against the Interests of the International Community' art 264 [Genocide]

Whoever, with intent to destroy, in whole or in part, a national, racial, religious or ethnic group:

(a) Kills members of the group or perpetrates a serious attack upon their physical or mental integrity;
(b) Subjects members of the group to conditions of existence likely to cause its total or partial physical destruction;
(c) Orders or takes measures aimed at preventing births within the group;
(d) Forcibly transfers the children of the group to another group,

shall be punished with imprisonment for life or for at least 10 years.

Tajikistan

Penal Code (Tajikistan) s 1 c 1 art 398 'Genocide'

Acts committed with the intent to fully or partially destroy a national, ethnic, racial or religious group through its full or partial physical extermination, forcible reduction of child-bearing ability, transfer of children from one of these human groups to another, causing grave injury to the health of group members, or the creation of living conditions leading to the physical destruction of members of the group, are punishable by imprisonment for 15 to 20 years or the death penalty.

Tonga

Genocide Act (No 8 of 1969) c 19

(1) A person commits an offence of genocide if he commits any act falling within the definition of 'genocide' in Article II of the Genocide Convention as set out in the Schedule to this Act.
(2) A person guilty of an offence of genocide shall on conviction on indictment—
    (a) if the offence consists of the killing of any person, be sentenced to death or to imprisonment for life;
    (b) in any other case, be liable to imprisonment for a term not exceeding 14 years.
(3) Proceedings for an offence of genocide shall not be instituted except by or with the consent of the Solicitor-General.

Schedule

Article II of Genocide Convention

In the present Convention, genocide means any of the following acts committed with intent to destroy, in whole or in part, a national, ethnical, racial or religious group, as such:

(a) Killing members of the group;
(b) Causing serious bodily or mental harm to members of the group;
(c) Deliberately inflicting on the group conditions of life calculated to bring about its physical destruction in whole or in part;
(d) Imposing measures intended to prevent births within the group;
(e) Forcibly transferring children of the group to another group.

Trinidad and Tobago

Genocide Act 1977 s 3

In this Act 'the Genocide Convention' means the Convention on the Prevention and Punishment of the Crime of Genocide approved by the General Assembly of the United Nations on 9th December 1948.

Offence of genocide

(1) A person who commits any act falling within the definition of 'genocide' in Article II of the Genocide Convention as set out in the Schedule is liable on conviction on indictment—
   (a) to the same punishment as is provided for murder if the Act committed was the one specified in paragraph (a) of the said Article II; or
   (b) to imprisonment for 14 years in any other case.
(2) No proceedings shall be instituted under this Act except by or with the consent of the Director of Public Prosecutions.

Tuvalu

Laws of Tuvalu (1978) c 8: Penal Code pt 8 art 62

(1) A person commits the felony of genocide if he commits any of the following acts with the intention to destroy, in whole or in part, a national, ethnical, racial or religious group, as such—
   (a) Killing members of the group;
   (b) Causing serious bodily or mental harm to members of the group;
   (c) Deliberately inflicting on the group conditions of life calculated to bring about its physical destruction in whole or in part;

(d) Imposing measures intended to prevent births within the group;
(e) Forcibly transferring children of the group to another group.

(2) A person guilty of the felony of genocide shall on conviction—
(a) if the offence consists of the killing of any person, be sentenced to imprisonment for life;
(b) in any other case, be liable to imprisonment without the option of a fine for 14 years (section 26 notwithstanding).

(3) Proceedings for an offence of genocide shall not be instituted except by or with the consent of the Attorney-General.

Uganda

International Criminal Court Bill (19 Apr 2004) art 7 sch 1

Article 7 [Genocide]

(1) A person is liable on conviction on indictment to the penalty specified in subsection (3) who, in Uganda or elsewhere—
(a) Commits genocide; or
(b) Conspires or agrees with any person to commit genocide, whether that genocide is to take place in Uganda or elsewhere.

(2) For the purposes of this section, 'genocide' is an act referred to in Article 6 of the [ICC] Statute.

Ukraine

Criminal Code of Ukraine (1 Sep 2001) c 20 art 442

(1) Genocide, meaning a wilfully committed act for the purpose of the total or partial destruction of any national, ethnic, racial, or religious group through the extermination of members of any such group, or inflicting grave bodily injuries on them, or the creation of conditions of life calculated to lead to the total or partial physical destruction of the group, or decreasing or preventing childbearing in the group, or the forceful transfer of children from one group to another, shall be punishable by imprisonment for 10 to 15 years, or by life imprisonment.

(2) Public calls to commit genocide, and also creating materials with calls to commit genocide for the purpose of distribution, or distribution of such materials, shall be punishable by arrest for a term up to 6 months, or by imprisonment for up to 5 years.

United Kingdom

International Criminal Court Act 2001 c 17 ss 50–52, 58–59 sch 8 ¶1 art 6

For the purpose of this Statute, 'genocide' means any of the following acts committed with intent to destroy, in whole or in part, a national, ethnical, racial or religious group, as such:

(a) Killing members of the group;
(b) Causing serious bodily or mental harm to members of the group;
(c) Deliberately inflicting on the group conditions of life calculated to bring about its physical destruction in whole or in part;
(d) Imposing measures intended to prevent births within the group;
(e) Forcibly transferring children of the group to another group.

United States

Genocide Implementation Act of 1987 (The Proxmire Act) (1988) 18 USC s 1091
s 1091 [Genocide]

(a) *Basic Offence.* Whoever, whether in time of peace or in time of war, in a circumstance described in subsection (d) and with the specific intent to destroy, in whole or in substantial part, a national, ethnic, racial or religious group as such—
  (1) Kills members of that group;
  (2) Causes serious bodily injury to members of that group;
  (3) Causes the permanent impairment of the mental faculties of members of the group through drugs, torture (mental/physical), or similar techniques;
  (4) Subjects the group to conditions of life that are intended to cause the physical destruction of the group in whole or in part;
  (5) Imposes measures intended to prevent births within the group; or
  (6) Transfers by force children of the group to another group; or attempts to do so,

  shall be punished as provided in subsection (b).
(b) *Punishment for Basic Offence.* The punishment for an offence under subsection (a) is
  (1) in the case of an offence under subsection (a)(1), where death results, by death or imprisonment for life and a fine of not more than $1,000,000, or both; and
  (2) a fine of not more than $1,000,000 or imprisonment for not more than 20 years, or both, in any other case.
(c) *Incitement Offence.* Whoever in a circumstance described in subsection (d) directly and publicly incites another to violate subsection (a) shall be fined not more than $500,000 or imprisoned not more than 5 years, or both.
(d) *Required Circumstance for Offences.* The circumstance referred to in subsections (a) and (c) is that—
  (1) the offence is committed within the United States; or

(2) the alleged offender is a national of the United States (as defined in section 101 of the Immigration and Nationality Act [8 USC s 1101]).

(e) *Non-applicability of Certain Limitations.* Notwithstanding section 3282 of this title, in the case of an offence under (a)(1), an indictment may be found, or information instituted, at any time without limitation.

s 1092 [Exclusive remedies]

Nothing in this chapter shall be construed as precluding the application of State or local laws to the conduct proscribed by this chapter, nor shall anything in this chapter be construed as any substantive or procedural right enforceable by law by any party in any proceeding.

s 1093 [Definitions]

As used in this chapter—

(1) the term 'children' means the plural and means individuals who have not attained the age of 18 years;
(2) the term 'ethnic group' means a set of individuals whose identity as such is distinctive in terms of common cultural traditions or heritage;
(3) the term 'incites' means urges another to engage imminently in conduct in circumstances under which there is a substantial likelihood of imminently causing such conduct;
(4) the term 'members' means the plural;
(5) the term 'national group' means a set of individuals whose identity as such is distinctive in terms of nationality or national origins;
(6) the term 'racial group' means a set of individuals whose identity as such is distinctive in terms of physical characteristics or biological descent;
(7) the term 'religious group' means a set of individuals whose identity as such is distinctive in terms of common religious creed, beliefs, doctrines, practices, or rituals; and
(8) the term 'substantial part' means a part of a group of such numerical significance that the destruction or loss of that part would cause the destruction of the group as a viable entity the nation of which such group is a part.

Public Law No 110–141 (21 Dec 07) 'Genocide Accountability Act of 2007' s 2

Section 1091 of title 18, United States Code, is amended by striking subsection (d) and inserting the following:

(d) *Required Circumstance for Offences.* The circumstance referred to in subsections (a) and (c) is that—
    (1) the offence is committed in whole or in part within the United States;
    (2) the alleged offender is a national of the United States (as that term is defined in section 101 of the Immigration and Nationality Act [8 USC s 1101]);

(3) the alleged offender is an alien lawfully admitted for permanent residence in the United States (as that term is defined in section 101 of the Immigration and Nationality Act [8 USC s 1101]);
(4) the alleged offender is a stateless person whose habitual residence is in the United States; or
(5) after the conduct required for the offence occurs, the alleged offender is brought into, or found in, the United States, even if that conduct occurred outside the United States.

Uruguay

Implementation of the Rome Statute of the International Criminal Court 2003 (17 Jan 2003) art II (2)(B)

Article 2 incorporates to the internal law [of Uruguay] the crime of genocide whose definitions and elements are set forth in article 6 of the [ICC] Statute. These normative descriptions are complemented by the Elements of the Crimes referred to in article 9 of the [ICC] Statute, which although not strictly binding at the same level as the Statute, are clearly considered bound to the Statute as interpretive provisions.

Venezuela

Legislative Proposal on the Implementation of the Rome Statute of the International Criminal Court (25 Jul 2002) art 5(1)(a) and n 26

[Incorporates ICC Statute art 6 by reference]

Index

The manufacturer's authorised representative in the EU for product
safety is Oxford University Press España S.A. of El Parque Empresarial
San Fernando de Henares, Avenida de Castilla, 2 - 28830 Madrid
(www.oup.es/en or product.safety@oup.com). OUP España S.A. also acts
as importer into Spain of products made by the manufacturer.
Printed and bound by CPI Group (UK) Ltd, Croydon, CR0 4YY
18/09/2026
02218916-0001